On Macintosh Programming

On Macintosh Programming: Advanced Techniques

DANIEL K. ALLEN

Addison-Wesley Publishing Company, Inc.

Reading, Massachusetts Menlo Park, California New York
Don Mills, Ontario Wokingham, England Amsterdam Bonn
Sydney Singapore Tokyo Madrid San Juan

Library of Congress Cataloging-in-Publication Data

Allen, Daniel K.
    On Macintosh programming : advanced techniques / Daniel K. Allen.
        p.   cm.
    ISBN 0-201-51737-X
    1. Macintosh (Computer)--Programming. I. Title
QA76.8.M3A445   1990   89-39855
005.265--dc20   CIP

This book was written, organized, indexed, and formatted by the author, using the following tools: Apple Macintosh SE 2.5/40 with Radius Accelerator 16, Apple LaserWriter Plus, Microsoft Word 4.0, Microsoft Excel 1.5, Apple HyperCard 1.2.2, Apple MPW 2.0 and 3.0, and many of the tools presented in this book.

Sponsoring Editor: Carole McClendon
Technical Editor: Tony Meadow
Technical Reviewers: Paul Finlayson and Tom Taylor
Cover Design: Doliber Skeffington
Text Design: Total Concept Associates
Set in 11-point Times Roman by Perry McIntosh

0-201-51737-X

ABCDEFGHIJ-AL -89
First printing, December 1989

To
Mom and Dad
Grandma and Grandpa
Fluffernutter

CONTENTS

CHAPTER 5   SANE   162

CHAPTER 6   MPW   209

ACKNOWLEDGMENTS

I could not have written this book without the support and help of many people. Thanks first go to Carole McClendon, Joanne Clapp, Rachel Guichard, and the rest of the Addison-Wesley staff for their editing, help, understanding, and encouragement, and to Tony Meadow of Bear River Associates for his help with technical editing. I would like to thank those at Apple who supported me in writing this book, especially Jean Louis Gasseé, Mike Holm, and the entire HyperCard team.

Thanks go to Dan Winkler for his insights and calm attitude toward everything; to Rick Auricchio for "The Meaning of ls," plane flights, and children's clothes; to Brian McGhie for maintaining the A-trap and low memory lists; to Larry Tesler for being instrumental in hiring me at Apple in early 1985; to Mark Neubieser for the Script Interpreter and Thursday Mexican lunches; to Steve Goldberg for the TFS Monkey and Roo-Roo jokes; to Erich Ringewald for the About Box and condominium; and to Carl Madsen for the UNIX mail and Nikon buying sprees.

For genius, a special thanks to my friends Bill Atkinson, Steve Capps, Jerome Coonen, and Donn Denman. These are some of the best Macintosh programmers in the world, and I am grateful to have worked with them and learned so much from them. For inspiration, thanks to Hugh W. Nibley, Truman G. Madsen, and Wilfred C. Griggs, three professors at Brigham Young University who taught me how to appreciate history, philosophy, and the Greek language, respectively.

For years of friendship, thanks to Rob Boody, Ken Davis, Paul Finlayson, Gary Howard, Mike Holm, Rich Mead, Steve Monfort, Doug Phillips, and Tom Taylor. A special thanks to Paul and Tom for reviewing this book for technical accuracy; to Doug for being a great munging partner; to Rob for the moral support that only a Boodelian individual can give (thanks for the Brautigans); and to Mike, thanks for the garlic bread, fro-yos, and beverages.

My family has been very supportive and loving during this major undertaking. A special thanks to my parents Daniel R. and Elizabeth V. Allen for the weekends in Paradise; to my sister Laura and her husband Woody Edvalson, Uncle Joseph K. Allen, Uncle T. K. Allen, and to my grandparents J. Knight and Alice R. Allen, for their support. Honorable mention should be made of my second cousin once removed, Robert E. Allen II, who gave me my first job years ago and helped me get my first Macintosh on January 27, 1984.

Lastly—but most importantly—I thank my dear wife and companion, Elizabeth Tobin Allen, for her support, gentle prodding, and infinite understanding. Without her, this would never have been finished. And thanks to Andrew Kegan and Rachel Elizabeth, our two greatest joys in life, for the cutest smiles and loving spirits.

PREFACE

This book shows both by precept and by example how easy it is to write Macintosh software. Programming the Macintosh is easy if you understand how the Macintosh works and hard if you do not. This book strives to teach how the Macintosh works.

Before now this material has not existed all in one place. I have tried to distill the important information needed for programming into one book, based upon my personal experience of more than five years of programming on the Mac. In fact, this is one book I wish I had had five years ago.

The programs found in this book are not artificial. They are useful, real programs. I wrote them to solve actual problems, and have found them to be handy tools that I use daily. In addition to being useful in their own right, they serve to illustrate how to program the Macintosh and how different languages are used in practice.

In order to fully utilize this book, you will need to roll your sleeves up and get into programming, because much of the reference material in this book is designed to be used while you are programming. You cannot write good software in a vacuum; this book is designed to be a programming companion. In addition to reference materials such as this book, programming for me requires a large block of uninterrupted time to concentrate, lots of music, munchies, and cold drinks. (Your mileage may vary.) In any case, make sure you have a good comfortable environment with all the necessary resources at hand when writing software.

Do not be afraid to try new things and to experiment. For example, HyperCard, MultiFinder, the Finder, and the original Mac ROMs were all written *without* an Engineering Reference Specification (ERS). They were prototyped and played with; they were written and rewritten, with each iteration becoming better. Iterate. Take the programs in this book and expand on them. Suggestions for improving many of the programs are given with the program listings.

There is also some historical information scattered throughout this book, including specific names of people who worked on various pieces of software at Apple. I feel it is important to record the names of these people here, as no other history has been written documenting their achievements. I apologize to those whose names I have forgotten; this history is necessarily limited, coming from only one person's perspective.

Disclaimer

I alone have written this book, and the opinions expressed herein are solely mine. I have tried to make this book as accurate as possible, but I can give no formal guarantee of accuracy. Furthermore, neither my employer, Apple Computer, nor my publisher, Addison-Wesley, are to be held responsible for any of the content of this book.

Although the programs are copyrighted, they may be freely copied and distributed, but neither the source code nor the resulting binary code for any program may be sold. These programs are to be used, learned from, and improved upon. Anyone wishing to incorporate these sources in other products or on a CD-ROM should contact me first. Source code for the programs found in this book may be obtained on an 800 KB Sony 3.5-inch Macintosh HFS disk as MPW text files for $20.00. To order this disk or to send correspondence to the author about this book, its source code, and other Apple-related issues, write to:

Dan Allen
1013 Suffolk Way
Fairfield, CA 94533

All correspondence, questions, comments, witty remarks, bug reports, and suggestions are welcomed at either of these electronic mail addresses: `dan@apple.com` on the UNIX/USENET network or `ALLEN.DAN` on AppleLink.

On Macintosh Programming

INTRODUCTION

This book covers the subject of Macintosh programming at the intermediate to advanced level. In order to get the most from this book, you should have some experience with programming in C or Pascal, and some experience in programming the Macintosh.

You will be looking at a lot of source code as you read this book. The code provides examples of stand-alone applications, MPW tools, desk accessories, INITs, HyperCard XCMDs, and other types of code. A number of languages are used: C, Pascal, 68000 assembly language, MPW Shell command language, and HyperTalk. Obviously, it pays to be multilingual these days.

This book will not replace *Inside Macintosh* or the documentation for your development system. Instead, it is an attempt to point out some of the important, interesting, or commonly misunderstood aspects of Macintosh programming. You will not find a detailed explanation of all the MPW tools in here, for example, but you will find an explanation of how the MPW Shell manages tools, not to mention the source code for more than a dozen different MPW tools.

How This Book Is Organized

This book takes a bottom-up approach to understanding how the Macintosh works. The Macintosh architecture is covered in the first five chapters, and the tools used to create software are explored in the final five chapters. Why are the low-level details first? Just as the foundation of a house must be built before anything else, you need to understand the basics of the Macintosh architecture before you can begin developing software.

Each chapter begins with descriptive and reference material, which is followed by source code that illustrates the topic at hand. A recommended reading list is given in each chapter.

Chapter 1 begins with a look at the various layers of the Macintosh architecture. Then the lowest-level layer is explored, including the A-trap dispatcher, low-memory globals, register saving conventions, and other basics of the Macintosh architecture.

Chapter 2 covers the Macintosh operating system, including memory and process management, the file system, and device drivers. MultiFinder is also discussed.

Chapter 3 covers QuickDraw, the graphics kernel of the Macintosh that forms the foundation for the Toolbox.

Chapter 4 presents the Toolbox and its various Managers. The System file, resources, windows, menus, and dialogs are explored, and user interface issues are discussed.

Chapter 5 discusses the Standard Apple Numerics Environment, or SANE. The Macintosh is first-rate for numerical analysis, so this chapter is essential reading for anyone doing scientific or engineering programming.

Chapter 6 shifts gears to a discussion of Apple's prime development environment: the Macintosh Programmer's Workshop, or MPW. The MPW Shell and its script language are presented, followed by a look at the various MPW Tools that come with MPW. Make, Link, and MPW Shell scripts are used to build various types of software.

The remainder of the book shows the various languages in use through many examples. Assembly language examples can be found in Chapter 7, C examples in Chapter 8, Pascal examples in Chapter 9, and HyperTalk scripts—as well as XCMDs in C and Pascal—are found in Chapter 10.

The appendix contains an ASCII table. The bibliography is an annotated list of books and publications you may find useful while you develop your skills in programming the Macintosh.

Conventions

Hexadecimal numbers are preceded by a dollar sign (or in C source code by `0x`); all other numbers are in decimal format. All Macintosh ROM routine names, file names, and source code listings are in the `Courier` font. Variable names begin with a lowercase letter, and routine names start with an uppercase letter.

History of Macintosh

The remainder of the introduction gives a brief personal history of the Macintosh. You may choose to skip this section on a first reading if you want to dive right into the technical details. However, knowing about the history of the Macintosh is important to a programmer because it explains why parts of the Mac OS are the way they are.

The first computers were built in the 1940s, but the notion of a personal computer did not surface until the middle of the 1970s. At this time the Santa Clara Valley, just forty miles south of San Francisco, was ripe for a revolution in personal computing. Some years earlier in this valley, the integrated circuit revolution had already been begun by such hardware pioneers as Fairchild, Varian, Hewlett-Packard, Intel, National Semiconductor, Advanced Micro Devices, and Amdahl. That revolution earned the valley the title "Silicon Valley," and the area has retained its title—and its leading role in computer-related technology—ever since.

The personal computer revolution began within the small Silicon Valley city known as Cupertino, which was largely made up of orchards until the 1970s. Apple began life in the area of Cupertino just south of Highway 280 near Stevens Creek Boulevard and

Highway 9 (also known as DeAnza Boulevard or the Sunnyvale-Saratoga road). This area includes Bubb Road, where Apple's first office began, and Bandley Drive, where Apple buildings today form the main Apple campus.

A central meeting place for many of Apple's early employees was Sunnyvale's Homestead High School. Steve Jobs (Apple employee #0 and #2), Steve Wozniak (Apple employee #1), Bill Fernandez (Apple employee #4), Chris Espinosa (employee #8), and Dan Allen (employee #7849) all attended Homestead during the 1970s.

Steve Wozniak and Bill Fernandez experimented together on some early machines, experimentation that over time led to the Apple I and the birth of Apple Computer. The Apple I led to the famous Apple II and then the infamous Apple III. The Apple IIe, IIc, IIGS, and the IIc Plus are the more recent members of this family, built using the Motorola 6502 processor.

In 1979, Jef Raskin began creating a computer at Apple that was to be an appliance for the home. It used a Motorola 6809 8-bit processor and a 5.25-inch disk drive, and it was called the Macintosh.

Meanwhile the Xerox Corporation had gathered a unique team of people developing new metaphors and ideas about using computers. In the 1970s, the Xerox Palo Alto Research Center (PARC) was designing some of the first workstations that incorporated bit-mapped graphics, windows, icons, and a new device called a mouse. (The mouse was actually designed in the 1960s at the Stanford Research Institute.) At PARC, Alan Kay, Dan Ingalls, and Adele Goldberg created the language Smalltalk while Larry Tesler worked on icons and modeless word processors; in time Kay, Ingalls, and Tesler all came to work for Apple. While at PARC, Niklaus Wirth, who had created Pascal in the early 1970s, worked on a successor language called Modula. Later Wirth developed his own system, called Lilith, that contained Modula-2, a bit-mapped display, windows, pop-up menus, and a three-button mouse, but it was never a commercial success.

Some of the people who developed these ideas at PARC were lured by Steve Jobs to come to work for Apple Computer. Together, they worked to bring many of the powerful ideas found at PARC to the world at a reasonable price. Apple employees spent three years and a lot of money working on their own implementation and extension of the PARC workstation concepts, which led to an amazing computer named after a girl in Steve Jobs's life.

1983

In January, 1983, Apple introduced Lisa, a novel computer with a Motorola 68000 microprocessor running at 5 MHz, 16 KB of ROM, 1 MB of RAM, two 5.25-inch 860 KB floppy disk drives, a 5 MB hard disk, a built-in 12-inch bit-mapped black-and-white display of 720 by 364 oval pixels, and a mouse. A choice of two printers was offered: a dot matrix printer that offered integrated printing of text and graphics and a daisy wheel printer that offered just letter-quality text.

Lisa had a multitasking operating system that was concealed from the user by the metaphor of a Desktop, with folders and documents that were graphically illustrated by the use of icons. Files were manipulated by pointing at, clicking on, and dragging icons with the mouse. Options available to the user were accessed via pull-down menus. Different fonts, sizes, and styles could be specified, displayed on screen, and then printed just as seen on screen. Although most of these features had been implemented previously in places like Xerox PARC, most people had never before been exposed to them. The friendly user interface found on Lisa was a revolutionary giant step toward making powerful software easy to use.

Lisa offered a set of applications that had a degree of integration previously not seen. Data could be passed between applications by the use of a clipboard, and text and graphics could be combined in a single document. These applications—known collectively as the Lisa 7/7 and bundled with Lisa—included the following:

- LisaCalc   spreadsheet
- LisaDraw   object graphics
- LisaGraph   business graphics and charts
- LisaList   file manager
- LisaProject   project management
- LisaTerm   terminal emulation
- LisaWrite   word processing

Unfortunately, Lisa was ahead of its time. The price, $9,995, was too high for most people.

1984

On January 24, 1984, Apple introduced Macintosh. Like Lisa, Macintosh was ahead of its time, but it had a more reasonable price of $2,495. Macintosh had a Motorola 68000 microprocessor running at 7.83 MHz, 64 KB of ROM, 128 KB of RAM, one 3.5-inch 400 KB internal floppy disk, a 9-inch internal black-and-white bit-mapped display, and a mouse. Macintosh also used the Desktop metaphor, but its operating system was singletasking. The Macintosh screen had 72 square pixels per inch in a 512-by-342 configuration. To complement the Macintosh's screen, the ImageWriter printer could print all text and graphics seen on the screen, using a resolution of 144 dots per inch (dpi). The printer came in standard and wide-carriage models.

Macintosh was bundled with three applications: a word processor called MacWrite, a bit-mapped graphics program called MacPaint, and a Desktop organizer called the Finder. The Finder was originally started by Bruce Horn, but in late 1983 Steve Capps began to write more of the code. Early versions of the Finder were developed using the Lisa Monitor and were written all in assembly language, like most of the Macintosh software. MacPaint was written by Bill Atkinson as a demonstration program to show off his earlier work, QuickDraw, which was ported from Lisa. Originally, the program now known as WriteNow was going to be shipped with the Mac, but MacWrite, written by Randy Wigginton (another early Apple employee), made it into the box instead.

Later, Apple added MacDraw (a port of LisaDraw by Mark Cutter), MacProject (a port of LisaProject by Solosoft), MacTerminal (Martin Haerberli), MacPascal (Think), and MacBasic (Donn Denman). MacBasic—although announced and completed—tragically was never shipped. Little third-party software was developed for Lisa, but the world of third-party software for Macintosh was explosive. Microsoft's Word, Chart, File, MultiPlan, and Basic all helped foster interest in Macintosh in the critical first months of 1984. In the product's first 100 days on the market, 50,000 Macs were sold.

When the Macintosh was introduced, Lisa was revised to have a single 400 KB 3.5-inch Sony floppy disk, and the base model had only 512 KB of RAM. It was called Lisa 2.

In September, 1984, Apple introduced Macintosh 512K, which was the original Macintosh with 512 KB of RAM, or four times the memory of the original Macintosh. This greater memory (provided by the use of 256 KB chips), combined with the availability of external 3.5-inch 400 KB disk drives, opened up a new market for larger and more sophisticated software packages.

1985

In January, 1985, Apple introduced the LaserWriter, which was a 300-dpi printer based on the Canon CX laser printer engine. It was billed as Apple's "most powerful computer," including a Motorola 68000 microprocessor running at 12 MHz, 1.5 MB of RAM, and 512 KB of ROM. The LaserWriter had in ROM a new page description language called PostScript, created by Adobe Systems.

Along with the LaserWriter, Apple also introduced its AppleTalk local area network, which allowed devices such as the LaserWriter to be shared by up to 32 users. At this time, the main engineering network in Apple's Bandley 2 building was running more than 65 nodes out of a theoretical maximum of 254 devices. Maze Wars was being played by a majority of the engineers on this network; this heavy use caused the network to come to its knees, and EtherTalk was soon being considered.

As Lisa sales slowed, Apple renamed Lisa 2 to Macintosh XL. Apple also released an emulation package for Lisa called MacWorks, which allowed the Mac XL to run Macintosh software. Only a few months later, Apple discontinued the Lisa/Mac XL altogether. Later in the year Steve Jobs left Apple and formed NeXT.

Later in 1985 came software that really began to take advantage of the Macintosh platform. Part of this development was due to the May Software Supplement, which provided a massive amount of information to developers. Harvey Alcabes gathered more than a dozen disks and thousands of pages of documentation for this publication. Major third-party releases later in the year included an integrated package from Lotus called

Jazz, Microsoft's Excel spreadsheet, and Aldus' PageMaker, a page composition program especially tuned to work with the LaserWriter. Together, these and other programs began the desktop publishing revolution.

A major software innovation was also created by Andy Hertzfeld: Switcher, a small application that allowed multiple applications to coexist. It was written entirely in 68000 assembly language using MDS and went through many iterations and releases, culminating in Switcher 5.2. Although it was not as reliable as MultiFinder eventually was, it certainly laid the application groundwork for MultiFinder. Erich Ringewald began to maintain Switcher in late 1985 but soon decided to rewrite it completely.

In September, 1985, the Hard Disk 20, along with the Hierarchical File System (HFS), allowed Macintoshes to work with large numbers of files much more efficiently, and a new ImageWriter II printer offered faster printing, AppleTalk support, and color printing.

The Hard Disk 20 with the Macintosh 512K used a 400K Boot Disk with a RAM-based version of HFS that augmented the original flat Macintosh File System (MFS). The later 128 KB ROMs of the Mac Plus had HFS built in, which ended the days of the Boot Disk. HFS was originally called TFS, for Turbo File System. The name came from a project called Turbo Mac that began in late 1984. Turbo Mac was to be a faster Mac in the original Mac box, but the project was scrapped in early 1985. The Macintosh Plus project replaced it, and it included TFS under the name of HFS.

HFS was written by Pat Dirks and Bill Bruffy, with some help from Larry Kenyon, the author of MFS. HFS was tested by Mark Neubieser, Steve Goldberg, and Dan Allen using the Neubian "Script Interpreter" with Goldberg's "Monkey" scripts for exhaustive testing.

Finder 4.1 was released in May, 1985, the last and best of the MFS-only Finders. Finder 5.0 was the first Finder that supported HFS. It shipped with the Hard Disk 20 disk after a long season of Finders whose code names all began with the letter "S." The code name replaced the word "Special" in the menu bar. Some of these names were Swizzle, Sushi, and Spam. Those were the halcyon days…

1986

In January, 1986, Apple introduced the Macintosh Plus, which added support for external peripherals through a Small Computer Standard Interface (SCSI) port. It had a larger-capacity 3.5-inch Sony floppy disk drive. The new drive used double-sided disks that held 800 KB. The drive was also faster and quieter than older drives. The Macintosh Plus increased standard memory to 1 MB, expandable to 4 MB via the use of SIMMs modules. The ROMs were expanded from 64 KB to 128 KB and featured HFS and faster versions of the Resource Manager and QuickDraw. MacWrite and MacPaint were no longer bundled with each Macintosh that Apple shipped.

The Mac Plus began the trend toward smaller connectors, with its mini DIN-8 serial connections replacing the earlier DB-9 connectors. It also began the trend toward larger keyboards, with a built-in (rather than optional) numeric keypad; the new keyboard was variously code-named the Saratoga, Nimitz, or Dörfer.

The Mac Plus ROMs were done in about six months by a very small group of people. Ed Colby and Eric Harslem led Ernie Beernink, Bill Bruffy, Steve Capps, Jerome Coonen, Donn Denman, Pat Dirks, Larry Kenyon, Bryan McGhie, and Erich Ringewald to create new sets of ROMs almost daily in late 1985. Each new set of high and low ROMs were given interesting names, such as Happy Landing, Hoist Lanyard, Land Ho, Hearty Laughter, Halle Lujah, Lonely Hearts (the final ROM that shipped with the original Mac Plus), and Lonely Heifer (a single ROM patched in slightly later Mac Pluses to fix the infamous SCSI bug). Note the nautical theme, due in large part to Ed Colbydörfer and Jerome Coonenmüller.

Along with the usual bug fixes and optimizations, the new ROMs offered much greater speed than the original 64K ROMs. A major speed-up in QuickDraw was achieved by the classical trade-off of space for speed: loops were unwound by in-lining the code. There was also new code in the ROMs for the SCSI Manager and Time Manager. Several of the resources normally found in the System file (including the float-ing-point packages) were also put in ROM. There was no wasted space in the ROMs.

The Macintosh 128K and 512K became part of history as the Macintosh 512Ke slowly replaced them as the new low end of Apple's Macintosh lineup. The 512Ke was the original Mac 512K with the new 128 KB ROMs and 800 KB disk drive that the Mac Plus offered. The 512Ke therefore had the original 512K motherboard—no SIMMs modules—and retained the DIN-9 connectors for the serial ports. Original Macintosh owners could upgrade their computers to either the Mac 512Ke or the Mac Plus level.

Along with the Macintosh Plus came the LaserWriter Plus, an upgraded version of the original LaserWriter with 1 MB of ROM containing more built-in PostScript fonts. The Mac Plus originally shipped with System 3.0 and Finder 5.1, but it took until June to release the classic System 3.2 and Finder 5.3 that was to be the Mac Plus standard for about one year.

1987

In January of 1987 came AppleShare, an application requiring a dedicated Macintosh to provide shared access of remote file server volumes with password protection over the AppleTalk network. AppleShare provided the second reason for people to install a network. Multiple volumes could be set up on one server.

In March, 1987, Apple introduced two new computers: the Macintosh SE and the Macintosh II. On the outside, the Mac SE was basically a Mac Plus with a small slot added for more peripherals, but on the inside the Mac SE had been redesigned in a major way. A lot of the logic of the Mac Plus was put into custom gate arrays, thus reducing cost and increasing reliability. The video interlace overhead was reduced, making the SE about 25 percent faster than a Mac Plus.

The SE had 1 MB of RAM (expandable to 4 MB), 256 KB of ROM, a SCSI port, and its own internal expansion connector. It was offered in two versions: with two internal 800 KB drives, or with one 800 KB floppy and a 20 MB built-in hard disk. Because of this internal hard disk option, a fan was required. Unfortunately, the original SE "air motion device" was loud; SEs made since early 1988 have a quieter fan.

The SE project was known at various times as Freeport, Maui, Mac±, and originally, as Aladdin. Many inside Apple joked that SE stood for Slightly Enhanced, but the official meaning of SE as System Expansion is quite appropriate. Third parties created a wide variety of cards to utilize this slot: for example, 68020/68881 accelerator cards, EtherTalk cards, 8086 PC cards, and cards for large displays.

The extra space in the SE ROMs is largely wasted. Each machine begins with the ROMs of the previous machine as a starting point, so the Mac Plus ROMs were the starting point for the Mac SE. The SE team choose 256 KB ROMs because they were the same size as the Mac II ROMs, which needed the room for things like Color QuickDraw. Some new code was shared between the SE and II, such as the Apple Desktop Bus (ADB) Manager, but there was so much free space left—and so little time to develop good tested code to fill that space—that the SE team ended up putting in several digitized pictures of themselves. To see the photos, go into MacsBug, set the program counter to $0041D89A, and then Go. To stop the photos, reset the machine.

The Macintosh II was the first Macintosh to use a different processor. The Mac II came with a 16.67 MHz Motorola 68020 and a 16.67 MHz Motorola 68881 floating-point coprocessor. Standard RAM was 1 MB, expandable to 8 MB, and 256 KB of ROM was included. Actually the Mac II was designed to hold 128 MB of RAM on the motherboard when 16 Mbit memory chips become available. The Mac II ROMs were quite a project because the developers had to work with a new 32-bit microprocessor and bus in 32-bit mode, as well as working with color across multiple monitors.

One internal 800 KB floppy disk drive was standard, with room for a second optional 800 KB drive. The Mac II also accommodated an internal SCSI hard disk, as well as external SCSI devices through the SCSI bus. The Mac II had six slots using the NuBus architecture, and it offered a NuBus video card that supported up to 256 colors chosen from a palette of 16 million colors. The same Apple Video Card worked with either color or black-and-white monitors and offered 16 levels of gray or 16 colors in its standard configuration. Optional RAM fully populated the card and offered the 256 colors or grays. The Mac II opened the world of color to Macintosh users.

The Mac II is a descendant of several interesting 68020 projects proposed internally at Apple in 1985. These projects were called Jonathon, Mid Mac, and Big Mac. Jonathon fizzled, and the chief architect of Big Mac left with Steve Jobs to form NeXT. This left Mid Mac—also known as Little Big Mac—as the main expandable Mac project. It took its first formal step with a full hardware specification under the name of Milwaukee. Milwaukee then was known variously as Becks (another beer), Ikki ("bottoms up" in Japanese), Paris (because of Jean Louis Gasseé's involvement), and Reno (both the city of Reno and the Mac II have slots).

At the Boston Mac World Expo in August of 1987 came two very important pieces of software: HyperCard and MultiFinder. HyperCard was an all new type of software, a blend between a programming environment, a flexible text-retrieval system, and a souped-up MacPaint. Written by Bill Atkinson and known as WildCard during its two-year development, HyperCard has become a very useful and powerful tool for many different applications. It is discussed in more detail in Chapter 10.

MultiFinder was a cooperative multitasking system designed by Erich Ringewald. Contrary to what the press thought, MultiFinder was a completely different piece of software from Hertzfeld's Switcher. Written largely in MPW C, MultiFinder was variously known as Twitcher, Oggler, and Juggler. Phil Goldman and Erich Ringewald split the work with the aid of an AppleShare file server and GCS: the Goldman Control System. More on MultiFinder can be found in Chapter 2. Both HyperCard and MultiFinder became bundled with the Macintosh.

Also unveiled at the Boston MacWorld was a faster and sharper ImageWriter LQ with a 27-pin dot matrix print head offering 216-dpi resolution and a 15-inch-wide carriage. Other peripherals included EtherTalk software and cards for the Mac SE and Mac II, as well as a FAX modem.

It was a busy year for system software: Finder 5.4 was released with AppleShare in January; System 4.1 and Finder 5.5 were released in April of 1987 with the Mac II; System 4.2, Finder 6.0, and MultiFinder 1.0 were bundled as System Tools 5.0 in October; and the System was revised to 4.3 for System Tools 5.1 in December.

1988

Three refined LaserWriters appeared at the start of 1988, with the introduction of the expandable LaserWriter II. The LaserWriter II offered a single laser print engine—the Canon SX—and three different modular controller cards, thus allowing an upgrade path.

The basic LaserWriter IISC controller was a QuickDraw-based 300-dpi card that contained a 7.5 MHz 68000 microprocessor and 1 MB of RAM. It had a single SCSI port that restricted the printer's use to a single Macintosh. The LaserWriter IINT controller contained a 12 MHz 68000 microprocessor, 1 MB of ROM, and 2 MB of RAM. This PostScript based card configured the LaserWriter II to be similar to a LaserWriter Plus, which it replaced. The LaserWriter IINTX controller, with its 16.67 MHz 68020 microprocessor, offered the fastest printing yet. It retained the 1 MB of ROM and 2 MB of RAM of the IINT, but added the ability to expand both ROM and RAM up to 12 MB. It also could have its own dedicated hard disk to hold fonts.

In addition, Apple got into the CD-ROM arena with its CD SC drive, with full support for the High Sierra and ISO 9660 standards. To users, the CD SC drive acted like a much larger and write-protected SCSI hard disk. A single removable plastic CD-ROM with a diameter of 120 mm could be partitioned to hold multiple formats, including HFS (Macintosh) files, Apple II ProDos files, MS-DOS, and CD-Audio, with a capacity totaling 550 MB per compact disc. (The CD-Audio people spell "disc" with a "c," whereas in the computer world, "disk" is spelled with a "k.")

The Apple flatbed Scanner provided 300-dpi resolution with 16 levels of gray scale information to help provide the same resolution input to the Macintosh that LaserWriters output. The scanner came with AppleScan and HyperScan software. Bill Atkinson's HyperScan brought images directly into HyperCard and thus was especially fast and easy to use. It offered a new style of dithering called *diffusion* that made scanned images very attractive.

System Tools 6.0 debuted in April of 1988, with Finder 6.1, System 6.0, and MultiFinder 6.0. It took until September, when System 6.0.2 was released, to get the bugs out of the System software. HyperCard 1.2 came early in the year offering many new features, and HyperCard version 1.2.2, which fixed 1.2's bugs, came late in November.

In September, 1988, Apple introduced the Macintosh IIx, the company's first 68030-based Macintosh. This enhanced version of the Macintosh II featured 4 MB of RAM standard and a FDHD 1.4 MB disk drive that could read and write 3.5-inch disks for Macintosh, Apple II, and IBM formats. A faster Motorola 68882 floating-point coprocessor replaced the Mac II's earlier 68881 coprocessor. The Mac IIx standard configurations offered internal 40 MB and 80 MB hard disks. At this time, a new configuration of the Macintosh SE also was offered, providing 2 MB of RAM and an internal 40 MB 3.5-inch hard disk.

1989

In January, 1989, Apple introduced the Macintosh SE/30, which featured Mac II logic in the classic Macintosh form factor, thus retaining the 9-inch built-in monitor. Like the Macintosh IIx, the SE/30 had a 68030 microprocessor running at 16.67 MHz, a 68882 floating-point coprocessor also at 16.67 MHz, 1 MB of RAM expandable to 8 MB, a FDHD 1.4 MB 3.5-inch floppy disk drive, and an internal 40 MB hard disk. A version with 4 MB of RAM and an 80 MB 3.5-inch internal hard disk was also offered. (The 3.5-inch internal 40 MB and 80 MB hard disks were particularly quiet and fast, unlike the slow and noisy 20 MB 3.5-inch internal drives.) The Mac SE/30 had Color QuickDraw in ROM, so a color video card could be connected to an external color monitor through its unique 122-pin bus. To support the new machine, System 6.0.3 was released with the SE/30.

In March, 1989, Apple introduced the Macintosh IIcx, a Macintosh IIx in a case about half as wide as a Mac II, with only 3 NuBus slots instead of 6. At 14 pounds it was the lightest Mac made to date. It had a 68030 and a 68882, both running at 16.67 MHz, 1 MB of RAM expandable to 8 MB, and the 1.4 MB 3.5-inch floppy disk. Options included a 40 MB internal hard disk, or 4 MB of RAM and an 80 MB hard disk. Along with the IIcx came two new monitor choices: a portrait full-page display and a two-page display, as well as three NuBus cards: a low-cost 1-bit black-and-white display card, a card for the portrait display, and a card for the two-page display. The Mac IIx was also offered in several new RAM/disk configurations: 1 MB/no hard disk, 1 MB/40 MB 3.5-inch internal hard disk, and 4 MB/160 MB internal 5.25-inch hard disk. A 160 MB 5.25-inch external SCSI hard disk was also offered.

In September, 1989, the long-awaited Portable Macintosh was finally unveiled. Roughly equivalent in functionality to the Macintosh SE, the Portable weighed 15 pounds and was rather large for a laptop, but it ran up to 12 hours on a charge of its lead-acid batteries. Its long battery life was due to a special Power Manager chip that slowed the processor and put the machine to sleep when possible. It came with a CMOS version of the 68000 running at 16 MHz, 1 MB of static RAM (expandable to 4 MB), a ROM slot, a 1.4 MB floppy drive, and an optional 40 MB hard disk. The display was an active matrix LCD with 640 x 400 pixel resolution, while the full-size non-detachable keyboard could accept either a trackball or a numeric keypad. Perhaps the nicest touch was a beautiful carrying case.

The Macintosh IIci was also introduced in September. The Macintosh IIci was a IIcx with a faster 25 MHz 68030, a built-in video card for all Apple monitors (except the Two Page Display), and a slot for an optional memory cache board. The on-board video avoided NuBus by using main memory as the SE/30 did, thus freeing up an otherwise used slot. The new 512 KB ROM was 32-bit clean and incorporated 32-bit Color QuickDraw. Parity checking RAM was another option. A/UX release 1.1.1 was also introduced, supporting Apple's flavor of UNIX on the Mac II, Mac IIx, Mac IIcx, Mac IIci, and SE/30 machines.

As Apple continues to create new models of Macintosh, compatibility becomes of greater importance to those who create Macintosh software. Understanding the basics of the Macintosh architecture will help you dramatically in this process.

## CHAPTER 1

THE MACINTOSH ARCHITECTURE

Important components of the architecture of the Macintosh are presented in this chapter. First, we will look at the world of software from the applications programmer's point of view. Next, we will take a brief look at the hardware side of the Macintosh and then examine how memory is used by the operating system. Finally, we will look at the heart of the Macintosh operating system, the trap dispatcher.

Code for three MPW tools is presented: `ATrap`, which looks up an A-trap given either its name or number; `LoMem`, which looks up low-memory globals by name or number; and `Ascii`, which displays the Macintosh character set.

The Macintosh Software Architecture

In its broadest sense, the Macintosh software architecture can be described as a set of three layers, each layer of software building upon the previous layer. Each software layer also emphasizes a particular piece of hardware.

Layer one is the world of bits, bytes, and assembly language. The first layer is chiefly concerned with the manipulation of hardware and basic system resources. Software that performs these functions, known as system software, usually just means an operating system; an operating system is the software that manages the fundamental resources of the computer, which are memory, processes, and files. The Macintosh has added two higher levels of system software: a standard graphics kernel called QuickDraw and a collection of user interface components collectively called the Toolbox.

Code written at this level is usually machine-dependent, although assembly language code can usually be written to work across a range of similar machines. In the case of the Macintosh, the vast majority of the instructions found in 68000 assembly language will run on all varieties of Macintoshes. The newer, more sophisticated 68020 and 68030 processors, however, offer instructions that are not available in 68000 assembly language. Programs and compilers that use these new instructions will not run on older Macs that use the 68000.

The native Macintosh operating system contained in ROM on all Macintoshes is written in assembly language, both for speed and for the full freedom to access the processor and memory. For these reasons, many of the most popular applications found on

1

personal computers today—for example, Lotus 1–2–3, WriteNow, WordPerfect, Reflex, and Turbo Pascal—are written in assembly language.

Assembly language code can be hard to maintain. It does not have to be that way—use of the MPW Structured Macro package, for example, makes assembly language code appear more like Pascal—but assembly language code often regresses to sloppy, "spaghetti" code. Everything that takes place in the Macintosh, no matter how it is initially coded, is actually performed as assembly language instructions executed by the microprocessor, so an *understanding of assembly language is essential for a good Macintosh programmer*. Some types of bugs are difficult to find and fix unless you have at least a good reading knowledge of assembly language.

Layer two is the world of high-level computer languages, such as C and Pascal. The second layer begins to attribute meaning to bits and bytes. Most of the meaning of a given computation at this level is stored symbolically, with information or data broken into word-sized chunks rather than bits or bytes. The definition of a word on a Macintosh is usually considered to be 32 bits.

High-level languages are usually better than assembly language to write applications with, because they abstract the messy details of addressing modes and bit twiddling that are part of layer-one programming. High-level languages also have their own library routines to insulate programmers from the operating system.

Layer three is the world of applications. Applications include word processors, spreadsheets, databases, graphics, and communication packages. Many of these applications include ways for users to customize applications with a macro or scripting language. (*Customize* is the "user friendly" way of saying *program*.) Such programming involves working with Excel macros, HyperTalk scripts, and fourth-generation database query languages (4GLs), for example. These offer a simple, high-level approach to using the Macintosh ROM resources. Bits and bytes are—or at least should be—completely hidden at this level. This level of computing interacts with information at the document or stream level; it is the level that most "end users" see.

Unfortunately, with each increase in data abstraction and power comes a corresponding decrease in speed and efficiency. Most of the layer-three applications that contain languages use interpreters rather than compilers and hence are not suited for large or complex jobs.

There are several notable layer-three tools, however, that you will find very useful. These tools are also good representatives of what can be created with the tools of layers one and two:

- HyperCard   Hypertext, graphics, scripting (Apple)
- Excel   Data and statistical analysis, charting, macros (Microsoft)
- Word   Documenting code, style sheets (Microsoft)

- More   Outlining, desktop presentations (Semantec)
- MacDraw   Object graphics (Claris)
- PageMaker   Desktop publishing (Aldus)
- Illustrator   PostScript graphics (Adobe)

The Macintosh Hardware Architecture

The Macintosh—like any computer—is composed of three major types of hardware: memory (both RAM and ROM), a central processing unit (CPU), and several I/O devices. As shown in the following table, each of these pieces of hardware has an influence on the Macintosh architecture because of specific low-level protocols and conventions that have been adopted for using these devices.

Hardware Element(s)	Architecture Element
Memory	Memory map
I/O	Memory mapped RS-232, SCSI
CPU	Register saving conventions
CPU, Memory	Parameter passing conventions
CPU, Memory	A5 World
Memory	Low-memory globals
Memory	A-trap dispatcher / system routines

Memory Map

One of the best ways to learn about how the Macintosh works is to begin with a detailed look at the memory map, which will show you where things are located. Although the actual addresses in memory differ from model to model, the same basic elements are present on all flavors of Macintosh.

Each of the major parts of the Macintosh (memory, CPU, and I/O devices) interacts with the memory map in different ways. The following table gives a simple view of the Macintosh Plus memory, shown with high memory descending to low memory. Other versions of the Macintosh are slightly different.

Address	Memory Map for the Macintosh Plus
$EFFFFF	End of VIA space
$E80000	Beginning of VIA space
$DFFFFF	End of IWM space
$D00000	Beginning of IWM space
$BFFFFF	End of SCC write
$B00000	Beginning of SCC write
$09FFFF	End of SCC read
$090000	Beginning of SCC read
$5FFFFF	End of SCSI
$580000	Beginning of SCSI
$41FFFF	End of ROM
$400000	Beginning of ROM
$3FFFFF	End of RAM (with 4 MB of RAM installed)
varies	Sound buffer
varies	System Error Handler area
varies	Main Screen (ScrnBase)
varies	MacsBug, if installed
varies	RAM cache, if installed
varies	Jump table (A5)
varies	Application and QuickDraw globals (A5)
varies	Stack (A7)
varies	Beginning of the application heap (ApplZone)
$001600	Beginning of the system heap (SysZone)
$000E00	Beginning of the Toolbox A-trap table
$000800	More low-memory globals
$000400	Beginning of the OS A-trap table
$000100	Beginning of low-memory global area
$000000	Beginning of RAM; Motorola vectors

Memory Mapped I/O

The higher locations in the memory map are devoted to *memory mapped I/O*. The chips that control the peripherals are seen by the CPU as living at the various addresses shown in the table above. These locations vary between models of the Macintosh, but can be determined by examining certain special locations in low RAM. Our exploration into the memory map will concentrate on examining RAM, where the most important things are happening as far as you are concerned, but we will start by reviewing quickly what the basic I/O devices are on the Mac.

At the top of the map is the 6522 Versatile Interface Adapter, or VIA. This chip interfaces with the keyboard, mouse, and real-time clock, and it contains two microsecond timers. It also is involved with the disk drives, sound, video, serial interface, and SCSI interrupts. On the Mac SE and later computers, this chip deals with the keyboard and mouse through the custom Apple Desktop Bus (ADB) chip.

Next on the map is the Integrated Woz Machine, or IWM. This custom Apple chip controls the Sony floppy disk drives as well as the original Apple Hard Disk 20. The maximum data transfer rate for the IWM is about 500 Kbits per second (Kbaud).

The next major chip is a Zilog Z8530 Serial Communications Controller, or SCC, which is a programmable dual-channel chip that also converts between parallel and serial. It controls the twin RS-422 (a more noise-immune version of RS-232) serial ports found on all Macs, and thus is involved with printers, modems, and AppleTalk. AppleTalk transmits at about 230.4 Kbaud, but the serial ports can actually get up to about 500 Kbaud under ideal circumstances.

The last important device is the NCR 5380 Small Computer System Interface chip, or SCSI for short. This byte-oriented interface can be used to connect up to seven peripherals to the Mac and is designed for fast hard disks and the like. It can transfer 170 K bytes per second on the Mac Plus all the way up to 1.4 M bytes per second on the Mac II. (Note that these figures are bytes: multiply by 8 to compare with the transfer rates of the other chips.)

Register Saving Conventions

Although you can see many of the I/O devices in the memory map, the CPU itself does not appear anywhere in this map. The 68000 processor is what actually moves things around in the memory map, via the bus. The Motorola 68000 has 16 main registers, a program counter, and a status register. More recent members of the 68xxx family have additional registers. Floating-point chips have 8 floating-point (FP) registers and three status registers.

The 68000 registers are organized into a set of 8 data registers and a set of 8 address registers. Another aspect of the Macintosh architecture dictates what some of these registers must be used for, with other registers being left for your arbitrary use (or the use of a compiler). The basic register conventions are shown in the following table.

68000 Register	Use Within Macintosh Architecture
A7	Stack pointer
A6	Local stack frame pointer; preserved by ROM
A5	Global data pointer; preserved by ROM
A4	Free to use; preserved by ROM
A3	Free to use; preserved by ROM
A2	Free to use; preserved by ROM
A1	Scratch; preserved by just OS routines
A0	Scratch; OS ROM routines return results here

continued

continued from page 5

68000 Register	Use Within Macintosh Architecture
D7	Free to use; preserved by ROM
D6	Free to use; preserved by ROM
D5	Free to use; preserved by ROM
D4	Free to use; preserved by ROM
D3	Free to use; preserved by ROM
D2	Free to use; preserved by just OS routines
D1	Free to use; preserved by just OS routines
D0	Scratch; OS ROM routines return results here
PC	Program counter; specifies which instruction to execute

Parameter Passing Conventions

Another aspect of the Macintosh register conventions deals with the way parameters are passed to ROM routines. Most operating system routines are register-based, but unfortunately not all are. Parameters are usually passed to routines in D0, A0, and sometimes A1, with results returned in D0 and sometimes A0.

The other style of calling is called *stack-based.* Most Toolbox routines, but not all, are stack-based. Parameters are passed using Pascal conventions, which occur in the following order.

1. Space is reserved on the stack for a result if the routine is a function.
2. The parameters are pushed on the stack, from left to right.
3. The trap is called.
4. The called routine removes its own parameters.
5. The function result (if any) is put on the stack.
6. The routine returns via an RTS.

These conventions are called *Pascal calling conventions,* and they are used throughout the Toolbox and in the Pascal compiler. The C compiler has a different set of calling conventions, unless the `pascal` keyword is used. The following table presents a comparison of the calling conventions of C and Pascal.

Parameter	MPW Pascal	MPW C 3.0
Order of evaluation:	Left to right	Right to left
Remover of params:	Callee	Caller
Boolean	1 byte (0 or 1)	4 bytes, sign ext.
-128..127	1 byte	4 bytes, sign ext.
Integer, char	2 bytes	4 bytes, sign ext.
-32767..32767	2 bytes	4 bytes, sign ext.
LongInts	4 bytes	4 bytes
Pointers	4 bytes	4 bytes
SW SANE types	Address of extended	10 byte values
68881 SANE types	Address of extended	12 byte values
Structure <= 4 bytes	Rec/Str/Array passed	struct passed
Structure > 4 bytes	4 byte Ptr to structure	struct passed
Pascal VAR params	4 byte Ptr to VAR	—
C style arrays	—	4 byte Ptr to array

Many of the Toolbox routines are functions that return values. Again, all of the Toolbox uses the Pascal conventions, but for comparison, the following table shows how function results are allocated and returned with both C and Pascal.

Function Results	MPW Pascal	MPW C 3.0
Allocator of result	Caller	—
Remover of result	Caller	—
Boolean	2 bytes (in high byte)	Register D0
-128..127	2 bytes	Register D0
Integer, char	2 bytes	Register D0
-32767..32767	2 bytes	Register D0
LongInts, Pointers	4 bytes	Register D0
Real	4 bytes	Reg D0,D1,A0 or FP0
Double,Extended	4 byte Ptr to temp	Reg D0,D1,A0 or FP0
Structure <= 4 bytes	Rec/Str/Array passed	Reg D0 - Ptr to struct
Structure > 4 bytes	4 byte Ptr to structure	Reg D0 - Ptr to struct

A5 World

An A5 world is that portion above an application's heap that contains its stack, global data, and jump table. Register A5 is actually a pointer to a pointer to QuickDraw global data. Positive offsets from A5 refer to jump table entries. (See the "Segment Loader" section in chapter 2 for more information.) Global data is stored below where A5 points, so negative offsets refer to global variables.

One A5 world is allocated per running application. Desk accessories, XCMDs, and definition procedures do not have their own A5 worlds. Unless an A5 world is faked, therefore, these lesser citizens do not have global data and multiple code segments.

When you are writing certain types of code—code that can be called during interrupts or from a patched out A-trap, or code in a definition procedure—it is important to remember that such code cannot rely upon having a known A5 world. Instead, you should write such types of code so that they save and restore A5 if they use global variables. The current application A5 can be retrieved from the low- memory global `CurrentA5` at $904.

Low-memory Globals

Low-memory globals maintain state information about the machine, display, keyboard, disk drive, OS, and Toolbox; they allow hardware to vary from machine to machine while maintaining software compatibility.

You should use low-memory globals in preference to hard-wired values, but A-traps are better than either from a compatibility perspective. In other words, you should use the A-trap `TickCount` rather than using the low-memory location `Ticks`. Unfortunately, many of the useful low-memory variables do not have A-trap interfaces. There is usually a much greater chance of your code having future incompatibilities with System software if you are using low memory than if you are not. Nevertheless, low memory is definitely the most efficient way to access state information, as there is no trap overhead. If you must use low-memory globals, at least try to avoid writing to low memory—that is, reading from low memory is safer than writing to it.

The A-trap Dispatcher

The real heart or "Grand Central Station" of the Macintosh architecture is the A-trap dispatcher. Virtually all requests for services from the Macintosh are vectored through this flexible mechanism. It is called the A-trap dispatcher because all system calls on the Macintosh are implemented with 68xxx instructions that begin with binary 1010, or hex A—hence A-trap. All 68xxx processors have set aside all instructions beginning with hex A for just such uses.

The A-trap dispatcher is set up by the Macintosh during the boot process. The original 64 KB ROM had just one table of traps, with the lower-numbered traps being for the operating system and the higher-numbered traps for the Toolbox. Since the introduction of the 128 KB ROM, this table has been expanded and separated into two tables that reside in low memory beneath the system heap.

The A-trap dispatcher looks up the current address of a specified routine and then calls that routine. By using `GetTrapAddress` and `SetTrapAddress,` you can change these tables to refer to different routines than the normal ROM routines. Such changes to the trap tables are usually done by Apple in order to fix bugs, but there are many other nifty uses as well. Some of the functions that can be accomplished by patching out traps and/or doing pre- and post-processing around traps include the following:

- By intercepting the `Open` and `Close` calls, the MPW Shell can support its windows over files abstraction. (It also uses the low-memory global `FSQueueHook` to do this.)
- By intercepting Memory Manager calls, the MPW Shell can mark blocks of memory allocated by MPW tools.
- HyperCard intercepts the `DrawMenuBar` trap to draw its padlock when a stack is locked.
- MultiFinder intercepts many Event Manager and Window Manager traps to allow multiple applications to share the screen.

Not all routines are implemented on all Macs. For example, none of the Color QuickDraw and Palette Manager calls are implemented on a Mac Plus. One trap is guaranteed always to be unimplemented: $A89F. To determine if a trap is available, do a `GetTrapAddress` on the trap in question and a `GetTrapAddress` on the official unimplemented trap $A89F. If their addresses are the same, the trap is questionable; do not use it.

An A-trap word begins with binary 1010 in bits 15 through 12, as mentioned above. Bit 11 is set for Toolbox traps and cleared for OS traps. Bit 10 is the auto-pop bit for Toolbox traps and is a flag for OS traps. All of the details of an A-trap word are normally handled by the libraries and interfaces found that are part of MPW.

The auto-pop bit is rarely used any more. If this bit is set, it is assumed that two return addresses were pushed on the stack (old compilers JSRed to the trap word rather than putting the A-trap in-line), and the trap dispatcher pops the trap's return address off the stack so that the flow returns directly to the calling program. This mechanism was set up for older development environments that could not generate in-line A-trap instructions.

Bit 9 is reserved for future use for Toolbox traps and is another flag for OS traps. Bits 8 to 0 constitute the A-trap number for Toolbox traps; bits 7 to 0 make up this number for OS traps. Bit 8 for OS traps is set if the trap dispatcher does not preserve A0 because the routine returns a result there. If the bit is clear, the trap dispatcher will save and restore A0.

The following list presents examples of the flag bits in OS trap words.

- If bit 9 is set in memory manager calls that allocate memory, the requested memory will be zeroed upon allocation; if clear, the memory is left in an unknown "garbage" state.

- If bit 10 is set in a memory manager call, the call applies to the system heap; if clear, the call applies to the current zone, usually the application heap.

- If bit 9 is set for a device driver call, the call is executed immediately; if clear, it is not.

- If bit 9 is set for a file system call, the call is an HFS call; if clear, it is an MFS call. This indicates the expected size of the parameter block that will be passed to these routines.

- If bit 10 is set for a file system or device driver call, the call is to be executed asynchronously; if clear, the routine is executed synchronously.

- If bit 9 is set for calls to GetTrapAddress and SetTrapAddress, the new trap numbering (two separate tables) is used; if clear, the old 64 KB ROM conventions apply.

- If bit 10 is set for calls to GetTrapAddress and SetTrapAddress, Toolbox traps are assumed; if clear, OS traps are assumed.

- If bit 9 is set for RelString and EqualString calls, the comparison ignores diacriticals.

- If bit 10 is set for RelString and EqualString calls, the comparison is case-sensitive.

- If bit 8 is set for calls to PostEvent in 128 KB ROMs or later, A0 will return a pointer to the event queue entry. This new routine is called `PPostEvent`.

Of course, all of these details are normally handled for you by the system and your development environment, but knowing these details does help when debugging. In fact, MacsBug, the assembly level debugger, is a useful tool in exploring low memory and A-traps.

ATrap—C Tool

This MPW tool is useful for quickly looking up A-traps by name or number. Look-up is case-sensitive, and all entries that match the given string are output. Thus, typing `Menu` or `Color` will list most of the traps that deal with menus or color, for example. The names of A-traps are standardized but sometimes are written differently for assembly language and Pascal. In the end, it is the trap number that really matters.

Improving ATrap

Here are some suggestions for improving `ATrap`:

- `ATrap` uses the ANSI C standard library routine `strstr`, which was not present for MPW C 2.0. Add this functionality if needed.
- Add the full *Inside Macintosh* parameters for each trap.

```
/*
 *  ATrap.c - Looks up by trap number the name of a Macintosh trap
 *          - Alternately dumps a list of all trap names and numbers
 *          - Written by Dan Allen 10/30/88
 *          - Name lookup added 2/1/89
 */

#include  <CType.h>
#include  <StdIO.h>
#include  <String.h>

typedef unsigned short word;

typedef struct trap {
  char   *name;
  word   num;
} trap;

static trap list[] = {
"Open",0xA000,"Close",0xA001,"Read",0xA002,
"Write",0xA003,"Control",0xA004,"Status",0xA005,
"KillIO",0xA006,"GetVolInfo",0xA007,"Create",0xA008,
"Delete",0xA009,"OpenRF",0xA00A,"Rename",0xA00B,
"GetFileInfo",0xA00C,"SetFInfo",0xA00D,"UnmountVol",0xA00E,
"MountVol",0xA00F,"Allocate",0xA010,"GetEOF",0xA011,
"SetEOF",0xA012,"FlushVol",0xA013,"GetVol",0xA014,
"SetVol",0xA015,"InitQueue",0xA016,"Eject",0xA017,
"GetFPos",0xA018,"InitZone",0xA019,"GetZone",0xA01A,
"SetZone",0xA01B,"FreeMem",0xA01C ,"MaxMem",0xA01D,
"NewPtr",0xA01E,"DisposePtr",0xA01F,"SetPtrSize",0xA020,
```

```
"GetPtrSize",0xA021,"NewHandle",0xA022,"DisposeHandle",0xA023,
"SetHandleSize",0xA024,"GetHandleSize",0xA025,"HandleZone",0xA026,
"ReallocHandle",0xA027,"RecoverHandle",0xA028,"HLock",0xA029,
"HUnlock",0xA02A,"EmptyHandle",0xA02B,"InitApplZone",0xA02C,
"SetApplLimit",0xA02D,"BlockMove",0xA02E,"PostEvent",0xA02F,
"OSEventAvail",0xA030,"GetOSEvent",0xA031,"FlushEvents",0xA032,
"VInstall",0xA033,"VRemove",0xA034,"OffLine",0xA035,
"MoreMasters",0xA036,"ReadParam",0xA037,"WriteParam",0xA038,
"ReadDateTime",0xA039,"SetDateTime",0xA03A,"Delay",0xA03B,
"CmpString",0xA03C,"DrvrInstall",0xA03D,"DrvrRemove",0xA03E,
"InitUtil",0xA03F,"ResrvMem",0xA040,"SetFilLock",0xA041,
"RstFilLock",0xA042,"SetFilType",0xA043,"SetFPos",0xA044,
"FlushFile",0xA045,"GetTrapAddress",0xA046,"SetTrapAddress",0xA047,
"PtrZone",0xA048,"HPurge",0xA049,"HNoPurge",0xA04A,
"SetGrowZone",0xA04B,"CompactMem",0xA04C,"PurgeMem",0xA04D,
"AddDrive",0xA04E,"RDrvrInstall",0xA04F,"RelString",0xA050,
"ReadXPRam",0xA051,"WriteXPRam",0xA052,"ClkNoMem",0xA053,
"UprString",0xA054,"StripAddress",0xA055,"LwrString",0xA056,
"SetAppBase",0xA057,"InsTime",0xA058,"RmvTime",0xA059,
"PrimeTime",0xA05A,"PowerOff",0xA05B,"** Free **",0xA05C,
"SwapMMUMode",0xA05D,"NMInstall",0xA05E,"NMRemove",0xA05F,
"HFSDispatch",0xA060,"MaxBlock",0xA061,"PurgeSpace",0xA062,
"MaxApplZone",0xA063,"MoveHHi",0xA064,"StackSpace",0xA065,
"NewEmptyHandle",0xA066,"HSetRBit",0xA067,"HClrRBit",0xA068,
"HGetState",0xA069,"HSetState",0xA06A,"TestManager",0xA06B,
"InitFS",0xA06C,"InitEvents",0xA06D,"SlotManager",0xA06E,
"SlotVInstall",0xA06F,"SlotVRemove",0xA070,"AttachVBL",0xA071,
"DoVBLTask",0xA072,"OSReserved",0xA073,"** Free **",0xA074,
"SIntInstall",0xA075,"SIntRemove",0xA076,"CountADBs",0xA077,
"GetIndADB",0xA078,"GetADBInfo",0xA079,"SetADBInfo",0xA07A,
"ADBReInit",0xA07B,"ADBOp",0xA07C,"GetDefaultStartup",0xA07D,
"SetDefaultStartup",0xA07E,"InternalWait",0xA07F,"GetVideoDefault",0xA080,
"SetVideoDefault",0xA081,"DTInstall",0xA082,"SetOSDefault",0xA083,
"GetOSDefault",0xA084,"PmgrOp",0xA085,"SetIOPMsgInfo",0xA086,
"IOPMsgAccess",0xA087,"IOPMoveData",0xA088,"SCSIAtomic",0xA089,
"Sleep",0xA08A,"CommMgr",0xA08B,"** Free **",0xA08C,
"** Free **",0xA08D,"** Free **",0xA08E,"** Free **",0xA08F,
"SysEnvirons",0xA090,"SndDisposeChannel",0xA801,"SndAddModifier",0xA802,
"SndDoCommand",0xA803,"SndDoImmediate",0xA804,"SndPlay",0xA805,
"SndControl",0xA806,"SndNewChannel",0xA807,"InitProcMenu",0xA808,
"GetCVariant",0xA809,"GetWVariant",0xA80A,"PopUpMenuSelect",0xA80B,
"RGetResource",0xA80C,"Count1Resources",0xA80D,"Get1IxResource",0xA80E,
"Get1IxType",0xA80F,"Unique1ID",0xA810,"TESelView",0xA811,
"TEPinScroll",0xA812,"TEAutoView",0xA813,"SetFractEnable",0xA814,
"SCSIDispatch",0xA815,"Pack8",0xA816,"CopyMask",0xA817,
"FixATan2",0xA818,"XMunger",0xA819,"GetZone",0xA81A,
"SetZone",0xA81B,"Count1Types",0xA81C,"MaxMem",0xA81D,
"NewPtr",0xA81E,"Get1Resource",0xA81F,"Get1NamedResource",0xA820,
"MaxSizeRsrc",0xA821,"NwHandle",0xA822,"DsposeHandle",0xA823,
"SetHandleSize",0xA824,"GetHandleSize",0xA825,"InsMenuItem",0xA826,
"HideDItem",0xA827,"ShowDItem",0xA828,"HLock",0xA829,
```

```
"HUnLock",0xA82A,"Pack9",0xA82B,"Pack10",0xA82C,
"Pack11",0xA82D,"Pack12",0xA82E,"Pack13",0xA82F,
"Pack14",0xA830,"Pack15",0xA831,"FlushEvents",0xA832,
"ScrnBitMap",0xA833,"SetFScaleDisable",0xA834,"FontMetrics",0xA835,
"GetMaskTable",0xA836,"MeasureText",0xA837,"CalcMask",0xA838,
"SeedFill",0xA839,"ZoomWindow",0xA83A,"TrackBox",0xA83B,
"TEGetOffset",0xA83C,"TEDispatch",0xA83D,"TEStylNew",0xA83E,
"Long2Fix",0xA83F,"Fix2Long",0xA840,"Fix2Frac",0xA841,
"Frac2Fix",0xA842,"Fix2X",0xA843,"X2Fix",0xA844,
"Frac2X",0xA845,"X2Frac",0xA846,"FracCos",0xA847,
"FracSin",0xA848,"FracSqrt",0xA849,"FracMul",0xA84A,
"FracDiv",0xA84B,"CompactMem",0xA84C,"FixDiv",0xA84D,
"GetItemCmd",0xA84E,"SetItemCmd",0xA84F,"InitCursor",0xA850,
"SetCursor",0xA851,"HideCursor",0xA852,"ShowCursor",0xA853,
"UprString",0xA854,"ShieldCursor",0xA855,"ObscureCursor",0xA856,
"SetEntry",0xA857,"BitAnd",0xA858,"BitXor",0xA859,
"BitNot",0xA85A,"BitOr",0xA85B,"BitShift",0xA85C,
"BitTst",0xA85D,"BitSet",0xA85E,"BitClr",0xA85F,
"WaitNextEvent",0xA860,"Random",0xA861,"ForeColor",0xA862,
"BackColor",0xA863,"ColorBit",0xA864,"GetPixel",0xA865,
"StuffHex",0xA866,"LongMul",0xA867,"FixMul",0xA868,
"FixRatio",0xA869,"HiWord",0xA86A,"LoWord",0xA86B,
"FixRound",0xA86C,"InitPort",0xA86D,"InitGraf",0xA86E,
"OpenPort",0xA86F,"LocalToGlobal",0xA870,"GlobalToLocal",0xA871,
"GrafDevice",0xA872,"SetPort",0xA873,"GetPort",0xA874,
"SetPBits",0xA875,"PortSize",0xA876,"MovePortTo",0xA877,
"SetOrigin",0xA878,"SetClip",0xA879,"GetClip",0xA87A,
"ClipRect",0xA87B,"BackPat",0xA87C,"ClosePort",0xA87D,
"AddPt",0xA87E,"SubPt",0xA87F,"SetPt",0xA880,
"EqualPt",0xA881,"StdText",0xA882,"DrawChar",0xA883,
"DrawString",0xA884,"DrawText",0xA885,"TextWidth",0xA886,
"TextFont",0xA887,"TextFace",0xA888,"TextMode",0xA889,
"TextSize",0xA88A,"GetFontInfo",0xA88B,"StringWidth",0xA88C,
"CharWidth",0xA88D,"SpaceExtra",0xA88E,"OSDispatch",0xA88F,
"StdLine",0xA890,"LineTo",0xA891,"Line",0xA892,
"MoveTo",0xA893,"Move",0xA894,"ShutDown",0xA895,
"HidePen",0xA896,"ShowPen",0xA897,"GetPenState",0xA898,
"SetPenState",0xA899,"GetPen",0xA89A,"PenSize",0xA89B,
"PenMode",0xA89C,"PenPat",0xA89D,"PenNormal",0xA89E,
"Unimplemented",0xA89F,"StdRect",0xA8A0,"FrameRect",0xA8A1,
"PaintRect",0xA8A2,"EraseRect",0xA8A3,"InverRect",0xA8A4,
"FillRect",0xA8A5,"EqualRect",0xA8A6,"SetRect",0xA8A7,
"OffSetRect",0xA8A8,"InsetRect",0xA8A9,"SectRect",0xA8AA,
"UnionRect",0xA8AB,"Pt2Rect",0xA8AC,"PtInRect",0xA8AD,
"EmptyRect",0xA8AE,"StdRRect",0xA8AF,"FrameRoundRect",0xA8B0,
"PaintRoundRect",0xA8B1,"EraseRoundRect",0xA8B2,"InvertRoundRect",0xA8B3,
"FillRoundRect",0xA8B4,"ScriptUtil",0xA8B5,"StdOval",0xA8B6,
"FrameOval",0xA8B7,"PaintOval",0xA8B8,"EraseOval",0xA8B9,
"InvertOval",0xA8BA,"FillOval",0xA8BB,"SlopeFromAngle",0xA8BC,
"StdArc",0xA8BD,"FrameArc",0xA8BE,"PaintArc",0xA8BF,
"EraseArc",0xA8C0,"InvertArc",0xA8C1,"FillArc",0xA8C2,
```

```
"PtToAngle",0xA8C3,"AngleFromSlope",0xA8C4,"StdPoly",0xA8C5,
"FramePoly",0xA8C6,"PaintPoly",0xA8C7,"ErasePoly",0xA8C8,
"InvertPoly",0xA8C9,"FillPoly",0xA8CA,"OpenPoly",0xA8CB,
"ClosePoly",0xA8CC,"KillPoly",0xA8CD,"OffsetPoly",0xA8CE,
"PackBits",0xA8CF,"UnpackBits",0xA8D0,"StdRgn",0xA8D1,
"FrameRgn",0xA8D2,"PaintRgn",0xA8D3,"EraseRgn",0xA8D4,
"InvertRgn",0xA8D5,"FillRgn",0xA8D6,"BitMapRgn",0xA8D7,
"NewRgn",0xA8D8,"DisposeRgn",0xA8D9,"OpenRgn",0xA8DA,
"CloseRgn",0xA8DB,"CopyRgn",0xA8DC,"SetEmptyRgn",0xA8DD,
"SetRectRgn",0xA8DE,"RectRgn",0xA8DF,"OffsetRgn",0xA8E0,
"InsetRgn",0xA8E1,"EmptyRgn",0xA8E2,"EqualRgn",0xA8E3,
"SectRgn",0xA8E4,"UnionRgn",0xA8E5,"DiffRgn",0xA8E6,
"XorRgn",0xA8E7,"PtInRgn",0xA8E8,"RectInRgn",0xA8E9,
"SetStdProcs",0xA8EA,"StdBits",0xA8EB,"CopyBits",0xA8EC,
"StdTxMeas",0xA8ED,"StdGetPic",0xA8EE,"ScrollRect",0xA8EF,
"StdPutPic",0xA8F0,"StdComment",0xA8F1,"PicComment",0xA8F2,
"OpenPicture",0xA8F3,"ClosePicture",0xA8F4,"KillPicture",0xA8F5,
"DrawPicture",0xA8F6,"** Free **",0xA8F7,"ScalePt",0xA8F8,
"MapPt",0xA8F9,"MapRect",0xA8FA,"MapRgn",0xA8FB,
"MapPoly",0xA8FC,"PrGlue",0xA8FD,"InitFonts",0xA8FE,
"GetFontName",0xA8FF,"GetFNum",0xA900,"FMSwapFont",0xA901,
"RealFont",0xA902,"SetFontLock",0xA903,"DrawGrowIcon",0xA904,
"DragGrayRgn",0xA905,"NewString",0xA906,"SetString",0xA907,
"ShowHide",0xA908,"CalcVis",0xA909,"CalcVBehind",0xA90A,
"ClipAbove",0xA90B,"PaintOne",0xA90C,"PaintBehind",0xA90D,
"SaveOld",0xA90E,"DrawNew",0xA90F,"GetWMgrPort",0xA910,
"CheckUpdate",0xA911,"InitWindows",0xA912,"NewWindow",0xA913,
"DisposeWindow",0xA914,"ShowWindow",0xA915,"HideWindow",0xA916,
"GetWRefCon",0xA917,"SetWRefCon",0xA918,"GetWTitle",0xA919,
"SetWTitle",0xA91A,"MoveWindow",0xA91B,"HiliteWindow",0xA91C,
"SizeWindow",0xA91D,"TrackGoAway",0xA91E,"SelectWindow",0xA91F,
"BringToFront",0xA920,"SendBehind",0xA921,"BeginUpdate",0xA922,
"EndUpdate",0xA923,"FrontWindow",0xA924,"DragWindow",0xA925,
"DragTheRgn",0xA926,"InvalRgn",0xA927,"InvalRect",0xA928,
"ValidRgn",0xA929,"ValidRect",0xA92A,"GrowWindow",0xA92B,
"FindWindow",0xA92C,"CloseWindow",0xA92D,"SetWindowPic",0xA92E,
"GetWindowPic",0xA92F,"InitMenus",0xA930,"NewMenu",0xA931,
"DisposeMenu",0xA932,"AppendMenu",0xA933,"ClearMenuBar",0xA934,
"InsertMenu",0xA935,"DeleteMenu",0xA936,"DrawMenuBar",0xA937,
"HiliteMenu",0xA938,"EnableItem",0xA939,"DisableItem",0xA93A,
"GetMenuBar",0xA93B,"SetMenuBar",0xA93C,"MenuSelect",0xA93D,
"MenuKey",0xA93E,"GetItmIcon",0xA93F,"SetItmIcon",0xA940,
"GetItmStyle",0xA941,"SetItmStyle",0xA942,"GetItemMark",0xA943,
"SetItemMark",0xA944,"CheckItem",0xA945,"GetItem",0xA946,
"SetItem",0xA947,"CalcMenuSize",0xA948,"GetMHandle",0xA949,
"SetMenuFlash",0xA94A,"PlotIcon",0xA94B,"FlashMenuBar",0xA94C,
"AddResMenu",0xA94D,"PinRect",0xA94E,"DeltaPoint",0xA94F,
"CountMItems",0xA950,"InsertResMenu",0xA951,"DelMenuItem",0xA952,
"UpdtControl",0xA953,"NewControl",0xA954,"DisposeControl",0xA955,
"KillControls",0xA956,"ShowControl",0xA957,"HideControl",0xA958,
"MoveControl",0xA959,"GetCRefCon",0xA95A,"SetCRefCon",0xA95B,
```

```
"SizeControl",0xA95C,"HiliteControl",0xA95D,"GetCTitle",0xA95E,
"SetCTitle",0xA95F,"GetCtlValue",0xA960,"GetMinCtl",0xA961,
"GetMaxCtl",0xA962,"SetCtlValue",0xA963,"SetMinCtl",0xA964,
"SetMaxCtl",0xA965,"TestControl",0xA966,"DragControl",0xA967,
"TrackControl",0xA968,"DrawControls",0xA969,"GetCtlAction",0xA96A,
"SetCtlAction",0xA96B,"FindControl",0xA96C,"Draw1Control",0xA96D,
"Dequeue",0xA96E,"Enqueue",0xA96F,"GetNextEvent",0xA970,
"EventAvail",0xA971,"GetMouse",0xA972,"Stilldown",0xA973,
"Button",0xA974,"TickCount",0xA975,"GetKeys",0xA976,
"WaitMouseUp",0xA977,"UpdtDialog",0xA978,"CouldDialog",0xA979,
"FreeDialog",0xA97A,"InitDialogs",0xA97B,"GetNewDialog",0xA97C,
"NewDialog",0xA97D,"SelIText",0xA97E,"IsDialogEvent",0xA97F,
"DialogSelect",0xA980,"DrawDialog",0xA981,"CloseDialog",0xA982,
"DisposeDialog",0xA983,"FindDItem",0xA984,"Alert",0xA985,
"StopAlert",0xA986,"NoteAlert",0xA987,"CautionAlert",0xA988,
"CouldAlert",0xA989,"FreeAlert",0xA98A,"ParamText",0xA98B,
"ErrorSound",0xA98C,"GetDItem",0xA98D,"SetDItem",0xA98E,
"SetIText",0xA98F,"GetIText",0xA990,"ModalDialog",0xA991,
"DetachResource",0xA992,"SetResPurge",0xA993,"CurResFile",0xA994,
"InitResources",0xA995,"RsrcZoneInit",0xA996,"OpenResFile",0xA997,
"UseResFile",0xA998,"UpdateResFile",0xA999,"CloseResFile",0xA99A,
"SetResLoad",0xA99B,"CountResources",0xA99C,"GetIndResource",0xA99D,
"CountTypes",0xA99E,"GetIndType",0xA99F,"GetResource",0xA9A0,
"GetNamedResource",0xA9A1,"LoadResource",0xA9A2,"ReleaseResource",0xA9A3,
"HomeResFile",0xA9A4,"SizeRsrc",0xA9A5,"GetResAttrs",0xA9A6,
"SetResAttrs",0xA9A7,"GetResInfo",0xA9A8,"SetResInfo",0xA9A9,
"ChangedResource",0xA9AA,"AddResource",0xA9AB,"AddReference",0xA9AC,
"RmveResource",0xA9AD,"RmveReference",0xA9AE,"ResError",0xA9AF,
"WriteResource",0xA9B0,"CreateResFile",0xA9B1,"SystemEvent",0xA9B2,
"SystemClick",0xA9B3,"SystemTask",0xA9B4,"SystemMenu",0xA9B5,
"OpenDeskAcc",0xA9B6,"CloseDeskAcc",0xA9B7,"GetPattern",0xA9B8,
"GetCursor",0xA9B9,"GetString",0xA9BA,"GetIcon",0xA9BB,
"GetPicture",0xA9BC,"GetNewWindow",0xA9BD,"GetNewControl",0xA9BE,
"GetRMenu",0xA9BF,"GetNewMBar",0xA9C0,"UniqueID",0xA9C1,
"SysEdit",0xA9C2,"KeyTrans",0xA9C3,"OpenRFPerm",0xA9C4,
"RsrcMapEntry",0xA9C5,"Secs2Date",0xA9C6,"Date2Secs",0xA9C7,
"SysBeep",0xA9C8,"SysError",0xA9C9,"PutIcon",0xA9CA,
"TEGetText",0xA9CB,"TEInit",0xA9CC,"TEDispose",0xA9CD,
"TextBox",0xA9CE,"TESetText",0xA9CF,"TECalText",0xA9D0,
"TESetSelect",0xA9D1,"TENew",0xA9D2,"TEUpdate",0xA9D3,
"TEClick",0xA9D4,"TECopy",0xA9D5,"TECut",0xA9D6,
"TEDelete",0xA9D7,"TEActivate",0xA9D8,"TEDeactivate",0xA9D9,
"TEIdle",0xA9DA,"TEPaste",0xA9DB,"TEKey",0xA9DC,
"TEScroll",0xA9DD,"TEInsert",0xA9DE,"TESetJust",0xA9DF,
"Munger",0xA9E0,"HandToHand",0xA9E1,"PtrToXHand",0xA9E2,
"PtrToHand",0xA9E3,"HandAndHand",0xA9E4,"InitPack",0xA9E5,
"InitAllPacks",0xA9E6,"Pack0",0xA9E7,"Pack1",0xA9E8,
"Pack2",0xA9E9,"Pack3",0xA9EA,"Pack4",0xA9EB,
"Pack5",0xA9EC,"Pack6",0xA9ED,"Pack7",0xA9EE,
"PtrAndHand",0xA9EF,"LoadSeg",0xA9F0,"UnloadSeg",0xA9F1,
"Launch",0xA9F2,"Chain",0xA9F3,"ExitToShell",0xA9F4,
```

```
"GetAppParms",0xA9F5,"GetResFileAttrs",0xA9F6,"SetResFileAttrs",0xA9F7,
"MethodDispatch",0xA9F8,"InfoScrap",0xA9F9,"UnloadScrap",0xA9FA,
"LoadScrap",0xA9FB,"ZeroScrap",0xA9FC,"GetScrap",0xA9FD,
"PutScrap",0xA9FE,"Debugger",0xA9FF,"OpenCPort",0xAA00,
"InitCPort",0xAA01,"CloseCPort",0xAA02,"NewPixMap",0xAA03,
"DisposePixMap",0xAA04,"CopyPixMap",0xAA05,"SetCPortPix",0xAA06,
"NewPixPat",0xAA07,"DisposePixPat",0xAA08,"CopyPixPat",0xAA09,
"PenPixPat",0xAA0A,"BackPixPat",0xAA0B,"GetPixPat",0xAA0C,
"MakeRGBPat",0xAA0D,"FillCRect",0xAA0E,"FillCOval",0xAA0F,
"FillCRoundRect",0xAA10,"FillCArc",0xAA11,"FillCRgn",0xAA12,
"FillCPoly",0xAA13,"RGBForeColor",0xAA14,"RGBBackColor",0xAA15,
"SetCPixel",0xAA16,"GetCPixel",0xAA17,"GetCTable",0xAA18,
"GetForeColor",0xAA19,"GetBackColor",0xAA1A,"GetCCursor",0xAA1B,
"SetCCursor",0xAA1C,"AllocCursor",0xAA1D,"GetCIcon",0xAA1E,
"PlotCIcon",0xAA1F,"OpenCPicture",0xAA20,"OpColor",0xAA21,
"HiliteColor",0xAA22,"CharExtra",0xAA23,"DisposeCTable",0xAA24,
"DisposeCIcon",0xAA25,"DisposeCCursor",0xAA26,"GetMaxDevice",0xAA27,
"GetCTSeed",0xAA28,"GetDeviceList",0xAA29,"GetMainDevice",0xAA2A,
"GetNextDevice",0xAA2B,"TestDeviceAttribute",0xAA2C,
"SetDeviceAttribute",0xAA2D,
"InitGDevice",0xAA2E,"NewGDevice",0xAA2F,"DisposeGDevice",0xAA30,
"SetGDevice",0xAA31,"GetGDevice",0xAA32,"Color2Index",0xAA33,
"Index2Color",0xAA34,"InvertColor",0xAA35,"RealColor",0xAA36,
"GetSubTable",0xAA37,"UpdatePixMap",0xAA38,"MakeITable",0xAA39,
"AddSearch",0xAA3A,"AddComp",0xAA3B,"SetClientID",0xAA3C,
"ProtectEntry",0xAA3D,"ReserveEntry",0xAA3E,"SetEntries",0xAA3F,
"QDError",0xAA40,"SetWinColor",0xAA41,"GetAuxWin",0xAA42,
"SetCtlColor",0xAA43,"GetAuxCtl",0xAA44,"NewCWindow",0xAA45,
"GetNewCWindow",0xAA46,"SetDeskCPat",0xAA47,"GetCWMgrPort",0xAA48,
"SaveEntries",0xAA49,"RestoreEntries",0xAA4A,"NewCDialog",0xAA4B,
"DelSearch",0xAA4C,"DelComp",0xAA4D,"SetStdCProcs",0xAA4E,
"CalcCMask",0xAA4F,"SeedCFill",0xAA50,"** Free **",0xAA51,
"** Free **",0xAA52,"** Free **",0xAA53,"** Free **",0xAA54,
"** Free **",0xAA55,"** Free **",0xAA56,"** Free **",0xAA57,
"** Free **",0xAA58,"** Free **",0xAA59,"** Free **",0xAA5A,
"** Free **",0xAA5B,"** Free **",0xAA5C,"** Free **",0xAA5D,
"** Free **",0xAA5E,"** Free **",0xAA5F,"DelMCEntries",0xAA60,
"GetMCInfo",0xAA61,"SetMCInfo",0xAA62,"DispMCInfo",0xAA63,
"GetMCEntry",0xAA64,"SetMCEntries",0xAA65,"MenuChoice",0xAA66,
"** Free **",0xAA67,"** Free **",0xAA68,"** Free **",0xAA69,
"** Free **",0xAA6A,"** Free **",0xAA6B,"** Free **",0xAA6C,
"** Free **",0xAA6D,"** Free **",0xAA6E,"** Free **",0xAA6F,
"** Free **",0xAA70,"** Free **",0xAA71,"** Free **",0xAA72,
"** Free **",0xAA73,"** Free **",0xAA74,"** Free **",0xAA75,
"** Free **",0xAA76,"** Free **",0xAA77,"** Free **",0xAA78,
"** Free **",0xAA79,"** Free **",0xAA7A,"** Free **",0xAA7B,
"** Free **",0xAA7C,"** Free **",0xAA7D,"** Free **",0xAA7E,
"** Free **",0xAA7F,"** Free **",0xAA80,"** Free **",0xAA81,
"** Free **",0xAA82,"** Free **",0xAA83,"** Free **",0xAA84,
"** Free **",0xAA85,"** Free **",0xAA86,"** Free **",0xAA87,
"** Free **",0xAA88,"** Free **",0xAA89,"** Free **",0xAA8A,
```

```
"** Free **",0xAA8B,"** Free **",0xAA8C,"** Free **",0xAA8D,
"** Free **",0xAA8E,"** Free **",0xAA8F,"InitPalettes",0xAA90,
"NewPalette",0xAA91,"GetNewPalette",0xAA92,"DisposePalette",0xAA93,
"ActivatePalette",0xAA94,"SetPalette",0xAA95,"GetPalette",0xAA96,
"PmForeColor",0xAA97,"PmBackColor",0xAA98,"AnimateEntry",0xAA99,
"AnimatePalette",0xAA9A,"GetEntryColor",0xAA9B,"SetEntryColor",0xAA9C,
"GetEntryUsage",0xAA9D,"GetEntryUsage",0xAA9E,"CTab2Palette",0xAA9F,
"Palette2CTab",0xAAA0,"CopyPalette",0xAAA1
};

#define OFFSET  144

main(int argc,char *argv[])
{
  word  i,n;
  trap  *p;

  if (argc == 2 &&
      sscanf(argv[1],"%hX",&i) == 1 &&
      i > 0xA000 &&
      i < 0xAAA1)
  {
    n = i & 0x03FF; /* hex lookup */
    if (i > 0xA800)
      printf("%4X  %s\n",list[n+OFFSET].num,list[n+OFFSET].name);
    else
      printf("%4X  %s\n",list[n].num,list[n].name);
    return 0;
  }

  i = sizeof(list)/sizeof(trap);
  if (argc == 2 && isalpha(argv[1][0])) {   /* dump matches */
    for (p = &list[0]; i--; p++)
      if (strstr(p->name,argv[1]))
        printf("%X\t%s\n",p->num,p->name);
  } else {                                  /* or whole table */
    for (p = &list[0]; i--; p++)
      printf("%X\t%s\n",p->num,p->name);
  }
  return 0;
}
```

LoMem — C Tool

LoMem is almost a carbon copy of the `ATrap` tool above, but this version looks up low-memory globals rather than A-traps.

Improving `LoMem`

Here is a suggestion for one way in which `LoMem` might be improved: `LoMem` uses the ANSI C standard library routine `strstr`, which was not present in the MPW C 2.0 libraries. Add this functionality if needed.

```
/*
 *  LoMem.c - Looks up by memory by name or number
 *          - Written by Dan Allen 2/1/89
 */

#include  <CType.h>
#include  <StdIO.h>
#include  <String.h>

typedef unsigned short word;

typedef struct mem {
  char   *name;
  word   num;
} mem;

static mem list[] = {
"Unassigned",0x0000,"ResetSPPC",0x0004,"BusError",0x0008,
"AddrErr",0x000C,"Illegal",0x0010,"ZeroDiv",0x0014,
"ChkError",0x0018,"TrapVErr",0x001C,"Privileg",0x0020,
"Trace",0x0024,"Line1010",0x0028,"Line1111",0x002C,
"Unassigned",0x0030,"Coproces",0x0034,"FmtErrVect",0x0038,
"Uninited",0x003C,"Unassig2",0x0040,"Spurious",0x0060,
"AutoInt1",0x0064,"AutoInt2",0x0068,"AutoInt3",0x006C,
"AutoInt4",0x0070,"AutoInt5",0x0074,"AutoInt6",0x0078,
"AutoInt7",0x007C,"TRAPtble",0x0080,"FP-68881",0x00C0,
"reserved",0x00DC,"PMMU",0x00E0,"SMgrOldCore",0x00E0,
"reserved",0x00EC,"MonkeyLives",0x0100,"SysCom",0x0100,
"ScrVRes",0x0102,"ScrHRes",0x0104,"ScreenRow",0x0106,
"MemTop",0x0108,"BufPtr",0x010C,"StkLowPt",0x0110,
"HeapEnd",0x0114,"TheZone",0x0118,"UTableBase",0x011C,
"MacJmp",0x0120,"DskRtnAdr",0x0124,"PollRtnAddr",0x0128,
"DskVerify",0x012C,"LoadTrap",0x012D,"MmInOK",0x012E,
"CPUFlag",0x012F,"DskWr11",0x012F,"ApplLimit",0x0130,
"SonyVars",0x0134,"PWMValue",0x0138,"PollStack",0x013A,
"PollProc",0x013E,"DskErr",0x0142,"SysEvtMask",0x0144,
"SysEvtBuf",0x0146,"EventQueue",0x014A,"EvtBufCnt",0x0154,
```

```
"RndSeed",0x0156,"SysVersion",0x015A,"SEvtEnb",0x015C,
"DSWndUpdate",0x015D,"FontFlag",0x015E,"IntFlag",0x015F,
"VBLQueue",0x0160,"Ticks",0x016A,"MBTicks",0x016E,
"MBState",0x0172,"Tocks",0x0173,"KeyMap",0x0174,
"KeyMap",0x0174,"KeypadMap",0x017C,"{**unknown**}",0x0180,
"KeyLast",0x0184,"KeyTime",0x0186,"KeyRepTime",0x018A,
"KeyThresh",0x018E,"KeyRepThresh",0x0190,"Lvl1DT",0x0192,
"Lvl2DT",0x01B2,"UnitNtryCnt",0x01D2,"VIA",0x01D4,
"SCCRd",0x01D8,"SCCWr",0x01DC,"IWM",0x01E0,
"GetParam",0x01E4,"SPValid",0x01F8,"SysParam",0x01F8,
"SPATalkA",0x01F9,"SPATalkB",0x01FA,"SPConfig",0x01FB,
"SPPortA",0x01FC,"SPPortB",0x01FE,"SPAlarm",0x0200,
"SPFont",0x0204,"SPKbd",0x0206,"SPPrint",0x0207,
"SPVolCtl",0x0208,"SPClikCaret",0x0209,"SPMisc1",0x020A,
"CDeskPat",0x020B,"Time",0x020C,"BootDrive",0x0210,
"JShell",0x0212,"SFSaveDisk",0x0214,"KbdVars",0x0216,
"KbdLast",0x0218,"JKybdTask",0x021A,"KbdType",0x021E,
"AlarmState",0x021F,"MemErr",0x0220,"JFigTrkSpd",0x0222,
"JDiskPrime",0x0226,"JRdAddr",0x022A,"JRdData",0x022E,
"JWrData",0x0232,"JSeek",0x0236,"JSetUpPoll",0x023A,
"JRecal",0x023E,"JControl",0x0242,"JWakeUp",0x0246,
"JReSeek",0x024A,"JMakeSpdTbl",0x024E,"JAdrDisk",0x0252,
"JSetSpeed",0x0256,"NiblTbl",0x025A,"FlEvtMask",0x025E,
"SdVolume",0x0260,"Finder",0x0261,"SoundPtr",0x0262,
"SoundVars",0x0262,"SoundBase",0x0266,"SoundVBL",0x026A,
"SoundDCE",0x027A,"SoundActive",0x027E,"SoundLevel",0x027F,
"CurPitch",0x0280,"SoundLast",0x0282,"Switcher",0x0282,
"SwitcherTPtr",0x0286,"RSDHndl",0x028A,"ROM85",0x028E,
"PortAUse",0x0290,"PortBUse",0x0291,"ScreenVars",0x0292,
"JGNEFilter",0x029A,"Key1Trans",0x029E,"Key2Trans",0x02A2,
"SysZone",0x02A6,"ApplZone",0x02AA,"ROMBase",0x02AE,
"RAMBase",0x02B2,"BasicGlob",0x02B6,"ExpandMem",0x02B6,
"DSAlertTab",0x02BA,"ExtStsDT",0x02BE,"SCCASts",0x02CE,
"SCCBSts",0x02CF,"SerialVars",0x02D0,"ABusVars",0x02D8,
"FinderName",0x02E0,"DoubleTime",0x02F0,"CaretTime",0x02F4,
"ScrDmpEnb",0x02F8,"ScrDmpType",0x02F9,"TagData",0x02FA,
"BufTgFNum",0x02FC,"BufTgFFlg",0x0300,"BufTgFBkNum",0x0302,
"BufTgDate",0x0304,"DrvQHdr",0x0308,"PWMBuf2",0x0312,
"MacPgm",0x0316,"Lo3Bytes",0x031A,"MinStack",0x031E,
"DefltStack",0x0322,"MMDefFlags",0x0326,"GZRootHnd",0x0328,
"GZRootPtr",0x032C,"GZMoveHnd",0x0330,"DSDrawProc",0x0334,
"EjectNotify",0x0338,"IAZNotify",0x033C,"CkdDB",0x0340,
"NxtDB",0x0342,"MaxDB",0x0344,"FlushOnly",0x0346,
"RegRsrc",0x0347,"FLckUnlck",0x0348,"FrcSync",0x0349,
"NewMount",0x034A,"DrMstrBlk",0x034C,"FCBSPtr",0x034E,
"DefVCBPtr",0x0352,"VCBQHdr",0x0356,"FSBusy",0x0360,
"FSQHead",0x0362,"FSQTail",0x0366,"RgSvArea",0x036A,
"WDCBsPtr",0x0372,"HFSVars",0x0376,"DefVRefnum",0x0384,
"HFSDSErr",0x0392,"CurDirStore",0x0398,"ErCode",0x03A2,
"Params",0x03A4,"FSTemp8",0x03D6,"FSTemp4",0x03DE,
"FSQueueHook",0x03E2,"ExtFSHook",0x03E6,"DskSwtchHook",0x03EA,
```

```
"ReqstVol",0x03EE,"ToExtFS",0x03F2,"FSFCBLen",0x03F6,
"DSAlertRect",0x03F8,"OSTable",0x0400,"GrafBegin",0x0800,
"JHideCursor",0x0800,"JShowCursor",0x0804,"JShieldCursor",0x0808,
"JScrnAddr",0x080C,"JScrnSize",0x0810,"JInitCrsr",0x0814,
"JSetCrsr",0x0818,"JCrsrObscure",0x081C,"JUpdateProc",0x0820,
"ScrnBase",0x0824,"MTemp",0x0828,"RawMouse",0x082C,
"Mouse",0x0830,"CrsrPin",0x0834,"CrsrRect",0x083C,
"TheCrsr",0x0844,"CrsrAddr",0x0888,"JAllocCrsr",0x088C,
"JSetCCrsr",0x0890,"JOpcodeProc",0x0894,"CrsrBase",0x0898,
"CrsrDevice",0x089C,"SrcDevice",0x08A0,"MainDevice",0x08A4,
"DeviceList",0x08A8,"CrsrRow",0x08AC,"{**unknown**}",0x08AE,
"QDColors",0x08B0,"CrsrVis",0x08CC,"CrsrBusy",0x08CD,
"CrsrNew",0x08CE,"CrsrCouple",0x08CF,"CrsrState",0x08D0,
"CrsrObscure",0x08D2,"CrsrScale",0x08D3,"{**unknown**}",0x08D4,
"MouseMask",0x08D6,"MouseOffset",0x08DA,"JournalFlag",0x08DE,
"JSwapFont",0x08E0,"WidthListHand",0x08E4,"JournalRef",0x08E8,
"{**unknown**}",0x08EA,"CrsrThresh",0x08EC,"JCrsrTask",0x08EE,
"WWExist",0x08F2,"QDExist",0x08F3,"JFetch",0x08F4,
"JStash",0x08F8,"JIODone",0x08FC,"CurApRefNum",0x0900,
"LaunchFlag",0x0902,"FondState",0x0903,"CurrentA5",0x0904,
"CurStackBase",0x0908,"LoadFiller",0x090C,"CurApName",0x0910,
"SaveSegHandle",0x0930,"CurJTOffset",0x0934,"CurPageOption",0x0936,
"HiliteMode",0x0938,"{**unknown**}",0x0939,"LoaderPBlock",0x093A,
"PrintErr",0x0944,"ChooserBits",0x0946,"CoreEditVars",0x0954,
"ScrapSize",0x0960,"ScrapHandle",0x0964,"ScrapCount",0x0968,
"ScrapState",0x096A,"ScrapName",0x096C,"ScrapTag",0x0970,
"RomFont0",0x0980,"ApFontID",0x0984,"SaveFondFlags",0x0986,
"FMDefaultSize",0x0987,"CurFMInput",0x0988,"CurFMSize",0x098A,
"CurFMFace",0x098C,"CurFMNeedBits",0x098D,"CurFMDevice",0x098E,
"CurFMNumer",0x0990,"CurFMDenom",0x0994,"FOutError",0x0998,
"FOutFontHandle",0x099A,"FOutBold",0x099E,"FOutItalic",0x099F,
"FOutULOffset",0x09A0,"FOutULShadow",0x09A1,"FOutULThick",0x09A2,
"FOutShadow",0x09A3,"FOutExtra",0x09A4,"FOutAscent",0x09A5,
"FOutDescent",0x09A6,"FOutWidMax",0x09A7,"FOutLeading",0x09A8,
"FOutUnused",0x09A9,"FOutNumer",0x09AA,"FOutDenom",0x09AE,
"FMDotsPerInch",0x09B2,"FMStyleTab",0x09B6,"ToolScratch",0x09CE,
"WindowList",0x09D6,"SaveUpdate",0x09DA,"PaintWhite",0x09DC,
"WMgrPort",0x09DE,"DeskPort",0x09E2,"OldStructure",0x09E6,
"OldContent",0x09EA,"GrayRgn",0x09EE,"SaveVisRgn",0x09F2,
"DragHook",0x09F6,"TempRect",0x09FA,"OneOne",0x0A02,
"MinusOne",0x0A06,"TopMenuItem",0x0A0A,"AtMenuBottom",0x0A0C,
"IconBitmap",0x0A0E,"MenuList",0x0A1C,"MBarEnable",0x0A20,
"CurDeKind",0x0A22,"MenuFlash",0x0A24,"TheMenu",0x0A26,
"SavedHandle",0x0A28,"MBarHook",0x0A2C,"MenuHook",0x0A30,
"DragPattern",0x0A34,"DeskPattern",0x0A3C,"DragFlag",0x0A44,
"CurDragAction",0x0A46,"FPState",0x0A4A,"TopMapHndl",0x0A50,
"SysMapHndl",0x0A54,"SysMap",0x0A58,"CurMap",0x0A5A,
"ResReadOnly",0x0A5C,"ResLoad",0x0A5E,"ResErr",0x0A60,
"TaskLock",0x0A62,"FScaleDisable",0x0A63,"CurActivate",0x0A64,
"CurDeactive",0x0A68,"DeskHook",0x0A6C,"TEDoText",0x0A70,
"TERecal",0x0A74,"ApplScratch",0x0A78,"GhostWindow",0x0A84,
```

```
"CloseOrnHook",0x0A88,"ResumeProc",0x0A8C,"SaveProc",0x0A90,
"SaveSP",0x0A94,"ANumber",0x0A98,"ACount",0x0A9A,
"DABeeper",0x0A9C,"DAStrings",0x0AA0,"TEScrpLength",0x0AB0,
"{**unknown**}",0x0AB2,"TEScrpHandle",0x0AB4,"AppPacks",0x0AB8,
"SysResName",0x0AD8,"SoundGlue",0x0AE8,"AppParmHandle",0x0AEC,
"DSErrCode",0x0AF0,"ResErrProc",0x0AF2,"TEWdBreak",0x0AF6,
"DlgFont",0x0AFA,"LastTGLobal",0x0AFC,"TrapAgain",0x0B00,
"KeyMVars",0x0B04,"ROMMapHndl",0x0B06,"PWMBuf1",0x0B0A,
"BootMask",0x0B0E,"WidthPtr",0x0B10,"AtalkHk1",0x0B14,
"AtalkHk2",0x0B18,"FourDHack",0x0B1C,"{**unknown**}",0x0B20,
"HWCfgFlags",0x0B22,"TimeSCSIDB",0x0B24,"TopMenuItem",0x0B26,
"AtMenuBottom",0x0B28,"WidthTabHandle",0x0B2A,"SCSIDrvrs",0x0B2E,
"TimeVars",0x0B30,"BtDskRfn",0x0B34,"BootTmp8",0x0B36,
"{**unknown**}",0x0B3E,"T1Arbitrate",0x0B3F,"JDiskSel",0x0B40,
"JSendCmd",0x0B44,"JDCDReset",0x0B48,"LastSPExtra",0x0B4C,
"AppleShare",0x0B50,"MenuDisable",0x0B54,"MBDFHndl",0x0B58,
"MBSaveLoc",0x0B5C,"BNMQHd",0x0B60,"Twitcher1",0x0B64,
"{**unknown**}",0x0B68,"Twitcher2",0x0B7C,"RMgrHiVars",0x0B80,
"RomMapInsert",0x0B9E,"TmpResLoad",0x0B9F,"IntlSpec",0x0BA0,
"SMgrCore",0x0BA0,"RMgrPerm",0x0BA4,"WordRedraw",0x0BA5,
"SysFontFam",0x0BA6,"SysFontSize",0x0BA8,"MBarHeight",0x0BAA,
"TESysJust",0x0BAC,"HiHeapMark",0x0BAE,"SegHiEnable",0x0BB2,
"FDevDisable",0x0BB3,"CMVector",0x0BB4,"XFSGlobs",0x0BB8,
"ShutDownQHdr",0x0BBC,"NewUnused",0x0BC0,"LastFOND",0x0BC2,
"FONDID",0x0BC6,"App2Packs",0x0BC8,"MAErrProc",0x0BE8,
"MASuperTab",0x0BEC,"MimeGlobs",0x0BF0,"FractEnable",0x0BF4,
"UsedFWidths",0x0BF5,"FScaleHFact",0x0BF6,"FScaleVFact",0x0BFA,
"{**unknown**}",0x0BFE,"SCSIBase",0x0C00,"SCSIDMA",0x0C04,
"SCSIHsk",0x0C08,"SCSIGlobals",0x0C0C,"RGBBlack",0x0C10,
"RGBWhite",0x0C16,"{**unknown**}",0x0C1C,"RowBits",0x0C20,
"ColLines",0x0C22,"ScreenBytes",0x0C24,"IOPMgrVars",0x0C28,
"NMIFlag",0x0C2C,"VidType",0x0C2D,"VidMode",0x0C2E,
"SCSIPoll",0x0C2F,"SEVarBase",0x0C30,"MMUFlags",0x0CB0,
"MMUType",0x0CB1,"MMU32bit",0x0CB2,"WhichBox",0x0CB3,
"MMUTbl",0x0CB4,"MMUTblSize",0x0CB8,"SInfoPtr",0x0CBC,
"ASCBase",0x0CC0,"SMGlobals",0x0CC4,"TheGDevice",0x0CC8,
"CQDGlobals",0x0CCC,"AuxWinHead",0x0CD0,"AuxCtlHead",0x0CD4,
"DeskCPat",0x0CD8,"SetOSDefKey",0x0CDC,"LastBinPat",0x0CE0,
"DeskPatEnable",0x0CE8,"{**unknown**}",0x0CEA,"ADBBase",0x0CF8,
"WarmStart",0x0CFC,"TimeDBRA",0x0D00,"TimeSCCDB",0x0D02,
"SlotQDT",0x0D04,"SlotPrTbl",0x0D08,"SlotVBLQ",0x0D0C,
"ScrnVBLPtr",0x0D10,"SlotTICKS",0x0D14,"PowerMgrVars",0x0D18,
"AGBHandle",0x0D1C,"TableSeed",0x0D20,"SRsrcTblPtr",0x0D24,
"JVBLTask",0x0D28,"WMgrCPort",0x0D2C,"VertRRate",0x0D30,
"SynListHandle",0x0D32,"LastFore",0x0D36,"LastMode",0x0D3E,
"LastDepth",0x0D40,"FMExist",0x0D42,"SavedHilite",0x0D43,
"{**unknown**}",0x0D44,"MenuCInfo",0x0D50,"MBProcHndl",0x0D54,
"MBSaveLoc",0x0D58,"MRect",0x0D58,"MBFlash",0x0D5C,
"MenuCInfo",0x0D5C,"ChunkyDepth",0x0D60,"CrsrPtr",0x0D62,
"{**unknown**}",0x0D64,"PortList",0x0D66,"MickeyBytes",0x0D6A,
"QDErr",0x0D6E,"VIA2DT",0x0D70,"SInitFlags",0x0D90,
```

```
"DTQFlags",0x0D92,"DTQueue",0x0D92,"DTskQHdr",0x0D94,
"DTskQTail",0x0D98,"JDTInstall",0x0D9C,"HiliteRGB",0x0DA0,
"TimeSCSIDB",0x0DA6,"DSCtrAdj",0x0DA8,"IconTLAddr",0x0DAC,
"VideoInfoOK",0x0DB0,"EndSRTPtr",0x0DB4,"SDMJmpTblPtr",0x0DB8,
"JSwapMMU",0x0DBC,"SdmBusErr",0x0DC0,"LastTxGDevice",0x0DC4,
"PmgrHandle",0x0DC8,"LayerPalette",0x0DCC,"ToolTable",0x0E00,
"SystemHeap",0x1E00
};

main(int argc,char *argv[])
{
  word  i,n;
  mem   *p;

  if (argc -- 2 && sscanf(argv[1],"%hX",&n) == 1 && n <= 0x1E00) {
    i = sizeof(list)/sizeof(mem); /* hex lookup */
    for (p = &list[0]; i--; p++)
      if (n == p->num)
        printf("%X\t%s\n",p->num,p->name);
  }

  i = sizeof(list)/sizeof(mem);
  if (argc == 2 && isalpha(argv[1][0])) {   /* dump matches */
    for (p = &list[0]; i--; p++)
      if (strstr(p->name,argv[1]))
        printf("%X\t%s\n",p->num,p->name);
  } else {                                  /* or whole table */
    for (p = &list[0]; i--; p++)
      printf("%X\t%s\n",p->num,p->name);
  }
  return 0;
}
```

Ascii—C Tool

Another convention used in the Macintosh is the ASCII character set, which is defined only for values from 0 to 127. In addition, the Macintosh uses the values 128 to 255 to hold foreign characters and symbols.

Ascii is a simple MPW tool that lists all of the Macintosh character set. It includes decimal and hex numbers along with the characters themselves. Obviously, the appearance of this table of characters will vary according to what font you select. The full names of the control characters are also shown, and Macintosh-specific keys are mentioned where applicable.

```c
/*
 *  Ascii.c - Lists the ASCII character set
 *          - Written by Dan Allen 12/16/87
 *          - Control characters added 1/4/88
 *
 */

#include <StdIO.h>

char *controlChars[] = {
  "NUL - Null",
  "SOH - Start of Heading",
  "STX - Start of Text",
  "ETX - End of Text / Enter key",
  "EOT - End of Transmission",
  "ENQ - Enquiry",
  "ACK - Acknowledge",
  "BEL - Bell",
  " BS - Backspace",
  " HT - Horizontal Tab",
  " LF - Line Feed",
  " VT - Vertical Tab",
  " FF - Form Feed",
  " CR - Carriage Return",
  " SO - Shift Out",
  " SI - Shift In",
  "DLE - Data Link Escape",
  "DC1 - Device Control 1",
  "DC2 - Device Control 2",
  "DC3 - Device Control 3",
  "DC4 - Device Control 4",
  "NAK - Negative Acknowledge",
  "SYN - Synchronous Idle",
  "ETB - End of Transmission Block",
  "CAN - Cancel",
  " EM - End of Medium",
  "SUB - Substitute",
  "ESC - Escape / Clear key on keypad",
```

```
  " FS - File Separator / Left arrow key",
  " GS - Group Separator / Right arrow key",
  " RS - Record Separator / Up arrow key",
  " US - Unit Separator / Down arrow key"
};

main()     /* --> stdout */
{
  int    i;

  for (i = 0;  i <= 31;  i++)
    printf("%d\t$%X\t%s\n",i,i,controlChars[i]);
  for (i = 0;  i <= 255;  i++)
    printf("%d\t$%X\t%c\n",i,i,i);
  for (i = 33;  i <= 128;  i++) {
    if (i % 8) printf("%3d %c  |",i,i);
    else printf("%3d %c\n",i,i);
  }
  return 0;
}
```

Conclusion

In this chapter, we have looked at several important components of the Macintosh architecture:

- Levels of software
- The memory map
- Memory mapped input/output
- Register saving and parameter passing conventions
- The A5 world of an application
- Low-memory globals
- A-trap dispatcher

Three MPW tools were listed: ATrap, which looks up A-traps by name or number; LoMem, which looks up low-memory globals by name or number; and Ascii, which displays the Macintosh character set.

Recommended Reading

The best reference about the Macintosh hardware is the *Macintosh Family Hardware Reference*, published jointly by Apple and Addison-Wesley.

The most accessible source of information about the Macintosh architecture is found in *Inside Macintosh*. The best sources for learning about how the Macintosh works are the ROM listings; unfortunately, the official commented ROM listings have a very restricted distribution. Even inside of Apple they are given only to those with a serious "need to know."

The next best thing to commented ROM listings is an uncommented ROM listing, which is at the fingertips of anyone who knows MacsBug, the Macintosh debugger, and assembly language. While in MacsBug, simply type `IL @2AE` and you will see the beginning lines of the ROM in 68000 assembly language. If you want to see the code for a particular routine—let's pick at random the QuickDraw `Random` function—just type in MacsBug `IL Random`.

The experimental method is often the fastest and most accurate way of determining how the Macintosh works. Write a short test program and see what the Mac actually does. Although documentation is important, in the end it is the actual behavior of the Mac that becomes accepted as the Macintosh architecture.

## CHAPTER 2

THE MACINTOSH OPERATING SYSTEM

Every computer has an operating system that manages the machine's fundamental resources. Traditionally, an operating system tracks processes, files, and input/output. The following table shows the basic functions performed by the various important parts of the operating system on the Macintosh.

Part of OS	Macintosh Manager
Process, booting	Start code
Process, memory management	Memory Manager
Process, process management	Segment Loader, MultiFinder
File system	File Manager
I/O	Device Manager

Note that graphics, windows, menus, and the like are *not* part of the operating system. These are higher-level pieces of system software that will be discussed in later chapters, especially in chapters 3 and 4. Note also that the Finder has nothing to do with the Macintosh operating system; it is an application just like HyperCard or the MPW Shell. This chapter concentrates upon the three fundamental subsystems of the operating system as found on the Macintosh: process management, the file system, and the input/output system. The AppleTalk network manager is also discussed briefly. We will then tie these topics together by examining the start code and the Macintosh boot process. At the end of this chapter is code for OSPeek, a desk accessory that lets you look at the inside of the Macintosh operating system (OS); ADBKey, an INIT that turns the power-on key into a programmer's switch; and Zero, an MPW tool that reinitializes disks.

Process Management

The original Macintosh permitted a single process to be active. As the machine started up, the system's boot code was the single active process. The boot sequence then gave control to the Finder, which in turn gave control to a single application at a time. Switcher and MultiFinder changed the Macintosh from a single-process machine to a multitasking machine that handled multiple processes running simultaneously.

Process management on the Macintosh is broken down into several different parts, the Memory Manager, Segment Loader, and MultiFinder being the three most important.

The Memory Manager

A fundamental part of the Macintosh operating system is the Memory Manager. It is used by almost every part of the operating system and Toolbox, as well as by applications. To be a successful Macintosh programmer, you must understand the Memory Manager, as it is critical to a bug-free application. By far the greatest cause of bugs on the Macintosh is incorrect use of memory and the Memory Manager. The Macintosh's methods for allocating memory are quite different from most computers, so learn them well.

The Memory Manager was originally written in Pascal and was actually part of LisaWrite! It was then translated by Bud Tribble into assembly language while being ported to the Macintosh. Later, Martin Haeberli, Larry Kenyon, and Jerome Coonen continued work on it.

One decision to be made for any given project is whether to use a language's library routines or to call the Memory Manager directly. For example, to dynamically allocate memory, you could call the Macintosh OS `NewPtr` routine directly. This could be done from assembly language, C, or Pascal. However, if you were writing in C, you could also call `malloc`; likewise, in Pascal you could call `New`. These library routines in turn call the Memory Manager. Few languages have library routines to cover all of the needs of a Macintosh programmer, so try to use the Memory Manager routines in preference to a language's library routines. As the Macintosh OS evolves, your code will have fewer compatibility problems if you have used the Memory Manager routines.

Why is the Memory Manager so hard to use? Much of the blame is due to its virtually unique use of handles to access memory. A handle is a pointer to a special pointer to a (possibly) relocatable block of memory. Why this extra level of indirection? Well, if blocks of memory can move around—rather than being fixed—memory can be used much more efficiently. In the days of the original 128 KB Macintosh, memory was at a premium, and handles provided a more efficient form of memory management.

The operation of the Macintosh Memory Manager can be compared to that of the U.S. Postal Service, as is shown in the following table of correspondences.

Memory Manager	U.S. Postal Service
Heap zone	City
Subzone	Zip code
Pointer	Street address
Handle	Post Office Box
Master pointer block	Post Office
`malloc` block	Apartment numbers

Heap Zones and Subzones. The Memory Manager allocates and manages chunks of memory that are found in a *heap*. A heap is a contiguous piece of memory that is allocated and maintained by the Memory Manager on a dynamic basis. At least two heaps are active at any time: the system heap and the application heap. The system heap is created while the Mac is booting up and is persistent until the Mac is shut down or rebooted. The application heap is created automatically when an application is launched under the Finder. Quitting an application causes the Finder's application heap to be created anew, because it is the application that is being launched.

In each of these heaps there is normally one *zone*. Heaps can also be subdivided into *subzones*, and in fact this is exactly what happens when MultiFinder is running. MultiFinder is the application that owns the application heap, and it creates inside its heap various subzones that are heaps in their own right. Each subzone contains an active Macintosh application. When an application is quit under MultiFinder, the single block of memory that MultiFinder allocated for the application is reclaimed. For the purposes of this discussion, the terms *heap, zone,* and *heap zone* will be used interchangeably.

The heap is the largest unit of memory. Subzones, or heaps inside of heaps, can be created. In a given heap (city), there can be multiple subzones (zip codes). Each heap zone contains blocks of memory. Memory blocks have varying attributes. For example, they can be locked or unlocked (a locked block cannot be moved until it is unlocked), purgeable or non-purgeable (a purgeable block can be disposed of if space is needed and it is not locked), relocatable or non-relocatable (a relocatable block can be moved if it is not locked). These different kinds of blocks are referenced using different methods.

Pointers. The simplest way to address memory is through the use of a pointer. Pointers refer to non-relocatable chunks of memory and are allocated by a call to the ROM routine `NewPtr`. Once a pointer is returned, the location of that block of memory is fixed, just as a street address is fixed. If the block of memory is disposed of or moved, any saved copies of the original pointer are invalid, as they still point to the same location in memory. Such a pointer is often called a *dangling pointer*. (The person moved and did not leave a forwarding address.)

Using non-relocatable blocks provides greater efficiency when compared with relocatable blocks, because there is no second level of indirection. If memory is tight, however, these fixed blocks often become "islands" in the heap zone, and they can cause a problem known as *fragmentation*. Thus, non-relocatable blocks should be used sparingly.

If there is not enough memory available to fill a `NewPtr` request for memory, a nil pointer—one whose value is zero—is returned. It is important to check all function results for nil pointers to ensure that your application is not writing into low memory.

Handles and Master Pointers. Handles are pointers that point to special pointers that point to relocatable blocks of memory (or objects as they are often called). Obviously, a second level of indirection is not as fast as more direct references, but the use of handles does increase the efficient use of memory. It is another example of the trade-off of time for space. Whereas use of a pointer requires a single dereferencing, use of a handle requires double dereferencing.

Handles are like having a Post Office box. An individual with a Post Office box can roam about the city without worrying about mail being properly delivered, because the Post Office always knows the current whereabouts of the addressee.

A pointer to a pointer is not a Memory Manager handle. That is, just because a declaration reads `char **foo` in C, or `foo ^^Char` in Pascal, does not mean that a "real" handle has been created. Handles come only from the Memory Manager through `NewHandle` and other similar calls.

What makes a handle "real" is that a handle points to a master pointer. Once allocated, master pointers always are in the same place in the heap. They are allocated in non-relocatable chunks called *master pointer blocks*. Because master pointer blocks are not relocatable themselves, you should allocate them in the early part of initializing an application by calling `MoreMasters`. This prevents heap fragmentation. Master pointers point to the current location of the relocatable object and are updated automatically by the Memory Manager when these objects are relocated.

Master pointers also contain attribute flags that specify whether the block is locked, purgeable, or a resource. In addition, the MPW Shell steals one of the extra bits to mark blocks of memory allocated by MPW tools. These extra bits have historically limited the Macintosh to only 24 bit addresses, because they are found in the upper 8 bits of each 32-bit master pointer. However, more recent Macs, such as the Mac II, have the potential to run in 32-bit mode. System 7.0 will provide support for running in 32-bit address space by moving these flags elsewhere.

Applications should never modify master pointers directly but instead should use the supplied ROM routines: `HLock`, `HUnlock`, `HPurge`, `HNoPurge`, `HSetRBit`, `HClrRBit`, `HGetState`, and `HSetState`. When you want to compare master pointers, your routine should call `StripAddress` in order to correctly compare the values of the pointers; otherwise these extra bits cause bogus results. `StripAddress` was new in the 256 KB ROMs but has been patched to the 128 KB ROMs in more recent versions of the System.

Allocating a relocatable block requires calling the routine `NewHandle`, which returns a handle. If this value is zero, it is referred to as a nil handle. A nil handle means that the Memory Manager was not able to allocate the memory asked for. It is important to check results for nil handles. Failure to do so will cause your application to write into location zero.

A good way to catch an application writing to location zero is to stuff a special illegal value into the long word at location zero, so that if location zero is used as a pointer you will cause a system error. A particularly good value was determined by Steve Capps to be $7739 5169. This particularly nasty number is odd (causes an address error on 68000-based Macs like the Mac Plus or Lisa) and references an illegal place in memory on all Macs (it also causes a bus error on a Lisa or Mac II, but no error at all on regular

Macs!). The best machine on which to debug your application is therefore the Lisa, as it is the only Mac that catches both address errors and bus errors!

A concept sometimes confused with nil handles is that of an empty handle. An empty handle starts off just like a regular handle—that is, it is a legal pointer to a master pointer. However, the master pointer itself is nil, meaning the object it once pointed to is no longer in memory. This occurs when an object is purged; a nil master pointer is analogous to the P.O. box number of someone who has moved out of a city.

Relocatable blocks are created as non-purgeable and unlocked. The general strategy of memory management is to allocate relocatable blocks as needed, locking them only for short periods in order to access them. If a block of memory is no longer needed, it should be freed. Memory can be reclaimed by calling `DisposePtr` or `DisposeHandle` to completely rid the heap of an object. The Memory Manager does not do much checking to see what kind of a handle or pointer you pass to it in the disposing process. If you pass a random "thing" that you claim is a handle, but that really is not a handle, the Memory Manager will try to dispose of it, with disastrous consequences: some arbitrary part of memory will be trashed! Therefore, make sure you pass actual handles and pointers to these routines.

An intermediate level of garbage collection, however, is available to relocatable objects: they can simply be marked purgeable. This means that the object will be disposed of if and when the Memory Manager needs more room in the heap, but not until then. This allows frequently accessed items to be cached in memory. If an item has been purged, the master pointer remains allocated but is nil. The relocatable object can be reallocated through a call to `ReallocHandle`, but it is up to the application to refill the contents of the memory.

Memory Allocation Algorithm. When the Memory Manager tries to fill a request for memory, it uses the following algorithm, stopping as soon as the request can be granted.

1 . Searches from the current roving location forward in the heap for the first free block that would accommodate the request.

2 . Compacts the heap by moving unlocked relocatable objects closer to each other, leaving a larger free space if possible.

3 . Grows the heap. This step is skipped if the heap has already been grown to its maximum size, which applications should do by calling `MaxApplLimit`.

4 . Purges unlocked, purgeable, relocatable objects, thus causing the master pointers of these objects to become updated to nil.

5 . The last-ditch effort is for the Memory Manager to call the application's (optional) grow zone function. In this routine, the application can unlock and make purgeable other objects in memory at its own discretion. Make sure not to call any routines whatsoever that allocate memory from within your grow zone

function, or the Mac will surely bomb ruthlessly. If the application has not registered a grow zone proc with the Memory Manager, this step is skipped.

6 . If all previous steps are taken with no success, the Memory Manager returns a nil pointer or nil handle according to the nature of the original request. In certain cases, however, the Memory Manager is unable to do even this, in which case a System Error #28 occurs: Out of Memory, and the bomb box appears.

Relocatable blocks of memory can be locked to improve efficient access to the object. Applications can lock and unlock relocatable objects through the HLock and HUnlock traps. (These calls are not needed for non-relocatable objects, because such objects cannot move.) Locked objects can cause the same fragmentation problems as non-relocatable objects, so objects should be locked only for short periods of time, accessed, and then unlocked. Unlocked objects are free to float around in the heap, and in fact they are almost guaranteed to do so.

Most calls to the Mac ROMs cause memory to be moved or purged. Almost all Toolbox calls move memory, and a fair percentage of OS calls do the same. This means that you should never trust a dereferenced handle across ROM calls, or trust dereferenced handles used in Pascal WITH statements across ROM calls. A helpful rule is to remember that straight, generic 68xxx code usually does not cause memory to change or be purged; many calls to library and system routines can change memory. The definitive lists of routines that move or purge memory are found as appendices in each volume of *Inside Macintosh*.

Memory Manager Routines. The Memory Manager is initialized at boot, along with the system heap. An application's heap zone is initialized automatically at launch by Launch calling SetApplBase and InitApplZone. In addition, an application can reinitialize any zone by calling InitZone. The application heap, under normal conditions, is set to a small (6 KB) size. The heap can be grown to its maximum size by MaxApplZone, a routine that is new with the 128 KB ROMs. Calling SetApplLimit is an indirect way of setting the stack size by setting the heap's size. MoreMasters should be called the appropriate number of times (for your application) to allocate master pointer blocks at application start-up to prevent later heap fragmentation.

The basic Memory Manager routines for allocating memory are NewPtr and NewHandle. Use DisposePtr and DisposeHandle to reclaim memory. Sizes of blocks can be manipulated with GetPtrSize, GetHandleSize, SetPtrSize, and SetHandleSize. These calls normally apply to the current heap, which can be determined using PtrZone, HandleZone, and GetZone and changed with SetZone. SetGrowZone is used to install a user function to be called when memory is tight, and BlockMove is an optimized routine for moving memory, even if it overlaps.

Additional routines for handles include routines to change the master pointer attributes: HLock, HUnlock, HPurge, HNoPurge, HSetRBit, HClrRBit, HGetState, and HSetState, the latter four of which were new with the 128 KB

ROMs. A handle can be recovered from a pointer to the relocatable block by RecoverHandle. An existing handle can be reallocated with ReallocHandle; if the handle is not nil, the memory it points to is purged before the new block is reallocated. An empty handle can be allocated with the NewEmptyHandle call, available with the 128 KB ROM and later versions.

Given a handle, a new handle that points to a copy of the original block can be created with HandToHand; or given a pointer to some data, a new handle that points to a copy of the data can be manufactured by PtrToHand. PtrToXHand is the same as PtrToHand but uses the passed existing handle instead of creating a new handle; PtrToXHand still copies the bytes pointed to. HandAndHand copies the data pointed to by the first handle onto the end of the data pointed to by the second handle; PtrAndHand copies the data pointed to by a pointer onto the end of the data pointed to by the handle.

To free space in a heap, use the following:

- FreeMem—returns total free space in the heap
- MaxMem—compacts, purges purgeables; returns size of largest contiguous block
- CompactMem—compacts, collects free space, but does not purge memory; returns size of largest contiguous block
- ResrvMem—automatically called by NewPtr; does not allocate space but frees up a contiguous chunk as low in memory as possible; compacts, purges
- PurgeMem—does not compact; just purges, trying to free up a block of specified size
- EmptyHandle—purges specified block; sets master pointer to nil

Space routines that were introduced with the 128 KB ROM include the following:

- MoveHHi—helps prevent heap fragmentation when called before locking a relocatable block
- StackSpace—returns number of bytes before the stack hits the heap
- PurgeSpace—returns total free space and the maximum contiguous block without changing the heap
- MaxBlock—returns the maximum contiguous block possible by compacting the current zone, without actually performing any compacting

The Segment Loader

The next major task of an operating system is to help provide more memory than there really is in the system. In sophisticated operating systems like UNIX, the operating system can page an image of memory to disk and bring it back in when needed. Such a system is called virtual memory and requires hardware support. Apple's own implementation of UNIX, called A/UX, requires a paged memory management unit (PMMU) in the form of a Motorola 68851 or a 68030 that has built-in memory management. System 7.0 will allow virtual memory under the Macintosh OS with the appropriate PMMU hardware.

In contrast, the standard Macintosh operating system provides only one simple mechanism for providing more memory: the Segment Loader, another Andy Hertzfeld creation. Any Macintosh application can be broken down into segments 32 KB or less in size. These segments are loaded into RAM from disk only when needed. The Segment Loader helps by knowing what routines are where, and it has only one task: to select and bring into memory automatically any needed CODE segment that is not already in memory. It does so by retrieving needed CODE segments from the resource fork of the currently executing application and placing them in the current application heap.

CODE resources are like any resource: they are relocatable objects. Obviously, CODE resources should be fixed when they are executing, so the Segment Loader locks their handles automatically when LoadSeg is called and unlocks them automatically when UnloadSeg is called . A CODE segment that is unlocked in the resource file is automatically moved (in 128 KB and later ROMs) to the top of the heap when the Segment Loader calls MoveHHi. If a CODE segment is marked locked in the resource file, it is simply left wherever the Memory Manager put it.

The mechanism used to locate needed CODE resources is straightforward. When an application is built, the linker prepares a list of intersegment jumps called a *jump table*. The Segment Loader automatically sets up the jump table when an application is launched. The jump table is stored on disk as the CODE 0 resource. It is always ID zero. The jump table is moved into an application's A5 World, which is the collective name for an application's global data space. As you can see in Figure 2–1, an A5 World consists of the application's QuickDraw globals, the jump table, the application's own global data, and its stack.

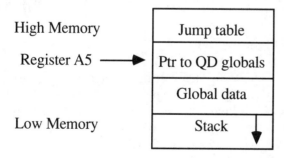

Figure 2–1: An A5 World

The format of the jump table is simple: each jump to a segment that is not currently in memory is just a call to the Segment Loader routine `LoadSeg`. Once a routine is in memory, the entry in the jump table is patched to be an actual `JMP` instruction to the routine in memory. An `UnloadSeg` call changes any affected entries back to `LoadSeg` calls and makes the `CODE` segment purgeable. `LoadSeg` and `UnloadSeg` are unusual for OS routines in that they are stack-based rather than register-based calls.

The Segment Loader does not at any time dispose of `CODE` resources; it only loads them. To dispose of unneeded `CODE` segments, have your application call the `UnloadSeg` routine when appropriate. It is sometimes definitely not appropriate to call `UnloadSeg`. For example, a routine should never unload itself. Your application should unload segments in the main event loop, or better yet, right after a segment is finished being used—that is, it should remove the print segments just after printing is finished.

`CODE` segments are given the default attributes of being purgeable by the MPW Linker, with the exception of segment 1 (the Main segment), which is always made non-purgeable, locked, and preloaded. These attributes, which are identical to the standard resource attributes of any resource, can be changed by specifying various linker options or by using ResEdit.

Segmentation Bugs. A special category of bugs can occur as a result of segmentation problems. If routine A of segment 1 calls a subroutine B of segment 2, and then segment 1 gets moved or purged, the return from segment 2 to segment 1 can be painful. A typical symptom of this problem you will see is that when the program counter is set to some random location in or out of memory, a bus, address, or illegal error occurs immediately. How does such an error occur?

Many paths can lead to such a situation. If routine B does an `UnloadSeg` on routine A, then segment 1 is as good as gone. Of course, the more complex the calling chain, the harder it is to find such errors, especially when mutual recursion between procedures is present. Such errors often come from a subtle change in segmentation directives in the sources, or perhaps from a change to the linker options. A source-level debugger is of little help in such a situation. Sometimes you can find the offending jump without too much effort by single-stepping in MacsBug.

Creating Processes Under the Finder

Launching an Application. The task of launching an application is related to the task of swapping segments. Before there was MultiFinder, the Segment Loader did most of this work. Things are quite different with MultiFinder active. We will describe here how things work *without* MultiFinder. For a description of how things work with MultiFinder, see the "MultiFinder" section later in this chapter.

The original Macintosh system software was single-tasking. It could run only one application at a time, the Finder being nothing more than an application itself. The `shellApp` and `startUpApp` names in the boot blocks are normally set to `Finder`. The start code then calls the `Launch` trap to run the Finder.

How is a new process created, or in Macintosh terms, launched? There are a variety of methods:

- Launch
- Chain
- Sublaunch

When a user double-clicks on an application to open it or launch it in a single-tasking Macintosh, the Finder then does what the start-up code does: it calls the `Launch` trap to open the application. However, there is a subtle but important change when the Finder calls `Launch`: the Finder also sets things up so that when the application quits, the Finder will itself be relaunched. This special kind of launch is called a *sublaunch*. Apple ships three applications with the ability to sublaunch:

- The Finder—the application that gives the Desktop illusion
- The MPW Shell—the application that gives a UNIX-like illusion
- HyperCard—the application that gives any illusion you like

The sublaunch mechanism was originally implemented separately by these applications, but it is now supported by `INIT` 13 in the System. A call to the `Launch` trap is treated as a sublaunch if bit 3 of the low-memory global byte called `Finder` at $261 is zero. Here is a bit of assembly language code that does this:

```
; PROCEDURE SubLaunch(appName: Str255)        ; under Finder

    ADD     #4,SP           ; pop return address
    LEA     $93A,A0         ; point to lomem LoaderPBlock
    MOVE.L  (SP),(A0)       ; stuff pointer to appName
    CLR.L   4(A0)           ; normal sound and screen
    BCLR    #3,$261         ; clear sublaunch bit in Finder
    _Launch                 ; DC.W $A9F2
```

Note that there is no `RTS` after `Launch`. This is because code following a sublaunch is never executed. The sublaunching application will resume execution by being relaunched as if it were running for the first time. Sublaunches can be nested—that is, you can launch HyperCard from the Finder, then launch MPW from HyperCard, and then launch MS Word from MPW. Quitting Word returns to MPW, quitting MPW returns to HyperCard, etc. Each subsequent quit operation "pops" back to the application before it.

Sublaunching is different from the ability to transfer to another application, a capability found in many different applications, such as Turbo Pascal or ResEdit. Transferring is a like a GOTO, whereas sublaunching is more like a subroutine. When an application calls `Launch`, a transfer normally occurs.

A further variant of `Launch` is chaining, which preserves the current application heap while starting up a new application. This allows data to be passed in one direction, namely, to the new application.

Quitting an Application. A process is reclaimed or destroyed by quitting. Although there are countless ways of exiting an application ungracefully, an application can be exited gracefully in two different ways:

- Upon an explicit call to `ExitToShell`, which is the best way out.
- Returning from the main routine of a program will cause a call to the `ExitToShell` routine automatically. (`ExitToShell` is pushed on the stack in the `Launch` code.) This behavior is handy for generic C MPW tools, for example.

`ExitToShell` zaps the current application heap and calls `Launch` to start the `shellApp`, which normally is the Finder.

MultiFinder

MultiFinder is an application that transforms the Macintosh into a multitasking computer. It was written by Erich Ringewald and Phil Goldman and is entirely separate from Switcher, an earlier attempt at multitasking that was written by Andy Hertzfeld.

When MultiFinder starts running it takes over quite a few of the operating system routines in order to perform its magic. Although there is still only one system heap and one application heap, MultiFinder creates the illusion of multiple application heaps within its own application heap. It can switch quickly between different applications by switching critical low-memory globals, switching A5 Worlds, and setting up the environment to look to any given application as if it were the only application running.

Within MultiFinder's application heap MultiFinder allocates partitions for each process. These partitions resemble individual application heaps, each containing its own heap, stack, and A5 World. The Finder occupies one such partition. When desk accessories are used, a small application called `DA Handler` occupies a partition. Background printing uses two different partitions: `Backgrounder` (started at boot) and `Print Monitor` (launched only when needed). The list of partitions to set up at system start-up is maintained by the Finder in a file called `Finder Startup` that resides in the System Folder.

When an application is double-clicked on in the Finder with MultiFinder running, the Finder does a special type of launch. It is a call to the regular `Launch` trap but with the high two bits set in the configuration word that maintains the parent process. This causes the Finder to continue running while the new "child" process runs. The child process is not linked to the parent process as in UNIX, however. If the high two bits are not set, the parent is terminated upon the spawning of the child process.

Here is some assembly code to launch an application under MultiFinder such that the launching application still lives:

```
; PROCEDURE MFLaunch(appName: Str255)

        LEA     mfBlk,A0        ; point to the extended length param block below
        MOVE.L  4(SP),(A0)      ; install ptr to appName
        MOVE.L  (SP)+,(SP)      ; pop appName
        _Launch                 ; DC.W $A9F2
        RTS                     ; and return flow to whoever just call this

mfBlk   DC.L    0               ; pointer to appName
        DC.W    0               ; normal sound and screen
        DC.W    'LC'            ; tag for extended param block
        DC.L    $00000004       ; length of extension
        DC.W    0               ; finder flags: normal
        DC.W    $4000           ; launch flags: a MultiFinder launch
```

`ExitToShell` works the same as it does when MultiFinder is not around, but in addition MultiFinder can "kill" an application if a system error occurs in that partition. This is because MultiFinder takes over some of the same vectors that MacsBug does. MultiFinder does not support the `Chain` trap.

MultiFinder introduces a new style of process scheduling known as cooperative multitasking. This method hinges upon MultiFinder's watching the event traps called by all standard Macintosh applications. A process switch can occur only when one of three traps is called: `GetNextEvent`, `WaitNextEvent`, or `EventAvail`. Three types of switching can occur: layer switching (A5 World and windows are switched), background switching (A5 World is switched, but windows are not), and update switching (A5 World is switched with update event). These various types of switching require that trap patches, completion routines, VBL tasks, and defprocs should not assume anything about register A5. When you are writing these routines, therefore, you should always save and restore register A5 accordingly.

Interprocess communication (IPC) is limited in the original version of MultiFinder to the use of "puppet strings," a simple method of passing a message to another application when switching between partitions. Microsoft uses this to implement its QuickSwitch facility between Word and Excel, for example.

The most prevalent form of interprocess communication on the Macintosh is the Clipboard. The Clipboard provides a simple but effective means of passing information. The Clipboard is normally handled by the Scrap Manager, but MultiFinder plays some tricks—as did Switcher—to coerce applications to get and put information on the global clipboard. Applications can also read and write to a common disk file as a means of passing information between processes.

The File System

The file system, also called the File Manager, is the single largest piece of operating system code in the Macintosh ROM. The original Macintosh File System (MFS) supports a single flat directory structure per volume, such as a Sony single-sided 400 KB disk. The Hierarchical File System (HFS) supports a hierarchical directory structure on 800 KB or larger volumes. Actually there is a way to create a 400 KB HFS volume: initialize a disk as single-sided while holding down the Option key. You can also create an 800 KB MFS volume if you have an old version of the System that did not know about HFS. To determine if HFS is installed, test the word FSFCBLen in low memory at $3F6. It is -1 on MFS-only systems and is positive for those machines with HFS installed.

MFS was designed and written by Larry Kenyon. HFS began life as the Turbo File System (TFS) and was developed during 1985 by Pat Dirks, Bill Bruffy, and Larry Kenyon for the Macintosh Plus and later machines.

Under MFS, file names may have up to 255 characters; file names under HFS are limited to 31 characters, and volume names are limited to 27 characters. Colons may not be used in a file or volume name for either system, because they are used to specify the full path name of a file.

Each file on the Macintosh has two *forks*: a resource fork, managed by the Resource Manager, and a data fork, managed by the programmer. A fork can be empty or nonexistent for a given file. In the case of an application file, all of the code, menus, dialogs, icons, and other resources are kept in the resource fork, and the data fork is usually empty. Document files created by an application are usually the inverse: in this case, the resource fork is unused, and all of a MacPaint graphic, HyperCard stack, or MS Word document lives in the data fork. There are exceptions, of course. Some applications store preference information in their data forks. The MPW Make tool stores default build rules in its data fork. HyperCard stacks can carry resources in their resource forks, with ICONs and XCMDs being popular residents.

Low- and High-level Routines

Two sets of calls are documented for you to use in file system routines, but actually only one set of file system calls exists. The so-called high-level routines are simply glue code found in MPW's Interface.o library. They are described in *Inside Macintosh* as being calls "not in ROM." These high-level routines are translated by the glue code into the only real calls, the so-called low-level routines.

Programming languages also offer routines to do file I/O. These routines ultimately call the low-level file system calls. The existence of such routines in programming languages further increases the number of choices available to you as a programmer. For example, using MPW C, you can choose among open (semi-standard UNIX/C library routine), fopen (ANSI C standard library routine with buffering), FSOpen (Mac high-level glue routine), and PBOpen (Mac low-level with minimal glue).

Param Blocks

All of the actual file-system traps use register D0 for returning result codes and register A0 to point to a ParamBlockRec. Through this somewhat complicated record, information is passed to and received from file system calls. Different calls interpret the record's fields differently. Here is a taste of what some of the cases of a ParamBlockRec look like, along with mention of the volume and file flags:

```
ParamBlockRec = RECORD
  qLink: QElemPtr;
  qType: INTEGER;
  ioTrap: INTEGER;
  ioCmdAddr: Ptr;
  ioCompletion: ProcPtr;
  ioResult: OSErr;
  ioNamePtr: StringPtr;
  ioVRefNum: INTEGER;
  CASE ParamBlkType OF
    IOParam:
        (ioRefNum: INTEGER;
        ioVersNum: SignedByte;
        ioPermssn: SignedByte;
        ioMisc: Ptr;
        ioBuffer: Ptr;
        ioReqCount: LONGINT;
        ioActCount: LONGINT;
        ioPosMode: INTEGER;
        ioPosOffset: LONGINT);
```

```
    FileParam:
        (ioFRefNum: INTEGER;
        ioFVersNum: SignedByte;
        filler1: SignedByte;
        ioFDirIndex: INTEGER;
        ioFlAttrib: SignedByte;          { -->   bit 7 set if file busy }
        ioFlVersNum: SignedByte;         {       bit 6 set if file protected }
        ioFlFndrInfo: FInfo;             {       bit 0 set if file locked }
        ioFlNum: LONGINT;
        ioFlStBlk: INTEGER;
        ioFlLgLen: LONGINT;
        ioFlPyLen: LONGINT;
        ioFlRStBlk: INTEGER;
        ioFlRLgLen: LONGINT;
        ioFlRPyLen: LONGINT;
        ioFlCrDat: LONGINT;
        ioFlMdDat: LONGINT);
    VolumeParam:
        (filler2: LONGINT;
        ioVolIndex: INTEGER;
        ioVCrDate: LONGINT;
        ioVLsBkUp: LONGINT;
        ioVAtrb: INTEGER;          { -->   bit 15 set if volume locked by software }
        ioVNmFls: INTEGER;         {       bit 7 set if volume locked by hardware  }
        ioVDirSt: INTEGER;         {       bit 6 set in VCB if any files open on vol}
        ioVBlLn: INTEGER;
        ioVNmAlBlks: INTEGER;
        ioVAlBlkSiz: LONGINT;
        ioVClpSiz: LONGINT;
        ioAlBlSt: INTEGER;
        ioVNxtFNum: LONGINT;
        ioVFrBlk: INTEGER);
    CntrlParam:
        (ioCRefNum: INTEGER;
        csCode: INTEGER;
        csParam: ARRAY [0..10] OF INTEGER);
END;
```

Types and Creators

Each file on the Macintosh has a specific type and creator. Types and creators are 32-bit codes, usually comprised of four letters. The creator signature is used by the Finder to display icons of applications and documents properly, and to launch the creator application when a document file's icon is opened by the user. File types are used to define types of documents that can be exchanged between applications. In creating new applications, you should not use existing file types in any way that would differ from existing usage—that is, a "STAK" should always be a HyperCard-compatible stack. Also, be careful not to confuse file types and creators with resource types, which use a similar 4-byte descriptor but for different purposes. The following table lists some popular types and creators.

Type	Creator	Software
ZSYS	MACS	System
ZSYS	MACS	MultiFinder
FNDR	MACS	Finder
APPL	maxb	MacsBug 5.5
cdev	sysc	General
PRER	LWRR	LaserWriter
LROM	LWRR	Laser Prep
APPL	MPS	MPW Shell 3.0
APPL	WILD	HyperCard 1.2.2
APPL	XCEL	MS Excel 1.5
APPL	MSWD	MS Word 4.0
APPL	MACA	MacWrite 4.6
APPL	MPNT	MacPaint 1.5
APPL	MDRW	MacDraw 1.9.5
APPL	MDPL	MacDraw II
TEXT	MPS	MPW Shell doc
MPST	MPS	MPW Shell tool
STAK	WILD	HyperCard stack
XLBN	XCEL	Excel worksheet
XLPG	XCEL	Excel macrosheet
WDBN	MSWD	Word 3 or 4 doc
WORD	MACA	MacWrite 4.6 doc
PNTG	MPNT	MacPaint 1.5 doc
DRWG	MDRW	MacDraw 1.9.5 doc
PICT	MDRW	MacDraw 1.9.5 pict
DRWG	MDPL	MacDraw II doc

Finder Information

A file's type and creator information is stored with each file's `FInfo`, or Finder information record. This record is actually only a small part of the information stored about each file; you can retrieve and change this record using the calls `GetFileInfo` and `SetFileInfo`. Here is a sample `FInfo` record, which in turn is part of a larger `ParamBlockRec`:

```
FInfo = RECORD
  fdType: OSType;
  fdCreator: OSType;
  fdFlags: INTEGER;
  fdLocation: Point;
  fdFldr: INTEGER;
END;
```

Volumes and files each have their own flag or attribute bits. In addition to those bits, the `FInfo` block has its own flags, which are interpreted as shown in the following table.

fdFlag Bit Number	Meaning if Bit Set
15	Finder's file lock
14	File is invisible
13	File has a bundle
12	System file—cannot rename
11	Bozo—cannot copy
10	Finder's busy file bit
9	Changed
8	Inited
7	No Inits
6	Shared
5	Always switch launch
0	File is on the Desktop

High-level File System Routines

The file system is initialized at boot time with a call to `InitFS`, so this should not be done by most applications. All queued file system calls can be terminated by a call to `InitQueue`.

To mount, unmount, put offline, and eject volumes, use calls to `MountVol`, `UnmountVol`, `Offline`, and `Eject`. An offline volume is seen on the Desktop but is largely unavailable otherwise. SetVol and GetVol handle the default volume to which file system calls go. To obtain detailed information about a volume, call GetVolInfo.

You can access files in many ways: by vRefNum and partial pathname, by full path name ("HD:System Folder:Finder"), or by vRefNum, dirID, and leaf name. You can also index through folders—which in HFS are actual directories.

The basic self-explanatory operations on files are accomplished by Create, Open, OpenRF (for opening the resource fork instead of the data fork), Read, Write, Close, Rename, and Delete. You can manipulate the logical length of a file with GetEOF and SetEOF, and you can change the physical length with Allocate. The file-pointer position within a file is handled by GetFPos and SetFPos. To lock and unlock an unopened file, use SetFilLock and RstFilLock. To retrieve information about a file, use GetFileInfo, and to change that information, use SetFileInfo and SetFileType. This last trap changes the version number of a file on MFS volumes but does not do anything on an HFS volume, because file version numbers are not supported in practice on any Mac volumes. It is largely a wasted trap because most routines fail if the file version number on MFS volumes is anything other than zero.

A file can be partially flushed to disk with FlushFile, but you must call FlushVol to ensure that writes and various low-level file system caches are flushed to the disk.

The 128 KB ROMs introduced many more routines. Virtually all of the routines mentioned above have a version that expects an HFS parameter block rather than the older and smaller MFS parameter blocks. These new HFS parameter blocks contain additional or changed fields to handle such things as real directories. You can tell which parameter block a file system routine expects by examining bit 9 in the trap word. If this bit is set, the HFS parameter block is expected.

In most cases, both versions of these calls perform the same operation, so you should use the older MFS calls whenever possible so that code will run on the original as well as newer Macintoshes. Allocate ($A010) is an exception, as it allocates space, contiguous or not, whereas AllocContig ($A210) is billed as a separate trap that allocates only contiguous disk space.

The Mac Plus 128 KB ROMs also have a trap called HFSDispatch ($A060) that offers many new file system calls using a word-sized routine selector passed in register D0. These routines largely give additional support for using directories. GetCatInfo, for example, allows you to index through all of the files in a directory. The routines that are available through this trap are shown in the following table.

Selector	Routine	Purpose
1	OpenWD	Opens a working directory
2	CloseWD	Closes a working directory
5	CatMove	Moves files/dirs
6	DirCreate	Creates a directory
7	GetWDInfo	Returns WD info
8	GetFCBInfo	Returns FCB info
9	GetCatInfo	GetFileInfo +
10	SetCatInfo	SetFileInfo +
11	SetVolInfo	Sets volume name
16	LockRange	Locks part of a file
17	UnlockRange	Unlocks part of a file

AppleShare (AS) also adds to HFSDispatch ($A060) new routines for supporting shared read/write access to files as well as permissions. If AppleShare is installed, the routines shown in the following table are present.

Selector	Routine	Purpose
48	GetVolParms	GetVolInfo for AS
49	GetLogInInfo	Returns login name
50	GetDirAccess	Get access permission
51	SetDirAccess	Set access permission
52	MapID	Gets name of usr/grp
53	MapName	Gets id given name
54	CopyFile	Duplicates a file on AS
55	MoveRename	Moves a file on AS
56	OpenDeny	AS version of Open
57	OpenRFDeny	AS vers. of OpenRF

Data Organization on Volumes

Each volume must have some information that describes the file system, such as boot blocks and file directories. An MFS 400 KB 3.5-inch floppy diskette has 800 512-byte blocks, numbered 0 through 799. They are arranged as shown in the following table.

Block #	Use
0 to 1	Boot blocks if bootable; otherwise zero
2 to 3	Master directory blocks; vol info; block map
4 to n	File directory
n+1 to 799	File contents

An HFS 800 KB 3.5-inch floppy diskette has 1600 512-byte blocks, numbered 0 through 1599. They are arranged as shown in the following table.

Block #	Use
0 to 1	Boot blocks if bootable; otherwise zero
2	Volume information block
3 to n	Volume bit map
n+1 to 799	File contents

Hard disks are organized in a way similar to that used for HFS floppies. The basic sector size of a hard disk must be large enough so that the number of sectors will fit in 16 bits. Thus, an 80 MB hard disk has sectors 1.5 KB in size. SCSI hard disk installation programs save a few blocks on the disk for storing the SCSI driver. Therefore, SCSI drivers are not kept anywhere within an HFS file system but must be retrieved by reading raw disk sectors. If 32 sectors were allocated for a SCSI driver, then the HFS boot blocks would actually be in sectors 32–33 of the disk.

On HFS volumes, the file directory is maintained by two invisible files called the extents tree file and the catalog tree file. These files are maintained by the B*-tree manager built into HFS and their existence is not acknowledged by the file system. Do not confuse them with the files used by the Finder for maintaining its icons. The Desktop file— or if the Desktop Manager is running, the Desktop DB and Desktop DF files—is invisible to the user but visible to any inquiring process.

An HFS volume information block—found in block 2 of the disk—is the same as the MFS volume block for the first 64 bytes. The HFS volume information block contains the basic information about a disk, including the number of files, space used and available, as well as pointers to the disk catalogs. The information provided in this block is shown in the following table.

Byte	Name - Size	Contents
0	drSigWord - word	HFS: $4244; MFS: $D2D7
2	drCrDate - long	init. date & time
6	drLsMod - long	last mod date & time
10	drAtrb - word	volume attributes
12	drNmFls - word	# of files
14	drVBMSt - word	first blk of vol bitmap
16	drAllocPtr - word	used internally
18	drNmAlBlks - word	# of alloc blocks
20	drAlBlkSiz - long	allocation block size
24	drClpSiz - long	default clump size
28	drAlBlSt - word	first blk in bitmap
30	drNxtCNID - long	next unused dir/file #
34	drFreeBks - word	# of unused alloc blks

continued

continued from page 45

Byte	Name - Size	Contents
36	drVN - byte	length of volume name
37	drVN+1 - bytes	the volume name chars
64	drVolBkUp - long	last bkup date & time
68	drVSeqNum - word	used internally
70	drWrCnt - long	volume write count
74	drXTClpSiz - long	extents tree clump size
78	drCTClpSiz - long	catalog tree clump size
82	drNmRtDirs - word	# dirs in root
84	drFilCnt - long	# files in volume
88	drDirCnt - long	# dirs in volume
92	drFndrInfo - 32 bytes	used by the Finder
124	drVCSize - word	used internally
126	drVCBMSize - word	used internally
128	drCtlCSize - word	used internally
130	drXTFlSize - long	length of extents tree
134	drXTExtRec - 12 bytes	extent rec for extents tree
146	drCTFlSize - long	length of catalog tree
150	drCTExtRec - 12 bytes	extent rec for catalog tree

The Input/Output System

Macintosh's input/output system, known as the Device Manager, handles the manipulation of devices used for input/output (I/O), including internal and external peripherals as well as desk accessories. The Device Manager was written by Andy Hertzfeld and Larry Kenyon.

Communication with each device is handled through a device driver. Device drivers respond to five different types of messages: `Open`, `Close`, `Control`, `Status`, and `Prime`. Driver calls include `Open`, `Close`, `Read`, `Write`, `Control`, `Status`, and `KillIO`.

Each Macintosh has a fixed-sized unit table that contains information about device drivers. This non-relocatable table lives in the system heap. The original Macintosh had 32 entries; the Mac Plus and SE have 48 entries; and the Mac II has 64 entries. The Mac II uses the extra entries for NuBus card slots. The following table presents a list of the standard devices by device number.

Device number	Device type
0	Reserved
1	Hard disk driver (HD-20)
2	.Print driver
3	.Sound driver
4	.Sony driver
5	.AIn (modem input)
6	.AOut (modem output)
7	.BIn (printer input)
8	.BOut (printer output)
9	.MPP AppleTalk driver
10	.ATP AppleTalk driver
11	Reserved
12-26	System desk accessories
27-31	Application desk accessories
32-39	SCSI drivers 0-7
40	.XPP AppleTalk driver
41-47	Reserved

Driver reference numbers are the two's complement—NEG.W—of the device or unit number. Driver names always begin with a period; desk accessory names always begin with a null (ASCII 0) character. If an Open call is made with a file name that does not begin with a period, the call is passed on to the File Manager. This method is similar to the UNIX operating system, which also treats files and devices in a unified manner. Because of this feature, the MPW Shell will not allow you to create or open a file whose name begins with a period, as the call would go to the Device Manager instead of the File Manager.

If you wanted to access raw blocks of a disk rather than files, you would go through the appropriate disk driver rather than the file system. The Sony disk driver is device 4, so its reference number (the two's complement of the device number) is -5. This would be plugged into the ioRefNum field of an IOParamBlock. The .Sony driver is opened automatically at boot, so no Open call needs to be made. To read and write blocks, you would use Read and Write calls.

AppleTalk

Local area networks—LANs—are becoming an increasingly essential part of computing systems. Different vendors systems are connected more and more often through the use of LANs. One of the great virtues of the Macintosh is the fact that every Mac has a LAN connection built into it. Thus, AppleTalk, which was designed by Gursharan Sidhu, is one of the most widely used networks ever made.

Originally, the term *AppleTalk* meant both a set of protocols and the medium of twisted pair cables. *LocalTalk* now refers to the original medium of twisted pair cables, and *EtherTalk* is an alternative medium that offers much faster transfer rates using different cabling and requiring an expensive card. *AppleTalk* is now understood to refer to the protocols that are related to the OSI network layers.

To access AppleTalk, you use standard `Read`, `Write`, and `Control` calls to the AppleTalk drivers. Two drivers are in ROM on 128 KB and later ROMs: .MPP and .ATP. The so-called AppleTalk Manager is a misnomer; it is not a ROM manager at all but is simply the glue code that properly calls the drivers. The AppleTalk Manager is not needed when you are using assembly language.

The layers of AppleTalk are presented in a top-down fashion in the following table.

Layer	Protocol	Driver	Comments
Presentation			
AFP	AppleTalk Filing	.XPP	Used by AppleShare
Session			
AFP	AppleTalk Session	.XPP	Links workstation & server
PAP	Printer Access	—	Supports LaserWriter
ZIP	Zone Information	—	
Transport			
ADSP	AppleTalk Data Stream	—	Socket-to-socket stream
ATP	AppleTalk Transaction	.ATP	Guarantees delivery
EP	Echo	—	Client of DDP
NBP	Name Binding	.MPP	Names to internet sockets
RTMP	Routing Table Maint.	—	Used internally by internet
Network			
DDP	Datagram Delivery	.MPP	Socket-to-socket delivery
Link Access			
ALAP	AppleTalk Link Access	.MPP	Node-to-node delivery
Physical			
—	LocalTalk	—	230 Kbaud twisted pair
—	EtherTalk	—	10 Mbaud coaxial cable

An AppleTalk network can have up to 255 nodes. Node-to-node delivery is done by sending up to 600-byte frames by ALAP. Each node can have multiple sockets. DDP uses ALAP to manage socket-to-socket delivery of 586-byte datagrams over internets.

Internet addresses are comprised of a 16-bit network number, an 8-bit node ID, and an 8-bit socket ID within that node.

ATP is the first level of transmission that does error checking to ensure a packet's contents are accurate. ATP assigns a 16-bit transaction ID and uses DDP, which in turn uses ALAP to guarantee socket-to-socket delivery of up to 8 ATP Packets, each with up to 578 bytes of user data, or a maximum of 4,624 bytes of user data. NBP assigns names to nodes.

Together, these protocols can be used easily to transfer information. A sample session is presented in the following table.

Client	Server	Comments
OpenATPSkt	OpenATPSkt	Connect to network
RegisterName	RegisterName	Register name on net
LookupName		Client will see server
SendRequest		Send request to server
	GetRequest	Server gets request
	SendResponse	Server sends data
	AddResponse	More packets sent
RemoveName	RemoveName	Become invisible
CloseATPSkt	CloseATPSkt	Disconnect from net

The Start Code and the Boot Process

The first piece of code to execute when a Macintosh is booted is called the *start code,* which is located as the first instructions of the Macintosh ROM. The start code, which was originally written by Larry Kenyon, begins by checking to see if a diagnostic ROM is installed. If one is installed, control is immediately turned over to it; otherwise, initialization next sets up the VIA and IWM chips, obtains the default sound volume from parameter RAM, draws a black screen, and then plays the boot beep. If the boot beep sounds, the CPU is okay.

Next comes a quick test of memory—both ROM and RAM—to determine its integrity. The memory test code for the Macintosh Plus was written by Jerome Coonen and is an interesting application of number theory to computer science. The ROM is checksummed against the first long word in the ROM address space, which is a checksum of the rest of the ROM. Various patterns are written to and then read from RAM to check its validity. The amount of RAM is also determined by the SizeSeriously routine at this time. If any memory is determined to have problems, the "Sad Mac" icon is displayed with a code specifying which chips are bad. The Sad Mac codes that might be displayed are shown in the following table.

Sad Mac Code	Meaning
01xxxx	ROM test
02xxxx	RAM test - bus subtest
03xxxx	RAM test - byte write
04xxxx	RAM test - mod3 test
05xxxx	RAM test - add uniqueness
0F0001	Bus error
0F0002	Address error
0F0003	Illegal instruction
0F0004	Zero divide
0F0005	Check instruction
0F0006	Trap instruction
0F0007	Privilege violation
0F0008	Trace
0F0009	Line 1010
0F000A	Line 1111
0F000B	Other exceptions
0F000C	Unimplimented trap
0F000D	NMI - interrupt button

If the first hex digit is 2-5, a memory chip failed to pass the RAM test. If this occurs, the last four digits (xxxx above) are the encoded position of the bad RAM chip. Starting with the third digit displayed from the left, the hex digits specify chips G12-G9, then G8-G5, then F12-F9, and finally F8-F5. Thus, an error code of 020800 means that chip G12 failed the bus subtest. Each bit represents a chip: row G is nearer the inside of the mother board; row F is closer to the outside.

System Error Handler

After the memory test is completed, all of memory is initialized to binary ones. Next, the System Error Handler written by Andy Hertzfeld and Ken Krugler is installed. This error handler sets all of the Motorola exception vectors to point into ROM. When one of these exceptions is hit the System Error Handler displays—using very minimal resources—the familiar "bomb box." The bomb box is actually INIT 2 of the System file, which is called by the ROM through the SysError routine as a last-resort method of informing the user that the Macintosh cannot proceed any further. The range of errors that may trigger the bomb box to appear includes—but is not limited to—the codes explained in the following table.

Bomb Box Code	Meaning
1	Bus error; invalid memory ref.; only XL & II
2	Address error; odd word data ref. w/68000
3	Illegal instruction; unrecognized bit pattern
4	DIVS or DIVU with divide by zero
5	CHK instruction failed; out of range
6	TRAPV instruction failed; overflow
7	Privilege violation; erroneous RTE?
8	The trace bit of the status register is set
9	The A-trap dispatcher failed (line 1010)
10	Unimplemented line 1111 instruction
11	Other Motorola hardware exceptions
12	Unimplemented A-trap routine
13	A interrupt vector is NIL, usually level 4-7
14	I/O Error; DCE purged
15	GetResource of CODE segment failed
16	Halt bit set in SANE environment
17	Package 0 not present
18	Package 1 not present
19	Package 2 not present
20	Package 3 not present
21	Package 4 not present
22	Package 5 not present
23	Package 6 not present
24	Package 7 not present
25	Out of memory; can't allocate request
26	GetResource of CODE 0 failed; can't launch
27	File system map has been trashed
28	Stack overflow (stack and heap collided)
30	Request user to reinsert offline disk
31	Not the disk I wanted
32	Hardware has overrun serial driver
33	Corrupt heap; ZcbFree is negative
40	Welcome to Macintosh greeting
41	Can't find the file named Finder; can't load it
42	Shutdown alert "You can now turn off…"
51	Unserviceable slot interrupt
64	Serial driver error masks
81	Bad opcode given to SANE Pack4
84	A menu has been purged
85	Can't find menu bar
86	Can't find menu
98	Can't find patch for particular Mac
99	Can't load patch resource
32767	General system error

On machines with 128 KB ROMs and later, a small version of MacsBug called MicroBug is installed at the same time as the System Error Handler. This debugger is installed via the `MacJmp` low-memory global pointer; you can enter MicroBug by pressing the interrupt programmer's switch (when a regular MacsBug is *not* installed). MicroBug supports MacsBug's G, DM, SM, TD, PC, and SR commands. It can also set and display individual A and D registers. A small Nub debugger that can communicate with another Macintosh through the serial port is also installed, but it has been little used.

Next in the boot process comes the main operating system initialization. This is where the Macintosh begins to take on its own personality, so to speak. `MemTop` is set to point to the top of physical memory. All interrupts are turned off. At this point, various low-memory globals are initialized to point to memory-mapped hardware, and the mouse and cursor are joined together.

The next step sets up the Vertical Blanking Manager (VBL). The video retrace triggers an interrupt 60 times each second (1/60 of a second = 1 tick) when the CRT gun is retracing back to the top of the screen before the next redraw. This level 1 interrupt has five main tasks to perform: increment the low-memory global called `Ticks`, update the cursor position, check keystrokes every 32 ticks, check the mouse state every other tick, and call other VBL tasks that are scheduled with the `VInstall` and `VRemove` routines.

At this point, more tables are set up, including the interrupt dispatch tables and the A-trap dispatch tables. The A-trap tables are set to point to the various OS and Toolbox routines in ROM, or to an unimplemented trap receiver. The ROM code does this by unpacking an encoded version of the trap table that is also located in ROM. The type of microprocessor is determined and the A-trap dispatcher is then started.

The boot code continues by reading the time and other saved parameters from parameter RAM. Next, the Memory Manager is initialized and the default system and application heaps are created. The SCC chip is initialized, the keyboard is fired up, and the Unit Table is set up with the Sony disk driver and sound driver opened. The asynch serial drivers and SCSI drivers are loaded but not opened. A default `GetNextEvent` filter is installed, the package dispatcher is initialized, and the Switcher table is installed. At this point, the first calls to QuickDraw change the black start-up screen to a gray boot screen with a disk icon. This first disk icon is in ROM and therefore cannot be changed.

Boot Blocks

Now the MacStart code tries to read in the boot blocks from the boot disk. Which disk is the boot disk? First the internal floppy is checked, then the external floppy, then it checks any chain of HD-20 hard disks of the IWM variety, and then it looks through SCSI devices, starting with device 7 down to 0. Internal SCSI hard disks are always SCSI ID 0. In the Macintosh SE and Mac II, this search path for a boot disk can be changed with the `cdev` named `Startup` in the Control Panel; this `cdev` stores the boot disk information in the extended parameter RAM that later Macs have. (A cdev is a piece of code that extends the functionality of the Control Panel DA. Other standard cdevs include Sound, Mouse, Keyboard, Color, etc.) Floppies that are found that do not have boot blocks are ejected and the search continues. If no boot disk can be found, the disk icon will contain a question mark.

What information do the boot blocks contain? The first two blocks (blocks zero and one) of any bootable Macintosh disk contain various start-up parameters. The first several parameters are shown in the following list, along with their defaults.

```
RECORD
   signature:    INTEGER;  { $4C4B or 'LK' }
   entryPoint:   Ptr;
   version:      INTEGER;  { $0017 for System 6.0 }
   page2Flags:   INTEGER;
   systemRsrc:   Str16;    {'System'}
   shellApp:     Str16;    {'Finder'}
   debugger:     Str16;    {'MacsBug'}
   debugger2:    Str16;    {'Disassembler'}
   startScrn:    Str16;    {'StartupScreen'}
   startupApp:   Str16;    {'Finder'}
   scrapFile:    Str16;    {'Clipboard File'}
   numFCBs:      INTEGER;  { max files open }
   numEvents:    INTEGER;  { max buffered events }
   heap128K:     LONGINT;  { Mac 128K system heap  }
   heap256K:     LONGINT;  { Mac 256K system heap  }
   heap512K:     LONGINT;  { Mac 512K system heap  }
END
```

A few more comments on boot blocks: the signature word contains the initials of Larry Kenyon, the chief architect of the original Macintosh File System. The startupApp name is set to MultiFinder, rather than Finder, when it is set to run. The boot blocks also show that there were once plans for a 256 KB Mac. In post-512 K Macs, the last of the three heap-size longs holds the actual value for other Macs. The start-up code also has its own defaults if these figures are too small, or if the boot block version is too old. The system heap is set to 128 KB with System 6.0 and a Mac II. (That's as big as all of the memory of the original 128 K Mac!)

A disk/file editing tool is useful when you need to examine or change the boot blocks. (My favorite is still Fedit, written by John Mitchell.) Later versions of the System file contain a copy of the boot blocks as resource boot 1. When the Finder does a disk-to-disk copy, it will copy the boot blocks as well.

Booting Continued

Now back to the boot sequence. After the boot disk has been found, the system heap is grown to the size specified in the boot blocks. The Event Manager is initialized by a call to InitEvents so that it has a buffer size that will handle the number of events specified in the boot blocks. The file system is initialized by a call to InitFS so that it has the maximum number of open files that the boot blocks indicate. Next, the boot disk is mounted and a system folder is looked for via the IOVFndrInfo field of a GetVolInfo call on the boot volume. This system folder is then set to be the default volume.

Another boot block parameter is checked as the start-up code looks to see if there is a boot screen present. The default file name is StartupScreen. If a file of that name is present, the QuickDraw bit map found in the data fork of the file is made the start-up screen by a call to CopyBits. If color QuickDraw is present, the resource fork is searched for a PICT 0 resource to display instead.

Next, the Resource Manager is fired up by a call to InitResources. For this to work, a System file whose name is specified in the boot blocks must be present. Normally, this file is called System. Once the System file is found, the Font Manager is initialized with a call to InitFonts and, unless there is a boot screen, the first Macintosh alert is displayed: "Welcome To Macintosh." This alert is contained in the DSAT 0 resource in the System file, and thus can be made international.

Booting—Installing MacsBug

The next step is to check for a debugger. The boot blocks actually have the ability to load and execute two different debuggers. If a file by the name of MacsBug or Disassembler is found, the system loads and executes that file. All versions of MacsBug since version 5 have a built-in disassembler, so the disassembler loading point is rarely used.

The process of loading MacsBug takes place as follows: First the boot-blocks code reserves some space (1,024 bytes) for MacsBug's own global variables. Then this code looks for the file specified in the boot blocks, as described above. If the file is not found, the global space is deallocated and the boot process continues normally without installing a debugger.

If MacsBug is found, the data fork (not the resource fork!) of the file is loaded onto the current stack, which is located immediately below the main screen buffer in memory. For historical reasons, the first block (512 bytes) of the MacsBug data fork is stripped off during this loading process. In any of the version 5 series of MacsBug, this otherwise unused block contained a brief history of the people who contributed to MacsBug. Unfortunately, the author of the version 6 series of MacsBug removed this nice use of otherwise wasted space and replaced it with spaces.

The boot code then executes a JSR (Jump Subroutine and Return) to MacsBug itself. MacsBug begins its installation process by checking to see if the mouse button is down. If it is, MacsBug aborts the installation and lets the boot process continue without installing itself. If the button is not down, MacsBug determines which kind of machine and microprocessor it is running on and configures itself accordingly. The code for MacsBug is loaded in high memory right beneath the screen on classic Macs, and it is almost at the very top of RAM on Mac IIs.

Any of the version 5 MacsBugs installed themselves into several of the Motorola vectors; MacsBug 6.0 installs itself into the low-memory global MacJmp at location $120 instead. At the successful completion of the installation, the message "MacsBug installed" is posted below the "Welcome to Macintosh" screen.

Booting—Installing Patches and INITs

The boot process then continues by checking the data fork of the System file, which contains the code that installs the patches to the OS and Mac ROMs. A patch is a tricky piece of code that either corrects bugs or adds features to the main Macintosh ROM routines.

Originally the patches themselves lived in the data fork, but in later versions of the Macintosh System file the code in the data fork simply loads a PTCH resource that contains all of the patches. There is a PTCH resource for each different Macintosh computer. They are keyed by ROM version number—for example, PTCH 630 is for the Macintosh SE. In addition, some ptch resources contain entire managers to be back-patched to earlier machines. For example, in System 6.0 there are several ptch resources that contain RAM-based code for Styled TextEdit, the Script Manager, and the Sound Manager.

Another mechanism is provided for developers and hackers: INITs. These useful resources allow you to patch and extend the system before any applications are running. Unfortunately, INITs can cause unexpected crashes if you do not use them properly. An example of an INIT is given at the end of the chapter.

The boot code looks for INIT resources 0–31 in the System file and JSRs to them. Some of these INIT resources are used by Apple to set up the keyboard maps (INIT 0 and INIT 1) and other localizable things. INIT 31 extends the system software further by looking for any files of type INIT that in turn contain resources of type INIT. These files must be in the System Folder in order to be found. This facility allows you to install your own start-up code without changing the System file.

A disk track cache is then set up from a resource of type cach. The name of the file containing the scrap—usually Clipboard—is then looked up from the boot blocks.

Finally, the start-up application is launched. Typically, the start-up application is the Finder, but you can set it to any other application via the Finder's Set Startup facility. This start-up application may be different from the "shell" application. Both names are mentioned in the boot blocks. At this point the System relinquishes control of the Mac to the start-up application.

OSPeek — Pascal Desk Accessory

You may find it useful at this point to examine the code for a driver. OSPeek is a handy desk accessory—recall that desk accessories are drivers—that is useful for "looking under the hood" of your Macintosh. It displays a graphical picture of what microprocessor, ROMs, and amount of memory are found on the Mac. It also shows the values of the some of the more important low-memory globals—in hex, of course. Figure 2–2 shows an example of OSPeek's display.

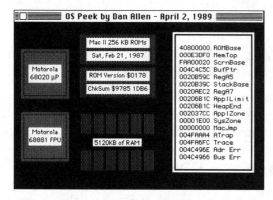

Figure 2–2: **OSPeek**'s Display

The value given for MemTop in Figure 2–2 is wrong because MultiFinder actually dummies up a false value that it stores in MemTop. After calling a special MultiFinder routine, we can find out the real value, which we did to show the 5 MB of RAM in this particular example.

The fun begins when you close OSPeek by clicking in its close box. When you do so, a Standard File dialog appears asking you to supply a file name. Clicking Okay then generates an MPW text file that lists every A-trap, along with an educated guess about the status of the routine. The trap can be either in ROM or in a RAM patch. If it is in RAM, OSPeek will also try to determine who patched the trap. Possible candidates include the System, MultiFinder, and the currently running application. Clicking Cancel will omit this process.

One tip on using OSPeek: hold down the Option key when bringing up OSPeek when MultiFinder is active. Bringing up desk accessories in MultiFinder normally launches a separate application known as the DA Handler. If you do not hold down the Option key, you will see the A-trap world of the DA Handler rather than of the application being examined. Holding down the Option key loads the DA into the application's heap rather than launching the separate DA layer. Alternately, you could just run without MultiFinder. In any case, examining the output of OSPeek for various applications can be instructive and revealing!

Here is the Makefile for OSPeek:

```
OSPeek    ƒ    OSPeek.p.o
    Link -o OSPeek.DRVW -w -rt DRVW=0 -sg OSPeek ∂
        "{Libraries}"DRVRRuntime.o OSPeek.p.o ∂
        "{Libraries}"Interface.o ∂
        "{PLibraries}"Paslib.o
    Rez -rd -c DMOV -t DFIL OSPeek.r -o OSPeek
    Delete OSPeek.DRVW
```

Now here is the Pascal code for the DA:

```
{ File OSPeek.p - Written by Dan Allen   }
{ Written May 1988 in Turbo Pascal; ported to MPW 14 Jan 1989 }
{ Tweaked 2 April 1989 }

{$R-} { No range checking   }

UNIT OSPeek;

INTERFACE

USES MemTypes,QuickDraw,OSIntf,ToolIntf,PackIntf;

FUNCTION DRVROpen      (ctlPB: ParmBlkPtr; device: DCtlPtr): OSErr;
FUNCTION DRVRControl   (ctlPB: ParmBlkPtr; device: DCtlPtr): OSErr;
FUNCTION DRVRStatus    (ctlPB: ParmBlkPtr; device: DCtlPtr): OSErr;
FUNCTION DRVRPrime     (ctlPB: ParmBlkPtr; device: DCtlPtr): OSErr;
FUNCTION DRVRClose     (ctlPB: ParmBlkPtr; device: DCtlPtr): OSErr;

IMPLEMENTATION

TYPE
  WordPtr = ^Integer;
  LongPtr = ^LongInt;
  ERPtr   = ^EventRecord;

FUNCTION  MFMemTop: LongInt; INLINE $3F3C,$0016,$A88F;
FUNCTION  GetRegA7: LongInt; INLINE $2E8F;
```

```pascal
(* ******** MAIN UTILITY ROUTINES ******** *)

FUNCTION AdrToLong(adr: LongInt) : LongInt;
VAR
  temp:      LongPtr;
BEGIN
  temp := Pointer(adr);
  AdrToLong := temp^;
END;

FUNCTION ByteToStr(address: Ptr) : Str255;
VAR
  theByte:     byte;
  theString:   Str255;
BEGIN
  theByte := address^;
  NumToString(theByte,theString);
  ByteToStr := theString
END;

FUNCTION CurAppName: Str255;
VAR
  p:   ^Str255;
BEGIN
  p := Pointer($910);
  CurAppName := p^;
END;

FUNCTION IntToHex(word: Integer): Str255;
VAR
  i,d:        Integer;
  hexStr:     Str255;
BEGIN
  hexStr := '0000';
  FOR i := 1 TO 4 DO
    BEGIN
      d := BAND(BSR(word,(4-i)*4),$000F);
      IF d < 10 THEN hexStr[i] := Chr(Ord('0')+d)
      ELSE hexStr[i] := Chr(Ord('A')+d-10);
    END;
  IntToHex := hexStr;
END;

FUNCTION LongToHex(address: LongInt) : Str255;
BEGIN
  LongToHex := Concat(IntToHex(HiWord(address)),
                      IntToHex(LoWord(address)));
END;
```

```
FUNCTION WordPtrToHex(address: WordPtr) : Str255;
BEGIN
  WordPtrToHex := IntToHex(address^);
END;


(* ******** MAIN DESK ACCESSORY ROUTINES ******** *)


FUNCTION DRVROpen(ctlPB: ParmBlkPtr; device: DCtlPtr): OSErr;
VAR
  savePort:   GrafPtr;
  myRect:     Rect;
BEGIN
  WITH device^ DO
    IF dCtlWindow = NIL THEN
      BEGIN
        SetRect(myRect,65,75,455,325);
        WindowPtr(dCtlWindow) := NewWindow(Pointer(0),myRect,
          'OS Peek by Dan Allen - April 2, 1989',
          TRUE, documentProc, Pointer(-1),TRUE, 0);
        WindowPeek(dCtlWindow)^.windowKind := dCtlRefNum;
        GetPort(savePort);
        SetPort(GrafPtr(dCtlWindow));
        SelectWindow(GrafPtr(dCtlWindow));
        TextMode(srcCopy); TextSize(9);
        SetPort(savePort);
      END;
  DRVROpen := NOErr;
END;

{ *** DRIVER CLOSE ROUTINE *** }

FUNCTION DRVRClose(ctlPB: ParmBlkPtr; device: DCtlPtr): OSErr;
VAR
  err:        OSErr;
  myRefNum:   Integer;

  mbExists:   Boolean; { is MacsBug installed ? }
  mfExists:   Boolean; { is MultiFinder installed ? }
```

```
busVector:  LongInt; { bus error handler address }
chkVector:  LongInt; { CHK instruction error handler address }
aTrapVec:   LongInt; { A-trap handler address }
macJmp:     LongInt; { MacsBug 6.0 funnel address }
bufPointer: LongInt; { end of the app's whole process space }
applLimit:  LongInt; { end of the app's heap }
applZone:   LongInt; { start of the app's heap }
romBase:    LongInt; { location of the ROM }
twitcher2:  LongInt; { MultiFinder's special low memory global }
unimpLoc:   LongInt; { location of the unimplemented A-trap }
aPoint:     Point;
reply:      SFReply;
theWatch:   CursHandle;

FUNCTION BufArea(address: LongInt) : Str255;
TYPE
  CodeTypes = (bufptr,mb5,mb6,mf,app);
VAR
  config: SET OF CodeTypes;
BEGIN
  config := [bufptr];
  IF macJmp <> 0 THEN config := config + [mb6];
  IF mbExists AND (macJmp = 0) THEN config := config + [mb5];
  IF mfExists THEN config := config + [mf];

  IF address < busVector THEN config := config - [mb5];
  IF address < BAND(macJmp,$00FFFFFF) THEN config := config - [mb6];
  IF mfExists AND (address < chkVector) THEN config := config - [mb5];
  IF mfExists AND (address > twitcher2+$4000) THEN config := config - [mf];
  IF mfExists AND (address < twitcher2-$2000) THEN config := config - [mf];
  IF address < bufPointer THEN config := config + [app];

  IF mb6 IN config THEN
    BufArea := 'MacsBug6.0'
  ELSE IF mb5 IN config THEN
    BufArea := 'MacsBug5.5'
  ELSE IF mf IN config THEN
    BufArea := 'MultiFinder'
  ELSE IF app IN config THEN
    BufArea := CurAppName
  ELSE
    BufArea := 'BufPtrArea';
END;
```

```
FUNCTION WhereAddr(address: LongInt) : Str255;
LABEL 9;
BEGIN
  IF (address > $00C00000) AND (address < $40000000) THEN
    BEGIN
      WhereAddr := 'RadiusROM';
      GOTO 9;
    END;
  IF address < applZone THEN
    WhereAddr := 'SysHeap'
  ELSE IF address < applLimit THEN
    WhereAddr := CurAppName
  ELSE IF address < romBase THEN
    WhereAddr := BufArea(address)
  ELSE IF address = unimpLoc THEN
    WhereAddr := 'Unimplemented'
  ELSE
    WhereAddr := 'ROM';
9:
END;


PROCEDURE OutString(a,b,c,d: Str255);
VAR
  len:  LongInt;
  p:    Ptr;
  out:  Str255;
BEGIN
  out := Concat(a,b,' = ',c,' ',d,CHR(13));
  len := Length(out);
  p := Pointer(LongInt(@out)+1);
  err := FSWrite(myRefNum,len,p);
END;


PROCEDURE TrapList(fileName: Str255; vRefNum: Integer);
LABEL 9;
VAR
  i:          Integer;
  a:          LongInt;
BEGIN
  busVector  := AdrToLong($8);
  chkVector  := AdrToLong($18);
  aTrapVec   := AdrToLong($28);
  bufPointer := AdrToLong($10C);
  macJmp     := AdrToLong($120);
  applLimit  := AdrToLong($130);
  applZone   := AdrToLong($2AA);
  romBase    := AdrToLong($2AE);
  twitcher2  := AdrToLong($B7C);
  unimpLoc   := GetTrapAddress($9F);
```

```
mfExists  := twitcher2 > 0;
mbExists  := (aTrapVec < romBase) OR (macJmp <> 0);

vRefNum := SetVol(NIL,vRefNum);
err := Create(fileName,0,'MPS ','TEXT');
err := FSOpen(fileName,vRefNum,myRefNum);
IF err <> 0 THEN GOTO 9;

FOR i := 2 TO 63 DO { Get vectors }
  BEGIN
    a := AdrToLong(i*4);
    OutString('Vector ',IntToHex(i*4),LongToHex(a),WhereAddr(a));
  END;

FOR i := 0 TO 255 DO { Get OS Traps }
  BEGIN
    a := NGetTrapAddress(i,OSTrap);
    OutString('OSTrap ',IntToHex(i+$A000),LongToHex(a),WhereAddr(a));
  END;

FOR i := 0 TO 511 DO { Get TB Traps }
  BEGIN
    a := NGetTrapAddress(i,ToolTrap);
    OutString('TBTrap ',IntToHex(i+$A800),LongToHex(a),WhereAddr(a));
  END;

IF ROMBase > $40000000 THEN
  FOR i := 512 TO 1023 DO { Get TB Traps }
    BEGIN
      a := NGetTrapAddress(i,ToolTrap);
      OutString('TBTrap ',IntToHex(i+$A800),LongToHex(a),WhereAddr(a));
    END;
9:  err := FSClose(myRefNum);
  END;
```

```
BEGIN
  LongInt(aPoint) := $00700070;
  SysBeep(5);
  SFPutFile(aPoint, 'Save vector & trap list:', 'TrapList.tx', NIL, reply);
  IF reply.good THEN
    BEGIN
      theWatch := GetCursor(watchCursor);
      SetCursor(theWatch^^);
      TrapList(reply.fName,reply.vRefNum);
    END;
  InitCursor;
  WITH device^ DO
    BEGIN
      DisposeWindow(GrafPtr(dCtlWindow));
      dCtlWindow := NIL
    END;
  DRVRClose := NOErr;
END;


FUNCTION DRVRPrime (ctlPB: ParmBlkPtr; device: DCtlPtr): OSErr;
BEGIN
  DRVRPrime := NoErr; (* not used by desk accessories *)
END;

FUNCTION DRVRStatus (ctlPB: ParmBlkPtr; device: DCtlPtr): OSErr;
BEGIN
  DRVRStatus := NoErr; (* not used by desk accessories *)
END;

FUNCTION DRVRControl(ctlPB: ParmBlkPtr; device: DCtlPtr): OSErr;
VAR
  savePort: GrafPtr;
  patBlack,patGray,patDkGray,patWhite: Pattern;

{ *** MAIN DRAWING ROUTINES *** }

  PROCEDURE DrawCPU;
  CONST
    xStart = 10; yStart = 40; width = 75;
  VAR
    myRect, m881Rect:   Rect;
    HWFlags:    Ptr;
    myStr:      Str255;
```

```
FUNCTION m68k(address: Ptr): Str255;
VAR
  theByte:    byte;
  theString:  Str255;
BEGIN
  theByte := address^;
  NumToString(theByte*10 + 68000,theString);
  m68k := theString
END;

BEGIN
  SetRect(myRect,xStart,yStart,xStart+width,yStart+width);
  m881Rect := myRect; OffsetRect(m881Rect,0,width+20);

  FillRoundRect(myRect,6,6, patGray); InsetRect(myRect,4,4);
  FrameRect(myRect); InsetRect(myRect,8,20);
  myStr := Concat('Motorola ',m68k(Pointer($12F)),' µP');
  TextBox(Pointer(LongInt(@myStr)+1),Length(myStr),myRect,teJustCenter);

  HWFlags := Pointer($B22);
  IF BAND(HWFlags^,$10) > 0 THEN
    BEGIN
      FillRoundRect(m881Rect,6,6, patGray); InsetRect(m881Rect,4,4);
      FrameRect(m881Rect); InsetRect(m881Rect,8,20);
      IF Ptr($12F)^ = $3 THEN
        myStr := 'Motorola 68882 FPU'
      ELSE
        myStr := 'Motorola 68881 FPU';
      TextBox(Pointer(LongInt(@myStr)+1),Length(myStr),
              m881Rect,teJustCenter);
    END;
END;

PROCEDURE DrawROM;
CONST
  width = 120; height = 45;
  xStart = 102; yStart = 18;
VAR
  romBase:       LongPtr;
  hiROM,loROM:   Rect;
  mtype:         LongInt;
  myStr:         Str255;
  burnDate:      Ptr;
  dateLen:       Integer;
BEGIN
  romBase := Pointer($2AE);
  SetRect(hiROM,xStart,yStart,xStart+width,yStart+height);
  loROM := hiROM; OffsetRect(loROM,0,50);
```

```
{ DRAW UPPER ROM }

   StringToNum(ByteToStr(Pointer(romBase^+8)),mtype);
   CASE mtype OF
     0:  BEGIN { Macintosh }
            IF (WordPtrToHex(Pointer(romBase^+8)) = '0069') THEN
              BEGIN
                myStr := 'Mac 64 KB ROMs';
                burnDate := Pointer(LongInt(romBase^)+$76C8);
                dateLen := 19;
              END
            ELSE
              BEGIN
                myStr := 'Mac+ 128 KB ROMs';
                burnDate := Pointer(LongInt(romBase^)+$1FFEF);
                dateLen := 16;
              END;
         END;

     1:  BEGIN { Milwaukee, Reno, Becks, Paris, OpenMac… }
            myStr := 'Mac II 256 KB ROMs';
            IF LongPtr(romBase^)^ = $97851DB6 THEN
              burnDate := Pointer(LongInt(romBase^)+$3FFEE)
            ELSE IF LongPtr(romBase^)^ = $9779D2C4 THEN
              burnDate := Pointer(LongInt(romBase^)+$3FF98)
            ELSE { Mac IIx offset }
              burnDate := Pointer(LongInt(romBase^)+$3FF9B);
            dateLen := 17;
         END;

     2:  BEGIN { Aladdin, Mawi, Freeport… }
            myStr := 'Mac SE 256 KB ROMs';
            burnDate := Pointer(LongInt(romBase^)+$3FFEE);
            dateLen := 17;
         END;
  -126:  BEGIN { Lisa as a MacXL - MacWorks 3.0 }
            myStr := 'MacWorks 3.0';
            burnDate := Pointer(LongInt(romBase^)+$30);
            dateLen := 12;
         END;
  OTHERWISE
         BEGIN { Unknown set OF ROMs }
            myStr := 'New Macintosh';
            burnDate := Pointer(LongInt(romBase^)+$3FF9B);
            dateLen := 17;
         END;
   END;
```

```
  FillRect(hiROM,patdkgray);
  InsetRect(hiROM,10,15); OffsetRect(hiROM,0,-10);
  TextBox(Pointer(LongInt(@myStr)+1),length(myStr),hiROM,teJustCenter);
  OffsetRect(hiROM,0,20); TextBox(burnDate,dateLen,hiROM,teJustCenter);

{ DRAW LOWER ROM }

  FillRect(loROM,patdkgray);
  InsetRect(loROM,10,15); OffsetRect(loROM,0,-10);
  myStr := Concat('ROM Version $',WordPtrToHex(Pointer(romBase^+8)));
  TextBox(Pointer(LongInt(@myStr)+1),Length(myStr),loROM,teJustCenter);

  OffsetRect(loROM,0,20);
  myStr := Concat('ChkSum $',WordPtrToHex(Pointer(romBase^)),' ',
                  WordPtrToHex(Pointer(romBase^+2)));
  TextBox(Pointer(LongInt(@myStr)+1),Length(myStr),loROM,teJustCenter);
END;

PROCEDURE DrawRAM;
VAR
  a,b:    Rect;
  i,j:    Integer;
  mem:    Str255;
  memTop: LongPtr;
BEGIN
  SetRect(a,104,138,119,168); b := a;
  FOR i := 1 TO 2 DO
    BEGIN
      IF i = 2 THEN
        BEGIN
          a := b; OffSetRect(a,0,55);
        END;
      FOR j := 1 TO 6 DO
        BEGIN
          FillRect(a,patdkgray);
          OffsetRect(a,20,0);
        END;
    END;
  MoveTo(122,185);
  IF GetTrapAddress($A88F) <> GetTrapAddress($9F) THEN
    NumToString(MFMemTop DIV 1024,mem)
  ELSE
    BEGIN
      memTop := Pointer($108);
      NumToString((memTop^) DIV 1024,mem);
    END;
  DrawString(Concat(' ',mem,'KB of RAM '));
END;
```

```
PROCEDURE DrawMemMap;
VAR
  i:  Integer;
  s:  Str255;
  r:  Rect;
BEGIN
  SetRect(r,249,14,376,226);
  PenNormal; FillRect(r,patWhite);
  PenSize(2,2); InsetRect(r,3,3); FrameRect(r);
  TextFont(monaco);
  FOR i := 1 TO 16 DO
    BEGIN
      CASE i OF
        1:  s := Concat(LongToHex(AdrToLong($2AE)),' ROMBase');
        2:  s := Concat(LongToHex(AdrToLong($108)),' MemTop');
        3:  s := Concat(LongToHex(AdrToLong($824)),' ScrnBase');
        4:  s := Concat(LongToHex(AdrToLong($10C)),' BufPtr');
        5:  s := Concat(LongToHex(AdrToLong($904)),' RegA5');
        6:  s := Concat(LongToHex(AdrToLong($908)),' StackBase');
        7:  s := Concat(LongToHex(GetRegA7),' RegA7');
        8:  s := Concat(LongToHex(AdrToLong($130)),' ApplLimit');
        9:  s := Concat(LongToHex(AdrToLong($114)),' HeapEnd');
       10:  s := Concat(LongToHex(AdrToLong($2AA)),' ApplZone');
       11:  s := Concat(LongToHex(AdrToLong($2A6)),' SysZone');
       12:  s := Concat(LongToHex(AdrToLong($120)),' MacJmp');
       13:  s := Concat(LongToHex(AdrToLong($28)),' ATrap ');
       14:  s := Concat(LongToHex(AdrToLong($24)),' Trace ');
       15:  s := Concat(LongToHex(AdrToLong($C)),' Adr Err');
       16:  s := Concat(LongToHex(AdrToLong($8)),' Bus Err');
      END;
      MoveTo(260,i*11+30);
      DrawString(s);
    END;
END;
```

```
{ *** MACINTOSH INTERFACE CODE *** }

  PROCEDURE DoUpdate;
  BEGIN
    StuffHex(@patBlack,   'FFFFFFFFFFFFFFFF');
    StuffHex(@patdkGray,  '77DD77DD77DD77DD');
    StuffHex(@patGray,    'AA55AA55AA55AA55');
    StuffHex(@patWhite,   '0000000000000000');
    WITH device^ DO
      BEGIN
        BeginUpdate(GrafPtr(dCtlWindow));
          FillRect(GrafPtr(dCtlWindow)^.portRect, patBlack);
          TextFont(geneva);
          DrawCPU;
          DrawROM;
          DrawRAM;
          DrawMemMap;
        EndUpdate(GrafPtr(dCtlWindow))
      END
  END;

{ *** MAIN DRIVER CONTROL ROUTINE *** }

BEGIN { Control }
  WITH device^ DO
    BEGIN
      GetPort(savePort);
      SetPort(GrafPtr(dCtlWindow));
      CASE ctlPB^.csCode OF
        accEvent: DoUpdate;
        goodBye:  IF DRVRClose(ctlPB,device) <> NOErr THEN SysBeep(10);
      END;
      SetPort(savePort);
    END;
  DRVRControl := NOErr;
END;


END. { of OSPeek UNIT }
```

ADBKey — Assembly Language INIT

Here is a short piece of code that will serve as an example of how to write an INIT. This INIT is written in assembly language; it converts the power-on key found on ADB keyboards to a direct MacsBug interrupt key. This key is a lot easier to use than the programmer's switch located on the side of the Macintosh.

```
* ADBKey INIT
* By Dan Allen 3 June 1988
* Converts the power-on key found on ADB keyboards to a MacsBug NMI key
* Select the following two lines in MPW and press enter to build the INIT
; Asm adb.a
; Link adb.a.o -o ADBKey -rt INIT=0 -t INIT -c adbk


            MAIN

            MOVEM.L    D3-D7/A2-A6,-(A7)
            SUB.W      #2,SP
            DC.W       $A974                 ; _Button
            MOVE.W     (SP)+,D0
            TST.W      D0
            BNE.S      @1                    ; branch when down

            BSR.S      Install
@1          MOVEM.L    (A7)+,D3-D7/A2-A6
            RTS

PatchBeg    MOVE.L     A0,-(A7)
            MOVE.L     $0CF8,A0              ; ADBBase
            CMPI.B     #$02,$0001(A0)        ; keyboard ?
            BNE.S      StdExit

            MOVE.L     $0008(A0),A0
            BCLR       #$07,$0013(A0)        ; clear key
            CMP.B      #$80,$183             ; check KeyMap
            BNE.S      StdExit

            CLR.B      $183                  ; does not spring back
            MOVE.L     (A7)+,A0
            MOVE.L     SavedNMI,-(A7)
            RTS

StdExit     MOVE.L     (A7)+,A0
            MOVE.L     SavedADB,-(A7)
            RTS
```

```
SavedADB   DC.L       0
SavedNMI   DC.L       0
PatchEnd

Install    MOVE.L     $2AE,A0                ; ROMBase
           ADD.W      #8,A0                  ; Machine Type
           TST.B      (A0)                   ; Mac Plus?
           BEQ.S      @9                     ; yes there is no ADB, cruise

           MOVE.L     #(PatchEnd-PatchBeg),D0
           DC.W       $A51E                  ; _NewPtr,Sys
           BNE.S      @9

           MOVE.L     a0,a1                  ; save ptr
           LEA        SavedADB,A0
           MOVE.L     $0064,(A0)
           LEA        SavedNMI,A0
           MOVE.L     $007C,(A0)
           LEA        PatchBeg,A0
           MOVE.L     #(PatchEnd-PatchBeg),D0
           DC.W       $A02E                  ; _BlockMove
           MOVE.L     A1,$0064

@9         RTS

           END
```

Zero — C Tool

Zero is an MPW tool written in C that quickly reinitializes floppy disks to a clean state. The default action of this tool is to erase the disk in the internal disk drive as normal. You can specify the external drive by using the -e option.

If you use the -m option, about 15 KB more space can be freed up on the disk. The program accomplishes this by reconfiguring the size of the HFS B-trees used to catalog the files on disk to their smallest possible size. This is useful when just a few large files occupy the disk. However, the system occasionally hangs if 32 or more files are put on such a disk, so be careful when using this option.

Another option (-z) configures the HFS B-trees to be much larger than normal. This greatly increases performance when hundreds of small files are to be stored on a disk. In fact, the original motivation for creating this tool was to make it easier to back up Maple, a symbolic math package for the Macintosh that has thousands of very small files. This option makes writing them to disk a much faster process.

By examining this tool, you will see how to fill out a parameter block and how to make a low-level file system call.

The tool is relatively straightforward and is useful for reinitializing old disks. If a disk has never been formatted, however, it should be erased normally once first because this tool calls only `DIZero`, not `DIFormat`.

Options for `Zero` give you the ability to change the allocation, clump, and B-tree sizes separately using the `-a`, `-b`, and `-c` options, or collectively by using the `-m` (maximum space) and `-z` (zillion files) options. By default, the disk is named "Untitled," but you can substitute any name by supplying the name as an argument to `Zero`.

Improving `Zero`

Here are some suggestions for improving `Zero`:

- If you are a paranoid user, you might want to add an option that allows confirmation when reinitializing disks that have files on them. Take into account hidden Desktop files.
- Experiment with different file system parameters on a hard disk. This will require a new option to specify drive numbers. When the user is erasing an entire hard disk, a special confirmation alert should be put up, saying "Are you sure you want to delete 2,147 files representing years' worth of work?" to make sure that the right disk is being zeroed.

```
/*
 *  zero.c   - Zeros floppy disks
 *           - Written by Dan Allen, 1/6/88
 *           - Fixed Mac II bomb 2/8/88
 *           - New options added 9/5/88
 *           - Brought forward to MPW C 3.0 10/11/88
 *           - Works with both 2.0 & 3.0 C compilers 1/8/89
 *           - Cleanup 2/15/89
 *           - Options & defaults changed; added disk options 6/10/89
 *
 *    Allocation size determined by: (1 + (numBlocks/64K)) * 512 bytes
 *    Clump size:  4 * allocation size
 *    B-Tree size determined by: numBlocks/64K * 512 bytes
 *
 */

#include <CType.h>
#include <DiskInit.h>
#include <Files.h>
#include <QuickDraw.h>
#include <StdIO.h>
```

```c
#ifdef  ghs /* check for MPW C 2.0 */
#define dizero  DIZero
#endif

typedef HFSDefaults     *HFSPtr;

#define INTERNAL        1
#define EXTERNAL        2
#define FMTDEFAULTS     (*((HFSPtr *) 0x39E))

static HFSDefaults      hfsVol = {'B','D',0,0,16,0};  /* std defaults */
static ParamBlockRec    volPB;
static Boolean          progFlag;
static char             *diskName = "Untitled";
static short            driveNum = INTERNAL;

main(int argc,char *argv[])
{
  short   err;
  int     i;
  HFSPtr  oldSettings;

  InitGraf(&qd.thePort);
  InitCursor();

  for(i = 1; i < argc; i++)
    if (argv[i][0] == '-')
      switch(tolower(argv[i][1])) {
        case 'a': hfsVol.abSize = atoi(argv[++i]);  break;
        case 'b': hfsVol.btClpSize = atoi(argv[++i]); break;
        case 'c': hfsVol.clpSize = atoi(argv[++i]); break;
        case 'e': driveNum = EXTERNAL; break;
        case 'm': hfsVol.abSize = 512; hfsVol.clpSize = 512;
                  hfsVol.btClpSize = 1024; break;
        case 'p': progFlag = true; break;
        case 'z': hfsVol.abSize = 512; hfsVol.clpSize = 2048;
                  hfsVol.btClpSize = 16384; break;
      }
    else diskName = argv[i];


  /* error check for bad sizes */
  hfsVol.abSize = Mult512(hfsVol.abSize);
  hfsVol.clpSize = Mult512(hfsVol.clpSize);
  hfsVol.btClpSize = Mult512(hfsVol.btClpSize);
```

```
  if (hfsVol.clpSize < hfsVol.abSize)
    hfsVol.clpSize = hfsVol.abSize;
  if (hfsVol.btClpSize < 2*hfsVol.abSize)
    hfsVol.btClpSize = 2*hfsVol.abSize;
  if (hfsVol.btClpSize < hfsVol.clpSize)
    hfsVol.btClpSize = 2*hfsVol.clpSize;
  if (progFlag)
    fprintf(stderr,"# abSize = %u  clpSize = %u  btClpSize = %u\n",
            hfsVol.abSize,hfsVol.clpSize,hfsVol.btClpSize);


  /* unmount and zero disk */
  volPB.volumeParam.ioVRefNum = driveNum;
  err = PBUnmountVol(&volPB);
  if (err) fprintf(stderr,"# Unmount err: %d\n",err);

  oldSettings = FMTDEFAULTS;  /* save undocumented low-memory */
  FMTDEFAULTS = &hfsVol;       /* set our parameters */
  err = dizero(driveNum, diskName); /* flame that disk ! */
  FMTDEFAULTS = oldSettings;  /* restore system defaults */
  if (err) {
    fprintf(stderr,"# DIZero err: %d\n",err);
    return 2;
  }
  return 0;
}

int Mult512(int arg)
{
  int num,rmd;

  num = arg / 512; rmd = arg % 512;
  if (rmd) return (num+1)*512;
  else return arg;
}
```

Conclusion

In this chapter, we have looked at the core of the Macintosh operating system:

- Memory Manager
- Segment Loader
- File Manager
- Device Manager
- AppleTalk

MultiFinder changed the way processes are handled, and these changes were described. We also looked in some detail at how the Macintosh OS boot sequence works.

Three pieces of code were also presented: a desk accessory (driver) that explores the insides of the Macintosh OS, an INIT, and an MPW tool that illustrates how to use the File Manager.

Recommended Reading

Inside Macintosh is—as always—the reference book of choice about the Mac OS. If you are interested in AppleTalk, try *Inside AppleTalk*. Apple's *Tech Notes* update these volumes.

For insights into how other operating systems work, there are several excellent UNIX-related texts. Bach's *The Design of the UNIX Operating System* gives some good insight into the UNIX kernel, and Comer's *Operating System Design, Volume 1: The Xinu Approach (Macintosh Edition)* actually implements a UNIX-like operating system for the Macintosh. Comer's text includes full source code in C. Another good book with C source code is Tanenbaum's *Operating Systems: Design and Implementation*.

## CHAPTER 3

QUICKDRAW

The most visible part of system software to end users is QuickDraw, the Macintosh graphics kernel. QuickDraw was designed to be fast and efficient. QuickDraw is device-dependent—that is, it is closely coupled to the Macintosh. However, QuickDraw is not part of the operating system. It is a separate layer built upon the operating system as a bridge to the Toolbox. The Toolbox will be examined in chapter 4.

QuickDraw can draw many different types of objects:

- Text—in varied fonts, sizes, and styles
- Lines—includes points, which are simply lines of length 1
- Rectangles—includes squares
- Round rectangles—a rectangle whose corners have been rounded
- Ovals—includes circles
- Arcs—part of an oval; filled arcs are called wedges
- Polygons—a collection of connected lines
- Regions—a collection of lines and framed rectangles, round rectangles, and ovals
- Pictures—a collection of any QuickDraw objects
- Patterns—8 pixel by 8 pixel bit maps
- Cursors—16 pixel by 16 pixel bit maps
- Icons—32 pixel by 32 pixel bit maps

Lines can vary in width and fill pattern. Shapes can be outlined and/or filled with patterns. QuickDraw also handles drawing into multiple locations on or off screen, and will clip to arbitrary regions.

Perhaps the most distinguishing attribute of QuickDraw is its ability to manipulate beautiful bit-mapped images quickly. This capability is due to QuickDraw's ability to draw arbitrary regions in an efficient manner. Regions are a collection of other simpler objects: lines and shapes (rectangles, ovals, round rectangles, wedges). The resulting image may be a very complex collection of points, but it is through such collections of points—such regions—that tools like MacPaint's lasso are made possible.

Virtually all drawing, whether to a screen or to an output device, goes through QuickDraw. This means that you do not have to worry much about which monitor your application's user has. There are many choices now: monochrome black and white,

4- and 8-bit gray scale, and 4-, 8-, and 32-bit color. You do not even have to worry if the user has more than one monitor—QuickDraw handles it all, even cutting and pasting graphics between a 32-bit color monitor and a monochrome black-and-white monitor, to give an example. There are exceptions to this rule, of course. To take full advantage of color, you should use the newer Color QuickDraw calls, and to take full advantage of the PostScript language, you need to write PostScript code.

In this chapter, we will look at QuickDraw in detail. First, we will look at classic QuickDraw, which is available on all Macintoshes ever made. Then we will look at Color QuickDraw, which was first implemented on the Macintosh II. We also give a summary of the Font Manager, which is intertwined with QuickDraw to build characters and draw text. Finally, we will look at printing and the Print Manager, which also uses QuickDraw extensively.

The code presented in this chapter includes Mandel, a Pascal application that will let you explore the Mandelbrot set; Graph, an MPW tool written in C that displays mathematical functions; and MacQ, a C application that simulates a book spinning on its axis in three dimensions.

QuickDraw was created by Bill Atkinson. It was originally written in Pascal for the Lisa, but eventually was reduced to about 24 KB of object code written in assembly language. QuickDraw was speeded up for the Macintosh Plus, and color was added by Ernie Beernink and Dave Fung for the Macintosh II. Both MacPaint and HyperCard were also written by Bill Atkinson and are excellent examples of what QuickDraw can do.

Graphics Ports

A GrafPort (or port for short) defines a drawing environment in which drawing can take place. A GrafPort contains quite a bit of information, and it is used so frequently that for the sake of speed it has been made a non-relocatable object. Before your program can do anything, it must initialize QuickDraw with a call to the InitGraf routine. This initializes QuickDraw's global variables. Space for these globals is handled by the linker and libraries when you are using MPW C or MPW Pascal. A convention of the Macintosh architecture is that register A5 always points to a pointer that points to the top QuickDraw variable, thePort. Global variables are referenced as negative offsets from register A5. Figure 3–1 shows what the QuickDraw portion of an A5 World looks like.

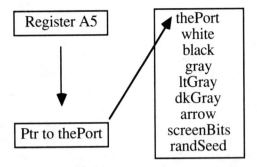

Figure 3–1: The QuickDraw Portion of an A5 World

After QuickDraw is initialized, a port can be opened and initialized by a call to `OpenPort`. A port already open can be reinitialized through a call to `InitPort`, closed through `ClosePort`, and associated with a device through `GrafDevice`. Creating a window through the Window Manager also creates a port. Although multiple ports can be open at the same time, only one port is active at a time. Most QuickDraw calls do not specify which port to use: they always use the current port. A QuickDraw global variable called `thePort` specifies the current port. Be sure to use the `SetPort` and `GetPort` routines to change ports. A common bug in QuickDraw programs is having the port set improperly. The symptoms of this bug include nothing being drawn or drawing being done in the wrong location. The solution is easy: use `SetPort` to specify the right port.

Clipping in a port is done to the `visRgn`, a field maintained by the Window Manager, and to the `clipRgn`, an arbitrary region at the disposal of the programmer. This `clipRgn` can be saved and restored with the use of `GetClip` and `SetClip`, respectively. You can also set the `clipRgn` to a rectangle using the `ClipRect` call. Each of these clipping operations changes the current port's clipping region, leaving the passed `RgnHandle` untouched.

Bit Maps

A *bit image* is a collection of bits in memory that all occur within a rectangle. Such images are always aligned to word boundaries and are stored in row major order. In other words, the first bit of a bit image is in the upper left corner, and the row bytes must be even. These bits or pixels fall between the points of the coordinate plane, so a rectangle of *m* x *n* pixels contains $(m-1)*(n-1)$ pixel elements. Zero bits are seen as white; one bits are black. When you add these additional pieces of information—row width in bytes and a boundary rectangle—to a pointer to the bit image, you have the QuickDraw data structure known as a *bit map*. The bit map data structure does not actually contain the image, just a pointer to the image—or, as they say in general semantics terminology, "the map is not the territory."

The Macintosh screen is itself a bit image. On a classic Mac, the bit image is 512 x 342 pixels in size, with a row width of 64 bytes. Such an image has 175,104 pixels that occupy 21,888 bytes in memory. A common software compatibility problem occurs when these values are hardcoded into a piece of software. The screen dimensions on any Macintosh are described by the QuickDraw global variable `screenBits`, which is a QuickDraw bit map. Using `screenBits` rather than hardcoding screen size will assure compatibility with future Macintoshes and screens of various sizes.

Each port has an associated bit map. To associate a bit map with a port, call `SetPortBits`. You might also want to use a common technique for drawing without flicker, which uses a second port and bit map located offscreen. Drawing takes place in the offscreen buffer, and `CopyBits` is called to transfer the image to the screen.

Bit maps are manipulated by the versatile `CopyBits` routine. Bit maps can also be compressed and uncompressed with `PackBits` and `UnpackBits`. The 128 KB ROM also added a `CopyMask` routine, two routines that work on the bit image itself, `SeedFill` and `CalcMask,` and a routine called `GetMaskTable` that returns a pointer to a special mask table in ROM. All of these routines help with things like lassoing an image in a painting program.

Coordinate Systems

The coordinate plane used by QuickDraw is a two-dimensional grid whose coordinates are in the range -32,768 to 32,767 and whose gridlines are infinitely thin. At the standard Macintosh screen resolution of 72 pixels per inch, the grid is more than 75 feet wide and tall. Coordinates increase the same way a page of English text is read, with the origin in the middle of the grid. The horizontal axis behaves like the standard Cartesian plane, with negative numbers left of the origin and positive numbers to the right. The vertical axis, however, is opposite the Cartesian plane: coordinates increase as you go down in QuickDraw. Points occur at the intersections of gridlines, and pixels occur between gridlines. A single pixel drawn at a point is therefore down and to the right of the point.

Two different coordinate systems are used by QuickDraw—local and global—and two different rectangles keep track of the coordinates. The `portRect` rectangle of a port specifies which part of the bit image will actually be drawn into, and the `portBits.bounds` rectangle always encloses the entire bit image specified by the port's bit map.

When a port is first created and initialized, its bit map refers to the whole screen, and both the `portBits.bounds` and `portRect` fields of the port enclose the entire screen. The default origin (0,0) is at the upper left corner of the screen. Local and global coordinates are identical when a port is first created and initialized.

All drawing and calculations in a port are done in local coordinates. If you want to use a different local coordinate system, call `SetOrigin` to change the coordinates of the `portRect` rectangle. The rectangle stays at the same relative location to the bit image and is the same size as before the call: only the numbers are changed. `SetOrigin` sets the coordinates of the top left corner of the `portRect`. The `portBits.bounds` and `visRgn` fields are adjusted accordingly. `PortSize` and `MovePortTo` are two other calls that change the coordinates, but they are normally used only by the Window Manager.

Global coordinates for a port are always fixed with the origin (0,0) at the top left corner of the port's bit image. To compare items in different ports, convert local coordinates to global coordinates via a call to `LocalToGlobal`, and convert them back with `GlobalToLocal`. `ScalePt`, `MapPt`, `MapRect`, `MapRgn`, and `MapPoly` help these entities to be manipulated across different ports and coordinate systems.

Graphics Operations

Each port has a graphics pen that is used for all drawing of objects, such as lines, rectangles, and regions, in that port. The pen always has a location that is a point on the QuickDraw plane, which can be set explicitly to an *x,y* coordinate by the `MoveTo` call, relatively by the `Move` call, or implicitly by most other drawing calls. Lines are drawn by the similar calls `LineTo` and `Line`. A pen's size is set by `PenSize`, its pattern is set by `PenPat`, and its set of default attributes is set by `PenNormal`. Pens can be hidden and shown with `HidePen` and `ShowPen`, and a set of attributes can be saved and restored with `GetPenState` and `SetPenState`. The current location of the pen can be determined with `GetPen`, and the state of an individual pixel on be tested with `GetPixel`.

QuickDraw also draws text. The Font Manager prepares the actual characters to be drawn. Each `GrafPort` contains fields that specify font, size, style, drawing mode, and amount of space to draw between characters for drawing text. You can set these fields with `TextFont` (by font family numbers), `TextFace` (bold, italic, underline, outline, shadow, condense, and extend), `TextSize` (in points), `TextMode` (various transfer modes), and `SpaceExtra`. Drawing is done with the `DrawChar`, `DrawString`, and `DrawText` routines, and information about the characters is returned by `CharWidth`, `StringWidth`, `TextWidth`, and `GetFontInfo`. `MeasureText` was added in the 128 KB ROM as a faster array version of `TextWidth`, but it works only with text displayed on the screen.

Your programs can draw many different shapes, including rectangles, rounded rectangles, ovals, arcs, polygons, and regions. Each of these shapes can be framed (empty interior), filled (with a specific pattern), painted (with the port's pattern), erased, and inverted. For rectangles, use these calls: `FrameRect`, `PaintRect`, `EraseRect`, `InvertRect`, and `FillRect`. The calls for other shapes are similar: for rounded rectangles, use `FrameRoundRect`, etc.; for ovals, use `FrameOval`, etc.; for arcs, use `FrameArc`, etc.; for polygons, use `FramePoly`, etc.; and for regions, use `FrameRgn`, etc.

QuickDraw defines three cumulative data types: polygons, regions, and pictures. Connected lines may be grouped together to form a polygon; lines and shapes with at least one closed loop may be grouped to form a region; and any arbitrary drawing operations may be grouped to form a QuickDraw picture. Opening one of these cumulative types is like turning on a tape recorder: all appropriate operations done until the object is closed are recorded as the definition of the object. OpenPoly, OpenRgn, and OpenPicture are balanced by ClosePoly, CloseRgn, and ClosePicture. Once grouped together, a polygon or region can be drawn in various flavors (for example, using PaintRgn, InvertPoly), and a picture can be drawn into an arbitrary rectangle with DrawPicture, thus allowing shrinking, distorting, and growing of the image. Only one of each cumulative type can be open per port at a given time. Memory for polygons and pictures is allocated automatically when they are opened, but memory for regions must be allocated manually by calling NewRgn. Memory is disposed of by KillPoly, DisposeRgn, and KillPicture. Pictures are often stored as PICT resources and can be retrieved by the GetPicture routine. PICTs are the means of transferring graphics between applications.

QuickDraw provides many calculation routines that help when you are using these graphical objects. You can set points using SetPt, combine them using AddPt and SubPt, test them with EqualPt, and transform them between coordinate systems with LocalToGlobal and GlobalToLocal. To determine angles, use PtToAngle, DeltaPoint, SlopeFromAngle, and AngleFromSlope. Rectangles can be set with SetRect; transformed with OffsetRect and InsetRect; tested with SectRect, PtInRect, EqualRect, and EmptyRect; and combined with UnionRect and Pt2Rect. You can translate polygons with OffsetPoly. To perform analogous operations on regions, use CopyRgn, SetEmptyRgn, SetRectRgn, RectRgn, OffsetRgn, InsetRgn, SectRgn, UnionRgn, DiffRgn, XorRgn, PtInRgn, RectInRgn, EqualRgn, and EmptyRgn.

You can also customize QuickDraw by overriding various bottleneck procedures. To do so, call SetStdProcs and set the procedures as desired. Individual routines may be changed by calling StdText, StdLine, StdRect, StdRRect, StdOval, StdArc, StdPoly, StdRgn, StdBits, StdComment, StdTxMeas, StdGetPic, and StdPutPic.

An example of why you may need to do such customizing can be found in the way HyperCard functions. HyperCard uses TextEdit to draw into an offscreen buffer. A problem arises because HyperCard does not want this offscreen buffer erased as it builds up its card and background layers. Normally TextEdit calls EraseRect before drawing text in response to TEUpdate; this action would clear the offscreen buffer. So it can draw its various layers properly, HyperCard takes over several of the QuickDraw bottleneck procedures to ensure that EraseRect is not called during TEUpdate.

QuickDraw pictures can be customized using PicComment. One use of this facility is to put printer-specific code into print code. For example, say that you wanted to send PostScript code directly to the LaserWriter. The following Pascal code would follow the standard opening of a page through PrOpenPage. This fragment would draw a single sentence of text, rotated 45 degrees. If an ImageWriter was being used, the following code would be ignored, with nothing being drawn. Each line of PostScript is sent through DrawString calls.

```
MoveTo(-32767,-32767);  { find some location not likely to be on the page }
Line(0,0);              { draw minimally to allow Print Mgr to define clipRgn }
PicComment(190,0,nil);  { turn on PostScript interpretation }
PicComment(194,0,nil);  { specify that DrawString calls contain PostScript }
DrawString('/Helvetica findfont 24 scalefont setfont'); { actual PostScript }
DrawString('200 200 moveto 45 rotate (Rotated text) show'); { more PostScript }
PicComment(191,0,nil);  { turn off PostScript interpretation of drawn text }
```

Patterns

Patterns are used to draw or fill objects. They are bit images 8 bits by 8 bits square that occupy 8 bytes of memory. The most common patterns exist as QuickDraw global variables: white, black, gray (50-percent gray), ltGray (25-percent gray), and dkGray (75-percent gray). Patterns can also be set by using StuffHex.

When a pattern is used as the "ink" for a graphics pen, the pen can paint using different transfer modes. Each port's graphics pen has a parameter called pnMode that specifies one of eight different degrees of transparency or opacity: Copy, Or, Xor, Bic (bit clear), and their inverses using either the source or a pattern as the ink. Each port also has two other patterns associated with it: a background pattern (usually white) set by BackPat and a fill pattern (the default is black).

Patterns are stored as resources in two different ways. A single 8-byte pattern, as described above, is a resource of type PAT, and it can be retrieved with GetPattern. In addition, a composite pattern resource type called PAT# contains multiple patterns. The system file includes a pattern list (PAT# 0) that contains the 38 standard MacPaint patterns.

Cursors

Another special QuickDraw data structure is the cursor, which is an image 16 bits by 16 bits. Actually a cursor has two such images: a mask and a data image. The mask allows the cursor to be black (data and mask are both one), white (mask is one, data is zero), transparent (mask and data both zero), or inverted (data is one, mask is zero). In addition, a point specifies where the cursor aligns with the mouse; this location is called the *hot spot*. The total size of a cursor is thus 68 bytes.

QuickDraw defines one common cursor as another global variable called `arrow`, whose shape is self-explanatory. Other commonly used cursors that are found in the System file are listed in the following table.

Cursor	Resource ID in System File
ibeamCursor	1
crossCursor	2
plusCursor	3
watchCursor	4

`InitCursor` starts with a clean slate and displays the arrow cursor. You can use the `GetCursor` function to retrieve a cursor and `SetCursor` to specify which resident cursor to use. The cursor can be shown and hidden with the `HideCursor`, `ShowCursor`, `ObscureCursor`, and `ShieldCursor` calls.

The rotating cursors that are used to show a spinning beachball in the MPW Shell or HyperCard, as well as the watch with rotating hands used in later versions of the Finder, are made possible by the MPW tool library of routines. These routines simply make repeated calls to `SetCursor` so often that the cursors appear animated. To use these routines, you will need the appropriate CursorCtl interface file, and should link with the `ToolLibs.o` library. The many related cursors are stored together as an `acur` resource.

Icons

Icons are the next larger QuickDraw data structure: 32 bits by 32 bits square. Icons are stored as resources in two different ways: an `ICON` resource is a single 128-byte icon, whereas an `ICN#` resource contains several 128-byte icons. Unlike a pattern list, an icon list does not begin with a count of the number of icons. To retrieve icons of the `ICON` variety, call the routine `GetIcon`, and to draw any icon in memory, use the `PlotIcon` routine.

The icons used in the Desktop file are stored in each application's resource file as icons of type `ICN#`, with two icons per `ICN#`. The first icon is used as the data image, and the second icon is a mask, in a manner similar to that used for cursors.

In order for an application to have its own icon show up on the Desktop, several conditions must be true of the application's resource fork:

- It must contain a `BNDL` resource: ID 128
- It must contain one or more `FREF` resources: ID 128, 129, 130 . . .
- It must contain one or more `ICN#` resources: ID 128, 129, 130 . . .
- A unique creator signature type, ID 0, must exist
- The bundle bit must be set

These resources are most easily created using ResEdit. The bundle bit can be set with ResEdit, Fedit, or in an MPW Shell script using the `SetFile` command. The first of the `FREF`/`ICN#` pairs refers to the applications icon (an `FREF` of `APPL`), and subsequent pairs give icons to documents owned by the application. (A text document `FREF` would be `TEXT`, for example.) Problems with icons being lost or transferred to other programs usually occur when the creator signature is not unique on a given volume.

Color QuickDraw

With the Macintosh II came a major revision of QuickDraw called Color QuickDraw. Color QuickDraw supports a variety of color schemes. The simplest color scheme used by Color QuickDraw has been in ROM on all Macs, and hence works on all Macs. GrafPorts have always had fields for a foreground color and a background color, which could be set by calls to `ForeColor`, `BackColor`, and `ColorBit`. These calls provide a limited set of colors useful for printing, but with the advent of Color QuickDraw on a Mac II they also reproduce 8 colors if a color monitor is present. These colors are actually modeled on a planar style of color, where each color plane or layer is drawn separately.

Color QuickDraw also supports chunky style graphics, where each pixel's color information is maintained contiguously in memory. For example, 8-bit color means that each pixel occupies a byte in memory. That byte can represent 256 different colors. A new data type called an `RGBColor` is used to specify colors, with each of the red, green, and blue components being represented by an unsigned integer. Thus 3 x 8 bits— 24 bits—of color information are represented in an `RGBColor`, which allows up to 16 million different colors to be specified.

Use of this new style of graphics requires a new type of port called a `CGrafPort`. `CGrafPort`s are created in the same way as old `GrafPort`s, but with the `OpenCPort`, `InitCPort`, and `CloseCPort` calls. Within these new ports are handles to blocks of information about color; thus, a colorized `BitMap` becomes a `PixMap` and a colorized `Pattern` becomes a `PixPat` (stored in the System file as a `ppat`). These new-style ports are the same size as the old ones, but they reinterpret the fields to allow more information. Specifically, the `BitMap` area is replaced by a `PixMapHandle` and a `portVersion` field, and several patterns were replaced with `PixPatHandles`, allowing `RGBColor` fields to be added. The new routines required to manipulate pixel maps and pixel patterns include `SetPortPix`, `NewPixMap`, `CopyPixMap`, `DisposPixMap`, `SeedCFill`, `CalcCMask`, `NewPixPat`, `DisposPixPat`, `GetPixPat`, `CopyPixPat`, `MakeRGBPat`, `PenPixPat`, and `BackPixPat`. Many existing routines, such as `CopyBits`, were simply extended to offer new functionality with the existing interface.

Most things therefore work the same in Color QuickDraw as in QuickDraw. The standard drawing routines stay intact, automatically drawing in the colors set by two new calls: `RGBForeColor` and `RGBBackColor`. These colors can also be determined by GetForeColor and GetBackColor. In fact, the only new color drawing operations added are FillCRect, FillCOval, FillCRoundRect, FillCArc, FillCRgn, and FillCPoly.

Individual pixels can be manipulated with GetCPixel and SetCPixel. There are also color cursors (in the System as type crsr) and icons (in the System as type cicn). AllocCursor, GetCCursor, SetCCursor, DisposCCursor, GetCIcon, DisposCIcon, and PlotCIcon work as expected. You can customize Color QuickDraw using SetStdCProcs; HiliteColor allows you to set the color of highlighted text; OpColor sets the RGB color for a few new transfer modes, and CharExtra supersedes SpaceExtra in a CGrafPort.

A new data structure introduced with Color QuickDraw, called a GDevice, allows multiple monitors to be connected to a Macintosh II family machine. A GDevice record maintains information about the size and depth of a screen. GDevices are manipulated by NewGDevice, InitGDevice, GetGDevice, SetGDevice, GetMainDevice, GetNextDevice, GetMaxDevice, GetDeviceList, SetDeviceAttributes, TextDeviceAttribute, and DisposGDevice. Start-up information about screen configurations is stored in the System as a scrn resource.

The Color Manager has the job of finding the best match from available colors for any given RGBColor request. It does this by setting up a *color table* through several new routines, including GetSubTable, GetCTSeed, ProtectEntry, ReserveEntry, SetEntries, RestoreEntries, and SaveEntries. Inverse tables are created by the Color Manager via MakeITable for finding approximate color matches. You can create customized searching and complementing routines using AddSearch, AddComp, DelSearch, DelComp, and SetClientID. In addition, you can convert colors using Color2Index, Index2Color, and InvertColor, and you can test them using RealColor. Errors are reported through QDError. Color tables are stored on disk as clut resources.

One final layer of color management has been added because of MultiFinder's requirements. Because there can be several applications competing for a limited number of colors, the Palette Manager was created to mediate between desirous applications. Programs use the Palette Manager much as they do the Color Manager. Initialization is done by InitPalettes and allocation with NewPalette, or a palette can be retrieved from a pltt resource by GetNewPalette. Color tables can be converted to palettes and vice versa with CTab2Palette and Palette2CTab, and individual entries can be changed with GetEntryColor, SetEntryColor, GetEntryUsage, and SetEntryUsage. Color tables can be animated by AnimateEntry and AnimatePalette. To associate a palette with a window, use the ActivatePalette, SetPalette, and GetPalette routines, and to specify specific palette colors, use PmForeColor and PmBackColor. When a palette is no longer needed, discard it using DisposePalette.

The Font Manager

The Font Manager, written by Andy Hertzfeld and Donn Denman, supports QuickDraw's needs for drawing text. Fonts can belong to a font family, which is identified by a name and a number. Each individual size in which a font is available is stored as a FONT resource, usually in the System. A font family is bundled together by a FOND resource. Apple's fonts are shown in the following table, with PostScript fonts marked with an asterisk. PostScript fonts are those fonts which are stored as bit maps in the System file and as outlines in the LaserWriter ROMs.

Font Name	Font Number	Style
Chicago	0 (system font)	Sans-serif
Application font	1 (usually Geneva)	-
New York	2	Serif
Geneva	3	Sans-serif
Monaco	4	Monospaced
Venice	5	Script
London	6	Old English script
Athens	7	Bold serif
San Francisco	8	Bizarre
Toronto	9	Sans-serif
Cairo	11	Hieroglyphics
Los Angeles	12	Script
Zapf Dingbats*	13	Symbols
Bookman*	14	Serif
Palatino*	16	Serif
Zapf Chancery*	18	Script
Times*	20	Serif
Helvetica*	21	Sans-serif
Courier*	22	Typewriter
Symbol*	23	Math symbols
Mobile*	24	Hieroglyphics
Avant Garde*	33	Sans-serif
New Century Schlbk*	34	Serif

The actual number of the font used as the application font is stored both in parameter RAM and in the low-memory global ApFontID at $984.

Most applications do not manipulate fonts directly, letting QuickDraw do it instead. However, you may still find many of the Font Manager calls useful. The Font Manager ensures that the system font is loaded when InitFonts is called. RealFont checks to see if a font of a specific size actually exists or whether scaling is needed. SetFontLock temporarily makes the most recently used font unpurgeable, and FMSwapFont returns a pointer to a font output record. The 128 KB ROM allows you to obtain more information via FontMetrics; it also allows you to use fractional scaling or to disable scaling with `SetFScaleDisable`. The 256 KB ROM adds `SetFractEnable` as a trap.

The Font/DA Mover can change font numbers in exceptional circumstances if two fonts have the same ID. To prevent problems, your applications should save font names rather than numbers. Font names and numbers can be converted back and forth with `GetFontName` and `GetFNum`.

The Print Manager

The Macintosh operating system supports printing in a device-independent manner. This capability was, until recently, unique to the Macintosh operating system. Almost all printing goes through QuickDraw, so the burden of supporting a new printer is assumed by the printer manufacturer, not (as is typical of other operating systems) by the application programmer.

The Print Manager works with the Chooser desk accessory to figure out which printer the user wants to use. When the printer is known, the Print Manager loads the correct device's printer driver, which installs its own set of QuickDraw bottleneck procedures. Your application may then draw the document page by page. In most applications, the same code is used both to display documents on the screen and to print them. This greatly improves the chances of an application's being WYSIWYG (what you see is what you get).

Although nearly all printing is done through QuickDraw, a few exceptions to this rule do exist. Most commonly, an application will write PostScript code directly, instead of letting the printer driver do the translation. This is done to take advantage of PostScript features not available in QuickDraw, such as text rotated to an arbitrary angle. As was pointed out above, you can write such PostScript enhancements in a compatible manner through the use of the `PicComment` calls supported in later versions of the LaserWriter driver.

Originally, print code was a large amount of glue code that needed to be linked into an application. This print code has since been moved into the 256 KB ROMs and back-patched in System 4.1 and later to the Macintosh Plus. Now all print routines go through a single trap called `PrGlue`.

To use the Print Manager, your application should begin by calling `PrOpen` to open printing. Next, a valid print record needs to be obtained. This can be accomplished in several ways. A print record may be stored with a document on disk, in which case your application simply needs to validate the print record with `PrValidate`. An all-new print record can be filled in with `PrintDefault`, and the Page Setup and Print dialogs can be accessed with `PrStlDialog` and `PrJobDialog`. `PrJobMerge` is useful for printing several jobs at once, such as printing from the Finder.

Once your application has validated this print record, it can begin the actual printing. Use `PrOpenDoc` to initialize a printing `GrafPort` and make it the current port. (This port is a superset of a QuickDraw `GrafPort`.) To print individual pages, use a call to `PrOpenPage` followed by QuickDraw calls for drawing the page in the current port, and terminated with a call to `PrClosePage`. When all pages have been printed, call `PrCloseDoc` to close the printing `GrafPort`. The resultant document will have been printed immediately (draft printing) or else will have been spooled to disk. In the latter case, your application will need to call `PrPicFile` to actually print the spooled document.

`Mandel` — Pascal Application

This demo program, which illustrates the use of QuickDraw, generates the Mandelbrot set, a mathematical set of points based on a type of recursive formula called a *fractal*. (Fractals were discovered by Benoit Mandelbrot.) A floating-point coprocessor greatly improves the execution time of this interactive application, and a color monitor provides some gorgeous hues. The About Box gives some hints to using the program.

One of the main advantages of this version of `Mandel`, which uses an algorithm devised by Paul Finlayson, is that it quickly draws a rough approximation to the Mandelbrot set, and then makes subsequent passes to further refine the image. This allows the viewer to see the set come into existence a lot sooner. Clicking on areas of the displayed set will zoom in on the selected area to allow further exploration.

Improving `Mandel`

Here are some suggestions for improving `Mandel`:

- Add better support for color. Possible enhancements include animation, selectable color ranges, and customizable color palettes.
- `Mandel` does not handle update events well. Add an off-screen bit-mapped image that contains all of the pixels as they are drawn. Update events could then be handled simply by doing a `CopyBits` call to copy the bits from offscreen to the main window.

Here is the Makefile:

```
POptions    = -mbg ch8 -mc68020 -mc68881 -r
PLibs =     "{PLibraries}PasLib.o" ∂
            "{PLibraries}SaneLib881.o" ∂
            "{Libraries}Interface.o" ∂
            "{Libraries}Runtime.o"
Mandel  ƒƒ  Mandel.r
    Rez -a -o Mandel Mandel.r -c maxb
Mandel  ƒƒ  Mandel.p.o {PLibs}
    Link -o Mandel -sg Main Mandel.p.o {PLibs}
Mandel  ƒƒ  {Worksheet}
    Setfile -a B -t APPL -c maxb -d . -m . Mandel
    Mandel
```

and here is the MPW Pascal code:

```
PROGRAM Mandel;

USES
  Memtypes,Quickdraw,OSIntf,ToolIntf,SANE;

TYPE
  WordPtr = ^Integer;

CONST
  CPU     = $12E;
  ROM85   = $28E;

  appleID = 128;
  fileID  = 129;
  editID  = 130;
  xID     = 131;
  yID     = 132;
  resID   = 133;

VAR
  colorQD:      Boolean;
  quitFlag:     Boolean;
  linearFlag:   Boolean;

  custPict:     Integer;
  numColors:    Integer;
  limit:        Integer;

  res:          Extended;
  centx, centy: Extended;
  xmin,xmax:    Extended;
  ymin,ymax:    Extended;
  delx,dely:    Extended;
```

```
str:            Str255;
f:              DecForm;

aColor:         RGBColor;
myRect:         Rect;
dragRect:       Rect;

myWindow:       WindowPtr;
aboutWindow:    WindowPtr;
appleMenu:      MenuHandle;
fileMenu:       MenuHandle;
editMenu:       MenuHandle;
xMenu:          MenuHandle;
yMenu:          MenuHandle;
resMenu:        MenuHandle;

PROCEDURE AboutDialog; FORWARD;
FUNCTION  CalcMandel(creal,cimag: Extended) : Integer; FORWARD;
FUNCTION  DoMenu(mResult: Longint) : Boolean; FORWARD;
PROCEDURE DrawMandel; FORWARD;
FUNCTION  EventCheck : Boolean; FORWARD;
PROCEDURE InitWorld; FORWARD;
PROCEDURE UpdateMenus; FORWARD;


PROCEDURE AboutDialog;
VAR
  oldPort: GrafPtr;
  tempRect: Rect;
BEGIN
  GetPort(oldPort);
  SetRect(tempRect,30,60,482,292);
  aboutWindow := NewWindow(nil, tempRect,'',TRUE, dBoxProc,
                           WindowPtr(-1),TRUE,0);
  SetPort(aboutWindow);

  ForeColor(redColor);
  TextFont(times); TextSize(36);
  MoveTo(8,30);
  DrawString('Mandel by Dan Allen');

  TextFont(courier); ForeColor(blueColor); TextSize(10);
  MoveTo(8,50);
  DrawString('Version     - 1.0 B1, built January 6, 1989 with MPW Pascal.');
  MoveTo(8,65);
  DrawString('Fractals    - Discovered by Benoit Mandelbrot.');
  MoveTo(8,80);
  DrawString('Software    - Classic black & white or Color QuickDraw.');
  MoveTo(8,95);
  DrawString('Hardware    - Use a MC68881/2 for a serious speedup.');
```

```
   MoveTo(8,115);
   DrawString('Click        - Zooms in by a factor of two.');
   MoveTo(8,127);
   DrawString('Option Click - Zooms out by a factor of two.');
   MoveTo(8,139);
   DrawString('Cmd Click    - Cycles through 6 classic locations.');
   MoveTo(8,151);
   DrawString('Shift Click  - Moves center but not magnification.');
   MoveTo(8,163);
   DrawString('Cmd Opt Click - Resets to standard Mandel view.');
   MoveTo(8,175);
   DrawString('MenuBar      - Shows coordinates of current screen center.');
   MoveTo(8,187);
   DrawString('Limits       - Number of loops to determine a pixel's color.');
   MoveTo(8,199);
   DrawString('Mod Colors   - Repeats colors Modulo the colors available.');
   MoveTo(8,211);
   DrawString('Linear Colors - Progression through the available colors.');

   REPEAT SystemTask UNTIL Button; { display until the user clicks mouse btn }
   DisposeWindow(aboutWindow);
   SetPort(oldPort);
   FlushEvents(mUpMask+mDownMask+activMask,0);
END;

FUNCTION CalcMandel(creal,cimag: Extended): Integer;
{ compute the actual value of the Mandelbrot set given a point }
VAR
   count:         Integer;
   zr2,zi2:       Extended;
   zreal,zimag:   Extended;
   zreal2,zreal1: Extended;
BEGIN
   zreal := creal; zimag := cimag; count := 0;
   zreal1 := 100; zreal2 := 200;
   REPEAT
     count := count + 1;
     zr2 := zreal*zreal; zi2 := zimag*zimag;
     zimag := 2*zreal*zimag + cimag;
     zreal := zr2 - zi2 + creal;
     IF zreal = zreal2 THEN count := 0;
     zreal2 := zreal1; zreal1 := zreal;
   UNTIL (count = 0) | (count = limit) | ((zr2 + zi2) > 4.0);
   CalcMandel := count;
END;
```

```
FUNCTION DoMenu(mResult: Longint) : Boolean;
LABEL 9;
VAR
  theItem:  Integer;
  theMenu:  Integer;
  temp:     Integer;
BEGIN
  DoMenu := TRUE;
  theMenu := HiWord(mResult); theItem := LoWord(mResult);
  CASE theMenu of
    appleID:
      IF (theItem = 1) THEN
        AboutDialog
      ELSE BEGIN
        GetItem(appleMenu, theItem, str);
        temp := OpenDeskAcc(str);
        SetPort(myWindow);
      END; {of appleID}
    fileID:
      CASE theItem of
        1:  BEGIN
              limit := 64;
              CheckItem(fileMenu, 1, TRUE);
              CheckItem(fileMenu, 2, FALSE);
              CheckItem(fileMenu, 3, FALSE);
            END;
        2:  BEGIN
              limit := 256;
              CheckItem(fileMenu, 2, TRUE);
              CheckItem(fileMenu, 1, FALSE);
              CheckItem(fileMenu, 3, FALSE);
            END;
        3:  BEGIN
              limit := 1024;
              CheckItem(fileMenu, 3, TRUE);
              CheckItem(fileMenu, 1, FALSE);
              CheckItem(fileMenu, 2, FALSE);
            END;
        5:  BEGIN
              linearFlag := FALSE;
              CheckItem(fileMenu, 5, TRUE);
              CheckItem(fileMenu, 6, FALSE);
            END;
        6:  BEGIN
              linearFlag := TRUE;
              CheckItem(fileMenu, 5, FALSE);
              CheckItem(fileMenu, 6, TRUE);
            END;
```

```
        8:   quitFlag := TRUE;
      END; { item CASE }
    editID:
      temp := Integer(SystemEdit(theItem - 1));
    OTHERWISE
      DoMenu := FALSE;
  END; {of menu CASE}
9:
  HiliteMenu(0);
END; {of DoMenu}

PROCEDURE DrawMandel;
LABEL 9;
VAR
  i,n,nx,ny:  Integer;
  xres,yres:  Integer;
  x,y,del:    Extended;
  aRect:      Rect;
BEGIN
  xres := myRect.right; yres := myRect.bottom;
  xmin := centx - res; xmax := centx + res;
  ymin := centy - res; ymax := centy + res;

  delx := (xmax-xmin)/(xres+1); dely := (ymax-ymin)/(yres+1);
  IF delx > dely THEN dely := delx ELSE delx := dely;
  i := xres;

  WHILE i > 0 DO
    BEGIN
      i := bsr(i,1);
      del := delx*i;
      y := ymax; ny := 0;

      WHILE ny < (yres-i) DO
        BEGIN
          x := xmin; nx := 0;
```

```
        WHILE nx < (xres-i) DO
          BEGIN
            n := CalcMandel(x,y);
            SetRect(aRect,nx,ny,nx+i,ny+i);
            IF colorQD & (numColors > 2) THEN { Color QuickDraw }
              BEGIN
                IF linearFlag THEN
                  BEGIN
                    IF (n = 0) | (n >= limit)
                    THEN n := numColors-1
                    ELSE n := n * numColors DIV limit;
                  END
                ELSE
                  BEGIN
                    IF (n = 0) | (n >= limit)
                    THEN·n := numColors-1
                    ELSE n := n MOD numColors;
                  END;
                Index2Color(n,aColor); RGBForeColor(aColor);
                FillRect(aRect,black);
              END
            ELSE { or patterns for those with black and white }
              BEGIN
                IF (n = 0) | (n >= 256) THEN
                  FillRect(aRect,black)
                ELSE IF n > 50 THEN
                  FillRect(aRect,dkgray)
                ELSE IF n > 10 THEN
                  FillRect(aRect,gray)
                ELSE IF n > 2 THEN
                  FillRect(aRect,ltgray)
                ELSE
                  FillRect(aRect,white);
              END;
            IF EventCheck THEN GOTO 9;
            IF quitFlag THEN GOTO 9;
            nx := nx + i; x := x + del;
          END; (* nx loop *)
        ny := ny + i; y := y - del;
      END; (* ny loop *)
    END; (* WHILE loop *)
  WHILE NOT quitFlag AND EventCheck DO
    ;
9:
END; { proc DrawMandel }
```

```
FUNCTION EventCheck : Boolean; { Mandel's main event loop }
LABEL 9;
VAR
  zIn, zOut:        Boolean; { zoom in, zoom out }
  theChar:          Char;
  myPart:           Integer;
  windSize:         LongInt;
  myEvent:          EventRecord;
  whichWindow:      WindowPtr;
BEGIN
  EventCheck := TRUE;
  IF GetNextEvent(everyEvent,myEvent) THEN
    CASE myEvent.what OF

      keyDown, autoKey:
        IF myWindow = FrontWindow THEN
          BEGIN
            theChar := CHR(Band(myEvent.message, charCodeMask));
            IF Band(myEvent.modifiers, cmdKey) <> 0 THEN
              IF DoMenu(MenuKey(theChar)) THEN GOTO 9;
          END; {of keyDown and autoKey}

      mouseDown:
        BEGIN
          myPart := FindWindow(myEvent.where, whichWindow);
          CASE myPart OF
            inMenuBar:
              IF DoMenu(MenuSelect(myEvent.where)) THEN GOTO 9;
            inSysWindow:
              BEGIN
                SystemClick(myEvent, whichWindow);
                IF colorQD THEN numColors := bsl(1,
                  CGrafPtr(myWindow)^.portPixMap^^.pixelSize);
                GOTO 9;
              END;
            inContent:
              BEGIN
                IF whichWindow <> FrontWindow THEN
                  SelectWindow(whichWindow)
                ELSE IF whichWindow = myWindow THEN
                  BEGIN
                    zIn := Band(myEvent.modifiers, cmdKey) <> 0;
                    zOut := Band(myEvent.modifiers, optionKey) <> 0;
                    IF zOut AND NOT zIn THEN
                      BEGIN   { optionKey = zoom out }
                        res := res*2;
                        GOTO 9;
                      END;
```

```
        IF zIn AND NOT zOut THEN
          BEGIN   { cmdKey = set to nifty zoomed area }
            CASE custPict OF
              1: BEGIN
                   centx := -0.55; centy := 0.6; res := 0.1;
                 END;
              2: BEGIN
                   centx := -0.92; centy := 0.26; res := 0.03;
                 END;
              3: BEGIN
                   centx := -1.253; centy := 0.046;
                   res := 0.001;
                 END;
              4: BEGIN
                   centx := -1.25316; centy := 0.0465;
                   res := 0.0005;
                 END;
              5: BEGIN
                   centx := -0.747; centy := 0.106;
                   res := 0.001;
                 END;
              6: BEGIN
                   centx := -0.74543; centy := 0.11301;
                   res := 0.00001;
                 END;
            END;
            custPict := custPict MOD 6 + 1; GOTO 9;
          END;
        IF zIn and zOut THEN
          BEGIN     { option cmd = reset to std view }
            centx := -0.8; centy := 0.0; res := 1.0;
            GOTO 9;
          END;
        IF Band(myEvent.modifiers, shiftKey) = 0
        THEN res := res*0.5;

        GlobalToLocal(myEvent.where);    { click = zoom in }
        centx := xmin + delx * myEvent.where.h;
        centy := ymax - delx * myEvent.where.v;
        GOTO 9;
      END;
    END; {of inContent}
inDrag:
  DragWindow(whichWindow, myEvent.where, dragRect);
```

```
        inGrow:
          BEGIN
            windSize := GrowWindow(whichWindow, myEvent.where,
                                   dragRect);
            SizeWindow(whichWindow, LoWord(windSize), HiWord(windSize),
                     TRUE);
            myRect := myWindow^.portRect;
            ClipRect(myRect);
            FillRect(myRect,white);
            GOTO 9;
          END;
        inGoAway:
          IF TrackGoAway(whichWindow,myEvent.where) THEN Halt;
        inZoomIn..inZoomOut:
          IF TrackBox(whichWindow, myEvent.where, myPart) THEN
            BEGIN
              ZoomWindow(whichWindow, myPart, FALSE);
              myRect := myWindow^.portRect;
              ClipRect(myRect);
              FillRect(myRect,white);
              GOTO 9;
            END;
        OTHERWISE
            ;
        END;
      END; {of mouseDown}

    activateEvt,app4Evt:
      BEGIN
        IF colorQD THEN numColors := bsl(1,
          CGrafPtr(myWindow)^.portPixMap^^.pixelSize);
        GOTO 9;
      END;
  END; { of event CASE }
  EventCheck := FALSE;
9:
END; { EventCheck }

PROCEDURE InitWorld;
BEGIN
  MaxApplZone;
  InitGraf(@thePort);
  InitFonts;
  InitWindows;
  InitMenus;
  TEInit;
  InitDialogs(nil);
```

```
      str[0] := CHR(1); str[1] := CHR(20);
      appleMenu := NewMenu(appleID, str);
      AppendMenu(appleMenu,'About Mandel…;(-');
      AddResMenu(appleMenu, 'DRVR');
      InsertMenu(appleMenu, 0);
      fileMenu := NewMenu(fileID,'Mandel');
      AppendMenu(fileMenu,'Limit = 64/1;Limit = 256/2;Limit = 1024/3;(-;');
      AppendMenu(fileMenu,'Mod Colors/M;Linear Colors/L;(-;Quit/Q');
      InsertMenu(fileMenu, 0);

      editMenu := NewMenu(editID,'Edit');
      AppendMenu(editMenu, 'Undo/Z;(-;Cut/X;Copy/C;Paste/V');
      InsertMenu(editMenu, 0);

      DrawMenuBar; InitCursor;

      SetRect(dragRect,-32768,-32768,32767,32767);
      myRect := ScreenBits.bounds;
      WITH myRect DO
        BEGIN
          top := top + 45; bottom := bottom - 10;
          left := left + 10; right := right - 10;
        END;

      colorQD := Band(WordPtr(ROM85)^,$C000) = 0;
      IF colorQD THEN
        BEGIN
          numColors := bsl(1,CGrafPtr(myWindow)^.portPixMap^^.pixelSize);
          myWindow := NewCWindow(nil,myRect,'Mandel',TRUE,zoomDocProc,
                                WindowPtr(-1),TRUE,0);
        END
      ELSE
        myWindow := NewWindow(nil,myRect,'Mandel',TRUE,zoomDocProc,
                                WindowPtr(-1),TRUE,0);

      SetPort(myWindow);
      FlushEvents(everyEvent,0);

(*  Mandel default position *)
      centx := -0.8; centy := 0.0; res := 1.0;
      limit := 256; CheckItem(fileMenu, 2, TRUE);
      linearFlag := FALSE; CheckItem(fileMenu, 5, TRUE);
      custPict := 1; f.digits := 5;
      quitFlag := FALSE;
END;
```

```
PROCEDURE UpdateMenus;
BEGIN
   { in a somewhat non-standard use of the menu bar, we will display }
   { the current location and magnification in the titles of 3 menus }
   { in order to change the text of a menu name, we must create a menu }
   { from scratch, so first let's delete the old menus... }

   DeleteMenu(xID); DeleteMenu(yID); DeleteMenu(resID);
   DisposeMenu(xMenu); DisposeMenu(yMenu); DisposeMenu(resMenu);

   f.style := FixedDecimal;
   Num2Str(f,centx,decStr(str));
   xMenu := NewMenu(xID,Concat('x = ',str));
   Num2Str(f,centy,decStr(str));
   yMenu := NewMenu(yID,Concat('y = ',str));

   f.style := FloatDecimal;
   Num2Str(f,res,decStr(str));
   resMenu := NewMenu(resID,Concat('res = ',str));

   InsertMenu(xMenu, 0); InsertMenu(yMenu, 0); InsertMenu(resMenu, 0);
   DrawMenuBar;
END;

BEGIN { Main }
   InitWorld;
   WHILE NOT quitFlag DO
     BEGIN
       UpdateMenus;
       DrawMandel;
     END;
   DisposeWindow(myWindow);
   ExitToShell;
END.
```

Mandel.r—Rez Source Code for Resources

```
/* Mandel.r - By Dan Allen */

#include "Types.r";

type 'maxb' { pstring; };

resource 'maxb' (0) {
    "Mandel 1.0 B1 by Dan Allen\n";
};

resource 'SIZE' (-1) {
    dontSaveScreen,
    acceptSuspendResumeEvents,
    enableOptionSwitch,
    canBackground,
    multiFinderAware,
    backgroundAndForeground,
    dontGetFrontClicks,
    ignoreChildDiedEvents,
    not32BitCompatible,
    reserved,reserved,reserved,reserved,reserved,reserved,reserved,
    64*1024,
    32*1024
};

resource 'FREF' (128) { 'APPL', 0, "" };

resource 'BNDL' (128) {
    'maxb', 0, { 'ICN#', { 0, 128 }; 'FREF', { 0, 128 } }
};

resource 'ICN#' (128, purgeable) {
    {   /* array: 2 elements */
        /* [1] */
        $"0000 0000 07FF FFE0 0800 0010 0800 0010 08FF FF10 0900 0090"
        $"0924 4890 096A D490 092A 5490 092A 5490 0924 4890 0912 2490"
        $"0935 6A90 0915 2A90 0915 2A90 0912 2490 0900 0090 08FF FF10"
        $"0800 0010 0800 0010 0800 0010 0800 0010 0800 FF10 0800 0010"
        $"0800 0010 0800 0010 0800 0010 07FF FFE0 0400 0020 0400 0020"
        $"0400 0020 07FF FFE0",
        /* [2] */
        $"0000 0000 07FF FFE0 0FFF FFF0 0FFF FFF0 0FFF FFF0 0FFF FFF0"
        $"0FFF FFF0 0FFF FFF0 0FFF FFF0 0FFF FFF0 0FFF FFF0 0FFF FFF0"
        $"0FFF FFF0 0FFF FFF0 0FFF FFF0 0FFF FFF0 0FFF FFF0 0FFF FFF0"
        $"0FFF FFF0 0FFF FFF0 0FFF FFF0 0FFF FFF0 0FFF FFF0 0FFF FFF0"
        $"0FFF FFF0 0FFF FFF0 0FFF FFF0 07FF FFE0 07FF FFE0 07FF FFE0"
        $"07FF FFE0 07FF FFE0"
    }
};
```

```
resource 'clut' (4, "DKA 4 Bit") {
    0x4, $8000,
    {   /* array ColorSpec: 16 elements */

        0, 65535, 65535, 65535,      /* White */
        1, 49151, 49151, 49151,      /* Lt Grey   */
        2, 32767, 32767, 32767,      /* Med Grey */
        3, 65535, 0, 0,              /* Red */
        4, 0, 65535, 0,              /* Green */
        5, 0, 0, 65535,              /* Blue */
        6, 65535, 65535, 0,          /* Yellow */
        7, 65535, 0, 65535,          /* Violet */
        8, 0, 65535, 65535,          /* Cyan */
        9, 0, 65535, 32767,          /* Mint */
        10, 0, 32767, 65535,         /* Sky Blue */
        11, 65535, 32767, 0,         /* Orange */
        12, 65535, 0, 32767,         /* Magenta */
        13, 32767, 65535, 0,         /* Light Green */
        14, 32767, 0, 65535,         /* Purple */
        15, 0, 0, 0,                 /* Black    */
    }
};
```

Graph — C Tool

Many people have complained that MPW cannot create graphical tools. It is not that it cannot be done; it is just that the methods for doing it have never been well documented. The tools that may be created must be modal in behavior, however, as the MPW Shell does not know what to do with a window it does not "own." Note that being modal does not mean that the window has to be a modal dialog; the window used in the following tool is created by calling `NewWindow,` and our tool provides its own modal behavior by simply not allowing certain things in its main event loop. During this time the MPW Shell is relatively dormant.

This tool uses basic QuickDraw calls to display various mathematical functions. Various functions are listed in a menu that this tool adds to the menu bar. Figure 3–2 shows a combined plot of the sine, cosine, tangent, and natural log functions as shown inside MPW.

Creating a graphical MPW tool is similar to creating a regular application, except that you should not initialize the Window or Menu Managers. The event processing used in this tool is simple: the tool takes all events but responds only to mouse- down events. If the mouse is clicked in the menu bar, the tool checks to see if the tool's special menu has been selected; if so, the tool draws a plot. Any other mouse clicks terminate the main event loop.

GRAPH — C TOOL **101**

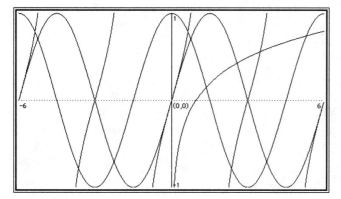

Figure 3–2: The Sine, Cosine, Tangent, and Natural Log Functions as Shown Inside MPW

Improving Graph

Here are some suggestions for improving Graph:

- If your Mac has a floating-point coprocessor, build a version of Graph with the -mc68881 option. Measure the tremendous performance increase.

- This tool plots only a fixed number of functions. Write an arbitrary expression evaluator that allows any function to be plotted.

- How would you expand the plotting area in the most Mac-like fashion? Certainly one option would be a dialog box in which coordinates could be entered, but that would not be too good for general exploring. How could clicking with the mouse greatly speed up exploring the coordinate plane?

- Extend the tool to plot complex functions with conformal mapping of contours shown in different colors. Does your tool still run on any Mac?

```c
/*
 *  Graph.c - Plots a function
 *        - Written by Dan Allen 11/22/88
 *        - Works with MPW 2.0 & 3.0 1/10/89
 *
 */

#include <Math.h>
#include <QuickDraw.h>
#include <Events.h>
#include <Windows.h>
#include <Menus.h>
#include <OSEvents.h>
```

```
#define PI       3.14159265358979323
#define MENUID   1000

#ifdef  ghs /* check for MPW C 2.0 */
#define NewMenu      NEWMENU
#define AppendMenu   APPENDMENU
#define DrawString   DRAWSTRING
#define FindWindow   FINDWINDOW
#define MenuSelect   MENUSELECT
#endif

short       halfX,halfY;
WindowPtr   wind;
EventRecord event;
MenuHandle  menu;

main()
{
  long      menuCmd;
  WindowPtr whichWind;

  InitWorld(); /* includes adding our own menu to the menu bar */
  while (1) {
    if (GetNextEvent(everyEvent,&event)) {
      if (event.what == mouseUp)
        break;
      if (event.what == mouseDown)
        if (FindWindow(event.where,&whichWind) == inMenuBar) {
          menuCmd = MenuSelect(event.where);
          if (menuCmd >> 16 == MENUID)
            switch (menuCmd & 0xFFFF) {
              case 1:   NewPlot(); break;
              case 3:   FSin(); break;
              case 4:   FCos(); break;
              case 5:   FTan(); break;
              case 7:   FAsin(); break;
              case 8:   FAcos(); break;
              case 9:   FAtan(); break;
              case 11:  FSinh(); break;
              case 12:  FCosh(); break;
              case 13:  FTanh(); break;
              case 15:  FLog(); break;
              case 16:  FLn(); break;
              case 17:  FExp(); break;
            }
          HiliteMenu(0);
        }
    }
  }
  DisposeWorld();
  return 0;
}
```

GRAPH — C TOOL   **103**

```
FSin()
{
  short     i;
  extended  y;

  MoveTo(-halfX,0);
  for(i = -halfX; i < halfX; i++) {
    y = sin((i*2*PI)/halfX)*halfY; /* parens needed for proper eval order */
    LineTo(i,-y);
  }
}

FCos()
{
  short     i;
  extended  y;

  MoveTo(-halfX,-halfY);
  for(i = -halfX; i < halfX; i++) {
    y = cos((i*2*PI)/halfX)*halfY; /* parens needed for proper eval order */
    LineTo(i,-y);
  }
}

FTan()
{
  short     i;
  extended  y;

  MoveTo(-halfX,0);
  for(i = -halfX; i < halfX; i++) {
    y = tan((i*2*PI)/halfX)*halfY; /* parens needed for proper eval order */
    LineTo(i,-y);
  }
}

FAsin()
{
  short     i;
  extended  y;

  MoveTo(-halfX,0);
  for(i = -halfX; i < halfX; i++) {
    y = asin((i*2*PI)/halfX)*halfY; /* parens needed for proper eval order */
    LineTo(i,-y);
  }
}
```

```
FAcos()
{
  short     i;
  extended  y;

  MoveTo(-halfX,0);
  for(i = -halfX; i < halfX; i++) {
    y = acos((i*2*PI)/halfX)*halfY; /* parens needed for proper eval order */
    LineTo(i,-y);
  }
}

FAtan()
{
  short     i;
  extended  y;
  MoveTo(-halfX,halfY);
  for(i = -halfX; i < halfX; i++) {
    y = atan((i*2*PI)/halfX)*halfY; /* parens needed for proper eval order */
    LineTo(i,-y);
  }
}

FSinh()
{
  short     i;
  extended  y;

  MoveTo(-halfX,0);
  for(i = -halfX; i < halfX; i++) {
    y = sinh((i*2*PI)/halfX)*halfY; /* parens needed for proper eval order */
    LineTo(i,-y);
  }
}

FCosh()
{
  short     i;
  extended  y;

  MoveTo(-halfX,0);
  for(i = -halfX; i < halfX; i++) {
    y = cosh((i*2*PI)/halfX)*halfY; /* parens needed for proper eval order */
    LineTo(i,-y);
  }
}
```

GRAPH — C TOOL   **105**

```
FTanh()
{
  short     i;
  extended  y;

  MoveTo(-halfX,halfY);
  for(i = -halfX; i < halfX; i++) {
    y = tanh((i*2*PI)/halfX)*halfY; /* parens needed for proper eval order */
    LineTo(i,-y);
  }
}

FLog()
{
  short     i;
  extended  y;

  MoveTo(0,halfY);
  for(i = 0; i < halfX; i++) {
    y = log10((i*2*PI)/halfX)*halfY; /* parens needed for proper eval order */
    LineTo(i,-y);
  }
}

FLn()
{
  short     i;
  extended  y;

  MoveTo(0,halfY);
  for(i = 0; i < halfX; i++) {
    y = log((i*2*PI)/halfX)*halfY; /* parens needed for proper eval order */
    LineTo(i,-y);
  }
}

FExp()
{
  short     i;
  extended  y;

  MoveTo(-halfX,0);
  for(i = -halfX; i < halfX; i++) {
    y = exp((i*2*PI)/halfX)*halfY; /* parens needed for proper eval order */
    LineTo(i,-y);
  }
}
```

```
NewPlot()
{
  EraseRect(&wind->portRect);
  PenPat(qd.ltGray);
  MoveTo(-halfX,0); LineTo(halfX,0);   /* X-axis */
  MoveTo(0,-halfY); LineTo(0,halfY);   /* Y-axis */
  PenPat(qd.black);
  TextSize(9);
  MoveTo(3,12); DrawString("\p(0,0)");
  MoveTo(halfX-10,12); DrawString("\p6");
  MoveTo(-halfX+2,12); DrawString("\p-6");
  MoveTo(3,-halfY+12); DrawString("\p1");
  MoveTo(3,halfY); DrawString("\p-1");
}

InitWorld()
{
  Rect   r;

  InitGraf(&qd.thePort);
  r = qd.screenBits.bounds;
  InsetRect(&r,20,40);
  wind = NewWindow(nil,&r,"",true,dBoxProc,(WindowPtr) -1,false,0);
  SetPort(wind);
  r = wind->portRect;
  halfX = (r.right - r.left)/2;
  halfY = (r.bottom - r.top)/2;
  SetOrigin(-halfX,-halfY);          /* sets coordinates of upper left corner */

  menu = NewMenu(MENUID,"\pFunction");
  AppendMenu(menu,"\pNew Plot;(-;Sin x;Cos x;Tan x;(-;ASin x;ACos x;ATan x;");
  AppendMenu(menu,"\p(-;Sinh x;Cosh x;Tanh x;(-;Log x;Ln x;Exp x");

  InsertMenu(menu,0);
  DrawMenuBar();
  FlushEvents(everyEvent,0);
  NewPlot();
  InitCursor();
}

DisposeWorld()
{
  DeleteMenu(MENUID);
  DisposeMenu(menu);
  DrawMenuBar();
  DisposeWindow(wind);
  FlushEvents(everyEvent,0);
}
```

MacQ — C Application

This stand-alone application is an example of the complex subject known as simulation. The mathematics and physics in this application are relatively complicated for the uninitiated, but it is a good example of putting a Macintosh interface onto some otherwise straight computational code. The first half of the application is the Mac interface portion that handles events, windows, and menus. Paul Finlayson did the dynamics and numerical analysis contained in the latter half of the application.

MacQ simulates the rigid-body dynamics of a book tumbling in space. The program optionally allows the user to specify a constant torque about one of the three principle axes. The simulation requires the simultaneous numerical integration of a set of seven first order differential equations. This program offers two different integrators: a simple Euler integrator for speed and a fourth-order Runge-Kutta integrator for accuracy.

MacQ is short for Mac Quaternion. A quaternion is a blend between a complex number and a vector; the concept was created by the father of modern vector analysis, William Hamilton. Some people have called quaternions "musty mathematics" because they were discovered in the mid-1800s and then forgotten, but they are experiencing a renaissance because they are an efficient technique for modeling rigid body kinematics. Part of the efficiency is obtained because the technique requires no trigonometric functions, but the real win for numerical integration results from the absence of singularities. Quaternion algebra is thus useful in many spacecraft dynamics applications, for example. Quaternions are sometimes called Euler's symmetric parameters.

Here is the Makefile:

```
COptions    = -mbg ch8 -mc68020 -mc68881 -elems881

CLibs =     "{CLibraries}CLib881.o" ∂
            "{CLibraries}Math881.o" ∂
            "{CLibraries}CSANELib881.o" ∂
            "{CLibraries}CInterface.o" ∂
            "{CLibraries}StdCLib.o" ∂
            "{CLibraries}CRuntime.o"

MacQ  ƒƒ  MacQ.r
    Rez -a -o MacQ MacQ.r -c PFDA
MacQ  ƒƒ  MacQ.c.o
    Link -w -o MacQ MacQ.c.o {CLibs} {Libs}
MacQ  ƒƒ  {Worksheet}
    Setfile -a B -c PFDA -t APPL -d . -m . MacQ
    MacQ
```

and here is the MPW C code:

```
/*  Quaternion Rotation Program
 *  Quaternion Algebra & Numerical Analysis by Dr. Paul Finlayson
 *  Macintosh User Interface by Dan Allen
 *
 *  Written originally on 6/13/1986 in Victorville, CA
 *  Ported from LightSpeedC to MPW C on 10/9/1986 in Cupertino, CA
 *  A few tweaks done on Tue, Apr 21, 1987 4:54:53 PM
 *  MPW 3.0 port and about box work on 1/14/89
 */

#include <Types.h>
#include <Memory.h>
#include <Resources.h>
#include <Quickdraw.h>
#include <Fonts.h>
#include <Events.h>
#include <Windows.h>
#include <Controls.h>
#include <Menus.h>
#include <TextEdit.h>
#include <Dialogs.h>
#include <Scrap.h>
#include <Desk.h>
#include <ToolUtils.h>
#include <SegLoad.h>

#include <Math.h>

/*    Mac Application Globals & Initialization Routines    */
# define appleID     128
# define runID       129
# define Go          1
# define Stop        2
# define Quit        3
# define axisID      130
# define torqueID    131
# define integID     132
# define LASTID      integID

# define HIWORD(aLong)   (((aLong) >> 16) & 0xFFFF)
# define LOWORD(aLong)   ((aLong) & 0xFFFF)
# define PEEK(address)   *((char *) address)
```

```
static Boolean      done = false,restart = true,hangout = false;
static short        curAxis = 2,curTorque = 0,curInteg = 1,xlimit,ylimit;
static PicHandle    pic1;
static WindowPtr    myWindow,whichWindow;
static MenuHandle   myMenus[6];
static Rect         myRect;
static EventRecord  myEvent;
static void InitWorld()
{
  short i;

  MaxApplZone();
  InitGraf(&qd.thePort);
  InitFonts();
  InitWindows();
  InitMenus();
  TEInit();
  InitDialogs(nil);

  if ( PEEK(0x12F) ) curInteg = 2;   /* default to Runge on 68020 */
  else curInteg = 1;                 /* default to Euler on 68000 */

  myRect = qd.screenBits.bounds;
  InsetRect(&myRect,10,10);
  myRect.top += 40;
  myWindow = NewWindow(nil,&myRect,"\pQuaternion Rotation Demo",true,
                       noGrowDocProc,(WindowPtr) -1,false,0);
  SetPort(myWindow);
  myRect = qd.screenBits.bounds;
  xlimit = myRect.bottom -= 40;
  ylimit = myRect.right -= 40;

  myMenus[appleID] = NewMenu(appleID,"\p\024");
  AppendMenu(myMenus[appleID],"\pAbout MacQuaternion...;(-;");
  AddResMenu(myMenus[appleID],'DRVR');

  myMenus[runID] = NewMenu(runID,"\pRun");
  AppendMenu(myMenus[runID],"\pGo/G;Stop/S;Quit/Q");

  myMenus[axisID] = NewMenu(axisID,"\pVelocity");
  AppendMenu(myMenus[axisID],"\pX Axis;Y Axis;Z Axis");

  myMenus[torqueID] = NewMenu(torqueID,"\pTorque");
  AppendMenu(myMenus[torqueID],"\pX Axis;Y Axis;Z Axis");

  myMenus[integID] = NewMenu(integID,"\pIntegrator");
  AppendMenu(myMenus[integID],"\pEuler/E;Runge/R");

  for (i = 128; i <= LASTID; i++) InsertMenu(myMenus[i],0);
  DrawMenuBar();
  InitCursor();
}
```

```
static void AboutDialog()
{
  long      i;
  GrafPtr   oldport;
  WindowPtr tempWind;
  Rect      tempRect;
  Handle    str;

  GetPort(&oldport);
  SetRect(&tempRect,30,60,482,292);
  tempWind = NewWindow(0,&tempRect,"",true,dBoxProc,(WindowPtr)-1,false,0);
  SetPort(tempWind);

  TextFont(times); TextSize(24);
  MoveTo(19,30);
  DrawString("\pMacQuaternion 1.0 B1");

  TextFont(geneva); TextSize(9);
  for(i = 0; i < 3; i++) {
    MoveTo(21,i*12+51);
    switch(i) {
      case 0: DrawString("\pMacintosh Interface by Dan Allen"); break;
      case 1: DrawString("\pNumerical Analysis by Paul Finlayson"); break;
      case 2: DrawString("\pQuaternions by William Hamilton"); break;
    }
    MoveTo(230,i*12+51);
    switch(i) {
      case 0: DrawString("\pJanuary 14, 1989"); break;
      case 1: DrawString("\pJune 13, 1986"); break;
      case 2: DrawString("\pOctober 16, 1843"); break;
    }
  }
  SetRect(&tempRect,20,83,442,170);
  str = GetResource('CSTR',128);
  HLock(str);
  i = SizeResource(str) - 1;
  TextBox(*str,i,&tempRect,0);
  HUnlock(str);
```

```
for(i = 0; i < 4; i++) {
  MoveTo(21,i*15+175);
  switch (i) {
    case 0: DrawString("\pREFERENCE"); break;
    case 1: DrawString("\p§41: Spinors"); break;
    case 2: DrawString("\p§8.6, p. 232"); break;
    case 3: DrawString("\pp. 511"); break;
  }
  MoveTo(110,i*15+175);
  switch (i) {
    case 0: DrawString("\pAUTHOR(s)"); break;
    case 1: DrawString("\pMisner, Thorne, Wheeler"); break;
    case 2: DrawString("\pGrant Fowler"); break;
    case 3: DrawString("\pJames R. Wertz"); break;
  }
  MoveTo(230,i*15+175);
  switch (i) {
    case 0: DrawString("\pTITLE"); break;
    case 1: DrawString("\p"Gravitation""); break;
    case 2: DrawString("\p"Analytical Mechanics, 3rd edition""); break;
    case 3: DrawString("\p"Spacecraft Attitude Determination and Control""");
            break;
  }
}
while (!Button()) SystemTask();
DisposeWindow(tempWind);
SetPort(oldport);
}


static void DoCommand(long mResult)
{
  short theItem,temp;
  char  name[255];

  theItem = LOWORD(mResult);
  switch (HIWORD(mResult)) {
    case appleID:
      if (theItem == 1) AboutDialog();
      else {
        GetItem(myMenus[appleID],theItem,name);
        temp = OpenDeskAcc(name);
        SetPort(myWindow);
      }
      break;
```

```
        case runID:
          switch (theItem) {
            case Go:
              restart = true; hangout = false; break;
            case Stop:
              hangout = true; break;
            case Quit:
              done = true; break;
          } break;
        case axisID:
          if (curAxis == theItem) curAxis = 0;
          else curAxis = theItem;
          restart = true; break;
        case torqueID:
          if (curTorque == theItem) curTorque = 0;
          else curTorque = theItem;
          restart = true; break;
        case integID:
          curInteg = theItem;
          restart = true; break;
    }
  HiliteMenu(0);
}

static void SetUpMenus()
{
  short i;

  CheckItem(myMenus[runID],Go,!hangout);
  CheckItem(myMenus[runID],Stop,hangout);

  for (i=1; i<=3; i++) {
    CheckItem(myMenus[axisID],i,(curAxis == i));
    CheckItem(myMenus[torqueID],i,(curTorque == i));
  }

  CheckItem(myMenus[integID],1,curInteg == 1);
  CheckItem(myMenus[integID],2,curInteg == 2);
}
```

```
static void MainEventLoop()
{
  static Rect dragRect = {-32767,-32767,32767,32767};

  switch (myEvent.what) {
    case mouseDown:
      switch (FindWindow(myEvent.where,&whichWindow)) {
        case inMenuBar:
          SetUpMenus();
          DoCommand(MenuSelect(myEvent.where));
          break;
        case inSysWindow:
          SystemClick(&myEvent,whichWindow);
          break;
        case inDrag:
          DragWindow(whichWindow,myEvent.where,&dragRect);
          break;
        default:
          break;
      }
      break;
    case keyDown:
    case autoKey:
      if (myWindow == FrontWindow() && myEvent.modifiers & cmdKey)
          DoCommand(MenuKey(myEvent.message & charCodeMask));
      break;
    default:
      break;
  }
}


/*    Quaternion Global Variables & Initialization Routines */

#define MAXPOINTS 21

static short      npars, npts;
static extended   Ixx,Iyy,Izz,IxxR,IyyR,IzzR,IyymIxx,IzzmIyy,IxxmIzz;
static extended   q[25],Tbr[4][4],h,t,Nx,Ny,Nz;
static extended   pt[MAXPOINTS][4],Tpt[MAXPOINTS][4],Tpt2d[MAXPOINTS][4],Xeye;
static extended   gr_a,gr_b,gr_c,gr_d;

static void initialize()
{
  /* number of integrated parameters, which are the following q[1..7] */
  npars=7;

  /* quaternion parameters themselves, e.g. the identity matrix */
  q[1]=0.; q[2]=0.; q[3]=0.; q[4]=1.;
```

```
  /* initial angular rotation rates */
  switch (curAxis) {
    case 0:
      q[5]=.02; q[6]=.02; q[7]=.02; break;
    case 1:
      q[5]=1.1; q[6]=.02; q[7]=.02; break;
    case 2:
      q[5]=.02; q[6]=1.1; q[7]=.02; break;
    case 3:
      q[5]=.02; q[6]=.02; q[7]=1.1; break;
  }

  /* moments of inertia */
  /* the middle valued moment of a rigid body is always the unstable axis */
  /* example: Ixx = 5; Iyy - 4; Izz = 3; the y axis is unstable */
  Ixx=5.; Iyy=4.; Izz=3.;

  /* reciprocals & diffs of the moments of inertia, precomputed for speed */
  IxxR = 1./Ixx; IyyR = 1./Iyy; IzzR = 1./Izz;
  IzzmIyy = Izz-Iyy; IxxmIzz = Ixx-Izz; IyymIxx = Iyy-Ixx;

  /* for an interesting demo, set Ny = 1.  This is torque applied to
     the unstable axis (q[5] = .02; q[6] = .1; q[7] = .02; )  */

  switch (curTorque) {
    case 0:
      Nx=0.; Ny=0.; Nz=0.; break;
    case 1:
      Nx=1.; Ny=0.; Nz=0.; break;
    case 2:
      Nx=0.; Ny=1.; Nz=0.; break;
    case 3:
      Nx=0.; Ny=0.; Nz=1.; break;
    default: ;
  }

  /* h is the integration step size, t is the initial starting time */
  h = .25; t = 0.;
}

static void normalize_qs()
{
  short       i;
  extended  qmagi;

/* Forces orthogonality of the transformation matrix
   defined by the quaternion parameters */

  qmagi = 1./sqrt(q[1]*q[1] + q[2]*q[2] + q[3]*q[3] + q[4]*q[4]);
  for (i = 1; i <= 4; q[i++] *= qmagi )
    ;
}
```

```
static void T_br(extended q[],extended t[4][4])
{
  extended q11,q22,q33,q44,q12,q13,q14,q23,q24,q34;

  /* Transformation from body to inertial reference */
  /* Compute squares and cross products of Quaternion parameter */

  q11 = q[1]*q[1]; q12 = q[1]*q[2]; q13 = q[1]*q[3]; q14 = q[1]*q[4];
                   q22 = q[2]*q[2]; q23 = q[2]*q[3]; q24 = q[2]*q[4];
                                    q33 = q[3]*q[3]; q34 = q[3]*q[4];
                                                     q44 = q[4]*q[4];

  /* Compute transformation from Body to Reference frame */

  t[1][1] = q11-q22-q33+q44; t[1][2] = 2*(q12-q34);    t[1][3] = 2*(q13+q24);
  t[2][1] = 2*(q12+q34);     t[2][2] =-q11+q22-q33+q44; t[2][3] = 2*(q23-q14);
  t[3][1] = 2*(q13-q24);     t[3][2] = 2*(q23+q14);    t[3][3] =
                                                        -q11-q22+q33+q44;
}

static void de(extended q[],extended dq[])
{
  /* the set of differential equations called by either integrator */
  /*  q[1],q[2],q[3],q[4] : Quaternion parameters */
  /*  q[5],q[6],q[7]      : wx,wy,wz              */

  /*  Quaternion parameter equations  */

  dq[1] = (             q[7]*q[2] - q[6]*q[3] + q[5]*q[4] ) * .5;
  dq[2] = (-q[7]*q[1]             + q[5]*q[3] + q[6]*q[4] ) * .5;
  dq[3] = ( q[6]*q[1] - q[5]*q[2]             + q[7]*q[4] ) * .5;
  dq[4] = (-q[5]*q[1] - q[6]*q[2] - q[7]*q[3]            ) * .5;

  /*  Euler's equations  */
  /*  See Grant R. Fowles' "Analytical Mechanics", §8.6 p.232 3rd edition */

  dq[5] = IxxR*( Nx - q[6]*q[7]*IzzmIyy );
  dq[6] = IyyR*( Ny - q[7]*q[5]*IxxmIzz );
  dq[7] = IzzR*( Nz - q[5]*q[6]*IyymIxx );
}

static void runge(short n,extended h,extended *t,extended y[])
{
  short    i;
  extended y1[25],f1[25],f2[25],f3[25],f4[25],h2;

  /*  Runge-Kutta 4th order numerical integrator - remarkably accurate */

  h2 = h/2;
  de(y,f1);
  for (i = 1; i <= n; y1[i] = y[i]+h2*f1[i], ++i );
  *t += h2;
```

```
    de(y1,f2);
    for (i = 1; i <= n; y1[i] = y[i]+h2*f2[i], ++i );

    de(y1,f3);
    for (i = 1; i <= n; y1[i] = y[i]+h*f3[i], ++i );
    *t += h2;

    de(y1,f4);
    for (i = 1; i <= n; y[i] += h/6*(f1[i]+2*(f2[i]+f3[i])+f4[i]), ++i);
}

static void euler(short n,extended h,extended *t,extended y[])
{
    short     i;
    extended  dy[25];

    /*  Euler 1st order numerical integrator - fast but not too accurate */

    de(y,dy);
    for ( i=1; i<=n; y[i]+=h*dy[i],++i );
    *t+=h;
}

static void define_object()
{
/*
  Database of coordinates representing a infinitely flat book
  If you wish to draw a more complicated object, simply add your
  datapoints to this database and set npts to the appropriate #
  of points up to MAXPOINTS - 1
*/

  npts=7; Xeye=10.;
  pt[1][1]=2.; pt[1][2]= 0.; pt[1][3]= 0.;
  pt[2][1]=0.; pt[2][2]= 3.; pt[2][3]= 0.;
  pt[3][1]=0.; pt[3][2]= 0.; pt[3][3]= 4.;
  pt[4][1]=0.; pt[4][2]=-2.; pt[4][3]= 3.;
  pt[5][1]=0.; pt[5][2]= 2.; pt[5][3]= 3.;
  pt[6][1]=0.; pt[6][2]= 2.; pt[6][3]=-3.;
  pt[7][1]=0.; pt[7][2]=-2.; pt[7][3]=-3.;
}

static void draw_object() /*  Transforms database and draws object */
{
    short    i,j,p;
    extended Xtemp;

    /*  Transform poshorts from Body to Reference frame   */
    for ( p=1; p<=npts; ++p )
      for ( i=1; i<=3; ++i )
        for ( j=1,Tpt[p][i]=0.; j<=3; ++j )
          Tpt[p][i]+=Tbr[i][j]*pt[p][j];
```

```
  /*  Map poshorts to 2-d  */
  for ( p=1; p<=npts; ++p )
  {
    Xtemp=Xeye/(Xeye-Tpt[p][1]);
    Tpt2d[p][2]=Xtemp*Tpt[p][2];
    Tpt2d[p][3]=Xtemp*Tpt[p][3];
  }
  /*  Draw object  */
  for (p=1; p<=3; ++p)
  {
    MoveTo( (short)(gr_b), (short)(gr_d) );
    LineTo( (short)(gr_a*Tpt2d[p][2]+gr_b), (short)(gr_c*Tpt2d[p][3]+gr_d) );
  }
  MoveTo( (short)(gr_a*Tpt2d[7][2]+gr_b), (short)(gr_c*Tpt2d[7][3]+gr_d) );
  for (p=4; p<=7; ++p)
    LineTo( (short)(gr_a*Tpt2d[p][2]+gr_b), (short)(gr_c*Tpt2d[p][3]+gr_d) );

}

static void scale( xmin,xmax,ymin,ymax )
  extended  xmin,xmax,ymin,ymax;
{
  gr_a = ( (extended) ylimit) / (xmax-xmin);
  gr_b =-gr_a*xmin;
  gr_c = ( (extended) xlimit) / (ymin-ymax);
  gr_d =-gr_c*ymax;
}

main()
{
  long  tickValue;

  InitWorld();
  define_object();          /* change this routine for different objects */
  scale(-8.,8.,-5.33,5.33); /* may need to change this depending on object */

  while(true) {
    if (restart) {
      initialize();
      restart = false;
    }

    if (curInteg == 1) euler(npars,h,&t,q);
    else runge(npars,h,&t,q);

    normalize_qs();
    T_br(q,Tbr);
```

```
    tickValue = TickCount();
    pic1 = OpenPicture(&myRect);
    draw_object();
    ClosePicture();
    EraseRect(&myRect);
    DrawPicture(pic1,&myRect);
    KillPicture(pic1);

    do {
      SystemTask();
      if (GetNextEvent(everyEvent,&myEvent)) MainEventLoop();
      if (done) ExitToShell();
    }
    while (hangout);
  }
}
```

MacQ.r—Rez Source Code for MacQ Resources

```
/*  MacQ.r  - Resource description for MacQ    */

#include "Types.r";

type 'CSTR' { cstring; };
type 'PFDA' { pstring; };

resource 'PFDA' (0) { "MacQuaternion 1.0 B1"; };

resource 'SIZE' (-1) {
  dontSaveScreen,
  acceptSuspendResumeEvents,
  enableOptionSwitch,
  canBackground,
  multiFinderAware,
  backgroundAndForeground,
  dontGetFrontClicks,
  ignoreChildDiedEvents,
  not32BitCompatible,
  reserved, reserved, reserved, reserved, reserved, reserved, reserved,
  64*1024,
  64*1024
};

resource 'FREF' (128) { 'APPL', 0, "" };
```

```
resource 'BNDL' (128) {
  'PFDA',
  0,
  { /* [1] */
    'ICN#',
    { /* array IDArray: 1 elements */
      /* [1] */
      0, 128
    };
    /* [2] */
    'FREF',
    { /* array IDArray: 1 elements */
      /* [1] */
      0, 128
    }
  }
};

resource 'ICN#' (128) {
  { /* array: 2 elements */
    /* [1] */
    $"FFFF FFFF 8000 0001 801F FE7F 807F FF01 807F FF7D"
    $"80FC 0701 80FC 0779 80F8 0601 80F8 0EF1 81F8 0C01"
    $"81F0 0DE1 81F0 1C01 83F0 1BC1 83E0 1801 83E0 3B81"
    $"87E0 3001 87E0 3701 87C0 3001 87C0 7601 8FC0 6001"
    $"8F80 6C01 8F86 6001 8F87 D801 9F07 C001 9F03 E021"
    $"9F03 F061 9F03 F0A1 9FFF F921 9FFF FDF1 8FFE 3C21"
    $"8000 1C21 FFFF FFFF";
    /* [2] */
    $"FFFF FFFF FFFF FFFF FFFF FFFF FFFF FFFF FFFF FFFF"
    $"FFFF FFFF FFFF FFFF FFFF FFFF FFFF FFFF FFFF FFFF"
    $"FFFF FFFF FFFF FFFF FFFF FFFF FFFF FFFF FFFF FFFF"
    $"FFFF FFFF FFFF FFFF FFFF FFFF FFFF FFFF FFFF FFFF"
    $"FFFF FFFF FFFF FFFF FFFF FFFF FFFF FFFF FFFF FFFF"
    $"FFFF FFFF FFFF FFFF FFFF FFFF FFFF FFFF FFFF FFFF"
    $"FFFF FFFF FFFF FFFF"
  }
};

resource 'CSTR'(128) {
  "This program models a specific rotating rigid body: an infinitely flat "
  "book.  The model is based on Euler's equations.  The graphics "
  "transformations and rotations are based on Quaternion theory.  "
  "The axis menu allows you to select the starting axis; the torque "
  "menu allows you to select which axis has a starting torque.  "
  "Either of two numerical integrators can be used: "
  "Euler's (for speed) or Runge (for accuracy).  "
  "Quaternions are a generalization of complex numbers to 4 dimensions.  "
  "In Quaternion theory, i^2 = j^2 = k^2 = ijk = -1.";
};
```

Conclusion

This chapter looked at how QuickDraw works—both classic and Color QuickDraw. It showed that QuickDraw relies upon the Font Manager to create the bit maps used by QuickDraw to draw text. The chapter also reviewed printing and explained that printing and drawing are closely related; in fact, they often use the same code in applications.

Speaking of code, this chapter presented three applications that use QuickDraw. `Mandel`, an application that explores the Mandelbrot set, can use either classic or Color QuickDraw. `Graph`, an MPW tool, demonstrates more uses for QuickDraw and how to create windows under the MPW Shell. Our final application, `MacQ`, shows how to wrap a Macintosh interface around a computational engine. As a bonus, `MacQ` illustrates the mathematics behind a true physical simulation.

Recommended Reading

Inside Macintosh, volume 1, chapter 6 and volume 5, chapters 4–8 are the places to read up on QuickDraw in its various flavors. For more reading on graphics in general, try Foley and Van Dam's *Fundamentals of Interactive Computer Graphics.* In the realm of image processing, Holzmann's *Beyond Photography: The Digital Darkroom* is lots of fun, and it includes C source code for an image transformation program.

Peitgen's *The Beauty of Fractals* is the source for information about the Mandelbrot set. With its gorgeous color plates, it is almost a coffee table book, but also contains a good technical appendix about writing your own fractal programs for fun and profit.

You will need a pretty good physics education to fully understand `MacQ`. Here is how you can get the necessary background on a shoestring. Start with a good introduction to physics from *The Feynman Lectures on Physics* by Richard Feynman. These lectures are the most lucid and readable introduction to physics around.

Next, to improve your mechanics, feast on Grant Fowles' *Analytical Mechanics.* It is the best intermediate-level mechanics text, with excellent material on rigid body motion. If you feel the need for a Ph.D.'s worth of mechanics, try Goldstein's *Classical Mechanics.*

Relativistic mechanics is one of my favorite diversions: Taylor and Wheeler's *Spacetime Physics* handles special relativity, and Misner, Thorne, and Wheeler's *Gravitation* is the Bible of general relativity. *Gravitation* is one of the most beautiful and fascinating books ever written, but prepare for a lifetime's worth of study to understand it, as the book weighs almost 1×10^{-27} meters! (Yes, you read meters! The book uses geometricized units.)

Once your mechanics are up to speed, try Kane's *Spacecraft Dynamics* and Wertz's *Spacecraft Attitude Determination and Control* for help in applying mechanics to real-world problems. Of course, handling real-world problems requires a good background in numerical analysis, so check the reading list for chapter 5 for those titles.

## CHAPTER 4

THE MACINTOSH TOOLBOX

The Macintosh Toolbox contains the various routines that together generate most of the standard behavior you see in most Macintosh applications. This behavior is known as the Desktop User Interface and is detailed in the *Apple Human Interface Guidelines: The Apple Desktop Interface* (Addison-Wesley, 1987). This chapter looks at some of the more important Toolbox Managers:

- Resource Manager
- Event Manager
- Window Manager
- Control Manager
- Menu Manager
- TextEdit
- Dialog Manager
- Desk Manager
- Scrap Manager
- Utilities
- Package Manager

Because many of the Managers are in ROM, many people mistakenly consider the Toolbox to be part of the operating system. It is not; rather, it is built on top of the operating system. The operating system handles memory, files, and I/O, and the Toolbox manages the user interface components, such as the windows, menus, and dialogs.

Much of the Macintosh's early success was the result of the functionality provided by the Toolbox, which allowed the uniform Desktop Interface. For the first time in the history of computers, developers were strongly encouraged to make their software follow a coherent, consistent set of interface guidelines. The resulting applications are easy to use, uniform, intuitive, and graphically impressive—all because of the use of the Toolbox. MS Windows (for MS-DOS), Presentation Manager (for OS/2), and the X Window System (for Unix) are among recent attempts to provide equivalent functionality for other computers.

Because programmers must learn how to use the hundreds of routines in the Macintosh Toolbox, the Macintosh has earned the reputation of being hard to program. It is true that there is a learning curve for programmers, but the results speak for themselves: learning about the Mac Toolbox is well worth it. Macintosh users tend to use more software than most other computer users, with six to eight applications being used regularly by the average Mac user as opposed to the one or two applications that most MS-DOS users tend to learn.

Few systems other than the Macintosh offer as neat a set of tools with which to create easy-to-use applications. Because the Toolbox routines are standard, all well-written Macintosh applications have a great deal in common, which makes learning a new Macintosh application easy after the first one has been mastered. This is not to say that all Macintosh programs are clones. The Toolbox still offers a high degree of latitude in its use and customization, allowing each Macintosh application to be unique.

In this chapter we will look at most of the important Managers in the Toolbox, one by one. The more useful calls for each of these Managers will be mentioned or described, to give you a feel for the functionality found in the Toolbox. (You should consult *Inside Macintosh* for greater detail.) Following these sections is the source code to several MPW tools that illustrate how to use the Resource Manager, as well as the source code to several FKEYs that show some tricks you can do with the Event Manager.

The Resource Manager

The concept of resources was unique to the Macintosh in 1984. A resource can be anything: code, data, text, graphics, icons, windows, fonts, sounds, or anything else you want. The Resource Manager was originally written by Bruce Horn and was updated by Brian McGhie. It allows code and data to be maintained as separate objects in the resource fork of a file. It also allows data to be initialized, something that Pascal does not allow. Because most parts of an application are individual resources, you can easily translate Macintosh applications into other languages without having to recompile code.

Any resource can be uniquely specified by using a resource type and a 16-bit signed resource ID number. All IDs less than 128 (including negative IDs) are reserved for system use. Resources can also have an optional resource name, which is a Pascal Str255.

Negative IDs actually are special IDs that have encoded information about another resource that "owns" that ID. Owned IDs are used so that the Font/DA Mover will automatically move resources such as menus and dialogs along with the desk accessory to which they belong. For example, a desk accessory is a resource of type DRVR, and its dialogs (DLOG) and dialog item lists (DITL) would have specially encoded owned IDs to indicate that they were owned by the DRVR. The two high bits of the ID (14 and 15) are always set for owned IDs. Bits 13 to 11 specify the type of the resource owner (all clear for a DRVR; other owners are WDEFs, MDEFs, CDEFs, PDEFs, and PACKs).

Bits 5 to 10 specify the owner's resource ID (thus a range of 0 to 63), and bits 0 to 4 are the ID of the owned resource (thus a range of 0 to 31).

A resource type is a 32-bit quantity usually composed of letters. (Lowercase resource types are reserved for use by Apple.) Resource types are case-sensitive. Most resource types with fewer than four letters pad the resource type with spaces. Many resource types already exist and have strict rules as to their structure, meaning, and use. The following tables present some of the most common resource types. The resource types in the first table were all defined in the original Macintosh.

Type	Resource Found in All Varieties of Macintosh
ALRT	Alert template for warning dialogs
BNDL	Bundle to associate an app with its documents
CDEF	Code for a custom control definition procedure
CNTL	Control template describing a control
CODE	Code segment (compiled code)
CURS	Cursor
DITL	Dialog item list specifying buttons
DLOG	Dialog template specifying size of dialog box
DRVR	Code for a device driver or desk accessory
DSAT	Startup alert table, "Welcome to Macintosh"
FKEY	Code for command shift keys, screen shots
FONT	A bit-mapped font
FREF	File reference
FRSV	A list of reserved fonts to not be removed
ICN#	Icon list (Desktop icons with masks)
ICON	Icon
INIT	Initialization resource, startup code
INTL	International resource used for localization
MBAR	A collection of menus
MDEF	Code for a custom menu definition procedure
MENU	A menu
PACK	Package (extra system code)
PAT	A pattern
PAT#	Pattern list (MacPaint patterns)
PDEF	Printer definition code
PICT	Picture (Scrapbook)
PREC	Print record information
SERD	RAM Serial driver
STR	Pascal string
STR#	A list of Pascal strings
TEXT	ASCII text (Scrapbook)
WDEF	Code for a custom window definition procedure
WIND	A window template

The Macintosh Plus put several new resources in ROM to save disk space and increase speed.

Type	ID	Resources in 128 KB ROM
CURS	1	IBeamCursor
CURS	2	CrossCursor
CURS	3	PlusCursor
CURS	4	WatchCursor
DRVR	2	.Print driver
DRVR	3	.Sound driver
DRVR	4	.Sony disk driver
DRVR	9	.MPP AppleTalk driver
DRVR	10	.ATP AppleTalk driver
FONT	0	System font name
FONT	12	Chicago 12
MDEF	0	Menu definition procedure
PACK	4	SANE arithmetic
PACK	5	SANE transcendentals
PACK	7	SANE binary-decimal
SERD	0	Serial driver
WDEF	0	Window definition procedure

Type	Resources Found in System 3.0 and Later
CACH	RAM cache code set in Control Panel
FMTR	3.5" disk formatter
FOND	Font family definition
NFNT	"New" Font
PRER	Non-serial printer Chooser code
PRES	Serial printer Chooser code
PTCH	ROM patches
RDEV	Network Chooser code
ROvr	ROM resource override code
ROv#	List to ROM resources to override
bmap	Bit maps used by the Control Panel
ctab	Used by Control Panel
insc	Installer script

Type	Resources Found in System 4.1 and Later
ADBS	Apple Desktop Bus driver
INT#	Integer list used by Find File DA
KCAP	Keyboard layout used by Key Caps DA
KCHR	ASCII mapping (software)
KMAP	Keyboard map (hardware)
KSWP	Keyboard script used by Script Manager
LDEF	Code for a custom list definition procedure
MBDF	Default menu definition
MMAP	Mouse tracking code
NBPC	Name Binding Protocol used by AppleTalk
SICN	Script symbol
atpl	AppleTalk resource
boot	Boot blocks in System file
itl0	Date & time formats
itl1	Day & month names
itl2	Pack6 sort hooks
itlb	Pack6 script bundles
itlc	Script Manager configuration
lmem	Globals to be switched by MultiFinder
mcky	Mouse tracking parameters
mppc	AppleTalk configuration code
snd	Sounds
snth	Synthesizer

Type	Color-related Resources Found on Mac II Machines
actb	Alert color table
cctb	Control color table
cicn	Color icon (color Mac at boot)
clst	Color icon list
clut	Color look up table
crsr	Color cursor
dctb	Dialog color table
fctb	Font color table
fint	Font information
gama	Color correction table
ictb	Dialog item color table
mctb	Menu color table
mitq	MakeITable memory requirements
nrct	Rectangle positions
pltt	Color palette
ppat	Pixel pattern
wctb	Window color table

Resource Maps

Each resource fork contains the actual resource data and an index to the data called a *resource map*. When a resource fork is opened, its resource map is read into memory. When any resource is actually read into memory, 12 bytes are used by the Memory Manager in addition to the actual size of the resource.

Through the resource map mechanism, the Resource Manager allows different places to be searched for resources. This chained searching of resource maps takes place automatically. When the Macintosh is first started up, the System file is opened as a general library of resources to be checked out by all executing applications.

Once opened, resource files are referred to by a 16-bit reference number, with the System file always being zero. Fonts and desk accessories, as well as many other resources used by applications, are stored in the System file, which is at the end of the chain of resource forks that are searched for resources when needed.

When an application is launched, its resource map is put at the top of the list of resource maps to search. This establishes a hierarchy of resource maps. A GetResource request begins searching with the current application's resources and then—if the resource specified is not found—follows the resource chain until it reaches the head of the chain, the System file. If the resource cannot be found anywhere, GetResource returns a nil handle. This mechanism allows you to write an application that overrides a standard system resource simply by having a resource of the same type and ID in your application's resource fork. You can use the UseResFile procedure to start the scope of a search somewhere "beneath" the most recently opened resource file.

There is a current limitation of 2,727 resources in any given file. Because the icons of applications are maintained as resources in the hidden Desktop file used by the Finder, there is a limit to the number of different applications with different icons that can be used on a given disk. If you archive lots of applications on a CD-ROM drive, you can easily hit this limit. The solution is to use the Desktop Manager, an INIT that comes with AppleShare that maintains icons and other Finder information in two hidden files called Desktop DB and Desktop DF. The Desktop information is kept in the data forks of these files and managed via B-trees rather than by being stored in the resource fork of the single Desktop file. Using the Desktop Manager greatly improves performance with large numbers of files on a hard disk, because the Resource Manager was not designed to be used as a database.

Resource Attributes

Each resource also has a set of resource attributes that specify how the resource is to be treated in memory. Starting with bit 1 of the attribute word, the resource attributes are: changed, preloaded, protected, locked, purgeable, and to be loaded into the system heap rather than the application heap.

To open a resource fork, use `OpenResFile` or `OpenRFPerm`, which return -1 if the file cannot be opened. There are routines to get information about resources, to modify resources, to change resource attributes, and to retrieve the resources themselves.

All resources are relocatable objects, and they may be manipulated by means of handles. These handles may be locked or otherwise marked if the resource attributes so indicate. If your program calls `SetResLoad(FALSE)` before `GetResource`, an empty handle (pointer to a nil master pointer) is returned and the resource is not read into memory. This should be done only for short periods of time, because many parts of the Toolbox expect `SetResLoad` to be turned on. Thus, leaving `SetResLoad FALSE` can cause a program to die a silent but painful death.

To access the actual resource, double dereference its handle. If the object or its attributes are changed, only the resource map is modified. The actual data is changed on disk only when the application terminates (the resource fork is automatically closed) or when `WriteResource`, `UpdateResFile`, or `CloseResFile` is called. Note that your application must call `ChangeResource` to tell the Resource Manager when a resource has been changed.

A resource that has the purgeable attribute set obviously can be purged by the operating system. Before using such a resource, make a call to `LoadResource` to ensure that the resource is in memory.

If a resource file is closed, all of its resources are purged. This can be a problem if you are still relying on such a resource. If you need a resource from a file that will be closed before you use the resource, the solution is as follows: before the resource file is closed, do a `DetachResource`. This routine will uncouple the actual data from the resource map.

You can copy a resource file most efficiently by using `OpenRF`, which will open the resource fork as if it was a data fork, without reading the resource map into memory. The resulting refNum can then be passed to `Read` the file. This is the way the Finder and MPW Shell copy resource forks, for example. It is not wise from a compatibility standpoint to have your application try to play Resource Manager itself when opening the file via `OpenRF`; it is best to always use the Resource Manager calls for manipulating individual resources. Be careful not to use both `OpenRF` and `OpenResFile` to open the same resource fork at the same time. It would be bad.

Resource Manager Routines

The Resource Manager is initialized by the System on start-up by a call to `InitResources`, and each time an application is launched `RsrcZoneInit` is also called automatically. To create a resource fork, use `CreateResFile`, and to open one, use `OpenResFile` or `OpenRFPerm` (the latter allows you to specify access privileges). `CloseResFile` does the obvious. Resource Manager errors are reported through `ResError`, which in a bulletproof application should be called after every Resource

Manager call to check if things went as expected. You can manipulate the ordering of resource maps with `CurResFile`, `HomeResFile`, and `UseResFile`.

Information about resources is available through calls to `CountTypes`, `GetIndType`, `CountResources`, `SizeResource`, `MaxSizeRsrc`, `GetResAttrs`, and `GetResInfo`. Create unique resource IDs through `UniqueID`. To bring resources into memory from disk, call `GetResource`, `GetNamedResource`, and `GetIndResource`.

The 128 KB ROMs also introduced a set of one-level-deep counterparts to many of these calls. They include `Count1Types`, `Get1IndType`, `Count1Resources`, `Unique1ID`, `Get1Resource`, `Get1NamedResource`, and `Get1IndResource`. `RGetResource` will also allow your application to look through ROMed resources. The one-deep calls are a way of looking in a single file without having the Resource Manager look at other files in the resource chain. They are useful for tools that list the actual resource contents of a file, for example.

When a resource has been purged and needs to be loaded back into memory, `LoadResource` will do the job. When a resource is no longer needed, `ReleaseResource` frees up the memory occupied by a specified resource. `DetachResource` may be called to make an existing RAM-resident resource a non-resource. In this case, if the resource file to which the resource belongs is closed, the resource will stay resident rather than being purged. `SetResLoad` allows empty handles to be returned rather than actually reading the resource in from disk.

Resources can be modified by `SetResInfo` and `SetResAttrs`. Calling `ChangedResource` notifies the Resource Manager that you want the changes to be written back to disk. These changes are not written until the file is closed, `UpdateResFile` is called, or the `WriteResource` routine is called explicitly. `SetResPurge` allows the Resource Manager to be called by the Memory Manager when purgeable (but perhaps changed) resources are about to be purged. The Resource Manager responds by writing changed resources via `WriteResource`. You can add and delete resources from a file using `AddResource` and `RmveResource`. Advanced routines include `RsrcMapEntry`, `GetResFileAttrs`, and `SetResFileAttrs`.

The Event Manager

Events and their proper handling are the core of all Macintosh applications. The Event Manager, which was written by Andy Hertzfeld, records and delivers events through an event queue on a FIFO (first in, first out) basis. The events are always returned on a priority basis, with priority one first, priority two next, etc. The defined events and their priorities are shown in the following table.

Event	Bit	Priority
(Not used)	0	Null events are 5
Mouse down	1	2
Mouse up	2	2
Key down	3	2
Key up	4	2
Auto key repeat	5	3
Update	6	4
Disk-inserted	7	2
Activate	8	1
(Reserved for future)	9	—
Network	10	2
Device driver	11	2
Application 1	12	2
Application 2	13	2
Application 3	14	2
Suspend/Resume	15	1

The events called Application 1, Application 2, and Application 3 in the preceding table are for a program's own use. A good use of them would be in a simulation application. However, they are gradually being taken over for system use. (Suspend/Resume used to be the Application 4 event.) If you do need your own events, use the Application 1 event and use the other fields of the EventRecord to signal various events.

The key routine of a Macintosh main event loop is its call to GetNextEvent to obtain the next queued event. MultiFinder uses this routine to give time to background applications. Before reporting an event to a requestor, GetNextEvent calls SystemEvent to see if the event belongs to a desk accessory. If it does, the event is given to the desk accessory rather than to the application. GetNextEvent returns an event record, which gives an event code, an event message, the time, mouse location, and modifier flags. Events are measured to a resolution of one tick, or 1/60th of a second. TickCount also returns the current number of ticks since the Macintosh was booted. Other flavors of GetNextEvent are also supported. WaitNextEvent adds a few more parameters for more precise tuning of background operation with MultiFinder, and EventAvail acts just like GetNextEvent but leaves the event in the queue rather than removing it.

GetOSEvent and OSEventAvail are register-based versions of GetNextEvent and EventAvail that do not call SystemEvent or process FKEYs. Finally, you can post an event to the queue with the register-based PostEvent, and you can clear events from the queue collectively or selectively with the register-based FlushEvents.

Although an InitEvents call does exist, FlushEvents is used instead to initialize the Event Manager when starting an application. InitEvents actually allocates space in the system heap for the event queue. It is automatically called once by the start-up code. If it were called again, the old queue would be left in the heap as garbage. In addition, the Event Manager relies upon the Window Manager. In the unusual circumstance that the Event Manager is needed without the Window Manager, the low-memory global WindowList should be set to NIL.

FKEYs

GetNextEvent also screens out FKEYs—key-down events in which the Command and Shift keys are held down when a non-keypad number is typed. The following table lists the Mac's predefined FKEYs.

FKEY Number	Location	Purpose
1	In ROM	Ejects internal disk
2	In ROM	Ejects external disk
3	In System file	Dumps screen to disk
4	In System file	Prints screen to IW

FKEYs 3 to 9 and zero can be added to or modified, but FKEYs 1 and 2 are in ROM and hence are unchangeable. Source code to a few example FKEYs is presented at the end of the chapter.

Mouse Events

In addition to using mouse-up and mouse-down events that return the mouse position in global coordinates, you can also find the current mouse location in the local coordinates of the current GrafPort with GetMouse, check to see if the mouse button is currently down with Button, check if the button is still down (without having been released) after a mouse-down event with StillDown, and finally distinguish a double click from a mouse-up with WaitMouseUp.

The modifiers field of the EventRecord also allows you to check whether the Option, Shift, or Command keys were down at the time of the mouse click. The only way to check for various keys while the mouse button is down is to check the current keymap via GetKeys.

For most buttons, your application should determine whether the button has been clicked on by checking for a mouse-up event; this gives the user the option to move off of the button as a means of canceling the operation of clicking on the button in the first place. Any button that could have destructive consequences should respond to a mouse-up rather than a mouse-down event.

Mouse-down events differ from mouse-up events in that an event is posted immediately. A good use of mouse-down events is illustrated by HyperCard. A button in a HyperCard stack that causes the next card of the stack to be revealed works better with a mouse-down handler than a mouse-up handler. The difference is subtle: a mouse-up type of button does its action exactly once, when the button is released, so only the next card can be reached with a mouse-up handler. A mouse-down type of button does its action at least once; if the script is written properly, the action is done over and over again until the mouse is finally released. For a non-destructive operation such as scanning through cards in a stack, a mouse-down handler is superior to a mouse-up handler.

Key Events

Key codes are reported via the event message field in two different ways. The standard—and most compatible—way is to rely upon the ASCII character code given in the low byte of the message. The second byte (bits 8 to 15) of the message field contains the actual key code, which varies between the various Macintosh keyboards. The third byte (bits 16 to 23) contains the ADB address on ADB keyboards. The keyboard-specific method is to use GetKeys, which returns a bit map of key codes.

Key-up events are rarely used. Auto-key events are posted at a rate based on the current low memory values of KeyThresh and KeyRepThresh, both of which are set by the Control Panel. In addition, the modifier flags field reports on the status of the keys that do not have their own key codes. The key modifier bits are set if the corresponding key is down. The currently defined modifiers are listed in the following table.

Modifier	Bit of the Modifier Flag Field
Window activate	0
Mouse up	7
Command	8
Shift	9
Caps Lock	10
Option	11
Control	12

The Macintosh, like almost all American computers, uses a variation of the ASCII character set. The only standard control characters used by Macintosh are Backspace (8), Tab (9) and Carriage Return (13). The Enter (3) and Arrow keys (28–31) are non-standard uses of these control characters. See Appendix A for a table of the Macintosh character set.

Activate and Update Events

Activate events are the highest-priority events and are never actually posted to the event queue. They occur whenever a window is clicked on to bring it to the top. A maximum of two such events can be pending: an deactivate of one window followed by a corresponding activate of another window. An update event is generated whenever a window's contents have been obscured and need to be redrawn. The event message for both events is a pointer to the window record of the appropriate window. Methods for handling activate and update events are discussed further in the Window Manager section of this chapter.

Other Events

Whenever a disk is inserted in the computer, a disk-inserted event is posted, with the message containing the drive number in the lower word of the event message and the File Manager result code in the high-order word. This result code is obtained through the automatic call the system makes to `MountVol` when this event is generated. If the result code is non-zero, a call to `DIBadMount` may be appropriate. This will bring up the standard disk-initialization dialogs.

Suspend and resume events are posted by MultiFinder when layers are being switched. Typically, your application should deactivate/activate its windows and export/import its scrap to the clipboard when it receives these events. Your application can also define and send events to itself by using `PostEvent`. Network events and device driver events are largely unused.

An obscure low-memory variable at $100 called `MonkeyLives` can be used when random events are posted to an application. MacPaint, for example, checks to see if this word of memory is other than $FFFF. If it is, MacPaint will not quit. This feature was used in the early days of Macintosh testing in conjunction with a desk accessory written by Steve Capps, called the Monkey, that posted random keyboard and mouse events for stress-testing purposes.

The Window Manager

The Window Manager handles multiple overlapping windows. Originally written in Pascal by Bill Atkinson for the Lisa, it was translated to assembly language by Andy Hertzfeld for the Macintosh.

The Window Manager is fired up by a call to `InitWindows` after QuickDraw and the Font Manager have been initialized. Among other things, this draws the Desktop, which is actually a special port called the `WMgrPort`. The routines `GetWMgrPort` and `GetCWMgrPort` return a pointer to this port. Drawing directly into the Window Manager Port has always been discouraged, but it is now dangerous when MultiFinder is running because many different applications share the screen.

The Window Manager allows different kinds of windows to be created. The standard types of windows are listed in the following table.

Window Definition ID	Window Name
0	Standard document
1	Modal dialog / alert box
2	Plain box (no shadow)
3	Plain box with shadow
4	Document with no grow box
8	Document with zoom box
12	Document with zoom, no grow
16	Rounded corner w/black title

You can create custom windows by writing a window definition (WDEF) procedure.

The Desktop is drawn as a rounded rectangle with a 16-pixel curvature at the corners, using pattern PAT 16 (or ppat if Color QuickDraw is installed) from the System file. In addition, the Mac II SetDeskCPat call sets the current color Desktop pattern. The size and shape of the current Desktop are stored in a RgnHandle kept in the low-memory global called GrayRgn at $9EE.

Each window has its own GrafPort, which is actually the first part of a larger WindowRecord. Windows have at least two regions: the content region is the region into which an application can draw, and the structure region is the entire window, including its frame, which the Window Manager draws.

Your application can create a window on the fly using NewWindow or NewCWindow, or it can retrieve a window's description from a WIND resource via GetNewWindow and GetNewCWindow. One advantage to the latter calls is that a custom color palette will be loaded automatically on Mac II family machines if a pltt resource of the same ID as the WIND resource is present in the resource file. SetWinColor and GetAuxWin allow the colors of a window on Mac IIs to be further modified. The default colors for windows are stored in a wctb resource of ID zero in the System file. Windows are usually closed by DisposeWindow. CloseWindow is a variant that does not release the window record memory.

Drawing in Windows

Drawing in a window should usually be done in response to an update event, and such drawing is bracketed with calls to BeginUpdate and EndUpdate. When your application needs to change the contents of a window, it can add areas to the current update region by calls to InvalRect and InvalRgn. The actual drawing can then be done in response to the official update event received via GetNextEvent. If the application knows that certain areas are up to date, it can call ValidRect and ValidRgn to inform the Window Manager of such areas.

The Window's title can be retrieved and changed with GetWTitle and SetWTitle; a window can be hidden or shown using HideWindow, ShowWindow, and ShowHide; a particular window can be made active (topmost) by a call to SelectWindow, which also deactivates any current active window and does the appropriate highlighting/

unhighlighting (a separate call to HiliteWindow is also provided). Windows can be rotated by BringToFront and SendToBack; the grow box is redrawn when needed by DrawGrowIcon, and the current front window can be determined by FrontWindow.

When there is a mouse event, a call to FindWindow determines which window was clicked in, and where. Window parts are categorized as shown in the following table.

Name	Value	Description
inDesk	0	None of the following
inMenuBar	1	In the main menu bar
inSysWindow	2	In a desk accessory
inContent	3	In the content region
inDrag	4	In the title bar
inGrow	5	In active grow box
inGoAway	6	In active go-away box
inZoomIn	7	To zoom smaller
inZoomOut	8	To zoom larger

Once the part is determined, the appropriate action should be taken. For example, the size and location of a window can be changed with DragWindow, GrowWindow, and ZoomWindow. TrackGoAway and TrackBox provide animation for these boxes in the title bar. In addition, SizeWindow and MoveWindow are provided for non-interactive window manipulation.

Auxiliary Window Routines

GetWindowPic and SetWindowPic are used to store a PicHandle in the Window Record. Setting this field causes the Window Manager to call DrawPicture instead of generating any update events for a window. This is especially useful for a window whose contents are static. GetWVariant returns a code about the type of window, with negative numbers being system windows (desk accessories). SetWRefCon and GetWRefCon are used to store an application-specific piece of information in the Window Record.

The PinRect and DragGrayRgn, utility routines called by DragWindow, are useful for dragging objects other than windows. Several low-level routines do the bulk of the window updating and region maintenance. They include CheckUpdate, ClipAbove, SaveOld, DrawNew, PaintOne, PaintBehind, CalcVis, and CalcVisBehind.

The Control Manager

The Control Manager, which was written by Andy Hertzfeld, handles controls such as buttons and check boxes, associating them with a window. The standard controls are listed in the following table.

Control Definition ID	Description
0	Simple button
1	Check box
2	Radio button
16	Scroll bar

You can also create custom controls known as CDEFs. Each control can also have an associated action procedure that provides a degree of animation when the control is being accessed.

Each control has one or more parts. The following table lists the various part codes for the standard controls.

Name	Value	Description
—	0	entire control active
inButton	10	regular button
inCheckBox	11	check box / radio btn.
inUpButton	20	scroll bar up arrow
inDownButton	21	scroll bar down arrow
inPageUp	22	scroll bar page up rgn
inPageDown	23	scroll bar page down
inThumb	129	scroll bar thumb
—	255	entire control inactive

Each control has a control record that contains information relating the control to a window; a link to the next control for the window; the window's title, size, and state; and a handle to its control definition function. No special initialization is needed for the Control Manager, but QuickDraw, the Font Manager, and the Window Manager do need to have been initialized.

Controls are either created by calling `NewControl` or brought in from disk as `CNTL` resources by calling `GetNewControl`. They can be disposed of individually by calling `DisposeControl`, or all controls for a given window can be disposed simultaneously by calling `KillControls`. Disposing of or closing a window automatically removes the controls.

If a user clicks on a control, `GetNextEvent` reports a mouse-down event that `FindWindow` reports to be associated with a certain window. If the window part is in the content region, your application can call `FindControl` to determine if a control was clicked on, and finally it can call `TrackControl`, `DragControl`, and `HiliteControl` to actually modify the control. The control's settings can be inspected and changed with `SetCtlValue`, `GetCtlValue`, `SetCtlMin`, `GetCtlMin`, `SetCtlMax`, and `GetCtlMax`.

To resize a window that has scroll bars, use `MoveControl` and `SizeControl` to change the size and position of its scroll bars. Other calls that affect the appearance of controls include `GetCTitle` and `SetCTitle`, which change the control's title, and `HideControl` and `ShowControl`, which make controls invisible or visible. Your application should always respond to update events by calling `DrawControls`, `Draw1Control`, or `UpdtControl`. This last routine is faster because it allows an update region to be specified.

Miscellaneous routines include `GetCRefCon` and `SetCRefCon`, which store 4 bytes of specific data in the Control Record (or a handle to a larger block of data); `TestControl`, a low-level utility called by other parts of the Control Manager; `GetCtlAction` and `SetCtlAction`, which manipulate a control's action procedure; `GetCVariant`, which returns the CDEF's variant control value; and for the Mac II, `GetAuxCtl` and `SetCtlColor`, which get and set colored controls. System defaults for control colors are kept in the System file as a `cctb` resource of ID zero.

The standard controls are not perfect for all situations. Sometimes a custom control (CDEF) needs to be created. When designing a user interface, consider how often a control is going to be used and how many different states it needs to represent. If only two states are needed, maybe a checked menu item would be better. Scroll bars may be appropriate for a word processor but perhaps are not the right navigational tool for hypertext. Make sure that operations that need to be executed often are accessible and quick to use.

The Menu Manager

The Menu Manager, which was written by Andy Hertzfeld, handles the pull-down menus used by applications. The Menu Manager is initialized by calling `InitMenus`. To create menus in memory, call `NewMenu`; to bring them in from `MENU` resources, call `GetMenu`. Items can be added to a specific menu through `AppendMenu`, `AddResMenu`, `InsertResMenu`, or `InsMenuItem`. Up to this point, the menus are not associated with the menubar. To do that, call `InsertMenu`. Hierarchical and pop-up menus can be formed by passing -1 as the behindID to `InsertMenu`. Finally, to actually see anything, call `DrawMenuBar`.

Certain characters, when they appear in a data string passed to `AppendMenu`, are given special interpretation; these characters are listed in the following table.

Character	Modifier	Definition
-		Creates a blank item
(		Disables item
;		Separates items
^	num	Uses ICON num
!	char	Marks item with char
<	B, I, U, O, S	Sets style of item
/	char	Keyboard equivalent

Menu items can be deleted by calling `DelMenuItem`, a whole menu can be removed by calling `DeleteMenu`, and all menus can be removed by calling `ClearMenuBar`. Finally, to release the memory used by the menus, call `DisposeMenu` for menus created by `NewMenu` and call `ReleaseResource` for menus brought in as resources via `GetMenu`.

Your application can bring in a set of menus from disk as a MBAR resource by calling `GetNewMBar`. It can save and restore menu bars by calling `GetMenuBar` and `SetMenuBar`. (`DrawMenuBar` still needs to be called after `SetMenuBar`.)

`MenuSelect` does the work of drawing menus when the user is browsing with the mouse down in the menubar. It returns a `LongInt` that contains the menu chosen in the high word and the item number returned in the low word. `MenuSelect` calls `SystemMenu` if the selected menu is owned by a desk accessory. Keyboard shortcuts are handled via `MenuKey`, which maps a character to a menu number and item number pair. A call to `Delay` for about 5 ticks will make sure the menu title is highlighted long enough to be visible. Once the menu number and item number pair are known, the appropriate routines can be called to process the menu request; a call to `HiliteMenu` is appropriate to unhighlight the menu when the operations are completed.

Menu items can be manipulated with `SetItem` and `GetItem`. Menus and items that are not appropriate at a given instant in time should be dimmed by a call to `DisableItem`. `EnableItem` allows a menu and/or items to again be chosen. Menu items can also be marked with `CheckItem`, `SetItemMark`, `GetItemMark`, `SetItemIcon`, `GetItemIcon`, `SetItemStyle`, and `GetItemStyle`.

Miscellaneous routines include `CalcMenuSize`, `CountMItems`, `GetMHandle`, `FlashMenuBar`, and `SetMenuFlash`. `InitProcMenu` should be called when a custom menu bar definition (MBDF) is used. Color menus are supported on the Mac II family of machines with `DelMCEntries`, `GetMCInfo`, `SetMCInfo`, `DispMCInfo`, `GetMCEntry`, and `SetMCEntries`. Default menu colors are stored as mctb 0 in the System file. Your application can manipulate hierarchical submenus with `GetItemCmd` and `SetItemCmd`, and it can use `PopUpMenuSelect` to handle pop-up menus. `MenuChoice` allows a Mac II to report the selection of a disabled menu item.

Menus and the User Interface

The use of hierarchical menus should be kept to a minimum, as they are quirky and frustrating for most users. They also encourage you to put too many items into the menus, thus making your applications complex. If you feel you need to use hierarchical menus because you have lots of menu items, sit down and rethink your design. Perhaps a simple dialog or even a single custom control could portray a wide range of options with a simpler interface. Imagine the complexity the Color Picker would have had if it had been done with hierarchical menus . . . not to mention the aesthetic disaster it would have been.

Pop-up menus, on the other hand, are an efficient technique that seems to work out well for options that are changed rarely or for choosing amongst a list of choices that need not be studied in order to decide what is needed. If a list of choices needs to be studied, consider creating a scrolling list using the List Manager, and forget menus altogether because holding the mouse down for long periods of time increases user stress.

Remember that each part of the Macintosh User Interface has its place, and learning the strengths and weaknesses of each part will allow you to develop much smoother programs than would result from your trying to shoehorn every choice into a menu.

TextEdit

TextEdit is a set of routines that are useful for basic text editing on quantities of text up to 32,000 characters. TextEdit was written by Steve Capps for editing text in dialog boxes, not as a true word processor. Originally there were plans for a more powerful set of text routines called CoreEdit that could be used by a word processor. CoreEdit never became part of System software; instead it became MacWrite.

To initialize TextEdit, call TEInit. QuickDraw, the Font Manager, and the Window Manager must already have been initialized. TENew creates a relocatable record that contains information about the text. TEDispose releases all memory used by TextEdit when the TERec is no longer needed.

To associate text with a TERec, call TEGetText and TESetText. Your program can give the user visual cues by calling TEIdle to flash the insertion point and TESetSelect to select text. TEActivate and TEDeactivate should be called to properly highlight and unhighlight the selection and insertion point when a window receives activate events. To draw text in response to update events, use TEUpdate; TextBox, which creates a temporary TERec, may also be used to draw text.

Your application can manipulate text by calling TEKey, TECut, TECopy, TEPaste, TEDelete, and TEInsert. The TextEdit scrap can be imported and exported by calling TEFromScrap, TEToScrap, TEScrapHandle, TEGetScrapLen, and TESetScrapLen. To recompute line starts, call TECalText, and to set up a custom word break routine, use SetWordBreak. Justification can be set via TESetJust, and text can be scrolled with `TEScroll` and `TEPinScroll`. Automatic scrolling can be enabled by calling `TEAutoView`, with `TESelView` causing the current selection to be scrolled into view.

Style TextEdit is found in ROM on newer Macs and is back-patched in the more recent Systems. It allows a single TERec to contain multiple fonts, sizes, styles, and colors. Various routines are provided to work with style runs, including `TEGetOffset`, `TEStylNew`, `TEStylPaste`, `TESetStyle`, `TEGetStyle`, `TEReplaceStyle`, `GetStylHandle`, `SetStylHandle`, `GetStylScrap`, `TEStylInsert`, `TEGetPoint`, and `TEGetHeight`. The `styl` resource format allows styled text to be shared between applications via the Clipboard.

The Dialog Manager

Dialogs are similar to windows, but controls are associated with them automatically. The Dialog Manager, written by Bruce Horn and Steve Capps, automatically handles many details of dealing with windows and events for the programmer.

Dialog boxes are usually of two types: modal and modeless. Modal dialog boxes do not go away and cannot be covered by other windows until the user performs some action. Modeless dialog boxes behave much like regular windows. Standard File's save and open dialogs are examples of modal dialogs.

A special simple case of a dialog is an alert, which is always modal. Both alerts and dialogs require a `DITL` resource that lists the items associated with the dialog. The standard item types that can be used in a dialog are listed in the following table.

Item Type	Description
0	Application defined item (dialogs only)
4	Standard button control
5	Standard check box control
6	Standard radio button control
7	Control defined in CNTL resource
8	Static text
16	Editable text (dialogs only)
32	Icon
64	QuickDraw picture
128	Add to other IDs if disabled

The Dialog Manager is initialized by calling `InitDialog`. A resume procedure pointer is optionally passed to this routine, which is stored in the low-memory global named `ResumeProc`. When a System Error occurs—a bomb—the dialog has two buttons: restart and resume. Resume is active only if the `InitDialog` call has set up a resume routine to call. Few applications support this, but the MPW Shell does.

To create a dialog on the fly, use `NewDialog` or `NewCDialog` (creates a color `GrafPort`); to create one from a `DLOG` resource, use `GetNewDialog`. You can dispose of a dialog with `DisposeDialog`, or if you supplied the memory for the DialogRecord, with `CloseDialog`. If a dialog may be needed, you can reserve memory for the dialog by calling `CouldDialog`, which brings the `DLOG` in from disk and makes it unpurgeable. `FreeDialog` makes it purgeable again. Color dialog defaults are stored in the System as `actb` 0 for alerts, `dctb` 0 for dialogs, and `ictb` for item lists.

To handle events in a modal dialog, call `ModalDialog`, which in turn calls `GetNextEvent` and `SystemTask`. Your application should provide a filter procedure that determines which events will cause `ModalDialog` to complete. This procedure is like a mini-main event loop.

Modeless dialogs are best treated by first calling `GetNextEvent` to obtain an event and then calling `IsDialogEvent`, which inspects the event to determine if it applies. If it does, the next step is to call `DialogSelect`, which actually handles most events. Your application will again need to have a filter procedure to provide application-specific control of actions in the dialog.

Detailed information about a dialog item is accessed with `GetDItem` and `SetDItem`, and individual items can be displayed or hidden by `ShowDItem` and `HideDItem`. `FindDItem` is useful for finding out which item is where so that the cursor can be changed if needed.

You can perform standard TextEdit operations on the editable text of a dialog box with the glue routines `DlgCut`, `DlgCopy`, `DlgPaste`, and `DlgDelete`. Static text can be changed by calling `ParamText`, and both static and editable text can be manipulated with `GetIText`, `SetIText`, and `SelIText`. The text of dialogs is by default always in the System font (that is, Chicago). To display static and editable text in a different font, set a low-memory global by calling the glue routine `DlgFont`; the titles of controls will still be displayed in the System font.

If you want a dialog to display information to the user without requiring any user interaction, use `DrawDialog`. `UpdtDialog` is a faster version that uses a supplied update region, normally the visRgn of the window. Normally, `DialogSelect` and `ModalDialog` handle all drawing and updating of a dialog.

Alerts are a special case of dialogs that incorporate sounds to inform the user of problems. Alerts are not as flexible as dialogs in the types of items they can support, but they are the most self-contained routines possible. A single ROM call creates a window, handles events and interactions with its own event procedures, tracks controls, draws and updates the window, and finally disposes of the window, returning a result. You can create alerts by calling `Alert`, `StopAlert`, `NoteAlert`, or `CautionAlert`, all of which retrieve `ALRT` resources. The latter three calls are the same as `Alert`, but they also draw one of three standard alert icons found in the System. `CouldAlert` and `FreeAlert` act analogously to the dialog routines of similar name. Alerts can use the system beep sound (the default), or you can install a custom sound routine by calling `ErrorSound`. Alerts do their work by calling `NewDialog`, `ModalDialog`, and `DisposeDialog`.

Dialogs and the User Interface

The Dialog Manager is not the sole component of a good user interface. Compared to menus, for example, dialogs are slow. Another drawback is that dialogs are usually modal, and a motto of Macintosh development has always been *no modes*! Then why are modal dialogs used? Well, if there is a major error, or if the program cannot proceed without getting the answer to a question, a modal dialog is perfect. It forces the user to concentrate on the problem at hand. Many choices are not that time-critical, however, and in such cases modeless dialogs or menus should be used instead.

An increasingly common dialog design problem has to do with buttons and their sizes and placement. Although this may seem like a minor issue, users have come to expect a standard user interface on the Macintosh, and it has recently become diluted.

All buttons should be 20 pixels high. Larger buttons are ugly; smaller buttons do not allow any room for the button's title.

The default button should be highlighted to identify the action that will take place when Return or Enter is pressed. Normally when users choose a menu item that brings up a dialog box, they want to do what the menu item suggested. Therefore, the default button should be the affirmative action, the "OK" or "Yes" option rather than the "No" or "Cancel" option. About the only exception to this I can think of is the erasing of an entire disk, which probably should have its default be "Cancel" because of the catastrophic nature of a possible mistake.

Even Apple has begun to forget this recommendation. For example, recent versions of the Font/DA Mover always ask, "Are you sure you want to remove that font?" when a user clicks on "Remove" and the default button says "Cancel." When users click on "Remove," 98 percent of the time they mean just that: they want the font removed. The appearance of the dialog with an option to cancel is forgiving enough for users who really did not want to remove the font. So if a dialog is to appear at all, the default should be "Yes, do what I just told you to do—that is, remove the font!"

If the environment becomes overly protective, and everything requires multiple confirmations and a dozen keystrokes just to do what the menu or button originally suggested, the Macintosh is complicating matters—and the computer is supposed to simplify our lives, right?

Another problem is that many applications that do highlight default buttons do so in an ugly manner, with the highlighting being too fat or too thin. It is a matter of aesthetics. An application needs to look clean and consistent. Here are three simple lines of Pascal that will create the standard highlight around a button whose rectangle has been retrieved via GetDItem:

```
PenSize(3,3);
InsetRect(displayRect,-4,-4);
FrameRoundRect(displayRect,16,16);
```

One final problem with dialog design has to do with the placement of buttons. Figure 4–1 shows an ideal dialog box.

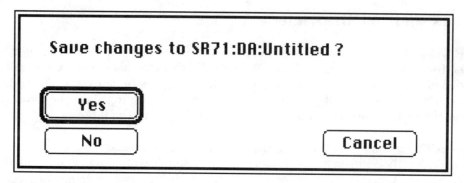

Figure 4–1: An Ideal Dialog Box

Why is this dialog ideal? The most common action is highlighted as the default, and the "Cancel" button is down and to the right of the other options that will alter data. *"Cancel" should always be down and to the right of other buttons.* Normally, it is desirable to save the changes, so the "Yes" option is rightly the default action. The "No" option also affects things: it will discard all of the user's work. But "Cancel" will effectively do nothing. If a user is wandering through menus bringing up dialog boxes, the "Cancel" button should be in the same location in all of these dialog boxes so that it is easy to back out of something that might not do what was desired.

Unfortunately, in some recent applications, the "OK" button has been put in the lower right corner, which is inconsistent with the Interface Guidelines.

It is nice to provide a keyboard equivalent for the three most common buttons. In this case (taken from the MPW Shell), the letter "Y" or Enter or Return will select "Yes"; the letter "N" will select "No"; and Command period (the universal cancel keyboard operation) will cancel the entire operation.

To summarize:

- Buttons are always 20 pixels high.
- Highlighting is always done with a 3-pixel pen, 4 pixels out from the button.
- "OK" or "Yes" is almost always the default and should be placed above "Cancel."
- "Cancel" is in the lower right corner and is very rarely the default.
- When there are just a few options, they should have keyboard equivalents.

The Desk Manager

The Desk Manager, written by Andy Hertzfeld, handles desk accessories, the original mini-applications that have proved to be so handy. Techniques for writing a desk accessory are covered in the device driver material found in chapter 2. The Desk Manager acts as the interface to desk accessories from the host applications point of view. Two excellent examples of desk accessory design are found in Donn Denman's Note Pad and Alarm Clock, my two personal favorites (see Figure 4–2).

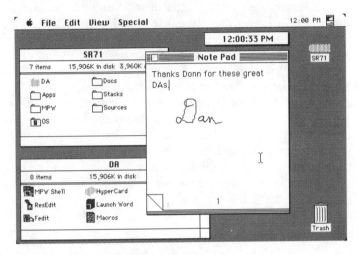

Figure 4–2: Desk Accessories

Desk accessories are always listed in the Apple menu, the very first menu on the menu bar. The first menu item is traditionally an "About" the application item, followed by a disabled line. Then a call to AddResMenu listing all DRVRs adds the names of the available desk accessories to the menu.

When a user makes a choice from the Apple menu (determined by MenuSelect), the application should call GetItem to return the desk accessory name. Then it can call OpenDeskAcc with this name to bring up the DA. CloseDeskAcc requires the driver's refNum, stored in the windowKind field for a DA's window. To give time to a desk accessory for periodic events (like the Alarm Clock's time), call SystemTask. This should be called in the application's main event loop or in interpreter loops so that DAs and drivers everywhere have the time they need for background processing.

When your application is processing events, if FindWindow reports a mouse click in a system window (DA), the application should call SystemClick; if MenuSelect reports a selection from the standard edit menu items (cut, copy, etc.) and a system window is at the front, it should call SystemEdit. SystemEvent and SystemMenu are called for you by their respective managers when needed. That's about all there is to supporting desk accessories.

The Scrap Manager

One of the most powerful yet simple innovations of the Macintosh is the Clipboard, designed by Andy Hertzfeld. Through the Clipboard, data can be passed between applications very easily. With the advent of Switcher, and now MultiFinder, this has become even easier.

Every application should support the Clipboard. Two standard types of data are widely supported: TEXT and PICTs. Your application should support the reading and writing of at least one of these, depending on the nature of the program, and ideally should read both. For example, a word processor should read and write TEXT to the Clipboard and should also be able to bring in a QuickDraw picture as a PICT resource. Your application can also create its own types, carrying more style and format information, if you like. That way a chunk of text with styles can be saved in the Scrapbook, for example, and can be brought back in later without any loss of information.

Using the Clipboard (or scrap) is simple. To figure out what is on the Clipboard, call InfoScrap. To clear the scrap, call ZeroScrap. To store something on the scrap, call PutScrap. Because PutScrap just adds to what is there already, several resource types can be on the scrap simultaneously. To read the scrap, call GetScrap.

The scrap can reside in memory and/or on the disk. If you want to force it to be read into memory, use LoadScrap, and to force it to be written to disk (to save RAM, for instance), call UnloadScrap.

Utilities

There are two sets of useful routines that are all too easy to ignore—the Operating System (OS) Utilities and the Toolbox Utilities.

OS Utilities

Strings may be compared with EqualString or UprString, and Enqueue and Dequeue are used by many OS routines to manage queues. A-trap addresses are manipulated with GetTrapAddress and SetTrapAddress, and parameter RAM is read by InitUtil and written to by WriteParam.

The current date and time, as measured in seconds since January 1, 1904, is returned by ReadDateTime and set with SetDateTime. This long word can be converted to and from a DateTimeRec by Date2Secs and Secs2Date. Two other handy routines include Delay and SysBeep.

Toolbox Utilities

Bit manipulations are supported by `BitTst`, `BitSet`, `BitClr`, `BitAnd`, `BitOr`, `BitXor`, `BitNot`, and `BitShift`. Routines for word manipulations include `HiWord`, `LoWord`, and `LongMul`. Pascal strings can be made relocatable by calling `NewString`, while an existing relocatable string can be changed with `SetString`. `GetString` returns the handle to a string located as a `STR` resource.

A general-purpose byte manipulator is found in the `Munger` function, which basically replaces a target string with a replacement string in a separate destination string. However, depending upon the six parameters passed to it, `Munger` can also do a simple insertion or deletion, or it can just return the location where the target string matches in the destination.

Package Manager

Packages are pieces of code that originally could not fit into ROM on the original Macintosh. Each package contains a set of routines that are selected by a selector passed to the package, along with the parameters to that routine. Since the 64 KB ROM, several of the packages have been put into the more recent and larger ROMs.

The Package Manager is initialized automatically when an application is launched by calling `InitAllPacks`, which in turn calls `InitPack` for each package. There is no public Pack 1, although a private copy of Pack 1 is used by ResEdit.

Pack 0—List Manager

This package debuted with the Macintosh Plus System disk after being developed for use by ResEdit. The List Manager depends on all managers up and through TextEdit in order to function properly. Lists are created with `LNew`, and columns and row can be added and deleted with `LAddColumn`, `LAddRow`, `LDelColumn`, and `LDelRow`; an entire list can be deleted with `LDispose`.

Within each row or column are cells manipulated with `LAddToCell`, `LClrCell`, `LGetCell`, `LSetCell`, `LCellSize`, `LGetSelect`, and `LSetSelect`. The mouse can be tracked with `LClick` and `LLastClick`. Cells can be navigated with `LFind`, `LNextCell`, `LRect`, `LSearch`, and `LSize`. Lists are displayed with `LDraw`, `LDoDraw`, `LScroll`, `LAutoScroll`, `LUpdate`, and `LActivate`. Custom list definitions are also possible.

Pack 2—Disk Initialization

This package contains the disk initialization code and alerts. DILoad brings the package into RAM and makes the code and alerts unpurgeable; DIUnload undoes this action. DIBadMount is the main routine that should be called when a disk-inserted event occurs with a result code in the high-order word of the event message. This means the disk that is inserted should (probably) be erased. DIBadMount puts up an alert and initializes the disk by calling DIFormat, DIVerify, and DIZero. These routines can also be called directly.

Pack 3—StdFile

Four routines are available for putting up standard dialogs for accessing files. SFPutFile allows the user to type a name for saving a file, and SFGetFile allows an existing file to be chosen for opening. SFPPutFile and SFPGetFile allow you to use custom dialog boxes.

Pack 4—SANE Arithmetic

Pack 4 contains the basic floating-point arithmetic functions of addition, subtraction, multiplication, division, remainder, and square root, along with most of the IEEE routines for the SANE environment. This package was disk-based on the original Macintosh, but since the Macintosh Plus, it has been in ROM. More information on SANE is found in chapter 5.

Pack 5—SANE Transcendentals

Pack 5 contains the logarithmic and trigonometric floating-point functions. This package was disk-based on the original Macintosh, but since the Macintosh Plus, it has been in ROM. More information on SANE is found in chapter 5.

Pack 6—International String Utilities

These routines use two resources of type INTL that are in the System file. These resources specify date, time, currency, and measurement formats for different countries. The current date and time are returned in a country-specific style as strings by the IUDateString and IUTimeString routines. IUDatePString and IUTimePString allow you to use a preferred format instead. Strings can be compared with IUMagString and IUMagIDString, the latter of which ignores secondary ordering. IUMetric indicates whether the metric system should be used, and the international resources can be manipulated with the IUGetIntl and IUSetIntl calls.

Pack 7—Binary-Decimal Conversions

This package was disk-based on the original Macintosh, but since the Macintosh Plus, it has been in ROM. It consists of two simple routines for converting integers to and from strings: NumToString and StringToNum. These routines are part of SANE.

Pack 12—Color Picker

Colors on the Macintosh are usually specified with a set of three colors: red, green, and blue. The main routine, called GetColor, allows a color dialog to be called up so that the user can interactively select a color, which is returned as an RGBColor. Several routines provide conversions between various color specifications, including CMY2RGB (cyan, magenta, yellow to RGB), HSL2RGB (hue, saturation, lightness to RGB), HSV2RGB (hue, saturation, value to RGB), and their inverses: RGB2CMY, RGB2HSL, and RGB2HSV. Two conversion routines, Fix2SmallFract and SmallFract2Fix, are provided for the data types used in the HSLColor and HSVColor types.

Dump — C Tool

This MPW tool dumps a hex and an ASCII view of a specified resource or of the entire data fork of any file. The tool is useful for quickly viewing resources.

Given a resource type, resource ID, and a file name, the specified resource will be displayed in hex with its corresponding ASCII version . If a resource type without an ID is specified, this tool functions like the UNIX tool strings: it shows the ASCII printable characters of all of the resources of that type. This is useful for perusing STR and STR# resources, for example.

```
/*
 *   Dump.c  - File or resource text dumper
 *           - Written by Dan Allen 7/13/88
 *           - SetResLoad calls added 9/1/88
 *           - Works on running Shell 12/21/88
 *           - Dumping strings fixed 12/26/88
 *           - Works with both 2.0 & 3.0 C compilers 1/8/89
 *           - Fixed bug when dumping strings 1/21/89
 *           - Spinning cursor added 2/1/89
 */
```

```
#include <CType.h>
#include <CursorCtl.h>
#include <Memory.h>
#include <Resources.h>
#include <StdIO.h>
#include <StdLib.h>
#include <Types.h>

#define fsRdPerm 1

#ifdef ghs /* check for MPW C 2.0 */
#define openrfperm  OpenRFPerm
#endif

typedef unsigned char byte;

Boolean printString;
long    size;
void    PrintBytes();

main(int argc,char *argv[])
{
  Boolean    purgeFlag;
  char       oldState;
  short      refNum,numRsrc,oldResFile;
  long       i;
  Handle     h;
  ResType    rt;

  if (argc < 2) {
    fprintf(stderr,"Dump [type [id]] file > stdout\n");
    return 1;
  }
```

```
  InitCursorCtl(nil);
  if (argc == 2) return DumpFile(argv[1]);
  if (argc == 3) printString = true;

  oldResFile = CurResFile();
  SetResLoad(false);
  refNum = openrfperm(argv[argc-1],0,fsRdPerm);
  SetResLoad(true);
  if (refNum == -1) {
    UseResFile(oldResFile);
    fprintf(stderr,"# OpenRFPerm failed for file: %s\n",argv[argc-1]);
    return 1;
  }

  rt = *((ResType *) argv[1]);
  numRsrc = (argc < 4) ? Count1Resources(rt) : 1;
  for (i = 1; i <= numRsrc; i++) {
    SpinCursor(-10);
    SetResLoad(false);
    h = (argc < 4) ? Get1IndResource(rt,i) : Get1Resource(rt,atoi(argv[2]));
    SetResLoad(true);
    if (h) size = SizeResource(h);
    else {
      UseResFile(oldResFile);
      fprintf(stderr,"# GetResource failed: #%d\n",ResError());
      return 2;
    }
    purgeFlag = *h ? false : true;
    oldState = HGetState(h);
    LoadResource(h);
    if (ResError()) {
      UseResFile(oldResFile);
      fprintf(stderr,"# LoadResource failed.\n");
      return 3;
    }
    HLock(h);
    PrintBytes(*h);
    HUnlock(h);
    HSetState(h,oldState);
    if (purgeFlag) EmptyHandle(h);
  }
  UseResFile(oldResFile);
  return 0;
}
```

```c
static void PrintBytes(byte *p)
{
  byte   c,s[256];
  long   i = 0,len = 0;

  while (size--) {
    c = *p++; i++;
    if (isprint(c)) {
      if (printString) putchar(c);
      else s[len] = c;
      len++;
    }
    if (!printString) {
      printf("%2.2X ",c);
      if (i % 16 == 0) {
        s[len] = '\0';
        printf("\t%s\n",s);
        SpinCursor(2);
        i = len = 0;
      }
    } else if (len > 80) {
      putchar('\n');
      SpinCursor(2);
      len = 0;
    }
  }
  if (!printString && len > 0) {
    s[len] = '\0';
    i = 16 - i;
    while (i--) printf("   ");
    printf("\t%s\n",s);
  }
}

static int DumpFile(char *fileName)
{
  char   *bufin;
  int    err;
  FILE   *input;

  input = fopen(fileName,"r");
  if (!input) {
    fprintf(stderr,"# Cannot open data fork of file %s\n",fileName);
    return 1;
  }
```

```
      fseek(input,0,2);
      size = ftell(input);
      if (size) {
        bufin = malloc(size);
        if (bufin) {
          fseek(input,0,0);
          fread(bufin,1,size,input);
          err = 0;
        }
        else {
          fprintf(stderr,"# Not enough heapspace: %d bytes needed\n",size);
          err = 2;
        }
      } else {
        fprintf(stderr,"# Zero length file: %s\n",fileName);
        err = 1;

      }
      fclose(input);
      if (!err) {
        PrintBytes(bufin);
        free(bufin);
      }
      return err;
}
```

ListRsrc — C Tool

This MPW tool is somewhat similar to the ResEqual that comes with MPW, but it has a nicer two-column format for comparing the resources found in different files. It is very useful, for example, in comparing two slightly different versions of the same application.

This tool also illustrates some of the trickier aspects of manipulating resources. Its use of UseResFile and SetResLoad calls allows it even to list resources from the currently open System or currently running Shell.

Improving ListRsrc

Here are some suggestions for improving ListRsrc:

- Right now ListRsrc considers two resources the same if they are the same type, ID, and size. However, the contents of the resources might be different. Add code to compare the actual bytes of the resources.

- Add an option that allows two individual resources to be considered the same if they are the same type and name rather than the same type and ID. This is useful for CODE resources.

```
/*
 *   ListRsrc.c  - Lists resources from 2 files in a 2 column comparison format
 *               - Written by Dan Allen 10/11/88
 *               - Works on running Shell (UseResFile) 12/21/88
 *               - Works with both 2.0 & 3.0 C compilers 1/8/89
 *               - Spinning cursors added 2/1/89
 *               - Second resource names added 2/6/89
 */

#include <CType.h>
#include <CursorCtl.h>
#include <Memory.h>
#include <Resources.h>
#include <StdIO.h>
#include <StdLib.h>
#include <String.h>
#include <Types.h>

#define fsRdPerm  1
#define MAXRSRC   1000

#ifdef ghs /* check for MPW C 2.0 */
#define getresinfo   GetResInfo
#define openrfperm   OpenRFPerm
#endif
```

```
typedef struct {
  ResType resType;
  short    resID;
  long     size1, size2;
  char     *name1, *name2;
} ResEntry;

static void      FillTable(), DumpTable();
static char      diffFlag,typeFlag,*file1,*file2;
static short     id,refNum1,refNum2,oldResFile,OpenRsrc();
static long      index;
static ResType   rt;
static ResEntry rsrc[MAXRSRC];

main(int argc,char *argv[])
{
  long  i;

  if (argc < 2) {
    fprintf(stderr,"ListRsrc [-d][-t TYPE] file1 [file2]\n");
    return 1;
  }
  InitCursorCtl(nil);
  oldResFile = CurResFile();
  for (i = 1; i < argc; i++) {
    if (argv[i][0] == '-')
      switch (tolower(argv[i][1])) {
        case 'd': diffFlag = true; /* only list resources w/different sizes */
                  break;
        case 't': typeFlag = true; /* only list resources of specified type */
                  rt = *((ResType *) argv[++i]);
                  break;
      }
    else {
      if (!file1) refNum1 = OpenRsrc(file1 = argv[i]);
      else if (!file2) refNum2 = OpenRsrc(file2 = argv[i]);
      else {
        UseResFile(oldResFile);
        fprintf(stderr,"# ListRsrc can only deal with two files at a time.\n");
        return 1;
      }
    }
  }
  if (file1) FillTable(refNum1);
  if (file2) FillTable(refNum2);
  UseResFile(oldResFile);
  DumpTable();
  return 0;
}
```

```c
char *AddName(char *name)
{
  char   *p;
  int    len;

  len = strlen(name);
  p = malloc(len+1);
  if (!p) {
    fprintf(stderr,"# Not enough memory for strcpy in AddName.\n");
    exit(4);
  }
  return strcpy(p,name);
}

void AddToTable(Handle h,long rsrcSize)
{
  char    name[256];
  short   id;
  int     i;
  ResType rt;

  if (index >= MAXRSRC) {
    fprintf(stderr,"# listrsrc's internal resource table is full.\n");
    exit(3);
  }

  getresinfo(h,&id,&rt,name);
  if (CurResFile() == refNum1) {
    rsrc[index].resType = rt;
    rsrc[index].resID = id;
    rsrc[index].size1 = rsrcSize;
    rsrc[index].name1 = AddName(name);
    index++;
  } else {
    for(i = 0; i < index; i++) {
      if (rt == rsrc[i].resType && id == rsrc[i].resID) {
        rsrc[i].size2 = rsrcSize;
        rsrc[i].name2 = AddName(name);
        return;
      }
    }
    rsrc[index].resType = rt;
    rsrc[index].resID = id;
    rsrc[index].size2 = rsrcSize;
    rsrc[index].name2 = AddName(name);
    index++;
  }
}
```

```
void DumpTable()
{
  int i;

  if (file2) {
    printf("Type  ResID     File 1       File 2      Name 1        Name 2\n");
    for(i = 79; i; i--) putchar('-');
    putchar('\n');
  }
  for(i = 0; i < index; i++) {
    if (diffFlag && rsrc[i].size1 == rsrc[i].size2) continue;
    printf("%.4s   %6d",&(rsrc[i].resType),rsrc[i].resID);
    printf("  %6u bytes",rsrc[i].size1);
    if (file2) printf("  %6u bytes",rsrc[i].size2);
    printf("     %-16s",rsrc[i].size1 ? rsrc[i].name1 : "");
    if (file2) printf("%-16s",rsrc[i].size2 ? rsrc[i].name2 : "");
    putchar('\n');
    SpinCursor(2);
  }
}

void FillTable(short refNum)
{
  short   numTypes,numRsrc;
  long    i,j,rsrcSize;
  Handle  h;

  UseResFile(refNum);
  numTypes = (typeFlag) ? 1 : Count1Types();
  for (i = 1; i <= numTypes; i++) {
    SpinCursor(-10);
    if (!typeFlag) Get1IndType(&rt,i);
    numRsrc = Count1Resources(rt);
    for (j = 1; j <= numRsrc; j++) {
      SetResLoad(false);
      h = Get1IndResource(rt,j);
      SetResLoad(true);
      if (h)
        rsrcSize = SizeResource(h);
      else {
        UseResFile(oldResFile);
        fprintf(stderr,"# GetResource failed: #%d\n",ResError());
        exit(2);
      }
      AddToTable(h,rsrcSize);
    }
  }
  UseResFile(oldResFile);
}
```

```
static short OpenRsrc(char *fileName)
{
  short refNum;

  SetResLoad(false);
  refNum = openrfperm(fileName,0,fsRdPerm);
  SetResLoad(true);
  if (refNum == -1) {
    fprintf(stderr,"# OpenRFPerm failed for file: %s\n",fileName);
    exit(1);
  }
  return refNum;
}
```

CleanRsrc — C Tool

This MPW tool deletes the entire contents of a file's resource fork. The MPW Shell does offer the built-in command `delete -r`, which can also remove a resource fork, but this tool checks first to see if there are any resources in the file. If there are, the fork is not deleted unless the `-f`(orce) option is being used.

Why such a tool? It was originally written to recover wasted space left by early versions of HyperCard in its stacks, but since then it has grown to have other uses as well. It is a simple and handy way to make a set of MPW text files all have the same font and size, because it can delete the MPSR resource that contains such information. (New MPSR resources are created automatically when such documents are opened.) Running this tool on MPW Pascal 3.0 source files will remove all of the automatic symbol information as well. (A script just to remove such information can be found in the Pascal chapter of this book.) If you run this tool on an application, you will end up deleting the entire application, so be careful!

This tool deletes the resource fork by opening the resource fork and setting the end of file to the zeroth byte.

```
/*
 * CleanRsrc.c  - Deletes resource forks of the specified files
 *                originally to gain wasted space in HyperCard Stacks.
 *              - Written by Dan Allen 11/24/87
 *              - Added -p and -n options 9/1/88
 *              - Works with both 2.0 & 3.0 C compilers 1/8/89
 */

#include  <CType.h>
#include  <CursorCtl.h>
#include  <Files.h>
#include  <Resources.h>
#include  <StdIO.h>
```

```
#ifdef ghs /* check for MPW C 2.0 */
#define openresfile OpenResFile
#define openrf      OpenRF
#endif

static char forceFlag, noModFlag, progFlag;

main(int argc,char *argv[])
{
  char      s[256],*p;
  short     i, j, err, refNum;
  long      savedDate;
  ParamBlockRec pb;

  InitCursorCtl(0);
  for(i = 1; i < argc; i++)
    if (argv[i][0] == '-')
      switch (tolower(argv[i][1])) {
        case 'f': forceFlag = true; break; /* force the fork to be deleted */
        case 'n': noModFlag = true; break; /* do not change mod date of file */
        case 'p': progFlag = true; break;  /* echo progress to stderr */
        default:  break;
      }

  if (argc < 2) {
    fprintf(stderr, "CleanRsrc [-f][-n][-p] files…\n");
    return 1;
  }
  for (i = 1; i < argc; i++) {
    if (argv[i][0] == '-') continue;

    if (noModFlag) {
      p = argv[i]; j = 1;
      while(*p) s[j++] = *p++;
      s[0] = j-1;
      pb.fileParam.ioNamePtr = s;
      pb.fileParam.ioVRefNum = 0;
      pb.fileParam.ioFVersNum = 0;
      pb.fileParam.ioFDirIndex = 0;
      err = PBGetFInfo(&pb,false);
      savedDate = pb.fileParam.ioFlMdDat;
    }
```

```
    refNum = openresfile(argv[i]);
    if (refNum == -1) continue;

    if (Count1Types() && !forceFlag) {
      if (progFlag)
        fprintf(stderr, "# File: %-19s - Rsrc fork not deleted.\n",argv[i]);
      CloseResFile(refNum);
      continue;
    }
    CloseResFile(refNum);

    err = openrf(argv[i],0,&refNum);
    if (err) {
      fprintf(stderr,"# ERROR: %d\tCannot open file %s\n",err,argv[i]);
      return 2;
    }
    err = SetEOF(refNum, 0);
    if (err) {
      fprintf(stderr,"# ERROR: %d\tCannot set EOF on file %s\n",
              err, argv[i]);
      return 3;
    }
    err = FSClose(refNum);
    if (err) {
      fprintf(stderr,"# ERROR: %d\tCannot close file %s\n", err, argv[i]);
      return 4;
    }
    if (noModFlag) {
      pb.fileParam.ioNamePtr = s;
      pb.fileParam.ioVRefNum = 0;
      pb.fileParam.ioFVersNum = 0;
      pb.fileParam.ioFDirIndex = 0;
      err = PBGetFInfo(&pb,false);
      pb.fileParam.ioFlMdDat = savedDate;
      err = PBSetFInfo(&pb,false);
    }
    if (progFlag)
      fprintf(stderr,"File %-19s # DELETED resource fork.\n",argv[i]);
  }
  return 0;
}
```

`MacsBugKey` — **Assembly Language FKEY**

This is the smallest possible FKEY. It simply drops into MacsBug. To get out of MacsBug, type the letter *g* and press Return. `MacsBugKey` is not as useful as the ADBKey INIT presented in chapter 2 for ADB-equipped Macs, but this FKEY will work on a Mac Plus. If MacsBug is not installed, this FKEY is a fast way of bringing up the bomb box!

```
;; MBKey by Dan Allen
; Select the following 2 lines and press enter to build into the current system
; Asm MacsBugKey.a
; Link -o "{System Folder}System" MacsBugKey.a.o -rt FKEY=6 -sg MacsBugKey


        MAIN
        STRING     ASIS

        bra.s      start
        dc.w       0,'FKEY',6,0
start   dc.w       $A9FF
        rts

        END
```

`RotateWindows` — **Assembly Language FKEY**

This FKEY allows you to cycle through the open windows in any application. It is especially useful in the Finder, where there is no Windows menu. If you have lots of folders open, these 30 bytes of code are pretty handy. . . .

```
; RotateWindows by Dan Allen.  Thanks to Brian Stearns for the idea.
; Select the following 2 lines and press enter to build into the current system
; Asm WRFKey.a
; Link -o "{System Folder}System" WRFKey.a.o -rt FKEY=5 -sg RotateWindows
```

```
        MAIN
        STRING    ASIS

        bra.s     start
        dc.w      0,'FKEY',5,0
start   clr.l     -(sp)              ; function result
        dc.w      $A924              ; FrontWindow: WindowPtr
        tst.l     (sp)               ; is there a window there?
        bne.s     @1                 ; yes, send it to the back
        add.w     #4,sp              ; no, pop stack pointer
        rts                          ; and return
@1      clr.l     -(sp)              ; zero means to the back
        dc.w      $A921              ; SendBehind(wind,behind: WindowPtr)
        rts

        END
```

MFSwitcher — Assembly Language FKEY

Switcher reserved the bracket keys to move between applications, but MultiFinder offers no keyboard facility to change layers. This FKEY partially solves this problem by allowing you to rotate through the various partitions through a simple technique: this FKEY clicks in the upper right corner of the menubar. MultiFinder detects the click and does the switch.

```
; MultiFinder FKEY Switcher
; Written by Dan Allen 2/6/1989
; Select the following 2 lines and press enter to build into the current system
; Asm Switch.a
; Link -o 'HD:System Folder:System' Switch.a.o -rt FKEY=9 -sg MFSwitcher

        MAIN
        STRING    ASIS

        bra.s     start
        dc.w      0,'FKEY',9,0       ; header for FKEY #9
start   tst.l     $B7C               ; test Twitcher2
        ble.s     exit               ; no MF? cruise…

        move.l    $830,-(sp)         ; save current Mouse position
        move.w    $BAA,d0            ; get MBarHeight
        lsr.w     #1,d0              ; divide by 2
        swap      d0
        move.w    $83A,d0            ; grab screen width from CrsrPin
        sub.w     #$18,d0            ; icon offset from right scrn edge
```

```
        move.l  d0,$830         ; stuff Mouse location

        move.w  #1,a0           ; mousedown event (msg undefined)
        dc.w    $A02F           ; PostEvent
        move.l  (sp)+,$830      ; restore Mouse
exit    rts

        END
```

Conclusion

The Toolbox is the foundation on which all Macintosh applications are built. This chapter looked at the important parts of the Toolbox:

- Resource Manager
- Event Manager
- Window Manager
- Control Manager
- Menu Manager
- TextEdit
- Dialog Manager
- Desk Manager
- Scrap Manager
- Utilities
- Package Manager

The code in this chapter illustrated the Resource Manager and the Event Manager. Code in other chapters will illustrate many of the other managers.

Recommended Reading

The single best resource for learning about the Toolbox is *Inside Macintosh*. It is the "Bible" of the Macintosh, and you should read it from cover to cover at least once and refer to it often thereafter. Apple's *Tech Notes* are an on-going addendum to *Inside Macintosh*; they correct errors and provide information about various techniques. Chernicoff's *Macintosh Revealed* is a useful supplement with an alternative view of the Toolbox.

## CHAPTER 5

SANE

This chapter looks at several numerics environments available to developers. The best known is SANE, the Standard Apple Numerics Environment, which is Apple's implementation of the IEEE 754 and IEEE 854 floating-point standards for floating-point arithmetic. (The 754 standard is a binary standard, and 854 is radix-independent.)

This chapter also examines how and when to use the 68881/68882 floating-point coprocessors, the numeric libraries that are part of various programming languages, and the `Fixed` and `Fract` series of traps provided also by the Macintosh OS.

The advantages and disadvantages of each of these various numerics environments are discussed. The trade-offs among speed, accuracy, and portability will be fairly obvious.

Following the discussion of numerics environments is the source code for various MPW tools that illustrate the usage of various numeric functions. The tools are:

- `NumTheory,` which calculates the properties of a given integer
- `Hash,` which measures and analyzes various hashing functions
- `Rand,` which statistically compares several random number generators
- `Solar,` which computes the current position of the sun and planets
- `Sun,` which is a more accurate model of just the sun
- `Det,` which calculates determinants of Finlayson matrices as a test of SANE

SANE Functionality

SANE adheres to the IEEE standards, which specify the following functionality:

- Single-, double-, and extended-precision data formats. (Only single is actually required by the standard.)
- Rounding modes, including round to nearest (tie cases round to even), and directed roundings: round toward $+\infty$, round toward $-\infty$, and round toward 0.
- The operations of add, subtract, multiply, divide, remainder, and square root, with results correctly rounded to the closest possible representation of the infinitely precise result.

- Roundings and conversions between the floating-point formats and integral values, as well as conversions between floating-point and decimal strings.

- Relational comparisons between floating-point numbers, with the four mutually exclusive relations of less than, equal, greater than, and unordered.

- Signed infinities, quiet and signaling NaNs (Not a Number), and signed zeros, including infinity arithmetic.

- Exceptions, including invalid operations, division by zero, overflow, underflow, and inexact operations, along with trap handlers to override the default behavior of exceptional conditions.

History of SANE

Software SANE began life July 3, 1982, when Jerome Coonen began his work on FP68K. Before coming to Apple, Jerome studied for his Ph.D. at the University of California at Berkeley with Professor W. Kahan, who was a major contributor to Hewlett-Packard's HP-38C and HP-15C calculators and the excellent Math ROMs for the HP-71B and HP-75C portable computers. Coonen and Kahan were two of the three primary authors of the early drafts which became the IEEE standards. Thus, it is no accident that Apple's implementation of IEEE arithmetic adheres scrupulously to these standards. Many members of the Apple Numerics Group also contributed, including David Hough, Colin McMaster, Kenton Hanson, Clayton Lewis, and Jim Thomas. In the end, however, it was Jerome who wrote almost every line of SANE in hand-coded 68000 assembly language.

SANE was implemented in three pieces, as shown in the following table.

Package	Name	Functionality
PACK 4	FP68K ($A9EB)	All IEEE except string conversions
PACK 5	Elems68K ($A9EC)	Log, exp, trig, financial functions
PACK 7	DecStr68K ($A9EE)	Decimal scanners and formatter

On the original Macintosh, SANE existed as RAM-based packages kept in the System file, but starting with the Macintosh Plus, SANE was put in ROM and it has stayed there ever since. Only three traps are consumed when the package interface is used. SANE's arguments are pushed onto the stack by address (PEA), first the source and then the destination. Finally a routine selector (opword) is pushed onto the stack to specify which operation to perform.

In addition to the requirements of the IEEE standards, Apple's SANE implements several items that are defined and recommended by the standard, as well as a few features not mentioned by the standard:

- `extended` and `comp` data formats with 80-bit accuracy (18–19 decimal digits)
- The exponential functions e^x, 2^x, $e^x - 1$, $2^x - 1$, x^y
- The logarithmic functions `ln`, `log2`, `ln(1+x)`, `log2(1+x)`
- The trigonometric functions `sin`, `cos`, `tan`, `atan`
- The miscellaneous functions `compound`, `annuity`, and `randomx`
- The auxiliary routines `scalb`, `logb`, `neg`, `abs`, `copysign`, `nextafter`, and `class` for inquiring about parts of numbers

Software SANE versus 68881 SANE

On Macs without a floating-point coprocessor, SANE comes in one flavor: extremely accurate but perhaps a bit slow for intensive number crunching. Most operation destinations are extended-precision, with the resulting intermediate math accurate to 80 or 96 bits.

On Macs equipped with a Motorola 68881 or 68882 floating-point coprocessor, there is a choice to be made. (The 68881 and the 68882 have identical functionality. The 68882 has been re-engineered with hardware pipelining so that, in carefully coded cases, it will run about twice as fast as the 68881. We will just refer to the 68881 and understand that the 68882 is included.) Much of SANE's functionality can be handled in hardware by these chips at much greater speeds, but sometimes with a loss in accuracy.

Although basic arithmetic (+, -, *, /, sqrt, rem), roundings, comparisons, and conversions are identical whether done in hardware or software, the other SANE functions can be less accurate when done by the 68881. For example, `atan(tan(0.5))` is exact with software SANE but not with MC68881 SANE. Software SANE functions, particularly trigonometric, generally provide better accuracy than the 68881. The elementary functions of the chips are generally accurate to double precision, however, and they *do* execute almost 100 times more quickly than software SANE functions.

You can choose which version of SANE to use by compiling code written with MPW C or MPW Pascal using various compile-time options. The `-mc68881` option specifies that you should use the 68881 directly for basic arithmetic and some other operations but use software SANE for the elementary functions. Thus, all results will be identical with or without this option turned on. On 68881-equipped machines, software SANE uses the 68881 for basic math functions, because they return the same results as the software packages and will therefore run faster than the software version.

If speed is desired at the expense of accuracy, the `-elems881` option generates code to call the chip directly for all functions that are available on the chip. If you plan to use either of these options, the math chip must be present or the program will bomb.

How about writing an application that has some modules compiled without direct 881 calls and some modules compiled with 881 calls? You may want to do this in an application that takes advantage of the 881 if it is around but that still will run on a machine that does not have the math chip. Well, there are a few problems with this. First, the extended data formats are different between software and 881 SANE: 80 bits versus 96 bits. The information content is the same, but an extra 16 bits of garbage is inserted between the exponent and mantissa with 881 SANE. This garbage must be taken into account if extendeds are to be used by both versions of SANE. Recent versions of the SANE libraries have routines such as `x96tox80` and `x80tox96` to help with these conversions.

The second problem is that MPW compilers generate 881 code that is executed in the first lines of the run-time initialization if any of the 881 options are specified. In order to have the application run on a machine without an 881, the main program segment must be compiled without any 881 options. A test can then be made to see if an 881 is present; if so, the separated compiled modules built with the 881 options can be called safely.

Portability Among Numeric Environments

The mathematical functions available on the Macintosh with software SANE (which we will refer here to as the PACKs), the 68881, and the standard library functions of C and Pascal create a real portability headache: which calls should you use? For example, if a 68881 is present the following functions are also provided:

- The logarithmic functions 10^x, `log10`
- The trigonometric functions `asin`, `acos`, `sinh`, `cosh`, `tanh`, `atanh`, and `sincos`
- The miscellaneous functions `modulo`, extract mantissa, set condition codes, and multiply and round to single or double precision

The following table shows which functions are implemented where and under what name. In the PACKs column, the hexadecimal selector value is given for those functions implemented by software SANE; in those cases where there are multiple routines that depend upon data format, the routine that returns extended precision is listed. The 68881 column lists the official Motorola names of the floating-point instructions as found in the *MC68881 User's Manual*.

The C routines listed in this table are those that are part of the ANSI C standard <math.h> library. They are implemented in MPW C either as calls to the packages or as direct in-line calls to the 68881, depending upon the state of the compile time flags. Apple extensions to the MPW 3.0 C compiler that appear when you are using the `-mc68881` and `-elems881` flags are marked in this table with an asterisk. These calls are *not* available unless this flag is used. Similarly, the Pascal routines listed are those that are part of ISO standard Pascal, and they, like the C routines, call either the packages or the 881, depending upon the `-mc68881` flag.

A confusing point is that all languages (assembly language, C, and Pascal) can call SANE library routines in addition to using their own standard routines, which are most likely implemented as calls to SANE themselves. For example, ANSI C does not support the IEEE-style remainder, so the table shows a blank for C. But MPW C fully supports SANE, so you can access the IEEE `remainder` function by linking to the `CSANELib.o` library, which will call the PACKs. Alternately, if the `-mc68881` option is turned on and the CSANELib881.o library is linked to instead, the library routine will simply call the chip.

Unless otherwise specified, all arguments and results are of type extended.

Function	PACKs	68881	C	Pascal
Arithmetic	FP68K			
Addition	$0000	FADD	+	+
Subtraction	$0002	FSUB	−	−
Multiplication	$0004	FMUL	*	*
Division	$0006	FDIV	/	/
Remainder, IEEE (rnd to nearest)	$000C	FREM		
Remainder, modulo (rnd to zero)		FMOD	fmod	
Negation	$000D	FNEG		
Absolute value	$000F	FABS	fabs	abs
Copy sign	$0011			
Square root	$0012	FSQRT	sqrt	sqrt
Nextafter	$0013			
Integer part, cur. rounding mode	$0014	FINT		
Integer part, rounded to zero	$0016	FINTRZ	trunc*	trunc
Integer part, rounded to -∞			floor	
Integer part, rounded to +∞			ceil	
Round, ties round away from zero				round
Integer & fractional parts			modf	
Scale x to [.5,1) and a power of 2			frexp	
Scale x by 2^i (i: integer)	$0018	FSCALE	ldexp	
Extract exponent (logb)	$001A	FGETEXP		
Extract mantissa		FGETMAN		
Logarithmic	Elems68K			
Log base e (ln or natural log)	$0000	FLOGN	log	ln
Log base 2	$0002	FLOG2	log2*	
Log (1+x), base e	$0004	FLOGNP1	ln1*	
Log (1+x), base 2	$0006			
Log base 10 (common log)		FLOG10	log10	
Exponential	Elems68K			
e^x (exponential, natural antilog)	$0008	FETOX	exp	exp
2^x	$000A	FTWOTOX	exp2*	
$e^x - 1$	$000C	FETOXM1	exp1*	
$2^x - 1$	$000E			
10^x (common antilog)		FTENTOX	exp10*	
x^i (i: integer)	$8010			
x^y	$8012		pow	

Function	PACKs	68881	C	Pascal
Trigonometric	Elems68K			
Sine	$0018	FSIN	sin	sin
Cosine	$001A	FCOS	cos	cos
Tangent	$001C	FTAN	tan	
Inverse sine		FASIN	asin	
Inverse cosine		FACOS	acos	
Inverse tangent	$001E	FATAN	atan	arctan
Angle of (x,y) in range [-π,π]			atan2	
Hyperbolic sine		FSINH	sinh*	
Hyperbolic cosine		FCOSH	cosh*	
Hyperbolic tangent		FTANH	tanh*	
Hyperbolic inverse sine				
Hyperbolic inverse cosine				
Hyperbolic inverse tangent		FATANH	atanh*	

NaNs and Infinities

The IEEE standard provides support in its data types for results that are not valid numbers. For example, the result of taking the square root of a negative number is not itself a real number. By using NaNs (Not A Number), this anomolous result can be returned. Dividing by zero can return infinity, another unique bit pattern. The following table lists the various NaN codes that software SANE implements.

NaN Code	Meaning
1	Invalid square root (sqrt(-1))
2	Invalid addition (+INF - INF)
4	Invalid division (0/0)
8	Invalid multiplication (0 x INF)
9	Invalid remainder or mod (x rem 0)
17	Invalid ASCII string conversion
20	Comp NaN to float
21	Attempt to creat NaN(0)
33	Invalid argument to trig routine
34	Invalid argument to inverse trig routine
36	Invalid argument to log routine
37	Invalid argument to x^i or x^y routine
38	Invalid argument to financial function
255	All 68881 NaNs
INF	1+INF
-INF	-1/0
-0	1/-INF

Remainders, Modulo, and Rounding

The IEEE standard requires, and SANE supports, four rounding modes: toward zero, toward negative infinity, toward positive infinity, and to nearest. Depending upon which mode is set, different functions are available. For example, calling the integer part routine with rounding to zero is the same as truncating, whereas rounding to positive infinity is the ceiling function.

Different types of remainder functions are available if you use different rounding modes as well. The following two tables show the various options available from several languages. The HP-71B—a hand-held BASIC computer that fully supports IEEE arithmetic—is also included for comparison.

Function	Asm w/881	ANSI C	ISO Pascal	Postscript	HP-71B
Int Arguments; Int Result					
Absolute value		abs	abs	abs	abs
Integer division (round to zero)	divs,divu	/	div	idiv	div
Remainder (from integer division)	divs,divu	%	mod	mod	rmd
Real Argument; Int Result					
Round to nearest, ties away from 0			round		
Integer part (same sign as arg)		(int)	trunc	cvi	ip
Real Arguments; Real Result					
Absolute value	abs	fabs	abs	abs	abs
Integer part (same sign as arg)	fint w/rnd to 0	modf		truncate	ip
Fractional part (same sign as arg)		modf			fp
Floor (greatest integer ≤ x)	fint w/rnd to -∞	floor		floor	int, floor
Ceiling (least integer ≥ x)	fint w/rnd to +∞	ceil		ceiling	ceil
Round to integer (near,+∞,-∞,zero)	fint,fintrz			round (pos)	

Function	Asm w/881	ANSI C	ISO Pascal	Postscript	HP-71B
Remainders					
Remainder = x - y* ToZero(x/y)	fmod	fmod			rmd
Reduction = x - y* ToNearest(x/y)	frem				red
Modulo = x - y* Floor(x/y)					mod

Remainder Theory	Periodicity	Interval	Rounding	Standard
Remainder = x - y* ToZero(x/y)	not periodic	(-|y|,0] [0,|y|)	Exact	ANSI Basic
Reduction = x - y* ToNearest(x/y)	|y| or 2|y|	[-|y|/2,|y|/2]	Exact	IEEE 754
Modulo = x - y* Floor(x/y)	|y|	(y,0] [0,y)	Inexact	Math

Fixed and Fract Arithmetic

In addition to the IEEE-compliant extended-precision routines, the Macintosh also has a fast set of routines that work with numbers in two fixed-point formats: `Fixed` and `Fract`. Both formats occupy the same size as a `LongInt`, or 32 bits. Although these formats do not support IEEE arithmetic (NaNs, infinities, multiple rounding modes), they are useful in certain domains where extended-precision accuracy is overkill and speed is critical. Their usefulness on an 881 machine, however, is questionable, because 881 calls giving full extended precision are actually faster than fixed-point math on such machines! The FixMath routines each have their own A-trap and use the Toolbox register conventions of passing their parameters on the stack. Jerome Coonen authored all of FixMath except for the trig routines, which Kenton Hansen wrote.

The `Fixed` format represents a number in the range ±0.00002 to ±32767.99998, with about 4.5 fractional digits of accuracy. The integer and sign are located in the high-order word, just like a standard integer. The fractional part is contained in the low-order word, with the most significant bit representing 1/2 and the least significant bit representing 1/65536. Addition and subtraction can be performed using normal math (`ADD.L`, `SUB.L`), and negation is done by 2's complement (`NEG.L`). Multiplication of two `Fixed` point numbers is done with `FixMul`, and division of two 16-bit integers returns a `Fixed` by calling `FixRatio`. A `FixDiv` that accepts `Fixed` numbers was added in the 128 KB ROMs. `FixRound` rounds `Fixed` numbers, with halfway ties being rounded up. The `HiWord` and `LoWord` routines allow you to access the integer and fractional parts, respectively. All of the FixMath routines were also improved in the 128 KB ROMs so that they handle exceptions in the spirit of the IEEE standard. For example, overflows return the maximum representable values $7FFFFFFF and $80000000, and division by zero returns the maximum value correctly signed to match the numerator.

The `Fract` format was introduced in the Mac Plus 128 KB ROMs, with bit 31 being the sign bit, bit 30 being an integer (0 or 1), and the remaining bits 29 to 0 being a fraction with about 8.5 digits of accuracy. Thus, the dynamic range of a `Fract` is approximately ±9e-10 to ±1.999999999. Like `Fixed` numbers, `Fract` numbers add and subtract just like `LongInts`. FracMul, FracDiv, FracSqrt, FracSin, FracCos, and `FixATan2` all accept and return `Fract`s. FracSqrt, however, treats its argument as an unsigned `Fract` in the range 0 to 3.999999999, because negative numbers are not allowed. With the addition of the `Fract` format came conversion functions: Long2Fix, Fix2Long, Fix2Frac, Frac2Fix, Fix2X, X2Fix, Frac2X, and X2Frac, where X denotes extended precision.

Fixed-point math is used by QuickDraw and the Font Manager in drawing text. A good use of `Fract` is found in the Map cdev which stores the `MachineLocation` latitude and longitude as type `Fract` in parameter RAM as fractions of a great circle of 90°. Thus, a latitude of 1.0 = 90°, a longitude of -2.0 = -180°, etc.

NumTheory — C Tool

This tool is just for fun. If you like number theory, this tool tells you everything that you wanted to know about a given number. (Well, actually, it only begins to tell you. The properties of numbers are endless....) These facts include:

- Prime numbers—The program either verifies primality of the specified number or lists the number's prime factors. Optionally, the program can generate a list of prime numbers by the Sieve of Eratosthenes.

- Perfect squares—If the input is the exact square root of a larger number, it is a perfect square. This is checked.

- Squarefree numbers—If the input number is not perfectly divisible by the squares of any smaller numbers, it is squarefree.

- Collatz sequences—A Collatz sequence is the sequence of numbers that occurs when even numbers are divided by 2 and odd numbers are multiplied by 3 and 1 is added. (It is sometimes referred to as the 3N+1 problem.) This tool checks the number of steps taken in the Collatz sequence until a cycle occurs. Optionally, the program can look for long Collatz sequences.

- Fibonacci numbers—If the input number is a Fibonacci number, the program lists which Fibonacci number it is. Optionally, the program can list Fibonacci numbers.

- Harmonic numbers—The -h option prints the nth harmonic number, which is the sum of the reciprocals of the first n integers.

Although this tool is mainly for fun, much of number theory is very important to computer science. The design and measurement of the running time of a particular algorithm, for example, relies heavily on the results and theories of number theory.

```c
/*
 *  NumTheory.c - Generates and checks primes, Collatz sequences, etc.
 *              - Written by Dan Allen 2/15/89
 */

#include <CursorCtl.h>
#include <Math.h>
#include <StdIO.h>
#include <StdLib.h>

pascal long TickCount() extern 0xA975;

#define FALSE    0
#define TRUE     1

static char collatzFlag,fibFlag,harmonicFlag,primeFlag,sieveFlag;
static unsigned seed = 1;

main(int argc,char *argv[])
{
  int       i;
  unsigned  n;
  extended  x;

  seed = TickCount(); n = RandKR();
  for (i = 1; i < argc; i++)
    if (argv[i][0] == '-')
      switch (argv[i][1]) {
        case 'c': collatzFlag = TRUE; break;
        case 'e': sieveFlag = TRUE; break;
        case 'f': fibFlag = TRUE; break;
        case 'h': harmonicFlag = TRUE; break;
        case 'p': primeFlag = TRUE; break;
      }
    else n = atoi(argv[i]);

  if (collatzFlag) Collatz(n);
  else if (fibFlag) Fibonacci(n);
  else if (harmonicFlag) Harmonic(n);
  else if (primeFlag) Factor(n | 1);
  else if (sieveFlag) Sieve();
  else {
    if (Factor(n)) Factorize(n);
    else printf("%u is prime.\n",n);
```

```
      i = x = sqrt(n);
      if (i == x) printf("%u is the perfect square of %u.\n",n,i);

      for (i = 2; i <= x; i++)
        if (n % (i*i) == 0) break;
      if (i > x && n > 2) printf("%u is squarefree.\n",n);

      i = Fibonacci(n);
      if (i >= 0) {
        printf("%u is the %d",n,i);
        switch(i) {
          case 1:  printf("st & 2nd"); break;
          case 3:  printf("rd"); break;
          default: printf("th");
        }
        printf(" Fibonacci number.\n");
      }
      printf("%u has a Collatz cycle of %u.\n",n,Collatz(n));
    }
    return 0;
}

int Collatz(unsigned m)    /* The 3N+1 problem */
{
  unsigned  i,j,n,num,max = 0;

  for (i = m; i <= 0xFFFFFFFF; i++) {
    j = 0; n = i;
    while (1) {
      j++; if (n < 2) break;
      n = n & 1 ? 3*n+1 : n/2;
    }
    if (!collatzFlag) return j;
    if (j > max) {
      max = j; num = i;
      printf("%6u -> %6u cycles\n",num,max);
    }
    if (i % 25 == 0) SpinCursor(1);
  }
}

int Factor(unsigned n)
{
  unsigned i,max,factor;
```

```
   if (n < 2) return 1;
   if (n == 2) return 0;
   if (n % 2 == 0) return 2;
   for (; n < 0xFFFFFFFF; n += 2) {
     max = ceil(sqrt(n));
     factor = 0;
     for (i = 3; i <= max; i += 2)
       if (n%i == 0) { factor = i; break; }
     if (!primeFlag) return factor;
     if (!factor) printf("%u is PRIME\n",n);
     SpinCursor(1);
   }
}

Factorize(unsigned n)
{
   unsigned f;

   if (n < 4) return;
   printf("%u = %u",n,f = Factor(n));
   while (TRUE) {
     n /= f;
     f = Factor(n);
     if (f) printf(" * %u",f);
     else break;
   }
   printf(" * %u\n",n);
}

int Fibonacci(unsigned n)
{
   unsigned  i,fn,fn1,fn2;

   if (!fibFlag) {
     if (n < 2) return n;
     fn = 2; fn1 = fn2 = 1;
     for (i = 3; fn <= n; i++) {
       if (fn == n) return i;
       fn2 = fn1;
       fn1 = fn;
       fn = fn1 + fn2;
     }
     return -1;
   }
   for (i = fn2 = 0,fn1 = 1,fn = 1; i < 48; i++) {
     printf("Fibonacci %3u = %10u\n",i,fn2);
     fn2 = fn1;
     fn1 = fn;
     fn = fn1 + fn2;
   }
}
```

```
Harmonic(unsigned n)
{
  unsigned  i;
  extended  h = 0.0;

  for(i = 1; i <= n; i++) {
    h += 1.0/i;
    printf("Harmonic %6u = %3.18f\n",i,h);
  }
}


int RandKR()
{
  seed = seed * 1103515245 + 12345;
  return (unsigned) (seed >> 16) % 32768;
}


#define MAXPRIME  8192
static char sieve[MAXPRIME];

Sieve()
{
  unsigned  i,j;

  for (i = 2; i < MAXPRIME; i++)
    sieve[i] = i & 1 ? TRUE : FALSE;
  for (i = 3; i < MAXPRIME; i++)
    if (sieve[i] == TRUE) {
      for (j = i + i; j < MAXPRIME; j += i)
        sieve[j] = FALSE;
    }
  for (i = 3; i < MAXPRIME; i++)
    if (sieve[i] == TRUE) printf("%u is prime.\n",i);
}
```

Hash — C Tool

Hashing is a powerful technique for finding items in a table. Most compilers use hashing to look up identifiers in their symbol tables. Different hash functions are suited for different types of data; this tool analyzes the resulting distributions of different hash functions. The tool uses a standard chi-square test, among other statistics, to measure how optimal these functions are.

Hash has a generalized hash routine that can take different arguments, thus creating different hash functions. Several interesting combinations of a multiplier and a modulus are set by the -e, -o, -q, and -t options, and any specific multiplier and modulus can be set by the -k and -m options. A random pair can be chosen with the -r option.

The default hash function is the same as the following simplified C function, where each character of the input string is added to a running total, with each intermediate total being multiplied by 255. This simple method is actually a good hash function.

```
int Hash255(unsigned char *s)
{
  unsigned h = 0;

  while(*s) {
    h += *s++;
    h *= 255;
  }
  return h % RANGE;
}
```

The input to Hash is simply a list of files to hash, with each line of each file being hashed on to determine an index into an array of 211 entries. In addition to the files given, Hash always tests one particularly interesting case: hashing the strings I100, I101 . . . I300. Many compilers, for example, could generate such a similar set of identifiers for internally generated temporary variables. However, many hash functions are poor at uniformly distributing a set of similar strings such as these.

The output of Hash reflects the degree of uniformity achieved by the hash function. The chi-square value should be—ideally—the same as the size of the hash table. Thus, the further removed the chi-square value is from this value of 211, the worse the hash function. The ratio value is another way of specifying this, with a ratio of 1 being ideal. Hash adds the variances of each file (as well as the I100–I300 test), thus weighting each of these equally; it then displays summary statistics. A progress option will display each individual test as well.

```
/*
 *  Hash.c  - Tests various hashing algorithms
 *          - Written by Dan Allen 2/12/1989
 *
 */

#include  <CursorCtl.h>
#include  <StdIO.h>
#include  <StdLib.h>

pascal long TickCount() = 0xA975;
#define RANGE 211                      /* size of hash table */
#define NUMI  300                      /* # of similar idents to hash */

char      progFlag;
unsigned  a[RANGE],n,runs;
unsigned  mult = 255,modu = 99999;     /* a very good hash function */
extended  tChi,tRatio;
```

```
main(int argc,char *argv[])
{
  char       str[256];
  unsigned   i;
  FILE       *input;
  InitCursorCtl(0);
  srand(TickCount());
  for(i = 1;  i < argc;  i++)
    if (argv[i][0] == '-')      /* process arguments */
      switch (argv[i][1]) {
        case 'e': mult = 44; modu = 11; break;         /* elevenths */
        case 'k': mult = atoi(argv[++i]); break;       /* konstant */
        case 'm': modu = atoi(argv[++i]); break;       /* modulus */
        case 'o': mult = 63; modu = 8; break;          /* octets */
        case 'p': progFlag = 1; break;                 /* progress */
        case 'q': mult = 256; modu = 4; break;         /* quads */
        case 'r': mult = rand() % 257;                 /* random */
                  modu = rand() % 14 + 2;
                  break;
        case 's': srand(atoi(argv[++i])); break;       /* seed */
        case 't': mult = 179; modu = 12; break;        /* twelvths */
      }
    else {                       /* process files */
      input = fopen(argv[i],"r");
      while (fgets(str,sizeof(str),input)) {
        a[Hash(str)]++;
        n++;
        SpinCursor(1);
      }
      fclose(input);
      stats(argv[i]);
    }

  for (i = 1;  i <= NUMI; i++) {
    sprintf(str,"I%d",i+99);
    a[Hash(str)]++;
    n++;
  }
  stats("I100 - I300");
  fprintf(stderr,
    "TOTAL: %2u\tChi = %3.3f\tr = %f\tMultiplier = %5u   Modulus = %5u\n",
    runs,tChi,tRatio,mult,modu);
  return 0;
}
```

```
stats(char *s)
{
  unsigned  i;
  extended  chi = 0.0,ratio = 0.0;
  extended  fabs(extended x);

  for (i = 0; i < RANGE; i++) {
    chi += a[i]*a[i];
    ratio += a[i]*(a[i]+1.0)/2.0;
    a[i] = 0;
  }
  chi = chi*RANGE/n - n;
  ratio = ratio/(n/(2.0*RANGE)*(n+2.0*RANGE-1.0));

  if (progFlag)
    fprintf(stderr,"N = %5u\tChi = %3.3f\tr = %f\t%s\n",n,chi,ratio,s);
  tChi += fabs(chi - RANGE); tRatio += fabs(ratio - 1.0); runs++;
  n = 0;
}


int Hash(unsigned char *s)
{
  unsigned  i,h = 0,t = 0;

  for (i = 1; *s; i++) {
    t *= mult;
    t += *s++;
    if (i%modu == 0) {
      h += t; t = 0;
    }
  }
  if (!h) h = t;
  return h % RANGE;
}
```

Rand — C Tool

Random numbers are another aspect of computer math that are often taken for granted. This tool allows several different random-number generators to be exercised, measured, and compared.

The Macintosh has two built-in random-number generators: the QuickDraw `Random`, which returns an integer in the range ±32767, and the SANE function `RandomX`, which returns an extended number in the range $1 \le x \le 2^{31} - 2$. In addition, C has its `rand()` function in its standard library. Kernighan and Ritchie recommend a particular function as a good random-number generator; this function is also implemented in this tool. Finally, from *Numerical Recipes in C*, we have Knuth's triple set of linear congruential generators. This tool will also encrypt or decrypt a simple one-line message. Statistical analysis using the chi-square method allows the program to evaluate how good each of these random number generators are.

Improving Rand

Here are some suggestions for improving Rand:

- Add the SANE RandomX function as yet another alternative random-number generator. How does its performance compare with the other generators?
- Read Knuth's *Seminumerical Algorithms*, the classic work on random numbers. Is anything really random? What is the difference between a random number and a pseudo-random number?
- Evaluate the Macintosh random-number generators using Knuth's spectral test, a very good technique for measuring randomness. How do these generators fare?
- Design and implement your own random-number generation technique.

```
/*
 *  Rand.c   - Generates random numbers
 *           - Written by Dan Allen 3/27/88
 *           - K&R generator added 11/23/88
 *           - Cleanup 2/15/89
 *           - Encrypting, QD Random, chi analysis added 2/21/89
 */

#include <CursorCtl.h>
#include <Math.h>
#include <QuickDraw.h>
#include <StdIO.h>
#include <StdLib.h>

#define TRUE     1
#define FALSE    0
#define MAXFREQ 5000

pascal long TickCount() extern 0xA975;

typedef unsigned char byte;
typedef unsigned long word;

static byte krFlag,libFlag,progFlag,qdFlag,*msg,cipher[4096];
static word seed,RandKR(),freq[MAXFREQ+1];
```

```
main(int argc,char *argv[])
{
  byte      c,*p,*q;
  word      high = 0,low = 0xFFFFFFFF,sum = 0;
  word      count = 1,i,x,t,maxNum = 1;
  extended  chi,y,fhigh = 0.0,flow = 1.0E4932,fsum = 0.0,Ran1();

  InitGraf(&qd.thePort);
  InitCursorCtl(0);
  t = seed = TickCount();
  for (i = 1; i < argc; i++)
    if (argv[i][0] == '-' && argv[i][2] == '\0')
      switch (argv[i][1]) {
        case 'c': count = atoi(argv[++i]); break;
        case 'k': krFlag = TRUE; maxNum = RAND_MAX; break;
        case 'l': libFlag = TRUE; maxNum = RAND_MAX; break;
        case 'm': msg = argv[++i]; break;
        case 'p': progFlag = TRUE; break;
        case 'q': qdFlag = TRUE; maxNum = RAND_MAX; break;
        case 's': seed = atoi(argv[++i]); break;
        default:
          fprintf(stderr,"Rand [-c num][-k|-l|-q][-m msg][-s seed] maxNum\n");
          return 1;
      }
    else maxNum = atoi(argv[i]);

  if (maxNum < 1) maxNum = 1;
  if (count < 1) count = 1;

  if (msg) {
    p = msg; q = cipher;
    while(c = *p++)
      *q++ = c ^ RandKR()%25;
    printf("Cipher: %s\n",cipher);
    return 0;
  }
```

```
if (krFlag) {
  maxNum++;
  for (i = 0; i < count; i++) {
    x = RandKR() % maxNum;
    if (x > high) high = x;
    if (x < low) low = x;
    if (x <= MAXFREQ) freq[x]++;
    sum += x;
    if (progFlag || count == 1) printf("%u\n",x);
  }
}
else if (libFlag) {
  srand(seed); maxNum++;
  for (i = 0; i < count; i++) {
    x = rand() % maxNum;
    if (x > high) high = x;
    if (x < low) low = x;
    if (x <= MAXFREQ) freq[x]++;
    sum += x;
    if (progFlag || count == 1) printf("%u\n",x);
  }
}
else if (qdFlag) {
  qd.randSeed = seed; maxNum++;
  for (i = 0; i < count; i++) {
    x = Random() % maxNum;
    if (x > high) high = x;
    if (x < low) low = x;
    if (x <= MAXFREQ) freq[x]++;
    sum += x;
    if (progFlag || count == 1) printf("%u\n",x);
    if (i % 16 == 0) SpinCursor(1);
  }
}
else {
  seed = -t;
  for (i = 0; i < count; i++) {
    y = Ran1(&seed)*maxNum;
    if (y > fhigh) fhigh = y;
    if (y < flow) flow = y;
    x = floor(y); if (x <= MAXFREQ) freq[x]++;
    fsum += y;
    if (progFlag || count == 1) printf("%.18f\n",y);
    if (i % 4 == 0) SpinCursor(1);
  }
}
```

```
    t = TickCount() - t;
    if (count > 1 && !progFlag) {
      for (i = x = 0; i <= MAXFREQ; i++)
        x += freq[i]*freq[i];
      chi = maxNum*x/count - count;
      if (krFlag || libFlag || qdFlag)
        printf("N: %u  Low: %u  Mean: %.2f  High: %u Chi: %.1f Time: %.2f sec\n",
               count,low,(extended)sum/count,high,chi,t/60.0);
      else
        printf("N: %u Low: %.2f Mean: %.2f High: %.2f Chi: %.1f Time:%.2f sec\n",
               count,flow,fsum/count,fhigh,chi,t/60.0);
    }
    return 0;
}

/* Recommended ANSI library routine */
/* From K&R 2nd edition, page 46 */
unsigned long RandKR()
{
    seed = seed * 1103515245 + 12345;
    return (seed >> 16) % RAND_MAX;
}

/*  Knuth's triple set of linear congruential generators */
/*  From Numerical Recipies in C, page 210 */
#define M1   259200
#define IA1 7141
#define IC1 54773
#define RM1 (1.0/M1)
#define M2   134456
#define IA2 8121
#define IC2 28411
#define RM2 (1.0/M2)
#define M3   243000
#define IA3 4561
#define IC3 51349

static extended Ran1(int *idum)
{
    static long ix1,ix2,ix3;
    static extended r[98];
    extended temp;
    static int iff = 0;
    int j;
```

```
if (*idum < 0 || iff == 0) {
  iff = 1;
  ix1 = (IC1 - (*idum)) % M1;
  ix1 = (IA1 * ix1 + IC1) % M1;
  ix2 = ix1 % M2;
  ix1 = (IA1 * ix1 + IC1) % M1;
  ix3 = ix1 % M3;
  for (j = 1; j <= 97; j++) {
    ix1 = (IA1 * ix1 + IC1) % M1;
    ix2 = (IA2 * ix2 + IC2) % M2;
    r[j] = (ix1 + ix2 * RM2) * RM1;
  }
  *idum = 1;
}
ix1 = (IA1 * ix1 + IC1) % M1;
ix2 = (IA2 * ix2 + IC2) % M2;
ix3 = (IA3 * ix3 + IC3) % M3;
j = 1 + ((97 * ix3) / M3);
if (j > 97 || j < 1) exit(3);
temp = r[j];
r[j] = (ix1 + ix2 * RM2) * RM1;
return temp;
}
```

Solar — Pascal Tool

This program presents one approach to modeling the solar system. It calculates the current position of the sun and planets. It uses matrices to do the coordinate system transformations from heliocentric to ecliptic to equatorial and finally to the horizon coordinate system. It solves Kepler's equation by Newton's method and uses a table lookup for sidereal time as well as the orbital elements. The tabular data for this program came from *Practical Astronomy with Your Calculator* by Peter Duffett-Smith. This program was written by Paul Finlayson.

Improving Solar

Here are some suggestions for improving Solar:

- Add command-line options to allow different dates, times, and locations to be input.
- Get the location of the Mac from the MachineLocation part of parameter RAM, like the Map cdev does.
- Solar currently displays its results as a table of text. Add a graphical interface that displays its results in a window.

Here is a generic Makefile for Pascal tools to be built with direct 68881 code.

```
# Generic Makefile for MPW Pascal tools & 68881 code

POptions    = -mbg ch8 -r -mc68020 -mc68881
PLibs =     "{PLibraries}PasLib.o" ∂
            "{PLibraries}SaneLib881.o" ∂
            "{Libraries}Interface.o" ∂
            "{Libraries}Runtime.o"

    ƒ  .p.o
  Link -o {Default} -sg Main {Default}.p.o {PLibs}
  Setfile -c 'MPS ' -t MPST -d . -m . {Default}
```

And here is the Pascal source code for `Solar`:

```
PROGRAM Solar;

(* Written by Dr. Paul Finlayson c. 1983 in Turbo Pascal on an HP-110 *)
(* Ported to Turbo on the Mac, and then to MPW Pascal by Dan Allen 8/22/87 *)

USES  SANE,OSUtils,Packages;

TYPE
  Vector  = ARRAY [0..2] OF Extended;
  Matrix  = ARRAY [1..9, 1..7] OF Extended;

VAR
  mon,day,year:         Integer;
  hrs,min,sec:          Integer;
  theSeconds:           LongInt;
  riseTime,setime,dhrs: Extended;
  lon,lat,tLAT:         Extended;
  lst,ra,dec,az,el:     Extended;
  dToR,rToD,timeZone:   Extended;
  planetPos, earthPos:  Vector;
  etoP:                 Vector;
  orbitdat:             Matrix;
```

```
FUNCTION ArcTan2(y,x: Extended): Extended;
{ ArcTan returned in the range -π to π }
VAR
  t: Extended;
BEGIN
  IF x = 0 THEN
    IF y > 0 THEN t := Pi ELSE t := - Pi
  ELSE
    t := ArcTan(y/x);
  IF x < 0 THEN
    IF y < 0 THEN t := t - Pi ELSE t := t + Pi;
  ArcTan2 := t;
END;

FUNCTION ArcCos(x: Extended): Extended;
BEGIN
  ArcCos := ArcTan2(Sqrt(1 - Sqr(x)),x);
END;

PROCEDURE PtoR(r,theta: Extended; VAR x,y: Extended);
{ polar to rectangular coordinate conversion }
BEGIN
  x := r * Cos(theta);
  y := r * Sin(theta);
END;

PROCEDURE RtoP(x,y: Extended; VAR r,theta: Extended);
{ rectangular to polar coordinate conversion }
BEGIN
  r := Sqrt(x * x + y * y);
  theta := ArcTan2(y,x);
END;

PROCEDURE StoR(r,theta,phi: Extended; VAR x,y,z: Extended);
{ spherical to rectangular coordinate conversion }
BEGIN
  z := r * Sin(phi);
  PtoR(r * Cos(phi),theta,x,y);
END;

PROCEDURE RtoS(x,y,z: Extended; VAR r,theta,phi: Extended);
{ rectangular to spherical coordinate conversion }
VAR
  r1: Extended;
BEGIN
  r := Sqrt(x * x + y * y + z * z);
  RtoP(x,y,r1,theta);
  phi := ArcTan2(z,r1);
END;
```

```
FUNCTION JD2(m,d,y: Integer): Integer;
{ Given a month,day,year, calculate Julian Day number }
{ JD2 = 1 on Jan 1, 1975 (Epoch 1975.0   JD 2442413) }
BEGIN
  JD2 := 367 * (y - 1950) - 7 * (y + (m + 9) DIV 12) DIV 4 +
       (275 * m) DIV 9 + d - 5749;
END;

FUNCTION Modulo(base, rmod: Extended): Extended;
{ Recursive definition of mathematical modulo }
BEGIN
  IF base >= rmod THEN
    Modulo := Modulo(base - rmod, rmod)
  ELSE
    IF base < 0.0 THEN
      Modulo := Modulo(base + rmod, rmod)
    ELSE
      Modulo := base;
END;

FUNCTION Pad(x: Integer): Str255;
{ prefix numbers with leading zeros if needed }
VAR
  s: Str255;
BEGIN
  NumToString(x,s);
  s := Concat('0',s);
  pad := Copy(s,Length(s) - 1,2);
END;

FUNCTION HMS(decimalHrs: Extended): Str255;
{ create HH:MM:SS style string from decimal time }
VAR
  dMin,dHrs:    Extended;
  hrs,min,sec:  Integer;
BEGIN
  dHrs := Modulo(decimalHrs + 1.0 / 7200,24.0);
  hrs := Trunc(dHrs);
  dMin := (dHrs - hrs) * 60.0;
  min := Trunc(dMin);
  sec := Trunc((dMin - min) * 60.0);
  HMS := Concat(pad(hrs), ':', pad(min), ':', pad(sec));
END;
```

```
FUNCTION Siderial(month,day,year: Integer;
          decHrs,Longitude,timeZone: Extended): Extended;
{ lookup siderial time given date, time, and location }
VAR
  dayOfYear:    Integer;
  ut,b,gst,lst: Extended;
BEGIN
  dayOfYear := JD2(month,day,year) - JD2(1,1,year) + 1;
  ut := decHrs + timeZone;
  IF ut > 24 THEN
  BEGIN
    dayOfYear := dayOfYear + 1;
    ut := ut - 24.0;
  END;
  CASE year OF
    1980: b := 17.411472;
    1981: b := 17.361677;
    1982: b := 17.377592;
    1983: b := 17.393506;
    1984: b := 17.409421;
    1985: b := 17.359625;
    1986: b := 17.375539;
    1987: b := 17.391453;
    1988: b := 17.407368;
    1989: b := 17.357573;
    1990: b := 17.373487;
    1991: b := 17.389402;
    1992: b := 17.405316;
    1993: b := 17.355521;
    1994: b := 17.371435;
    1995: b := 17.387349;
    1996: b := 17.403263;
    1997: b := 17.353468;
    1998: b := 17.369382;
    1999: b := 17.385297;
    2000: b := 17.401211;
  OTHERWISE { See Astronomonical Ephemeris for other years }
      WriteLn('Illegal year in function Siderial');
  END;
  gst := dayOfYear * 0.065709 - b + ut * 1.002743;
  lst := gst - longitude / 15.0;
  Siderial := Modulo(lst,24.0);
END;
```

```
PROCEDURE DateTime(VAR mon,day,year,hrs,min,sec: Integer;
            VAR decHrs: Extended);
{ Get current date and time from MacOS }
VAR
  t: DateTimeRec;
BEGIN
  GetDateTime(theSeconds);
  Secs2Date(theSeconds,t);
  mon := t.month;
  day := t.day;
  year := t.year;
  hrs := t.hour;
  min := t.minute;
  sec := t.second;
  decHrs := hrs + (min + sec / 60.0) / 60.0;
END;


PROCEDURE Kepler(m,a,ecc: Extended; VAR r,theta: Extended);
{
  Solve Kepler's equation by Newton's method where
  m   = mean anomaly
  a   = semi-major axis
  ecc = eccentricity
  r   = radius
  theta = true anomaly
}
VAR
  e,dE,lastdE,dMdE: Extended;
BEGIN
  e := m;
  dE := 9E9;
  REPEAT
    lastdE := dE;
    dMdE := 1 - ecc * cos(E);
    dE := (e - ecc * sin(E) - m) / dMdE;
    e := e - dE;
    dE := Abs(dE);
  UNTIL (dE = 0) OR (dE >= lastdE);
  theta := 2 * ArcTan2(Sqrt((1+ecc) / (1-ecc)) * Sin(e/2),Cos(e/2));
  r := a * (1-Sqr(ecc)) / (1+ecc * Cos(theta));
END;
```

```
PROCEDURE AxisRotate(axis: Integer; angle: Extended; VAR v: Vector);
{ Rotate coordinates of vector v through axis by angle }
VAR
   s,c,a:  Extended;
   k,j:    Integer;
BEGIN
   s := Sin(angle); c := Cos(angle);
   j := (axis + 1) MOD 3; k := (axis + 2) MOD 3;
   a := v[j];
   v[j] := c * v[j] + s * v[k];
   v[k] := c * v[k] - s * a;
END;

PROCEDURE EclipticCoords(m,a,ecc,argPer,incl,lonNode: Extended;
            VAR eclipticPos: Vector);
{ Heliocentric to ecliptic coordinates conversion }
VAR
   r,phi:  Extended;
BEGIN
   Kepler(m,a,ecc,r,phi);
   eclipticPos[2] := 0;
   PtoR(r,phi + argPer,eclipticPos[0],eclipticPos[1]);
   AxisRotate(0,-incl,eclipticPos);
   AxisRotate(2,-lonNode,eclipticPos);
END;

PROCEDURE EquatorialCoords(eclipticPos: Vector; VAR ra,dec: Extended);
{ Ecliptic to equatorial coordinate conversion }
VAR
   r: extended;
BEGIN
   AxisRotate(0,-23.43*dToR,eclipticPos);
   RtoS(eclipticPos[0],eclipticPos[1],eclipticPos[2],r,ra,dec);
END;

PROCEDURE HorizonCoords(ra,dec,lst,lat: Extended; VAR az,el: Extended);
{ Equatorial to horizon coordinate conversion }
VAR
   v: Vector;
   r: Extended;
BEGIN
   StoR(1,ra - lst * Pi / 12,dec,v[0],v[1],v[2]);
   AxisRotate(1,Pi/2 - lat,v);
   RtoS(-v[0],v[1],v[2],r,az,el);
END;
```

```
PROCEDURE ReadMat;
{ Initialize orbital elements for planets; see next proc for definitions }
{ From Duffet p. 100 }
BEGIN
  orbitdat[1,1] := 0.24085; (* Mercury *)
  orbitdat[1,2] := 320.66305;
  orbitdat[1,3] := 77.06645;
  orbitdat[1,4] := 0.205629;
  orbitdat[1,5] := 0.387099;
  orbitdat[1,6] := 7.00427;
  orbitdat[1,7] := 48.03494;

  orbitdat[2,1] := 0.61521; (* Venus *)
  orbitdat[2,2] := 310.97453;
  orbitdat[2,3] := 131.21928;
  orbitdat[2,4] := 0.006785;
  orbitdat[2,5] := 0.723332;
  orbitdat[2,6] := 3.39438;
  orbitdat[2,7] := 76.45475;

  orbitdat[3,1] := 1.00004; (* Earth *)
  orbitdat[3,2] := 99.53431;
  orbitdat[3,3] := 102.51044;
  orbitdat[3,4] := 0.016720;
  orbitdat[3,5] := 1.000000;
  orbitdat[3,6] := 0.0;
  orbitdat[3,7] := 0.0;

  orbitdat[4,1] := 1.88089; (* Mars *)
  orbitdat[4,2] := 249.62919;
  orbitdat[4,3] := 335.59881;
  orbitdat[4,4] := 0.093382;
  orbitdat[4,5] := 1.523691;
  orbitdat[4,6] := 1.84983;
  orbitdat[4,7] := 49.36466;

  orbitdat[5,1] := 11.86224;  (* Jupiter *)
  orbitdat[5,2] := 355.21414;
  orbitdat[5,3] := 13.91992;
  orbitdat[5,4] := 0.048460;
  orbitdat[5,5] := 5.202804;
  orbitdat[5,6] := 1.30450;
  orbitdat[5,7] := 100.19608;

  orbitdat[6,1] := 29.45771;  (* Saturn *)
  orbitdat[6,2] := 104.17278;
  orbitdat[6,3] := 92.55833;
  orbitdat[6,4] := 0.055630;
  orbitdat[6,5] := 9.538844;
  orbitdat[6,6] := 2.48933;
  orbitdat[6,7] := 113.43842;
```

```
  orbitdat[7,1] := 84.01247;   (* Uranus *)
  orbitdat[7,2] := 205.78286;
  orbitdat[7,3] := 170.25472;
  orbitdat[7,4] := 0.047250;
  orbitdat[7,5] := 19.181854;
  orbitdat[7,6] := 0.77316;
  orbitdat[7,7] := 73.87283;

  orbitdat[8,1] := 164.79558; (* Neptune *)
  orbitdat[8,2] := 249.91462;
  orbitdat[8,3] := 44.40592;
  orbitdat[8,4] := 0.008586;
  orbitdat[8,5] := 30.057960;
  orbitdat[8,6] := 1.77236;
  orbitdat[8,7] := 131.50506;

  orbitdat[9,1] := 246.378; (* Pluto *)
  orbitdat[9,2] := 202.3345;
  orbitdat[9,3] := 224.2580;
  orbitdat[9,4] := 0.246115;
  orbitdat[9,5] := 39.29976;
  orbitdat[9,6] := 17.14451;
  orbitdat[9,7] := 109.9965;
END;

PROCEDURE Planets(planetnum,mon,day,year: Integer;timeOfDay: Extended;
          VAR m,a,ecc,argPer,incl,lonNode: Extended);
{ Get orbital elements }
VAR
  quo:                   Integer;
  dse,le,lp,i,lan,period: Extended;
BEGIN
  period := orbitdat[planetnum,1]; { period in tropical years }
  le := orbitdat[planetnum,2];  { longitude at epoch 1980 in ° }
  lp := orbitdat[planetnum,3];  { longitude of perihelion in ° }
  ecc := orbitdat[planetnum,4]; { eccentricity of orbit }
  a := orbitdat[planetnum,5];   { semi-major axis in AU }
  i := orbitdat[planetnum,6];   { inclination of orbit in ° }
  lan := orbitdat[planetnum,7]; { longitude of ascending node in ° }

  argPer := (lp - lan) * dToR;  { argument of perihelion in radians }
  incl := i * dToR;             { inclination }
  lonNode := lan * dToR;        { longitude of ascending node in radians }

  dse := JD2(mon,day,year) + timeOfDay / 24.0;
  i := dse / (period * 365.25) + (le - lp) / 360.0;
  m := (i - Trunc(i)) * 2 * Pi;
END;
```

```
PROCEDURE PlanetCoords(planet,month,day,year: Integer; dHrs: Extended;
              VAR planetPos: Vector);
VAR
  m,a,ecc,argPer,incl,lonNode: Extended;
BEGIN
  IF planet = 0 THEN
    BEGIN
      planetPos[0] := 0;
      planetPos[1] := 0;
      planetPos[2] := 0;
    END
  ELSE
    BEGIN
      Planets(planet,month,day,year,dHrs,m,a,ecc,argPer,incl,lonNode);
      EclipticCoords(m,a,ecc,argPer,incl,lonNode,planetPos);
    END;
END;


PROCEDURE RiseSet(ra,dec,lat,lst,dHrs: Extended;
                  month,day,year: Integer;
                  VAR risetime,setime: Extended);
{ Determine times of rising and setting }
VAR
  theta,a: Extended;
BEGIN
  a := -Tan(lat) * Tan(dec);
  IF a < -1.0 THEN theta := Pi ELSE theta := ArcCos(a);
  risetime := dHrs + (ra - theta) * 12 / Pi - lst;
  setime := dHrs + (ra + theta) * 12 / Pi - lst;
END;


FUNCTION PlanetName(planetNum: Integer): Str255;
BEGIN
  CASE planetnum OF
    0: PlanetName := 'Sun    ';
    1: PlanetName := 'Mercury';
    2: PlanetName := 'Venus  ';
    3: PlanetName := 'Earth  ';
    4: PlanetName := 'Mars   ';
    5: PlanetName := 'Jupiter';
    6: PlanetName := 'Saturn ';
    7: PlanetName := 'Uranus ';
    8: PlanetName := 'Neptune';
    9: PlanetName := 'Pluto  ';
  END;
END;
```

```
PROCEDURE PlanetScreen;
VAR
  i,p:  Integer;
  s:    Str255;
BEGIN
  WriteLn('Latitude:      ', rToD * lat: 6: 2);
  WriteLn('Longitude:     ', lon: 6: 2);

  IUDateString(theSeconds,longDate,s);
  WriteLn('Date:          ',s);

  IUTimeString(theSeconds,TRUE,s);
  WriteLn('Local Time:    ',s);
  WriteLn('Universal Time: ',HMS(dHrs + timeZone));

  lst := Siderial(mon,day,year,dHrs,lon,timeZone);
  WriteLn('Siderial Time: ', HMS(lst));

  PlanetCoords(3,mon,day,year,dHrs,earthPos);
  WriteLn;
  WriteLn('': 12,
   'RA(HMS)   DEC(DMS)        AZ(deg)   EL(deg)     Rise(HMS) Set(HMS)' );
  WriteLn;

  FOR p := 0 TO 9 DO
    IF p <> 3 THEN
      BEGIN
        PlanetCoords(p,mon,day,year,dHrs,planetPos);
        FOR i := 0 TO 2 DO
          eToP[i] := planetPos[i] - earthPos[i];
        EquatorialCoords(eToP,ra,dec);
        IF dec < 0.0 THEN s := '-' ELSE s := ' ';
        HorizonCoords(ra,dec,lst,lat,az,el);
        RiseSet(ra,dec,lat,lst,dHrs,mon,day,year,risetime,setime);
        WriteLn(PlanetName(p), '     ',
                HMS(ra * 12 / Pi), ' ',
                s,
                HMS(rToD * Abs(dec)), '        ',
                rToD * az: 7: 2,' ',
                rToD * el: 7: 2, '       ',
                HMS(risetime),'  ',
                HMS(setime));
      END;
END;
```

```
BEGIN { main }
  ReadMat;
  dToR := Pi / 180;
  rToD := 180 / Pi;
  tLAT := 37.33; {Cupertino - PST}
  lon := 122.08;
  timeZone := 8.0;
  lat := tLAT * dToR;
  DateTime(mon,day,year,hrs,min,sec,dHrs);
  PlanetScreen;
END.
```

Sun — Pascal Tool

This program's approach to modeling the solar system shows only the sun rather than all of the planets as the previous program did. This version uses polynomial series with trigonometric coefficients to approximate the orbital elements, and they have a quoted accuracy of 1 minute of arc over a 300-year period of time. Coordinate trans-   formations are done by spherical trigonometric methods rather than by matrix transformations.

```
PROGRAM Sun;
{
  Written by Dan Allen, originally in HP BASIC on an HP-75C, Dec 1982.
  Ported to Macintosh Basic (MPL) 20 Feb 1988.
  Ported to Turbo Pascal on 18 Jul 1988.

  For more info see:
  "Explanatory Supplement to the Nautical Almanac & Astronomical Ephemeris"
  "Astrophysical Journal Supplement", Nov 1979.
}

USES
  OSUtils,SANE;

VAR
  m,d,y:        Integer;
  hour:         Integer;
  minute:       Integer;
  sec:          Integer;
  timeZone:     Integer;

  latitude:     Extended;
  longitude:    Extended;

  gmt:          Extended;
  gst,lst:      Extended;
  jc19,jd20:    Extended;
```

```
    sunLong:    Extended;
    sunAnom:    Extended;
    jupAnom:    Extended;
    moonLat:    Extended;
    moonLong:   Extended;
    meanElong:  Extended;
    lunAscNode: Extended;

    helioLong:  Extended;
    radiusAU:   Extended;
    e:          Extended;

    rightAscen: Extended;
    decl:       Extended;

    altitude:   Extended;
    azimuth:    Extended;


FUNCTION DtoR(x: Extended) : Extended; { degrees to radians }
BEGIN
  DtoR := x*pi/180;
END;

FUNCTION RtoD(x: Extended) : Extended; { radians to degrees }
BEGIN
  RtoD := x*180/pi;
END;

FUNCTION ArcSin(x: Extended) : Extended;
BEGIN
  ArcSin := Arctan(x/Sqrt(1-x*x));
END;

FUNCTION ArcCos(x: Extended) : Extended;
BEGIN
  ArcCos := 2*Arctan(Sqrt((1-x)/(1+x)));
END;

FUNCTION Modulo(x,y: Extended) : Extended;
VAR r:   RoundDir;
BEGIN
  r := GetRound;
  SetRound(Downward);
  Modulo := x - y * Rint(x/y);   { modulo using floor }
  SetRound(r);
END;
```

```
PROCEDURE ToJulian; { global date & time --> Julian date }
BEGIN
  gmt :=  hour + minute/60 + sec/3600 + timeZone;
  jd20 := 367.0*y - 7*(y+(m+9) DIV 12) DIV 4;
  jd20 := jd20 - 3*((y+(m-9) DIV 7) DIV 100 + 1) DIV 4;
  jd20 := jd20 + 275 * m DIV 9 + d - 730516.5 + gmt/24;
  jc19 := jd20/36525+1;
END;

PROCEDURE ToSiderial; { Julian Date --> approximate siderial time }
BEGIN
  gst := jc19 - gmt/876600;
  lst := Modulo((36000.76893 + 0.000387083*gst)*gst,360);
  lst := Modulo(lst + 15.04106863*gmt + 99.69098325,360);
END;

PROCEDURE FundArgs; { calculate approximate fundamental arguments }
BEGIN
  sunLong := jd20 * 0.9856473516 + 280.46592;
  sunAnom := jd20 * 0.98560026 + 357.52536;
  jupAnom := jd20 * 0.0830912148 + 20.35116;
  moonLat := jd20*13.229350272 + 93.27276;
  moonLong := jd20 * 13.1763964644 + 218.31624;
  meanElong := moonLong - sunLong;
  lunAscNode := moonLong - moonLat;
END;

PROCEDURE ToEcliptic; { fundamental args --> ecliptic coordinates }
BEGIN
  helioLong := Sin(DtoR(sunAnom)) * 691/360 + 0.02 * Sin(DtoR(2*sunAnom));
  helioLong := helioLong - 17/3600 * (Sin(DtoR(sunAnom)) + jc19);
  helioLong := helioLong - 7/3600*cos(DtoR(sunAnom-jupAnom))
               + Sin(DtoR(meanElong))/600;
  IF helioLong < 0 THEN helioLong := helioLong + 360;
  radiusAU := 1.00014 - Cos(DtoR(sunAnom))*0.01675
               - 0.00014 * Cos(DtoR(2*sunAnom));
END;
```

```
PROCEDURE ToEquatorial; { ecliptic --> equatorial conversion }
VAR
  q,q1,q2: Extended;
BEGIN
  e := Cos(DtoR(lunAscNode))/400 - jc19*47/3600 + 21107/900;
  sunLong := sunLong - Sin(DtoR(lunAscNode)) * 17/3600; { nutation }
  decl := (sin(DtoR(sunLong))*Cos(DtoR(helioLong))
          + Cos(DtoR(sunLong)) * Sin(DtoR(helioLong))) * Sin(DtoR(e));
  decl := RtoD(ArcSin(decl));
  q2 := (Sin(DtoR(sunLong)) * Cos(DtoR(helioLong))
          + Cos(DtoR(sunLong)) * Sin(DtoR(helioLong)));
  q1 := (1 - Cos(DtoR(e))) * q2;
  q := ArcTan((Sin(DtoR(helioLong)) - Cos(DtoR(sunLong)) * q1)
              / (Cos(DtoR(helioLong)) - Sin(DtoR(sunLong)) * q1));
  q := RtoD(q);
  rightAscen := (Modulo(sunLong,360) + q) / 15;
  IF rightAscen < 0 THEN rightAscen := rightAscen + 24;
END;

PROCEDURE ToHorizon; { equatorial --> horizon conversion }
VAR
  h1,h2:  Extended;
BEGIN
  h1 := Modulo(lst-rightAscen*15,360);
  h2 := h1 - longitude;
  altitude := ArcSin(Sin(DtoR(decl)) * Sin(DtoR(latitude))
              + Cos(DtoR(decl)) * Cos(DtoR(h2)) * Cos(DtoR(latitude)));
  altitude := RtoD(altitude);
  azimuth := (Sin(DtoR(decl)) * Cos(DtoR(latitude))
              - Cos(DtoR(decl)) * Cos(DtoR(h2)) * Sin(DtoR(latitude)));
  azimuth := RtoD(ArcCos(azimuth/Cos(DtoR(altitude))));
  IF latitude < 0 THEN azimuth := 180 - azimuth;
  IF (h2 > 0) AND (h2 < 180) THEN azimuth := Modulo(360-azimuth,360);
END;

PROCEDURE PrintResults;
  PROCEDURE Justify(i: Integer);
  BEGIN
    IF i < 10 THEN Write('0':0);
    Write(i:0);
  END;
BEGIN
  Write('Date      = ',m:0,'/');
  Justify(d);
  WriteLn('/',y:0);
```

```
          Write('Time       = ');
          Justify(hour);
          Write(':');
          Justify(minute);
          Write(':');
          Justify(sec);
          IF timeZone = 8 THEN WriteLn(' PST');
          IF timeZone = 7 THEN WriteLn(' PDT');
          WriteLn;
          WriteLn('Radius      = ',radiusAU:8:4,' AU  ',
                     'HelioLong = ',helioLong:8:4, ' °');
          WriteLn('Declination = ',decl:8:4,' °    ',
                     'RightAscn = ',rightAscen:8:4,' hr');
          WriteLn('Altitude    = ',altitude:8:4,' °    ',
                     'Azimuth   = ',azimuth:8:4,   ' °');
END;

PROCEDURE GetCurTime; { get current time from MacOS }
VAR
   secs: LongInt;
   dt:   DateTimeRec;
BEGIN
   GetDateTime(secs);
   Secs2Date(secs,dt);
   m := dt.month;
   d := dt.day;
   y := dt.year;
   hour := dt.hour;
   minute := dt.minute;
   sec := dt.second;
END;

BEGIN { main }
   latitude := 37.34; longitude := 122.0625; timeZone := 8;  { Cupertino }
   GetCurTime;
   ToJulian;
   ToSiderial;
   FundArgs;
   ToEcliptic;
   ToEquatorial;
   ToHorizon;
   PrintResults;
END.
```

Sun — C Tool

This is a C version of the previous program. It has additional argument processing that allows various locations and times to be specified as command-line arguments. It also is smart about the current Daylight Savings Time laws, which seem to change so often that few computers ever handle them properly.

Improving Sun

Here are some suggestions for improving Sun:

- Combine the best of Solar and Sun by doing matrix transformations for the coordinate system conversions but doing away with table look-up for the orbital elements and sidereal time.
- Add modeling for the path of the moon. *Caution:* the moon's motion is quite irregular compared to the sun and planets. Check your results against the astronomical and/or nautical almanacs.
- Create a more accurate model of the solar system, taking into account relativistic effects. Green's *Spherical Astronomy* shows that such effects actually are significant, and this book is a good source for the basic formulas. Use tensors where possible.
- Add graphics to these programs, with both accelerated and real-time options for viewing the modeled solar system.
- Make a desk accessory that shows the positions of the sun and moon in the sky.

```
/*
 *  Sun.c - Determines the position of the sun
 *        - Written by Dan Allen
 *        - First done on an HP-75C in HP Basic, Dec 1982.
 *        - Next ported to an HP-71B and HP Basic in mid 1984.
 *        - Next ported to Macintosh Basic 20 Feb 1988.
 *        - Next ported to Turbo Pascal on the Mac 18 Jul 1988.
 *        - Next ported to MPW Pascal Aug 1988.
 *        - Finally ported to MPW C on 2 Apr 1989.
 *
 * For more information see:
 * "Explanatory Supplement to the Nautical Almanac & Astronomical Ephemeris"
 * "The Astrophysical Journal Supplement Series", Volume 41:391-411, Nov 1979.
 *
 */
```

```
#include <Math.h>
#include <OSUtils.h>
#include <Sane.h>

#define TRUE    1
#define FALSE   0
#define RtoD(x) ((x)*180.0/pi())
#define DtoR(x) ((x)*pi()/180.0)

/*  Argument processing vars */
char   dateFlag,timeFlag;

/*  Default location is Cupertino, CA */
extended   latitude = 37.34;
extended   longitude = 122.0625;
extended   timeZone = 8.0;

/*  Main calculation vars */
int        m,d,y,hour,minute,sec;
extended   gmt,gst,lst,jc19,jd20;
extended   sunLong,sunAnom,jupAnom;
extended   moonLat,moonLong,meanElong,lunAscNode;
extended   helioLong,radiusAU,e;
extended   rightAscen,decl;
extended   altitude,azimuth;
extended   Modulo();

main(int argc,char *argv[])
{
  int i;

  for (i = 1; i < argc; i++) {
    if (sscanf(argv[i],"%d/%d/%d",&m,&d,&y) == 3) {
      dateFlag = TRUE;
      continue;
    }
    if (sscanf(argv[i],"%d:%d:%d",&hour,&minute,&sec) == 3) {
      timeFlag = TRUE;
      continue;
    }
```

```
      /* add your own custom locations below */
      if (strcmp(argv[i],"Fairfield") == 0) {
        latitude = 38.0 + 17.0/60.0;
        longitude = 122.0 + 1.0/60.0;
        timeZone = 8.0;
        continue;
      }
      if (strcmp(argv[i],"Palm Springs") == 0) {
        latitude = 33.0 + 49.0/60.0;
        longitude = 116.5;
        timeZone = 8.0;
        continue;
      }
      if (strcmp(argv[i],"Provo") == 0) {
        latitude = 40.0 + 14.0/60.0;
        longitude = 111.0 + 39.0/60.0;
        timeZone = 7.0;
        continue;
      }
    }

    if (!dateFlag) GetCurDate();
    if (!timeFlag) GetCurTime();
    if (DaylightSavings()) timeZone--;
    ToJulian();
    ToSiderial();
    FundArgs();
    ToEcliptic();
    ToEquatorial();
    ToHorizon();

    printf("Date         = %02d/%02d/%04d\n",m,d,y);
    printf("Time         = %02d:%02d:%02d\n",hour,minute,sec);
    printf("Radius (AU)  = %10.6f     Helio. Longitude = %10.5f °\n",
           radiusAU,helioLong);
    printf("Declination  = %10.6f °   Right Ascension  = %10.5f hr\n",
           decl,rightAscen);
    printf("Altitude     = %10.6f °   Azimuth          = %10.5f °\n",
           altitude,azimuth);
    return 0;
}

FundArgs() /* calculate approximate fundamental arguments */
{
    sunLong = jd20 * 0.9856473516 + 280.46592;
    sunAnom = jd20 * 0.98560026 + 357.52536;
    jupAnom = jd20 * 0.0830912148 + 20.35116;
    moonLat = jd20 * 13.229350272 + 93.27276;
    moonLong = jd20 * 13.1763964644 + 218.31624;
    meanElong = moonLong - sunLong;
    lunAscNode = moonLong - moonLat;
}
```

```
ToEcliptic() /* convert to ecliptic coordinate system */
{
  helioLong = sin(DtoR(sunAnom))*691.0/360.0 + 0.02*sin(DtoR(2.0*sunAnom));
  helioLong += -17.0/3600.0*(sin(DtoR(sunAnom)) + jc19);
  helioLong += -7.0/3600.0*cos(DtoR(sunAnom-jupAnom));
  helioLong += sin(DtoR(meanElong))/600.0;
  if (helioLong < 0.0) helioLong = helioLong + 360.0;
  radiusAU = 1.00014-cos(DtoR(sunAnom))*.01675 -.00014*cos(DtoR(2.0*sunAnom));
}


ToEquatorial() /* convert from ecliptic to equatorial coordinates */
{
  extended  q,q1,q2;

  e = cos(DtoR(lunAscNode))/400.0 - jc19*47.0/3600.0 + 21107.0/900.0;
  sunLong = sunLong - sin(DtoR(lunAscNode)) * 17.0/3600.0; /* nutation */
  decl  = sin(DtoR(sunLong))*cos(DtoR(helioLong));
  decl += cos(DtoR(sunLong))*sin(DtoR(helioLong));
  decl *= sin(DtoR(e));
  decl = RtoD(asin(decl));
  q2  = sin(DtoR(sunLong)) * cos(DtoR(helioLong));
  q2 += cos(DtoR(sunLong)) * sin(DtoR(helioLong));
  q1  = (1.0 - cos(DtoR(e))) * q2;
  q  = sin(DtoR(helioLong)) - cos(DtoR(sunLong))*q1;
  q /= cos(DtoR(helioLong)) - sin(DtoR(sunLong))*q1;
  q  = RtoD(atan(q));
  rightAscen = (Modulo(sunLong,360.0) + q) / 15.0;
  if (rightAscen < 0.0) rightAscen = rightAscen + 24.0;
}


ToHorizon() /* convert from equatorial to horizon coordinates */
{
  extended  h1,h2;

  h1 = Modulo(lst-rightAscen*15.0,360.0);
  h2 = h1 - longitude;
  altitude  = sin(DtoR(decl)) * sin(DtoR(latitude));
  altitude += cos(DtoR(decl)) * cos(DtoR(h2)) * cos(DtoR(latitude));
  altitude  = RtoD(asin(altitude));
  azimuth  = sin(DtoR(decl)) * cos(DtoR(latitude));
  azimuth -= cos(DtoR(decl)) * cos(DtoR(h2)) * sin(DtoR(latitude));
  azimuth  = RtoD(acos(azimuth/cos(DtoR(altitude))));
  if (latitude < 0.0) azimuth = 180.0 - azimuth;
  if (h2 > 0.0 && h2 < 180.0) azimuth = Modulo(360.0-azimuth,360.0);
}


int GregToJulian(int m,int d,int y) /* Gregorian to Julian conversion */
{
  return 367*y-7*(y+(m+9)/12)/4-3*((y+(m-9)/7)/100+1)/4+275*m/9+d+1721029;
}
```

```
ToJulian() /* set Julian epochs */
{
  gmt = hour + minute/60.0 + sec/3600.0 + timeZone;
  jd20 = GregToJulian(m,d,y) - 2451545.5 + gmt/24.0;
  jc19 = jd20/36525.0 + 1.0;
}


ToSiderial() /* approximate the siderial time */
{
  gst = jc19 - gmt/876600.0;
  lst = Modulo((36000.76893 + 0.000387083*gst)*gst,360.0);
  lst = Modulo(lst + 15.04106863*gmt + 99.69098325,360.0);
}


int DaylightSavings() /* check for Daylight Savings */
{
  int theSunday;

  if (m < 4 || m > 10) return FALSE;
  if (m == 4) {
    for(theSunday = 1; theSunday <= 30; theSunday++)
      if ((GregToJulian(4,theSunday,y)+1)%7 == 0) break;
    if (d < theSunday) return FALSE; else return TRUE;
  }
  if (m == 10) {
    for(theSunday = 31; theSunday > 0; theSunday--)
      if ((GregToJulian(4,theSunday,y)+1)%7 == 0) break;
    if (d < theSunday) return TRUE; else return FALSE;
  }
  return TRUE;
}


GetCurDate() /* get date from Mac OS */
{
  unsigned    secs;
  DateTimeRec dt;

  GetDateTime(&secs);
  Secs2Date(secs,&dt);
  m = dt.month;
  d = dt.day;
  y = dt.year;
}
```

```
GetCurTime() /* get time from Mac OS */
{
  unsigned    secs;
  DateTimeRec dt;

  GetDateTime(&secs);
  Secs2Date(secs,&dt);
  hour = dt.hour;
  minute = dt.minute;
  sec = dt.second;
}

extended Modulo(extended x,extended y) /* mathematical Modulo */
{
  extended  res;
  rounddir  r;

  r = getround();
  setround(DOWNWARD);
  res = x - y * rint(x/y);   /* modulo using floor */
  setround(r);
  return res;
}
```

Det — C Tool

This tool shows a neat technique for working with matrices in C. The technique solves the conformant array problem by allocating space for a matrix in two steps. First, a vector of pointers to each row of an array is allocated, and second, each row's actual space is allocated. The row pointers are stored in the first array. This technique allows C to pass different-sized arrays to standard matrix-processing routines. The rest of the tool is a collection of matrix routines that solve and print such matrices.

This tool solves a system of equations using the Gauss-Jordan method. A by-product of this operation is the determinant of a matrix. Two types of matrices are generated automatically and then solved. These matrices were chosen as good types of matrices to show off the excellent accuracy of SANE. The first type is a matrix we have called a Finlayson matrix, which is a square matrix whose elements are in a monotonically increasing sequence by row major order—that is, for the case $n = 3$, the Finlayson matrix is as shown in the following matrix.

$$\begin{bmatrix} 1 & 2 & 3 \\ 4 & 5 & 6 \\ 7 & 8 & 9 \end{bmatrix}$$

It can be shown that all Finlayson matrices 3 by 3 or larger are singular matrices—that is, their determinants are 0.

The second type of matrix is a Hilbert matrix. Hilbert matrices are ill-formed matrices, which means that their determinants are close to 0 but not actually 0. Small arithmetic errors are greatly magnified when a program is working with ill-formed matrices—just the kind of behavior that scientists and engineers do not need to distort their calculations. A 3-by-3 Hilbert matrix and its associated column vector are shown in the following example.

$$
\begin{bmatrix} 1 & \frac{1}{2} & \frac{1}{3} \\ \frac{1}{2} & \frac{1}{3} & \frac{1}{4} \\ \frac{1}{3} & \frac{1}{4} & \frac{1}{5} \end{bmatrix} \cdot \begin{bmatrix} x \\ y \\ z \end{bmatrix} = \begin{bmatrix} \Sigma \text{ row } 1 \\ \Sigma \text{ row } 2 \\ \Sigma \text{ row } 3 \end{bmatrix}
$$

The solution of the resulting system of equations is the column vector [x,y,z], all of whose elements should be exactly 1. Solutions that deviate do so because of round-off error. SANE's extended precision can actually solve a 10-by-10 Hilbert matrix, yielding the correct solution vector of all ones, without any round-off error. Few numerics environments can claim such accuracy.

This tool takes a single argument: the order of the matrix to create and solve. Thus, to solve a 100-by-100 matrix, you would simply type Det 100.

```
/*
 *  Det.c - Matrix Benchmark
 *         - Written by Dan Allen 10/4/88
 *         - Extended to include Hilbert matricies on 7/21/89
 *
 */

#include   <Math.h>
#include   <StdIO.h>
#include   <StdLib.h>

pascal long MacsBug() extern 0xA9FF;
pascal long TickCount() extern 0xA975;

extended SolveSys(extended **a,int m,int n);
extended **CreateMatrix(int a,int b,int c,int d);
void DestroyMatrix(extended **a,int a,int b,int c);
void PrintMatrix(extended **a, int m,int n);
void Error(char *text);
```

```
main(int argc,char *argv[])
{
  int        i,j,n,ticks;
  extended   **a,det,sum,t;

  if (argc != 2) return 1;

  n = atoi(argv[1]);
  if (n < 1) Error("negative array bounds specified");

  /* Create a "Finlayson" Matrix */
  ticks = TickCount();
  t = 1.0;
  a = CreateMatrix(1,n,1,n);
  for (i = 1; i <= n; i++)
    for (j = 1; j <= n; j++)
      a[i][j] = t++;
  det = SolveSys(a,n,n);
  DestroyMatrix(a,1,n,1);
  ticks = TickCount() - ticks;
  printf("FINLAYSON   Time = %.2f seconds    Det  = %.18e\n",ticks/60.0,det);

  /* Create a Hilbert Matrix */
  ticks = TickCount();
  a = CreateMatrix(1,n,1,n+1);
  for (i = 1; i <= n; i++) {
    sum = 0.0;
    for (j = 1; j <= n; j++) {
      t = 1.0/(i+j-1);
      a[i][j] = t;
      sum += t;
    }
    a[i][n+1] = sum;
  }
  det = SolveSys(a,n,n+1);
  ticks = TickCount() - ticks;
  printf("HILBERT     Time = %.2f seconds    Det  = %.18e\n",ticks/60.0,det);
  for (sum = 0.0, i = 1; i <= n; i++) sum += fabs(a[i][n+1] - 1.0);
  printf("Cumulative error = %.18e\n",sum);
  PrintMatrix(a,n,n+1);
  DestroyMatrix(a,1,n,1);

  return 0;
}
```

```
extended SolveSys(extended **a,int m,int n)
/* Gauss-Jordan method for solving sets of equations & inverting matrices */
{
   int         i,j,k,p;
   extended  det = 1.0,t;

   for (i = 1; i <= m; i++) {
     for (p = i; p <= m; p++)        /* find 1st non-zero pivot element */
       if (a[p][i] != 0.0) break;
     if (p > m) return 0.0;          /* singular matrix --> det = 0 */
     if (i != p) {                   /* swap rows if needed */
       for (k = 1; k <= n; k++) {
         t = a[i][k];
         a[i][k] = a[p][k];
         a[p][k] = t;
       }
       det = -det;
     }
     for (j = 1; j <= m; j++) {      /* add multiple of row */
       if (i == j) continue;
       t = a[j][i] / a[i][i];
       for (k = 1; k <= n; k++)
         a[j][k] -= t*a[i][k];
     }
   }
   for (i = 1; i <= m; i++)          /* compute determinant */
     det *= a[i][i];
   for (i = 1; i <= m; i++)          /* fix up right side */
     for (j = m+1; j <= n; j++)
       a[i][j] /= a[i][i];
   return det;
}

extended **CreateMatrix(int rowLow,int rowHi,int colLow,int colHi)
{
   int       i;
   extended  **m;

   m = malloc((unsigned) (rowHi-rowLow+1)*sizeof(extended *));
   if (!m) Error("out of memory for row pointers");
   m -= rowLow;

   for(i = rowLow; i <= rowHi; i++) {
     m[i] = malloc((unsigned) (colHi-colLow+1)*sizeof(extended));
     if (!m[i]) Error("out of memory for elements");
     m[i] -= colLow;
   }
   return m;
}
```

```
void DestroyMatrix(extended **a,int rowLow,int rowHi,int colLow)
{
  int i;

  for (i = rowHi; i >= rowHi; i--) free(a[i]+colLow);
  free(a+rowLow);
}

void PrintMatrix(extended **a,int m,int n)
{
  int   i,j;

  for (i = 1; i <= m; i++) {
    for (j = 1; j <= n; j++)
      printf("%.6f   ",a[i][j]);
    printf("\n");
  }
}

void Error(char *text)
{
  fprintf(stderr,"Error: %s\n",text);
  exit(2);
}
```

Conclusion

This chapter looked at the various numerics environments available under the Macintosh OS. These environments are as follows:

- SANE, the Standard Apple Numerics environment
  —Software SANE via the packages
  —68881 SANE for basic operations, software SANE for others
  —68881 SANE entirely
- MPW C and Pascal library routines (which in turn use SANE)
- Fixed and Fract routines

Next, this chapter presented the sources for several different MPW tools that used many of the SANE routines:

- NumTheory—A brief look at number theory
- Hash—Simple statistical analysis of hashing functions
- Rand—A comparison of several random-number generators

- `Solar`—A model of the solar system
- `Sun`—A more accurate model of just the sun's position
- `Det`—A test of SANE's accuracy when solving systems of equations

Recommended Reading

Source number one about SANE is Apple Computer's *Apple Numerics Manual,* now in its second edition. The Motorola reference works on the 68881/68882 floating-point chips are also invaluable.

Concrete Mathematics, by Graham, Knuth, and Patashnik, is a good introduction to the mathematics needed by computer scientists. Number theory, algorithm analysis, and other topics are covered in a readable style. If you are really interested in a heavily mathematical treatment of algorithm analysis, try Knuth's *Art of Computer Programming: Fundamental Algorithms* and then Purdom and Brown's *Analysis of Algorithms.*

Hashing is treated in Knuth's *Art of Computer Programming: Sorting and Searching* and Gonnet's *Handbook of Algorithms and Data Structures.* Knuth's *Art of Computer Programming: Seminumerical Algorithms* is the best reference concerning random numbers; it also covers floating-point arithmetic and lays the groundwork needed for symbolic algebra. Buchberger, Collins, and Loo's *Computer Algebra: Symbolic and Algebraic Computation* picks up where Knuth left off, but there is still a big need for a good book on the algorithms behind symbolic computation.

Numerical Recipes in C: The Art of Scientific Computing and *Numerical Recipes: The Art of Scientific Computing,* both by Press, Flannery, *et al.,* are an outstanding pair of volumes on numerical analysis. Both contain lots of source code illustrating many algorithms. The non-C version contains both Pascal and Fortran source code, into which tested algorithms can be plugged in quite easily. For more of the theory, but still at an understandable level, a personal favorite is Burdon, Faires, and Reynolds' *Numerical Analysis* which does a good job of outlining algorithms in a pseudo-code that translates easily to any language. An advanced treatment can be found in Ralston and Rabinowitz's *A First Course in Numerical Analysis,* a wonderful text.

For those interested in astronomy and celestial mechanics, Smart's *Textbook on Spherical Astronomy* has been the "Bible" for most of this decade. It is written in the charming style of the 1800s. Green's *Spherical Astronomy* is a modern derivative of Smart's work that includes a good relativistic treatment of stellar motion. Taff's *Celestial Mechanics* is the mathematically rigorous text on the subject. Finally, there are three "must-have" reference works: Allen's *Astrophysical Quantities* (something like a World Almanac for astronomers), Harwitt's *Astrophysical Concepts,* and the Royal Observatory's *Explanatory Supplement to the Nautical Almanac and Astronomical Ephemeris.* This final work details all of the formulas used to create the Nautical Almanacs.

## CHAPTER 6

MPW

The Macintosh Programmer's Workshop (MPW) is a professional environment for developing Macintosh software. It is similar to UNIX in that it is centered around a shell that can interpret and execute commands, but it is much more Mac-like than UNIX-like, with its mouse-based editor, user-definable menus, and custom dialogs.

MPW is one of the most powerful development environments around. Although it is generally conceived of as an environment for developing stand-alone Macintosh software, three groups of people will find MPW useful:

- Developers of stand-alone Macintosh software
- Anyone porting software from UNIX or MS-DOS—many scientific and engineering tools, for example, can be ported easily from other operating systems to run under the MPW Shell
- Anyone working with large amounts of text—MPW will let you edit a 10 MB text file, something that no word processor and few text editors will allow. MPW also makes it easy to write small scripts and tools that manipulate text. In Chapter 8, you will see many examples of text tools written in C.

This chapter looks at the history of MPW, the Shell language, and tools provided as part of MPW. The code in this chapter includes many scripts and an MPW tool. Finally, the scripts and code necessary to build a library are illustrated by the HyperCard XCMD library, which is utilized more in Chapter 10.

History of MPW

Development of MPW began late in 1984 when an Apple engineer named Rick Meyers was given the charge to create a development environment to suit Apple's own internal requirements. As the design of the MPW Shell progressed, it was seen that two different applications were needed: a UNIX-like command shell and a Mac-like mouse-based editor. A combination shell/editor was decided upon, with Dan Smith writing the shell and Jeff Parrish writing the editor. Rick Meyers led the project and also worked on the command interpreter portion of the shell. With the exception of a small amount of assembly language code, the Shell is written using MPW C and Rez, MPW's resource compiler.

MPW 1.0 was designed to support development on any Macintosh of its day that had 1 MB of RAM and at least 1.6 MB of disk space. It even worked on the Mac XL. The project started life as MPS, short for *Macintosh Programming System.* (It was later noticed that—coincidentally—MPS also stood for Meyers, Parrish, Smith!) The MPW Shell was begun by porting the MDS Edit program, which was the editor for the only other development system that then ran on the Macintosh (MDS Edit was written for Apple in C by Bill Duvall, formerly of Xerox PARC). Much of the early work on the Shell was done in C on three Apollo workstations. As the Lisa Workshop's Green Hills C compiler was ported to run under MPW, so the development of the MPW Shell moved to Macintosh.

Other elements of MPW included various tools and compilers. Ira Ruben wrote a completely new 68xxx assembler from scratch, as well as many of the other tools for MPW. Fred Forsman wrote two major utilities: `Make` and `Print`. Ken Friedenbach brought the Lisa Linker forward, with enhancements. Jim Thomas—then head of the Development Systems group—and Clayton Lewis of the Numerics group made sure that the Standard Apple Numerics Environment (SANE) was implemented properly across all of the languages. Johan Strandberg designed the Rez family of resource tools and Tom Taylor finished them. Gene Pope worked on ResEdit. Neal Johnson supervised the equates files, and Steve Hartwell (formerly of Bell Labs) ported the standard C libraries. Mike Shannon took over dealing with the Green Hills C compiler from Rick Meyers, and Al Hoffman, Ken Doyle, and Roger Lawrence brought Lisa Pascal forward.

Russ Daniels began work on a symbolic debugger (later to become SADE), but as that became too ambitious for the schedule, Dan Allen joined the team and rewrote MacsBug, the Macintosh assembly-level debugger. Russ contributed greatly as "Chief Heap Dump Analyzer" for the group. In addition to Russ, Chris Brown and at least 13 other people worked on testing the system, not to mention the many people who were beta-testers. Paul Zemlin was the product manager, and Harry Yee built the system for Apple's Software Configuration Management (SCM) group.

It took a year and a half to create MPW 1.0, which began distribution through the Apple Programmers and Developers Association (APDA) in September 1986. After that, the team grew substantially, and in July 1987, it released MPW 2.0 through APDA. MPW 2.0 required the 128 KB ROM and a hard disk, and it was shipped on 800 KB floppies. MPW 2.0 added some new tools, an improved Shell and MacsBug, compilers that generated 68020 and 68881 code, and interfaces and libraries to support the Macintosh II.

MPW 3.0 has the same hardware requirements as 2.0 and was released from APDA in early 1989. Tom Taylor led the project, which led to a brand new in-house C compiler written by Roger Lawrence, an integrated source code control system called Projector that was created by Peter Potrebic, a few more tools, and updated libraries and interfaces. Two all-new debuggers were also introduced: a rewritten MacsBug 6.0, which was created by Michael Tibbot and a source-level debugger based on the MPW Shell called SADE (Symbolic Application Debugging Environment), which was written by Russ Daniels and friends.

MPW Overview

MPW is versatile in what it can build. It was designed primarily for developing Macintosh stand-alone double-clickable applications. Many successful applications have been developed with MPW, including Apple's HyperCard, MPW itself, MacDraw II (now sold by Claris), Living Videotext's More (now Symantec), and many others. A substantial percentage of the successful Macintosh applications on the market today were designed and built using MPW.

Applications created with MPW are run and debugged outside of the MPW environment. When running under MultiFinder—Apple's recently introduced multitasking operating system—MPW can always be resident, thus allowing a fast return to the environment to continue the development cycle. MPW itself has at its heart a major Macintosh application, the MPW Shell, which will be discussed below.

MPW also supports the notion of an integrated tool, which is a generic line-oriented application that runs inside the MPW environment. Generally, such tools are things like language translators, text tools, and other non-graphical tools, but there are exceptions, such as MPW's own `Commando` tool. Integrated tools have the advantage over standard applications of being able to use the MPW Shell's environment and resources, thus freeing you from having to write a Macintosh application every time you need a small utility. Tools are also a good way to extend the system's functionality; they are discussed in more detail below.

Code is usually disguised as a resource of some kind in the Macintosh. MPW is able to create many different types of resources, including INITs, PACKs, MDEFs, WDEFs, DRVRs, and desk accessories. Even the Macintosh ROMs are built entirely with the same MPW system that is sold to the public.

A new resource type that is growing in popularity is the HyperCard XCMD, which allows HyperTalk to be extended by calling these compiled resources. Information on writing XCMDs with MPW is found in chapter 10.

The MPW Interface

MPW is a blend of Smalltalk and UNIX. From Smalltalk, MPW inherits an integrated environment and the ability to interpret commands when you simply select it and press the Enter key. The disk-based editor can edit multi-megabyte files, while still being quite fast because of effective use of memory. The editor is mainly mouse-based, but it does support several keyboard shortcuts, as well as cursor keys. As the editor is built in, you cannot easily use any other text editor—a disadvantage to those who prefer their own editors. The advantages of the integrated environment, however, far outweigh any disadvantages of the built-in editor.

From UNIX, MPW inherits the notion of a command shell. The command interpreter supports aliases, shell variables, structured constructs, I/O redirection, pipes, shell scripts, the sublaunching of tools and applications from MPW, and more. Its history mechanism is simple and easy to use: commands are maintained in a window called the Worksheet that is always present. The Worksheet is handled like any other open file by the editor. To execute any previous command, simply select the line (triple-clicking is one shortcut to doing this) and then press Enter or click with the mouse on the lower left corner of the window to execute the selection. (This corner also shows the name of the command that is currently executing.) Commands can be executed from any window, not just the Worksheet. The MPW Shell allows up to 20 open windows in addition to the Worksheet for MPW 3.0. Figure 6–1 shows a sample worksheet window.

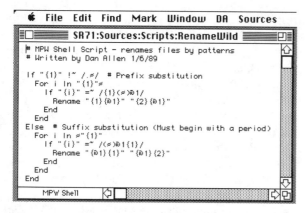

Figure 6–1: A Sample Worksheet Window

A window is considered to be a view into a file of the same name. This is a powerful concept when combined with I/O redirection. For example, if a tool's output is redirected to a particular file that is currently open, the output will be sent to the window as well as the file. This makes analyzing tool output easy, with one window containing various shell commands and a second window next to it saving the output from the commands.

MPW supports three types of commands: built-ins, tools, and scripts. If you issue MPW a command that is not a recognized built-in, MPW searches a user-definable search path of directories looking for a file of the same name. If the file is a regular MPW text file (file type of TEXT), it is interpreted as a shell command script. If the file is an MPW tool (file type of MPST), it is run as executable code. More details on the various built-ins and the operation of tools will be provided later. MPW can also launch any stand-alone Macintosh application. When you quit from an application, you will return to the MPW Shell.

Find-and-replace commands work on open windows, either in a literal mode similar to that found on most word processors or in a selection-expression mode in which you can do powerful text processing using commands reminiscent of UNIX's regular expressions. Numeric and string expressions are evaluated in the same way as the pattern portion of an awk script, regular expressions may be specified as in grep, and selections allow ranges of text in windows to be specified in powerful ways. Admittedly, selection expressions are the most arcane aspect of MPW and have a steep learning curve. This is one area of MPW that is drastically underused by most programmers.

Finally, MPW inherits from both Smalltalk and UNIX the ability to extend the system. MPW is flexible. From customizing a `UserStartup` shell script, to designing custom menus and keyboard equivalents that are tied into shell commands, to writing new tools, MPW is designed from the ground up to be configured the way you want it to be.

Shell Command Language

The MPW Shell language can be thought of as a programming language in its own right. It has variables, control structures, input/output facilities, support for subroutines, and so on. We will see examples of "programs" (often referred to as "scripts") later in this chapter.

MPW Commands are interpreted in seven steps when you press the Enter key (or equivalent):

1. Alias substitution
2. Evaluation of structured constructs
3. Variable and command substitution
4. Blank interpretation
5. File name generation
6. I/O redirection
7. Execution

We will look at each of these steps in turn.

Alias Substitution

Alias substitution is a simple macro mechanism for replacing one or more commands with a single term. As with the C preprocessor, the first step of command interpretation by the Shell is to scan for any words that may be aliases. If any are found, the alias is expanded. Aliases are created and destroyed by `Alias` and `Unalias`, respectively. All current aliases can be listed by simply typing `Alias`.

Evaluation of Structured Constructs

The next step of the command interpreter is to evaluate the structured constructs of a script. These allow conditional tests and iteration. The `If` statement allows multiway branching with multiple optional `Else If` clauses and an optional final `Else` clause. All structured statement openers (`Begin`, `For`, `If`, and `Loop`) must be alone on a line, and they require a matching `End` statement beginning on a separate line. Anything following an `End` is ignored until the next line.

The following table lists the structured commands that are built into MPW.

Name	Function
Begin	Group commands
Break	Break from For or Loop
Continue	Continue with next iteration of For or Loop
Evaluate	Evaluate an expression
Execute	Execute command file in the current scope
Exit	Exit from a command file
For	Repeat commands once per parameter
If	Conditional command execution
Loop	Repeat commands until Break

Loops are of two types: definite and indefinite. The definite loop is a variation on a `For` loop that resembles the UNIX tool `awk`'s `for` loop: it takes a list of parameters and sets a variable to those parameters. The indefinite loop starts simply with `Loop`. You may exit the loop using the `Break` command (which optionally has the form `Break If` expression . . .) or the `Exit` command, which terminates the entire script and optionally returns a result. The `Continue` statement is just like the C statement of the same name. There is no Goto.

Variable and Command Substitution

To refer to variables, enclose their names in braces. Variables are not typed: all variables evaluate to strings of text.

To create and destroy variables, use the `Set` and `Unset` commands. Their scope is local to the currently executing script. Scripts can call other scripts or themselves recursively, limited only by available memory. Each invocation of a script will have its own copy of local variables, which are implicitly declared by the use of `Set`.

If you want to make variables visible to nested scripts, export them with the `Export` command. Exported variables can also be hidden later using the `Unexport` command; they can also be overridden locally through the use of `Set`. To return lists of all currently set or exported variables, use the `Set` and `Export` commands without parameters.

If you run a script by using the `Execute` command rather than by just referring to the script's name, the script's scope stays the same as the global environment—no local scope is created. You should always execute a `Startup` script after it has been changed, rather than just referring to its name.

The MPW Shell sets several variables, including `Active`, `Aliases`, `AutoIndent`, `Boot`, `Command`, `Font`, `FontSize`, `ShellDirectory`, `Status`, `SystemFolder`, `Tab`, `Target`, `Windows`, `WordSet`, and `Worksheet`. Other variables that are referenced by the Shell include `Commands`, `Commando`, `Echo`, `Exit`, and `Test`.

The following table lists the variable and parameter commands that are built into MPW.

Name	Function
Alias	Define or write command aliases
Echo	Echo parameters
Export	Make variables available to commands
Parameters	Write parameters
Quote	Echo parameters, quoting if needed
Set	Define or write Shell variables
Shift	Renumber command file positional parameters
Unalias	Remove aliases
Unexport	Remove variable defs from the export list
Unset	Remove Shell variable definitions

Command substitution through the use of backquotes allows the results of a command that would normally go to standard output to be returned as a string, much like a function.

Blank Interpretation, File Name Generation, I/O Redirection, and Execution

Next in MPW's interpretation process comes blank interpretation. Blank spaces that have separated tokens are removed. Then file name generation allows selection expressions to expand to a list of file names for the current directory.

I/O redirection follows, sending `stdin`, `stdout`, and `stderr` to arbitrary destinations that are also specified by selection expressions. For example, using this mechanism, you can run a tool on just a selected portion of text in an open window. By default, standard output and standard error are sent to the location where the script began execution, usually the Worksheet.

After I/O redirection, the script is actually executed or interpreted. Evaluation of expressions takes place at this time.

MPW Shell Built-In Commands

The MPW Shell can accomplish most of the functions that the Finder provides. Obviously, the Shell is not as easy to use as the Finder, but the Shell does give you flexibility in manipulating files with the built-in file system commands shown in the following table. Many of these commands are similar to UNIX commands.

Name	Function
Catenate	Concatenate files
Delete	Delete files and directories
Directory	Set or write the default directory
Duplicate	Duplicate files and directories
Eject	Eject volumes
Equal	Compare files and directories
Erase	Initialize volumes
Exists	Confirm the existence of a file or directory
Files	List files and directories
Flush	Flush the tools that the Shell has cached
Mount	Mount volumes
Move	Move files and directories
Newer	Compare modification dates of files
NewFolder	Create a new folder
OpenFiles	List files that are open
Rename	Rename files and directories
SetFile	Set file attributes
Unmount	Unmount volumes
Volumes	List mounted volumes
Which	Determine which file the Shell will execute

As shown in the following table, a few other miscellaneous commands are provided.

Name	Function
Beep	Generate tones
Date	Write the date and time
Help	Write summary information
Quit	Quit MPW
Shutdown	Power down or restart the machine

The MPW Shell also provides built-in scriptable commands for most of the actions that normally would be done with the mouse or keyboard, thus facilitating build scripts that automate the production of software. Custom menus can be created, with scripts behind each menu item. A few standard dialogs are also available, and `Commando` allows you to create semicustom dialogs, which are useful for choosing command options and getting help on a particular command.

The following table lists MPW's built-in window, menu, and dialog commands.

Name	Function
AddMenu	Add a menu item
Alert	Display an alert box
Close	Close specified windows
Confirm	Display a confirmation dialog box
DeleteMenu	Delete user-defined menus and menu items
MoveWindow	Move window to h,v location
New	Open a new window
Open	Open file(s) in window(s)
Request	Request text from a dialog box
Revert	Revert window to previous saved state
RotateWindows	Send active (frontmost) window to back
Save	Save specified windows
SizeWindow	Set a window's size
StackWindows	Arrange windows diagonally
Target	Make a window the target window
TileWindows	Arrange windows in a tiled fashion
Windows	List windows
ZoomWindow	Enlarge or reduce a window's size

With its many built-in text commands, the MPW Shell can also act like a programmable word processor. The `Find` and `Replace` commands use selection expressions to specify complex text patterns, and markers allow ranges of text to be named and easily selected. Of course, the usual `Cut`, `Copy`, `Paste`, and the ever-needed `Undo` command allow text manipulation in open windows. Text can be selected and the cursor placed with the `Find` command.

The following table lists the text commands provided in MPW.

Name	Function
Adjust	Adjust lines
Align	Align text to left margin
Clear	Clear the selection
Copy	Copy selection to Clipboard
Cut	Copy selection to Clipboard and delete it
Find	Find and select a text pattern
Format	Set / display formatting options for a window
Mark	Assign a marker to a selection
Markers	List markers
Paste	Replace selection with Clipboard contents
Position	Display current line position
Replace	Replace the selection
Undo	Undo the last edit
Unmark	Remove a marker from a window

MPW Documentation

Several levels of help are provided with MPW. First, an on-line `help` command gives concise summaries of commands and their options, expression syntax and precedence, selections, and keyboard shortcuts. You can easily modify and extend this help system to include additional information.

A second level of help oriented toward building up command lines is an MPW tool called `Commando`. `Commando` was written by Tom Taylor in his spare time to provide a Mac-like dialog interface to tools. You can make any MPW tool `Commando`-compatible by adding a single `cmdo` resource to its resource fork. By typing a command name followed by the ellipsis character (or Option Enter), you can bring up a dialog that offers radio buttons, pop-up menus, check boxes, text fields, and on-line explanations of each option for that tool. The resulting command line is displayed dynamically in the dialog box, and can be copied or immediately executed. With every command in the MPW system "Commandoized," including the built-ins, `Commando` is a great way to explore new options and to learn about tools. `Commando` makes the manual pages generally unnecessary.

A third level of help comes through MPW Shell scripts that automate and guide a user through building an application, desk accessory, or tool. These powerful scripts, which are called collectively the Build scripts, install in the menubar two additional menus that allow directories to be changed quickly, as well as makefiles to be generated and run automatically. The Build scripts were written by Rick Meyers primarily to help a beginning user with the otherwise potentially overwhelming system, although they are useful anytime a quick tool needs to be cranked out. A list of the available scripts is provided in the following table.

Name	Function
BuildCommands	Show build commands
BuildMenu	Create the Build menu
BuildProgram	Build the specified program
CreateMake	Create a simple makefile
DirectoryMenu	Create the Directory menu
SetDirectory	Set the default directory

The final resource included with the system is the main *MPW Reference* manual, which fully describes the Shell and its commands. This manual has two parts: the Shell tutorial and the manual pages for the commands and tools.

MPW Tools

With the advent of the MPW Shell comes a new class of Macintosh software distinct from applications or desk accessories: MPW tools. An MPW tool is similar to a standard Macintosh application, but it runs as part of the MPW Shell and benefits from many services that the Shell provides. To get a bit more technical, an MPW tool is actually a coroutine resident within the MPW Shell's heap. The rules for writing tools are short, and they dictate, for example, that tools do not need to initialize the various Mac Toolbox managers or to deal with menus or events. MPW tools have these services performed for them by the MPW Shell.

The following paragraphs describe the launching of a tool and illustrate how an MPW tool fits into the Macintosh architecture.

A significant portion of the Shell needs to be active and resident in memory during the execution of a tool, but some code is unneeded, so the first step in preparing to launch a tool is for the Shell to unload some dormant code segments, thus allowing the tool more available heap space.

The second step is to open the tool's resource fork and allocate a cache entry. Tools are cached in memory upon their first execution. This makes subsequent executions of a cached tool much quicker. This speed advantage is noticeable when a compilation error is corrected and when code is recompiled, for example. Up to ten tools can be cached in RAM, with the oldest tools being purged from memory as additional space is required.

The third step in the launching of an MPW tool is to create a separate and distinct A5 World for the tool. What this means is that the MPW Shell does a type of context switch by setting up an area for the tool's A5 World in the Shell's own application heap. An A5 World in this context is collectively those areas of memory that in the Macintosh architecture depend upon the value contained in the A5 register of the 68xxx microprocessor. Such areas include the application's globals, QuickDraw's globals, and the intra-segment jump table. The MPW Shell takes care of allocating a non-relocatable block for the globals and also sets up the jump table (code segment 0 of any Mac application or tool). The tool's stack area, however, is shared with the stack of the MPW Shell, thus reducing memory requirements.

The fourth step in launching a tool is to set up the environment area, which is an area in memory containing the parameters being passed to the tool from the Shell. These are accessed in C, for example, via the standard `argv`, `argc` convention.

Finally, the Shell does a quick check of the heap for consistency and then calls the first routine in the tool's jump table. The MPW tool then effectively becomes the application in control.

Many of the common routines that an MPW tool may call, such as the file-system and memory allocation routines, are patched out or intercepted by the MPW Shell, thus allowing it to do I/O redirection and to perform its "windows over files" abstraction. When these routines are called by a tool, or when a `Readln` or `printf` instruction is called, the flow of execution returns to the Shell while it handles the tool's request.

Typical tools contain many instances where the path of execution is transferred back and forth—transparently to the programmer—between the MPW Shell and the MPW tool.

After the tool terminates, the Shell automatically performs several clean-up operations. It retrieves the status from the environment area, closes any files left open by the tool, and then frees up any memory that was allocated by the tool. These operations are possible because the Shell intercepts the memory allocation and file system calls. Tools executed later are thus given a clean environment in which to run.

If a tool goes into an infinite loop, or if you want to terminate the execution of a tool, the Shell provides a periodic Vertical Blanking (VBL) task that checks for a Command Period keyboard sequence, which will force a tool to be aborted and the environment to be cleaned up.

The real utility of an MPW tool is that generic code written for more traditional TTY environments will run in the Macintosh environment without any additional code support. `Readln`, `Writeln`, `scanf`, `printf`: they all work without your having to write a set of special QuickDraw commands to support them. Most utilities written to run in the UNIX environment are especially good candidates for an easy port to MPW tools.

MPW includes many different tools. Compilers, assemblers, and linkers are all MPW tools. There are text tools to analyze sources, object tools to create libraries and disassemble object code, and resource tools to create and verify resources. The following table shows a list of the full set of tools found in MPW.

Name	Function
Asm	MC68xxx Macro Assembler
Backup	Folder file backup
C	C compiler
Canon	Canonical spelling tool
CFront	C++ to C translator
Choose	Choose / list network file servers and printers
Commando	Present a dialog interface for commands
Compare	Compare text files
Count	Count lines and characters
DeRez	Decompile resources
DumpCode	Write formatted CODE resources
DumpFile	Display contents of any file
DumpObj	Write formatted object file
Entab	Convert runs of spaces to tabs
FileDiv	Divide a file into several smaller files
GetErrorText	Display error messages based on msg number
GetFileName	Display a Standard File dialog box
GetListItem	Display items for selection in a dialog box
Lib	Combine object files into a library file
Link	Link an application, tool, or resource
Make	Build up-to-date version of a program
MakeErrorFile	Create error message text file
MatchIt	Language-sensitive bracket matcher

Name	Function
Pascal	Pascal compiler
PasMat	Pascal programs formatter
PasRef	Pascal cross-referencer
PerformReport	Generate a performance report
Print	Print text files
ProcNames	Display Pascal procedure and function names
ResEqual	Compares the resources in two files
Rez	Resource compiler
RezDet	Detect inconsistencies in resources
Search	Search files for pattern
SetPrivilege	Set access rights for directories on file servers
SetVersion	Maintain version and revision number
Sort	Sort or merge lines of text
Translate	Translate characters
WhereIs	Find the location of a file

MPW Text Tools

Working with text is the most common task done on computers. The Macintosh is well suited to working with text, and in this chapter we will present the source code for several tools that make manipulating, searching, and summarizing text easier.

With the advent of the CD-ROM, more and more text will be available, but how will it be accessed? One major class of tools that work well with lots of text is made up of hypertext applications, such as Apple's HyperCard. (For more on hypertext, see the chapter on HyperCard.) When you are importing a large text database into HyperCard, doing a great deal of massaging of text up front before the actual importing operation can save a lot of time in the long run. Many of these tools were in fact created for the express purpose of importing megabytes of text into HyperCard.

MPW is a good companion environment for working with text, as the MPW Shell is one of the few programs that can actually open, edit, and work with multi-megabyte text documents. MPW's built-in commands that are useful in this context are `Catenate`, `Find`, `Replace`, `Cut`, `Copy`, and `Paste`. These commands are powerful because of their ability to use selection expressions, but they can also be quite slow when used on big files. MPW also contains several separate text tools, including `Canon`, `Compare`, `Count`, `FileDiv`, `Search`, and `Translate`.

`Find`, `Replace`, and `Search` are probably the most used of the text tools. `Find` and `Replace` are used to locate and replace text found in open windows, and `Search` can search through a list of open windows as well as closed files. All these commands use the same regular expression language, although `Find` and `Replace` can also specify selections in windows.

`Canon` allows a canonical list of spellings to be used throughout a file. It is essentially a tool for doing multiple search and replaces simultaneously. It can be used, for example, to ensure the uniform use of identifiers throughout a file. The input to `Canon` is a list of pairs of words, one pair per line. The first word in a line is the search string, and the second word in the line is the string that replaces all occurrences of the first string. If only one word is listed on a line, Canon makes sure that any occurrence of that word is in the proper case. Canon uses as its definition for words the notion of an identifier that is used in both C and Pascal: any letter or underscore followed by any number of letters, digits, and underscores.

Several additional text-processing tools written in C are presented in chapter 8, including TextTool, Sort, and Index.

MPW Object Tools

The primary object tool is Link, which takes different modules of compiled code and links them together. The output of the linker is made up of resources, the type of which depends upon what is being built. For example, the linker outputs CODE resources for applications, DRVR resources for desk accessories, etc.

Libraries of routines can be created with the Lib utility, which like the linker joins together different pieces of compiled code. Lib is similar to the linker, but its output is sent to other object files rather than to resources. (Remember that object files use the data fork rather than the resource fork of a file.)

DumpCode and DumpObj are disassemblers that allow inspection of compiled code. DumpCode works on resources of any type (usually CODE), and DumpObj reveals the contents of object files. A variant of DumpObj is presented later in this chapter: Obj is a tool written in C that lists the names and sizes of the various routines in a compiled object file.

MPW Resource Tools

Rez is the MPW resource compiler: it takes a textual description and creates a resource from it. (For more about resources, see chapter 4.) Rez uses a language that is similar in its syntax to C but that is especially crafted for describing Macintosh resources, such as ALRTs, DLOGs, DITLs, and MENUs. These and many other resources can textually be described in the Rez language. User-defined types are easily constructed; they aid in making programs easily localizable to foreign languages. To aid you in using Rez, MPW provides a companion resource decompiler called Derez that will derive source from existing resources.

Other than the MPW Shell itself, ResEdit is the only other application included with MPW. A familiar utility program to any Mac programmer, ResEdit is an interactive tool for creating, modifying, deleting, and moving resources. Using MPW Pascal or C, you can write custom editors and add them to the many editors already present in ResEdit. Sample code to extend ResEdit is included with MPW and ResEdit.

ResEdit was originally written by Steve Capps, who incidentally wrote many versions of the Finder. Rony Sebok wrote the template editor, and Gene Pope wrote most of the other pickers and editors.

A common way to work with resources is to create resources interactively with ResEdit, then Derez them to obtain a textual description of the resources. You can then maintain and build the resources with Rez.

MPW includes a few more resource tools. ResEqual is a comparison tool that is similar to diff in UNIX, except that it compares resources rather than text, showing all differences between two files. RezDet is a resource detective: it verifies a resource fork. It can also list the contents of a resource fork in several different formats. Chapter 4 contains the C source code to ListRsrc and CleanRsrc, two more useful resource tools. ListRsrc is a blend of ResEqual and RezDet: it lists the contents of two resource files in a two-column format that allows easy comparisons, and CleanRsrc will delete resource forks.

One last historical tidbit: why the different spellings of Rez and ResEqual? Well, ResEqual was named after ResEdit: both were written in Pascal. Meanwhile, Rez, DeRez, and RezDet had a whole different flavor, being written in C. Entire meetings were actually spent arguing the spelling of these tools, but the struggle for uniformity ended in a stalemate.

Startup — Shell Script

The first MPW Shell Script that you must understand is the start-up script. Startup is a text file that contains various directives that tell the Shell where things are. A file called UserStartup also exists to allow you to further customize MPW. Unfortunately, UserStartup has become just an extension of Startup for most people: they leave it untouched and thus get the default additional menus, etc.

A good way to get into MPW is to decide how you want your projects arranged and to rewrite the start-up files to your liking. My personal start-up file has encompassed both the standard Startup and UserStartup files. I do not even have a UserStartup file, which makes for even faster launching of the Shell.

The Shell script presented here is for such a system and probably will not be perfect for anyone else. It will require careful review and changes after any MPW updates. It is shown here so that you may get an idea of how to modify your own scripts. Figure 6–2 shows what my set-up looks like from the Finder.

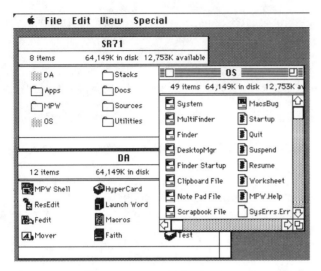

Figure 6–2: My Set-Up as Viewed from the Finder

The Shell's support files go into the System Folder, which is why this set-up is named OS. (There is nothing special about the name System Folder.) Naming this folder OS allows you to use the folder in scripts without having to quote it, because there are no spaces in its name.

The support files for MPW include the `Worksheet`, `Suspend`, `Resume`, `Quit`, `MPW.Help`, `SysErrs.err`, and `Startup` files. With these files in the System Folder, the MPW Shell can go anywhere, including on the Desktop, but when MultiFinder is in use, files on the Desktop are often inaccessible, so I use a folder to simulate the Desktop. The Poor Man's Search Path (PMSP) of HFS will allow the Shell to find its files in the System Folder.

A folder called MPW is placed in the root, and it in turn contains folders called Tools, Scripts, Libraries, and Interfaces. The Libraries and Interfaces folders have sub-folders for each language. Shell variables are set up in the `Startup` file to reflect this organization.

The following `Startup` file works with both MPW 2.0 and MPW 3.0, with the 3.0 version of the Shell containing additional shell variables that are not listed here. It is always wise to start your own `Startup` file from an existing `Startup` file and then begin hacking it.

```
## MPW Startup File by Dan Allen 1/13/89

## MPW Shell Variables ##
Export Active            # The pathname of the topmost window.
Export Aliases           # A comma separated list of the current aliases.
Export Boot              # The pathname of the boot disk.
Export Command           # The name of the currently executing command.
Export ShellDirectory    # The pathname of the directory of the MPW Shell.
Export Status            # The result of the last command executed.
Export SystemFolder      # The pathname of the System (blessed) folder.
Export Target            # The path of window underneath the active window.
Export Windows           # A comma separated list of open window pathnames.
Export Worksheet         # The pathname of the worksheet.
Set Exit 1 ; Export Exit # If non-zero, command files stop after an error.
Set Echo 0 ; Export Echo # If non-zero, commands are echoed.
Set Test 0 ; Export Test # If non-zero, tools and apps are not executed.


# Setup pathnames to common libraries and interfaces
Set MPW "{Boot}MPW:" ; Export MPW
Set Commando Commando ; Export Commando
Set AIncludes    "{MPW}Interfaces:AIncludes:" ; Export AIncludes
Set CIncludes    "{MPW}Interfaces:CIncludes:" ; Export CIncludes
Set PInterfaces "{MPW}Interfaces:PInterfaces:" ; Export PInterfaces
Set RIncludes    "{MPW}Interfaces:RIncludes:" ; Export RIncludes
Set Libraries    "{MPW}Libraries:Libraries:" ; Export Libraries
Set CLibraries   "{MPW}Libraries:CLibraries:" ; Export CLibraries
Set PLibraries   "{MPW}Libraries:PLibraries:" ; Export PLibraries


# Setup editor preferences
Set AutoIndent 1 ; Export AutoIndent
Set CaseSensitive 0 ; Export CaseSensitive
Set Font "Courier" ; Export Font
Set FontSize 9 ; Export FontSize
Set Tab 2 ; Export Tab
Set WordSet "a-zA-Z_0-9." ; Export WordSet


# Setup option preferences for two MPW tools that happen to support such things
Set PrintOptions "-f Courier -s 6 -h -hf Times -hs 9 -b2 -r"
Set PasMatOpts '-a -entab -h -k -o 120 -n -q -r -u -z'
Export PrintOptions ; Export PasMatOpts


## DKA Shell Variables ##
Set Sources "{Boot}Sources:" ; Export Sources
Set Tools "{Sources}Tools:" ; Export Tools
Set Scripts "{Sources}Scripts:" ; Export Scripts
Set wl "{Sources}WordLists:" ; Export wl
Set Commands ":,{Tools},{Scripts},{MPW}Tools:,{MPW}Scripts:" ; Export Commands
```

```
## MPW Aliases ##
Alias File Target
Alias v  Volumes -l
Alias ev Evaluate


## Unix Aliases - MPW already has date,echo,make,sort,whereis ##
Alias ar Lib
Alias cat Catenate
Alias cc 'C -mbg off'
Alias cd Directory
Alias cmp Equal
Alias cp Duplicate
Alias diff Compare -b
Alias df Volumes -l
Alias expr Evaluate
Alias grep Search
Alias ld Link '-w -t MPST -c "MPS " ∂
  "{Libraries}Stubs.o" "{Libraries}Interface.o" ∂
  "{CLibraries}CInterface.o" "{CLibraries}CRuntime.o" ∂
  "{CLibraries}StdClib.o" "{CLibraries}CSANELib.o" ∂
  "{CLibraries}Math.o" "{Libraries}ToolLibs.o"'
Alias ll Files -x tckrbm
Alias lr Files -m 5 -r
Alias ls Files -m 5
Alias man Help
Alias mkdir NewFolder
Alias mv Move
Alias nm obj    # src to this tool is in this book
Alias od dump   # src to this tool is in this book
Alias pr Print
Alias pwd Directory
Alias rm Delete
Alias sdb Sade
Alias source Execute
Alias tar Backup
Alias tr Translate
Alias wc Count
```

```
## DKA Aliases ##
# Two short cmds to clear the worksheet; 2nd executes output of make too
Alias ClearIt  'Open "{worksheet}" ; Clear •:∞ "{worksheet}"'
Alias DoIt 'Open "{worksheet}" ; Make > "{worksheet}" ; Find •:∞ "{worksheet}"'
# Cmds to save and restore directories; first 3 used by 1 letter cmds below
Alias sv 'Set oldDir `Directory`'
Alias rs 'Set Exit 0 ; Open ; Set Exit 1 ; cd "{oldDir}"'
Alias hist 'Set lastDir `Directory`'
Alias home 'hist ; cd "{ShellDirectory}"'
Alias back 'cd "{lastDir}"'
# One letter cmds to set my most accessed directories
Alias a 'hist ; cd "{Sources}ACPCode:"'
Alias b 'hist ; cd "{Boot}Stacks:Scriptures:"'
Alias h 'hist ; cd "{Sources}HCSrc:"'
Alias i 'hist ; cd "{Sources}CTools:"'
Alias m 'hist ; cd "{Sources}MBSrc:"'
Alias s 'hist ; cd "{Sources}ShellSrc:"'
Alias t 'hist ; cd "{Tools}"'
Alias w 'hist ; cd "{wl}"'
Alias x 'hist ; cd "{Sources}XCMD:"'
# Short cmds to launch most used apps
Alias xl Execute '"{Boot}Apps:MS Excel:MS Excel"'
Alias word Execute '"{Boot}Apps:MS Word:MS Word"'
Alias hc Execute '"{Boot}DA:HyperCard"'
Alias resedit Execute '"{Boot}DA:ResEdit"'
Alias mover Execute '"{Boot}DA:Mover" {SystemFolder}System'

## DKA Menus ##
DeleteMenu
AddMenu Find '(-' ''
# Find selection in target window, a very useful cmd key
AddMenu Find 'Find §{targ}/J' ∂
        'Find • "{target}" ; Find /`catenate < "{active}".§`/ ; Open "{Target}"'
# Set current window to canonical MPW size
AddMenu Find 'StdWind/∑' ∂
        'MoveWindow 36 22 "{Active}" ; SizeWindow 473 280 "{Active}"'
# Useful fast build-oriented menus
AddMenu DA 'Make/∫' 'DoIt'
AddMenu DA 'Build/B' 'ClearIt ; Build'
AddMenu DA 'Build HC/ß' 'ClearIt ; h; Build'
AddMenu DA 'Date Stamp/-' 'Echo -n `Date -s -d`'
AddMenu DA 'Change Stamp/=' 'Echo -n ∂ ∂{∂ DKA `Date -s -d`∂ ∂}'
AddMenu DA '(-' ''
AddMenu DA 'Open Startup' 'Open "{SystemFolder}Startup"'
AddMenu DA 'Open Makefile' 'Open Makefile'
AddMenu DA '(-' ''
AddMenu DA 'Files/L' 'ClearIt ; ll'
AddMenu DA 'Vol1 Name/1' 'Echo -n "`volumes 1`"'
AddMenu DA 'Vol2 Name/2' 'Echo -n "`volumes 2`"'
AddMenu DA 'Eject Disks/E' 'Eject 1 ≥ dev:null ; Eject 2 ≥ dev:null'
```

```
# Useful backup commands for moving files to/from floppies
AddMenu Sources 'Arriving Docs' ∂
        'ClearIt; Echo -n Backup -a -r -from 1 -to {Boot}Docs:'
AddMenu Sources 'Arriving Src' ∂
        'ClearIt; Echo -n Backup -a -r -from 1 -to {Sources}'
AddMenu Sources 'Arriving OS' ∂
        'ClearIt; Echo -n Backup -a -r -from 1 -to {SystemFolder}'
AddMenu Sources '(-' ''
AddMenu Sources 'Departing Docs' ∂
        'ClearIt; Echo -n Backup -a -r -to 1 -from {Boot}Docs:'
AddMenu Sources 'Departing Src' ∂
        'ClearIt; Echo -n Backup -a -r -t TEXT -to 1 -from {Sources}'
AddMenu Sources 'Departing OS' ∂
        'ClearIt; Echo -n Backup -a -r -to 1 -from {SystemFolder}'
AddMenu Sources '(-' ''
# These menus temporarily change dir to a specified dir for looking up files
AddMenu Sources 'HyperCard'      'sv ; h ; cd src ; rs'
AddMenu Sources 'MPW Shell'      'sv ; s ; cd src ; rs'
AddMenu Sources 'MacsBug'        'sv ; m ; cd src ; rs'
AddMenu Sources '(-' ''
AddMenu Sources 'DKA Scripts'    'sv ; cd "{Scripts}" ; rs'
AddMenu Sources 'XCMDs'          'sv ; x ; rs'
AddMenu Sources 'ACPCode'        'sv ; ac ; rs'
AddMenu Sources 'CTools'         'sv ; i ; rs'
AddMenu Sources '(-' ''
AddMenu Sources 'AIncludes'      'sv ; cd "{AIncludes}" ; rs'
AddMenu Sources 'CIncludes'      'sv ; cd "{CIncludes}" ; rs'
AddMenu Sources 'PInterfaces'    'sv ; cd "{PInterfaces}" ; rs'
AddMenu Sources 'RIncludes'      'sv ; cd "{RIncludes}" ; rs'
```

`MakeCTool` — Make Script

The second MPW script you need to understand is a Makefile. A Makefile is actually a combination of two languages: the MPW Shell command language and the `Make` language. If you understand that there are lines of `Make` and lines of the MPW command language in a Makefile, you have taken a big first step toward understanding Makefiles.

The following script is for building MPW C tools. It is a generic script that allows many different tools to be built with only a single script.

The first three lines are `Make` lines: they set `Make` variables that later will be incorporated in the script. (`COptions` also happens to be used by the default rules—more on that later.)

The `CLibs` line is continued over several lines by use of MPW's line continuation character, ∂. It too is a `Make` assignment that will later be interpreted by the Shell. That is why all of the quotes are present. The braces indicate a Shell variable that will be expanded by the Shell when it is interpreted.

The next section of the Makefile is what allows any C tool to be built. The idiom of
.ƒ.c.o is how Make says, "Any named argument to this script is a function of that argument followed by .c.o." So Make foo, for example, means that foo is a function of foo.c.o. The lines following this rule are output to stdout. In this case, the Makefile will link things, set the file type, delete the object file, and move the resulting tool into a Tools folder.

The next dependency is handled automatically by the default rules that reside in a sneaky place: the data fork of the Make tool itself! To dump these rules to standard output, type Catenate {MPW}Tools:Make or Catenate `which make`. (If you change the default rules by using Catenate to send text to the Make tool file, the file type will be changed to TEXT and Make will not be considered a tool, so be careful!)

One of the default rules says that any file ending in .c.o is dependent upon a file with the same name ending in just .c, or in other words, an object file depends upon a source file of the same root name. The default rules thus generate the line to call the compiler, adding the contents of the aforementioned COptions variable.

The following file is simply named Makefile. It resides in a folder called CTools with all of the source files for my various C Tools, many of which are presented in chapter 8. If this folder is the current directory, typing Make and the name of the tool desired will generate the appropriate list of build commands.

```
### C Tool Generic Makefile by Dan Allen 3/27/88

COptions  = -mbg ch8 # use old-style MacsBug names
LOptions  = -w -sg Main=STDIO,INTENV,SADEV,SACONSOL,CSANELib
SFOptions = -d . -m . -c "MPS " -t MPST

CLibs = "{Libraries}Stubs.o" ∂
        "{Libraries}Interface.o" ∂
        "{CLibraries}CInterface.o" ∂
        "{CLibraries}CRuntime.o" ∂
        "{CLibraries}StdClib.o" ∂
        "{CLibraries}CSANELib.o" ∂
        "{CLibraries}Math.o" ∂
        "{Libraries}ToolLibs.o"

    ƒ .c.o
  Link -o {Default} {LOptions} {Default}.c.o {CLibs}
  Setfile {SFOptions} {Default}
  Delete {Default}.c.o
  Move -y {Default} {Tools}
```

MakeCTool68881 — Make Script

This Makefile is almost identical to the previous Makefile, but the compiler options are different. The files to be linked against also are different when you are doing 68881 code generation. This file is named `Make881`.

```
### C Tool Generic Makefile for 68881 by Dan Allen 3/27/88

COptions   = -mc68020 -mc68881 -elems881 -mbg ch8
LOptions   = -w -sg Main=STDIO,INTENV,SADEV,SACONSOL,CSANELib
SFOptions  = -d . -m . -c "MPS " -t MPST

CLibs = "{CLibraries}CLib881.o" ∂
        "{CLibraries}Math881.o" ∂
        "{CLibraries}CSANELib881.o" ∂
        "{CLibraries}CInterface.o" ∂
        "{CLibraries}CRuntime.o" ∂
        "{CLibraries}StdCLib.o" ∂
        "{Libraries}Interface.o" ∂
        "{Libraries}ToolLibs.o"

     ƒ .c.o
  Link -o {Default} {LOptions} {Default}.c.o {CLibs}
  Setfile {SFOptions} {Default}
  Delete {Default}.c.o
  Move -y {Default} {Tools}
```

Build — Shell Script

This very short script automates the build process by calling `Make` (with an optional argument) and redirects the build steps that `Make` generates to a file named `make.build`. This file is then executed, thus building the piece of software that is the default item to be built in the current directory.

To use this script, simply change directory to the desired folder and type `build` followed by the magic Enter key; the build process begins for that project. Alternately, you can add special menus to Shell's menus to allow a command key equivalent to do this. This is demonstrated in the `Startup` script above. The `Date` and `Echo` commands in this simple script allow the progress of a build to be timed and watched, respectively.

```
Make {1} >make.build
  Date
    Set echo 1
      make.build
    Set echo 0
  Date
Delete make.build
```

BuildTools — Shell Script

This script calls the `Build` script that was just given, which in turn calls `Make`, which in turn uses `MakeCTool`, also given earlier. This script will automatically build all of the C tools whose sources reside in the CTools folder. Certain of these tools benefit greatly from having 68881 code generation. This script uses the `Make881` script above for those few tools.

Type `BuildTools` without any arguments to build all of the tools, or give `BuildTools` a list of arguments to build specific tools.

```
# BuildTool - automated build script for various MPW Tools
# Written by Dan Allen 4/1/88
# Modified last on 7/9/89

Set oldDir `Directory`
Set exit 0

Loop
  If {1} =~ /ctools/ || {1} == ""
    Directory {Sources}CSrc:
    Set start `Date -n`
    For j In ≈.c
      If "{j}" =~ /(≈)®1.c/           # this extracts the tool name w/o suffix
        Echo "Building {®1}..."
        # Certain tools really benefit from the 68881
        If {®1} =~ /det/ || {®1} =~ /graph/ || {®1} =~ /hash/ || ∂
          {®1} =~ /rand/ || {®1} =~ /sun/
          Make -f Make881 {®1} >{®1}.881 && {®1}.881 && Delete {®1}.881
        Else # the rest can be built normally
          Make {®1} >{®1}.build && {®1}.build && Delete {®1}.build
        End
      End
    End
    Set finish `Date -n`
    Echo "Built Tool Suite in `Evaluate {finish} - {start}` seconds"
  Else If `Exists -f {Sources}CTools:{1}.c` != ""
    Directory {Sources}CSrc:
    If {1} =~ /det/ || {1} =~ /graph/ || {1} =~ /hash/ || ∂
      {1} =~ /rand/ || {1} =~ /sun/
      Make -f Make881 {1} >{1}.881 && {1}.881 && Delete {1}.881
    Else
      Make {1} >{1}.build && {1}.build && Delete {1}.build
    End
  End
  Shift
  Break If {1} == ""
End

Directory "{oldDir}"
```

RenameWild — Shell Script

This script allows many files to be renamed at once, something that the built-in rename command cannot do. For example, if all files ending in .p.o need to be renamed to .o files, just type `RenameWild .p.o .o` .

```
# MPW Shell Script - RenameWild - renames files by patterns
# Written by Dan Allen 1/6/89

If "{1}" !~ /.≈/ # Prefix substitution
  For i In "{1}"≈
    If "{i}" =~ /{1}(≈)®1/
      Rename "{1}{®1}" "{2}{®1}"
    End
  End
Else        # Suffix substitution (Must begin with a period)
  For i In ≈"{1}"
    If "{i}" =~ /(≈)®1{1}/
      Rename "{®1}{1}" "{®1}{2}"
    End
  End
End
```

InitDisks —Shell Script

This script prompts you to initialize old disks. It uses two floppy disk drives and allows you to look at the contents of a disk before erasing it. The `zero` tool presented in chapter 2 is much faster, however.

```
# Script to prompt & initialize old disks in bulk quantities
# Written by Dan Allen 7/10/87

Set exit 0 ; Open -n temp
MoveWindow 15 150 temp ; SizeWindow 475 150 temp
Loop
  Mount 1 2 ≥ dev:null
  Loop
    For i In 1 2
      Set disk {i}
      Volumes -q {i} >temp ≥ dev:null
      Set nodisk {status}
      Set name "`catenate temp`" ≥ dev:null
      Break If !{nodisk}
    End
    If {nodisk}
      Confirm "Insert a Disk"
      If {status} != 0
        Close -n temp
        Exit 0
      End
    End
    Break If !{nodisk}
  End
  Files -x ktcmd "{name}" >temp ≥dev:stdout
  Confirm "Do you want to flame this disk?"
  If {status} == 0
    Erase -y {disk} ≥ dev:null
    If {status} == 2
      Erase -s -y {disk} ≥ dev:null
    End
    Rename -y `volumes {disk}` Untitled: ≥ dev:null
  End
  Eject {disk} ≥ dev:null
  Set nodisk 1
End
```

DeleteUnits —Shell Script

MPW Pascal 3.0 has a feature that automatically writes compressed symbol table information to the resource fork of units being compiled. This automatic load/dump feature greatly speeds up compile times, but these resources can also cause your files to become large. The following MPW Shell script deletes these unit resources.

Rez normally needs an input file. In this example, we pipe a very short input file to Rez by sending it from the Echo command's stdout through a pipe to Rez's stdin. The parameter −m ensures that the modification date does not get changed, and −a is required to do a delete operation with Rez.

```
# DeleteUnits
# Removes all unit resources from the list of files input to script
# Written by Dan Allen 12/2/88

For i In {Parameters}
  Echo "Delete 'unit';" | Rez -a -m -o "{i}"
End
```

CompareSources — Shell Script

This is another simple script; it is useful for comparing two different folders that contain (roughly) the same set of files, but perhaps from two different releases.

```
# CompareSources sourceDir destDir
# MPW Shell Script by Dan Allen
# Written 3/28/89; updated 6/29/89; updated 7/11/89

Set Exit 0                              # Ignore errors
Set oldDir `Directory`                  # Save current dir

Directory "{1}"                         # Go into source dir
set sourcePath `Directory`              # Get full pathname
set sourceFiles "`Echo ≈`"              # And list of files to diff
Directory "{oldDir}"                    # Pop back to saved dir

Directory "{2}"                         # Go into target dir
Set destPath `Directory`                # Get full pathname
If "{sourceFiles}" != "`Echo ≈`"        # Check for same # of files, same names
  Echo '# of files and/or names not the same between specified dirs!'
End
Directory "{oldDir}"                    # And pop back to orig dir

Echo "MASTER    {sourcePath}"           # Print folders to be compared
Echo "NEWSRC    {destPath}"
```

```
For i In {sourceFiles}                    # No quotes returns each filename
   Compare -b -n "{sourcePath}{i}" "{destPath}{i}"
End
```

LibList — Shell Script

This script creates a nice list of the various routines found in the libraries that ship with MPW, along with the names of the files in which they are found. The list makes a handy reference.

```
# LibList - Creates a list of library routines and the files they are in
# Uses TextTool, an MPW tool whose source is given in chapter 8

For i In {Libraries}≈.o {CLibraries}≈.o {PLibraries}≈.o
   DumpObj -n {i} | TextTool -d " " -s 4 -p {i} >> list
End
```

Obj — C Tool

This tool parses MPW object files, extracting size and name information; it was written because DumpObj did not provide the information desired. If files contain special symbol information generated for SADE, this tool may not work, as it has not yet been extended to parse the new MPW 3.0 object records.

```
/*
 * Obj.c    - Parses an MPW object file for module info
 *          - Written by Dan Allen 1/25/89
 *
 * For an alphabetized list of segments with the number of routines/segment:
 *     Obj ≈ | TextTool -s 3 -s 2 | Sort | Squash -c
 *
 * For a sorted list of the largest segments and their sizes:
 *     Obj ≈ | Sort -n -r
 */

#include <StdIO.h>
#include <StdLib.h>
#include <String.h>
#include <CursorCtl.h>

#define BUFSIZE    (32*1024)
#define DICTSIZE   5000
```

```
char   *dict[DICTSIZE];
int    modID,segID;
FILE   *input;

main(int argc,char *argv[])   /* files… --> stdout */
{
  void  GetDict(),Skip();
  char  *bufIn,*bufOut;
  int    c,i;

  InitCursorCtl(0);
  bufIn = malloc(BUFSIZE);
  if (bufOut = malloc(BUFSIZE)) setvbuf(stdout,bufOut,_IOFBF,BUFSIZE);
  if (argc == 1) {
    fprintf(stderr,"Obj files… > stdout\n");
    exit(1);
  }


  printf("Bytes\tRoutine\tSegment\tFile\n");
  for (i = 1; i < argc; i++) {
    input = fopen(argv[i],"r");
    if (bufIn) setvbuf(input,bufIn,_IOFBF,BUFSIZE);
    if (!input) {
      fprintf(stderr, "# Cannot open: %s\n", argv[i]);
      return 1;
    }
    while ( (c = getc(input) ) != EOF) {
      switch (c) {
        case 0: break;              /* pad record of a single null byte */

        case 1: Skip(3);            /* first record */
                break;

        case 2: getc(input);        /* last record */
                break;

        case 3: getc(input);        /* comment record */
                Skip(Get2() - 4);
                break;

        case 4: GetDict();          /* dictionary record */
                break;
```

```
       case 5: c = getc(input);      /* module record */
               if (c & 1) {          /* data module */
                 Skip(4);
                 modID = -1;
               }
               else {               /* code module */
                 modID = Get2();
                 segID = Get2();
               }
               break;

       case 6: Skip(7);             /* entry point record */
               break;

       case 7: Skip(5);             /* size record */
               break;

       case 8: getc(input);         /* contents record */
               c = Get2();
               if (modID != -1)
                 printf("%d\t%s\t%s\t%s\n",c,dict[modID],dict[segID],argv[i]);
               Skip(c - 4);
               break;

       case 9: getc(input);         /* reference record */
               Skip(Get2() - 4);
               break;

       case 10: getc(input);        /* computed reference record */
                Skip(Get2() - 4);
                break;
     default:
       fprintf(stderr,"# Unknown object record type: %d\n",c);
       return 2;
     }
   }
   fclose(input);
 }
 return 0;
}
```

```
int Get2()
{
  int i;

  i = getc(input);
  i <<= 8;
  i |= getc(input);
  if (i < 0) {
    fprintf(stderr,"# Bad object size\n");
    exit(2);
  }
  return i;
}

void Skip(int i)
{
  while(i--)
    if (getc(input) == EOF) {
      fprintf(stderr,"# Bad object file\n");
      exit(2);
    }
}

void GetDict()
{
  char *p;
  int    id,len,size;

  if (getc(input) == EOF) {
    fprintf(stderr,"# Bad object file\n");
    exit(2);
  }

  SpinCursor(2);
  size = Get2() - 6;
  id = Get2();
```

```
do {
  if (id >= DICTSIZE || id < 0) {
    fprintf(stderr,"# Dict array cannot hold ID: %d\n",id);
    exit(3);
  }
  len = getc(input);   /* get length byte */
  if (len < 0) {
    fprintf(stderr,"# Bad length byte for dictionary entry\n");
    exit(2);
  }
  dict[id] = p = malloc(len+1);
  if (!p) {
    fprintf(stderr,"# Not enough memory for malloc in GetDict()\n");
    exit(3);
  }
  id++;
  size -= len + 1;
  while(len--)
    *p++ = getc(input);
  *p = '\0';
} while (size > 0);
}
```

An XCMD Library Project

The next several files together form an example of how to create a library. A library is a central repository of useful routines that can be accessed using the Link tool. MPW includes many different libraries, some of which provide language support routines and others of which are interfaces to the Macintosh operating system and Toolbox. You can create a library of your own favorite and most useful routines for future use.

Before you can make a library, build instructions must exist for the library, so you need to create a Makefile. Next, you will need a description of the library routines that programs can use for a defined interface. These header files are usually put in a folder of interfaces to the libraries. Last, there is the actual source code to the library, the implementation of the useful routines.

The example provided here is a set of glue routines used in the development of XCMDs for HyperCard. In this case, within HyperCard are many routines called *call-backs* that XCMDs can use. The XCMD library interfaces to these callback routines. Many sample XCMDs are given in Chapter 10, where more information may be found on the art of writing XCMDs. This chapter concentrates on the details of creating a library.

This version of the XCMD library is written in MPW C. First comes a simple `Makefile` for building the library:

```
HyperXLib.o ƒ  HyperXLib.c.o
    C HyperXLib.c -mbg off
    Lib HyperXLib.c.o -o {Libraries}HyperXLib.o -Sym Off
    Delete HyperXLib.c.o
```

Next comes the Pascal interface to the libraries. This is put in the PInterfaces folder so that it may be found when used by XCMD sources.

```
(*
 *   HyperXCmd.p - XCMD and XFCN interface file
 *               - Modified by Dan Allen on 14 Oct 1988
 *               - Fully MPW 3.0 compatible 26 Oct 1988
 *)

UNIT HyperXCmd;

INTERFACE

USES
  MemTypes;

CONST

  { result codes }
  xresSucc      = 0;
  xresFail      = 1;
  xresNotImp    = 2;

TYPE
  XCmdPtr = ^XCmdBlock;
  XCmdBlock =
    RECORD
      paramCount: INTEGER;
      params:     ARRAY[1..16] OF Handle;
      returnValue: Handle;
      passFlag:   BOOLEAN;

      entryPoint: ProcPtr;    { to call back to HyperCard }
      request:    INTEGER;
      result:     INTEGER;
      inArgs:     ARRAY[1..8] OF LongInt;
      outArgs:    ARRAY[1..4] OF LongInt;
    END;
```

```
(* Message sending *)

PROCEDURE SendCardMessage(paramPtr: XCmdPtr; msg: Str255);
PROCEDURE SendHCMessage(paramPtr: XCmdPtr; msg: Str255);


(* Container access *)

FUNCTION  GetGlobal(paramPtr: XCmdPtr; globName: Str255): Handle;
PROCEDURE SetGlobal(paramPtr: XCmdPtr; globName: Str255; globValue: Handle);
FUNCTION  GetFieldByID(paramPtr: XCmdPtr; cardFieldFlag: BOOLEAN;
                    fieldID: INTEGER): Handle;
FUNCTION  GetFieldByName(paramPtr: XCmdPtr; cardFieldFlag: BOOLEAN;
                      fieldName: Str255): Handle;
FUNCTION  GetFieldByNum(paramPtr: XCmdPtr; cardFieldFlag: BOOLEAN;
                    fieldNum: INTEGER): Handle;
PROCEDURE SetFieldByID(paramPtr: XCmdPtr; cardFieldFlag: BOOLEAN;
                    fieldID: INTEGER; fieldVal: Handle);
PROCEDURE SetFieldByName(paramPtr: XCmdPtr; cardFieldFlag: BOOLEAN;
                      fieldName: Str255; fieldVal: Handle);
PROCEDURE SetFieldByNum(paramPtr: XCmdPtr; cardFieldFlag: BOOLEAN;
                    fieldNum: INTEGER; fieldVal: Handle);


(* String conversion *)

PROCEDURE BoolToStr(paramPtr: XCmdPtr; bool: BOOLEAN; VAR str: Str255);
PROCEDURE ExtToStr(paramPtr: XCmdPtr; num: Extended; VAR str: Str255);
PROCEDURE LongToStr(paramPtr: XCmdPtr; posNum: LongInt; VAR str: Str255);
PROCEDURE NumToStr(paramPtr: XCmdPtr; num: LongInt; VAR str: Str255);
PROCEDURE NumToHex(paramPtr: XCmdPtr; num: LongInt; nDigits: INTEGER;
                VAR str: Str255);
FUNCTION  StrToBool(paramPtr: XCmdPtr; str: Str255): BOOLEAN;
FUNCTION  StrToExt(paramPtr: XCmdPtr; str: Str255): Extended;
FUNCTION  StrToLong(paramPtr: XCmdPtr; str: Str255): LongInt;
FUNCTION  StrToNum(paramPtr: XCmdPtr; str: Str255): LongInt;
FUNCTION  PasToZero(paramPtr: XCmdPtr; str: Str255): Handle;
PROCEDURE ZeroToPas(paramPtr: XCmdPtr; zeroStr: Ptr; VAR pasStr: Str255);


(* Misc *)

FUNCTION  EvalExpr(paramPtr: XCmdPtr; expr: Str255): Handle;
PROCEDURE ReturnToPas(paramPtr: XCmdPtr; zeroStr: Ptr; VAR passStr: Str255);
PROCEDURE ScanToReturn(paramPtr: XCmdPtr; VAR scanPtr: Ptr);
PROCEDURE ScanToZero(paramPtr: XCmdPtr; VAR scanPtr: Ptr);
FUNCTION  StringEqual(paramPtr: XCmdPtr; str1,str2: Str255): BOOLEAN;
FUNCTION  StringMatch(paramPtr: XCmdPtr; pattern: Str255; target: Ptr): Ptr;
FUNCTION  StringLength(paramPtr: XCmdPtr; strPtr: Ptr): LongInt;
PROCEDURE ZeroBytes(paramPtr: XCmdPtr; dstPtr: Ptr; longCount: LongInt);

END.
```

Next comes the C header equivalent to be placed in the CIncludes folder:

```
/*
 *  HyperXCmd.h - HyperCard XCMD and XFCN header file
 *               - Modified by Dan Allen on 19 Oct 1988
 *               - Fully MPW 3.0 compatible 26 Oct 1988
 *
 */

#ifndef __HYPERXCMD__
#define __HYPERXCMD__

#ifndef __TYPES__
#include <Types.h>
#endif


/* result codes */

#define xresSucc    0
#define xresFail    1
#define xresNotImp  2

struct XCmdBlock {
    short paramCount;
    Handle params[16];
    Handle returnValue;
    Boolean passFlag;
    void (*entryPoint)();    /*to call back to HyperCard*/
    short request;
    short result;
    long inArgs[8];
    long outArgs[4];
} XCmdBlock;

typedef XCmdBlock *XCmdPtr;

/* Send messages */

pascal void SendCardMessage(XCmdPtr paramPtr,Str255 msg);
pascal void SendHCMessage(XCmdPtr paramPtr,Str255 msg);
```

```
/* Container access */

pascal void    SetGlobal(XCmdPtr paramPtr,Str255 globName,Handle globValue);
pascal Handle GetGlobal(XCmdPtr paramPtr,Str255 globName);
pascal Handle GetFieldByName(XCmdPtr paramPtr,Boolean cardFieldFlag,
                        Str255 fieldName);
pascal Handle GetFieldByNum(XCmdPtr paramPtr,Boolean cardFieldFlag,
                        short fieldNum);
pascal Handle GetFieldByID(XCmdPtr paramPtr,Boolean cardFieldFlag,
                        short fieldID);
pascal void    SetFieldByName(XCmdPtr paramPtr,Boolean cardFieldFlag,
                        Str255 fieldName,Handle fieldVal);
pascal void    SetFieldByNum(XCmdPtr paramPtr,Boolean cardFieldFlag,
                        short fieldNum,Handle fieldVal);
pascal void    SetFieldByID(XCmdPtr paramPtr,Boolean cardFieldFlag,
                        short fieldID,Handle fieldVal);


/* String conversion */

pascal void BoolToStr(XCmdPtr paramPtr,Boolean bool,Str255 str);
pascal void ExtToStr(XCmdPtr paramPtr,extended *myext,Str255 str);
pascal void LongToStr(XCmdPtr paramPtr,long posNum,Str255 str);
pascal void NumToStr(XCmdPtr paramPtr,long num,Str255 str);
pascal void NumToHex(XCmdPtr paramPtr,long num,short nDigits,Str255 str);
pascal Boolean StrToBool(XCmdPtr paramPtr,Str255 str);
pascal extended StrToExt(XCmdPtr paramPtr,Str255 str);
pascal long StrToLong(XCmdPtr paramPtr,Str255 str);
pascal long StrToNum(XCmdPtr paramPtr,Str255 str);
pascal Handle PasToZero(XCmdPtr paramPtr,Str255 passStr);
pascal void ZeroToPas(XCmdPtr paramPtr,char *zeroStr,Str255 passStr);


/* Misc */

pascal Handle EvalExpr(XCmdPtr paramPtr,Str255 expr);
pascal void ReturnToPas(XCmdPtr paramPtr,Ptr zeroStr,Str255 passStr);
pascal void ScanToReturn(XCmdPtr paramPtr,Ptr *scanHndl);
pascal void ScanToZero(XCmdPtr paramPtr,Ptr *scanHndl);
pascal Boolean StringEqual(XCmdPtr paramPtr,Str255 str1,Str255 str2);
pascal Ptr StringMatch(XCmdPtr paramPtr,Str255 pattern,Ptr target);
pascal long StringLength(XCmdPtr paramPtr,char *strPtr);
pascal void ZeroBytes(XCmdPtr paramPtr,Ptr dstPtr,long longCount);

#endif
```

Finally, there is the actual C source code for the HyperTalk callback routines. Note that this code can also be called from Pascal, or even from assembly language, because of the way that these routines—like virtually all Mac OS routines—use Pascal calling conventions. These conventions are enforced when you are using C by using the `pascal` keyword. The language in which this library was written does not matter to users.

```
/*
 *  HyperXLib.c - Library of HyperTalk callback routines
 *              - This file was originally called XCmdGlue.c
 *              - MPW C 3.0 compatible; ported by Dan Allen 10/19/88
 */

#include <HyperXCmd.h>

#define xreqSendCardMessage     1
#define xreqEvalExpr            2
#define xreqStringLength        3
#define xreqStringMatch         4
#define xreqSendHCMessage       5
#define xreqZeroBytes           6
#define xreqPasToZero           7
#define xreqZeroToPas           8
#define xreqStrToLong           9
#define xreqStrToNum            10
#define xreqStrToBool           11
#define xreqStrToExt            12
#define xreqLongToStr           13
#define xreqNumToStr            14
#define xreqNumToHex            15
#define xreqBoolToStr           16
#define xreqExtToStr            17
#define xreqGetGlobal           18
#define xreqSetGlobal           19
#define xreqGetFieldByName      20
#define xreqGetFieldByNum       21
#define xreqGetFieldByID        22
#define xreqSetFieldByName      23
#define xreqSetFieldByNum       24
#define xreqSetFieldByID        25
#define xreqStringEqual         26
#define xreqReturnToPas         27
#define xreqScanToReturn        28
#define xreqScanToZero          39   /* yes, it really is 39 */
```

```
/* The Callback routines */
pascal void SendCardMessage(XCmdPtr paramPtr,Str255 msg)
  /* Send a HyperCard message (a command with arguments) to the current card.
     msg is a pointer to a Pascal format string.  */
{
  paramPtr->inArgs[0] = (long)msg;
  paramPtr->request = xreqSendCardMessage;
  paramPtr->entryPoint();
}

pascal void SendHCMessage(XCmdPtr paramPtr,Str255 msg)
  /* Send a HyperCard message (a command with arguments) to HyperCard.
     msg is a pointer to a Pascal format string.  */
{
  paramPtr->inArgs[0] = (long)msg;
  paramPtr->request = xreqSendHCMessage;
  paramPtr->entryPoint();
}

pascal Handle GetGlobal(XCmdPtr paramPtr,Str255 globName)
/* Return a handle to a zero-terminated string containing the value of
   the specified HyperTalk global variable. */
{
  paramPtr->inArgs[0] = (long)globName;
  paramPtr->request = xreqGetGlobal;
  paramPtr->entryPoint();
  return (Handle)paramPtr->outArgs[0];
}

pascal void SetGlobal(XCmdPtr paramPtr,Str255 globName,Handle globValue)
/* Set the value of the specified HyperTalk global variable to be
   the zero-terminated string in globValue.  The contents of the
   Handle are copied, so you must still dispose it afterwards.  */
{
  paramPtr->inArgs[0] = (long)globName;
  paramPtr->inArgs[1] = (long)globValue;
  paramPtr->request = xreqSetGlobal;
  paramPtr->entryPoint();
}

pascal Handle GetFieldByName(XCmdPtr paramPtr,Boolean cardFieldFlag,
                             Str255 fieldName)
/* Return a handle to a zero-terminated string containing the value of
   field fieldName on the current card.  You must dispose the handle. */
{
  paramPtr->inArgs[0] = (long)cardFieldFlag;
  paramPtr->inArgs[1] = (long)fieldName;
  paramPtr->request = xreqGetFieldByName;
  paramPtr->entryPoint();
  return (Handle)paramPtr->outArgs[0];
}
```

```
pascal Handle GetFieldByNum(XCmdPtr paramPtr,Boolean cardFieldFlag,
                            short fieldNum)
/* Return a handle to a zero-terminated string containing the value of
   field fieldNum on the current card.  You must dispose the handle. */
{
  paramPtr->inArgs[0] = (long)cardFieldFlag;
  paramPtr->inArgs[1] = fieldNum;
  paramPtr->request = xreqGetFieldByNum;
  paramPtr->entryPoint();
  return (Handle)paramPtr->outArgs[0];
}


pascal Handle GetFieldByID(XCmdPtr paramPtr,Boolean cardFieldFlag,
                           short fieldID)
/* Return a handle to a zero-terminated string containing the value of
   the field whise ID is fieldID.  You must dispose the handle. */
{
  paramPtr->inArgs[0] = (long)cardFieldFlag;
  paramPtr->inArgs[1] = fieldID;
  paramPtr->request = xreqGetFieldByID;
  paramPtr->entryPoint();
  return (Handle)paramPtr->outArgs[0];
}


pascal void SetFieldByName(XCmdPtr paramPtr,Boolean cardFieldFlag,
                           Str255 fieldName,Handle fieldVal)
/* Set the value of field fieldName to be the zero-terminated string
   in fieldVal.  The contents of the Handle are copied, so you must
   still dispose it afterwards. */
{
  paramPtr->inArgs[0] = (long)cardFieldFlag;
  paramPtr->inArgs[1] = (long)'fieldName;
  paramPtr->inArgs[2] = (long)fieldVal;
  paramPtr->request = xreqSetFieldByName;
  paramPtr->entryPoint();
}


pascal void SetFieldByNum(XCmdPtr paramPtr,Boolean cardFieldFlag,
                          short fieldNum,Handle fieldVal)
/* Set the value of field fieldNum to be the zero-terminated string
   in fieldVal.  The contents of the Handle are copied, so you must
   still dispose it afterwards. */
{
  paramPtr->inArgs[0] = (long)cardFieldFlag;
  paramPtr->inArgs[1] = fieldNum;
  paramPtr->inArgs[2] = (long)fieldVal;
  paramPtr->request = xreqSetFieldByNum;
  paramPtr->entryPoint();
}
```

```
pascal void SetFieldByID(XCmdPtr paramPtr,Boolean cardFieldFlag,
                         short fieldID,Handle fieldVal)
/* Set the value of the field whose ID is fieldID to be the zero-
   terminated string in fieldVal.  The contents of the Handle are
   copied, so you must still dispose it afterwards. */
{
  paramPtr->inArgs[0] = (long)cardFieldFlag;
  paramPtr->inArgs[1] = fieldID;
  paramPtr->inArgs[2] = (long)fieldVal;
  paramPtr->request = xreqSetFieldByID;
  paramPtr->entryPoint();
}


pascal void BoolToStr(XCmdPtr paramPtr,Boolean bool,Str255 str)
 /* Convert a boolean to 'true' or 'false'. */
{
  paramPtr->inArgs[0] = (long)bool;
  paramPtr->inArgs[1] = str;
  paramPtr->request = xreqBoolToStr;
  paramPtr->entryPoint();
}


pascal void ExtToStr(XCmdPtr paramPtr,extended *myext,Str255 str)
 /* Convert an extended real number to decimal digits in a string.  */
{
  paramPtr->inArgs[0] = (long)myext;
  paramPtr->inArgs[1] = (long)str;
  paramPtr->request = xreqExtToStr;
  paramPtr->entryPoint();
}


pascal void LongToStr(XCmdPtr paramPtr,long posNum,Str255 str)
 /* Convert an unsigned long integer to a Pascal string. */
{
  paramPtr->inArgs[0] = (long)posNum;
  paramPtr->inArgs[1] = (long)str;
  paramPtr->request = xreqLongToStr;
  paramPtr->entryPoint();
}


pascal void NumToStr(XCmdPtr paramPtr,long num,Str255 str)
 /* Convert a signed long integer to a Pascal string. */
{
  paramPtr->inArgs[0] = num;
  paramPtr->inArgs[1] = (long)str;
  paramPtr->request = xreqNumToStr;
  paramPtr->entryPoint();
}
```

```pascal
pascal void NumToHex(XCmdPtr paramPtr,long num,short nDigits,Str255 str)
/* Convert an unsigned long integer to a hexadecimal number */
{
  paramPtr->inArgs[0] = num;
  paramPtr->inArgs[1] = nDigits;
  paramPtr->inArgs[2] = (long)str;
  paramPtr->request = xreqNumToHex;
  paramPtr->entryPoint();
}

pascal Boolean StrToBool(XCmdPtr paramPtr,Str255 str)
/* Convert the Pascal strings 'true' and 'false' to booleans. */
{
  paramPtr->inArgs[0] = (long)str;
  paramPtr->request = xreqStrToBool;
  paramPtr->entryPoint();
  return (Boolean)paramPtr->outArgs[0];
}

pascal extended StrToExt(XCmdPtr paramPtr,Str255 str)
 /* Convert a string of ASCII decimal digits to an extended long integer. */
{
  extended x;

  paramPtr->inArgs[0] = (long)str;
  paramPtr->inArgs[1] = &x;
  paramPtr->request = xreqStrToExt;
  paramPtr->entryPoint();
  return x;
}

pascal long StrToLong(XCmdPtr paramPtr,Str255 strPtr)
/* Convert a string of ASCII decimal digits to an unsigned long integer. */
{
  paramPtr->inArgs[0] = (long)strPtr;
  paramPtr->request = xreqStrToLong;
  paramPtr->entryPoint();
  return (long)paramPtr->outArgs[0];
}

pascal long StrToNum(XCmdPtr paramPtr,Str255 str)
/* Convert a string of ASCII decimal digits to a signed long integer.
   Negative sign is allowed. */
{
  paramPtr->inArgs[0] = (long)str;
  paramPtr->request = xreqStrToNum;
  paramPtr->entryPoint();
  return paramPtr->outArgs[0];
}
```

```
pascal Handle PasToZero(XCmdPtr paramPtr,Str255 passStr)
/* Convert a Pascal string to a zero-terminated string.  Returns a handle
   to a new zero-terminated string.  The caller must dispose the handle.
   You'll need to do this for any result or argument you send from
   your XCMD to HyperTalk. */
{
  paramPtr->inArgs[0] = (long)passStr;
  paramPtr->request = xreqPasToZero;
  paramPtr->entryPoint();
  return (Handle)paramPtr->outArgs[0];
}

pascal void ZeroToPas(XCmdPtr paramPtr,char *zeroStr,Str255 passStr)
/* Fill the Pascal string with the contents of the zero-terminated
   string.  You create the Pascal string and pass it in as a VAR
   parameter.  Useful for converting the arguments of any XCMD to
   Pascal strings. */
{
  paramPtr->inArgs[0] = (long)zeroStr;
  paramPtr->inArgs[1] = (long)passStr;
  paramPtr->request = xreqZeroToPas;
  paramPtr->entryPoint();
}

pascal Handle EvalExpr(XCmdPtr paramPtr,Str255 expr)
  /* Evaluate a HyperCard expression and return the answer.  The answer is
     a handle to a zero-terminated string. */
{
  paramPtr->inArgs[0] = (long)expr;
  paramPtr->request = xreqEvalExpr;
  paramPtr->entryPoint();
  return (Handle)paramPtr->outArgs[0];
}

pascal void ReturnToPas(XCmdPtr paramPtr,Ptr zeroStr,Str255 passStr)
/* zeroStr points into a zero-terminated string.  Collect the
   characters from there to the next carriage Return and return
   them in the Pascal string passStr.  If a Return is not found,
   collect chars until the end of the string. */
{
  paramPtr->inArgs[0] = (long)zeroStr;
  paramPtr->inArgs[1] = (long)passStr;
  paramPtr->request = xreqReturnToPas;
  paramPtr->entryPoint();
}
```

```
pascal void ScanToReturn(XCmdPtr paramPtr,Ptr *scanHndl)
/* Move the pointer scanPtr along a zero-terminated
   string until it points at a Return character
   or a zero byte.  */
{
  paramPtr->inArgs[0] = (long)scanHndl;
  paramPtr->request = xreqScanToReturn;
  paramPtr->entryPoint();
}

pascal void ScanToZero(XCmdPtr paramPtr,Ptr *scanHndl)
/* Move the pointer scanPtr along a zero-terminated
   string until it points at a zero byte.  */
{
  paramPtr->inArgs[0] = (long)scanHndl;
  paramPtr->request = xreqScanToZero;
  paramPtr->entryPoint();
}

pascal Boolean StringEqual(XCmdPtr paramPtr,Str255 str1,Str255 str2)
/* Return true if the two strings have the same characters.
   Case insensitive compare of the strings. */
{
  paramPtr->inArgs[0] = (long)str1;
  paramPtr->inArgs[1] = (long)str2;
  paramPtr->request = xreqStringEqual;
  paramPtr->entryPoint();
  return (Boolean)paramPtr->outArgs[0];
}

pascal Ptr StringMatch(XCmdPtr paramPtr,Str255 pattern,Ptr target)
/* Perform case-insensitive match looking for pattern anywhere in
   target, returning a pointer to first character of the first match,
   in target or NIL if no match found.  pattern is a Pascal string,
   and target is a zero-terminated string. */
{
  paramPtr->inArgs[0] = (long)pattern;
  paramPtr->inArgs[1] = (long)target;
  paramPtr->request = xreqStringMatch;
  paramPtr->entryPoint();
  return (Ptr)paramPtr->outArgs[0];
}

pascal long StringLength(XCmdPtr paramPtr,char *strPtr)
/* Count the characters from where strPtr points until the next zero byte.
   Does not count the zero itself.  strPtr must be a zero-terminated string. */
{
  paramPtr->inArgs[0] = (long)strPtr;
  paramPtr->request = xreqStringLength;
  paramPtr->entryPoint();
  return (long)paramPtr->outArgs[0];
}
```

```
pascal void ZeroBytes(XCmdPtr paramPtr,Ptr dstPtr,long longCount)
/* Write zeros into memory starting at destPtr and going for longCount
   number of bytes. */
{
  paramPtr->inArgs[0] = (long)dstPtr;
  paramPtr->inArgs[1] = longCount;
  paramPtr->request = xreqZeroBytes;
  paramPtr->entryPoint();
}
```

TwoCol — C Tool

As a final exercise in tool making, consider the task of printing MPW sources in two columns. You can go about the task in two ways: write a new Print tool from scratch, which requires learning about the Macintosh Print Manager, or write a preprocessor for the existing Print tool. This tool takes the latter course by preprocessing sources for Print.

Improving TwoCol

Here are some suggestions for improving TwoCol:

- This preprocessing is not the most efficient way to do things. Write a whole new tool that uses the Print Manager to print gorgeous two-column listings. Allow landscape or portrait orientation to be used.
- Add the ability to download PostScript to the LaserWriter.

```
/*
 * twocol.c  - Utility to create two columns of text in the same document
 *           - Written by Dan Allen 3/14/88
 *
 * The following MPW Shell script will print a TwoCol file:
 *
 *    EnTab -t 0 "{1}" | TwoCol | Print -f Courier -s 4 -h -b2 -hf Times -hs 9
 */

#include  <CursorCtl.h>
#include  <StdIO.h>
#include  <StdLib.h>
#include  <Types.h>

#define  BUFSIZE  32*1024
```

```
#define    TRUE       1
#define    FALSE      0

#define    PAGELEN    140
#define    LINELEN    105
#define    COLWIDTH   LINELEN+5
#define    TABWIDTH   2

static char a[PAGELEN][COLWIDTH+LINELEN+1];

main()
{
  char  c,*bufIn,*bufOut,*p,more = TRUE;
  int   i, tab;
  int   curChar = 0,curCol = 0,curLine = 0;

  InitCursorCtl(0);
  if (bufIn = malloc(BUFSIZE)) setvbuf(stdin,bufIn,_IOFBF,BUFSIZE);
  if (bufOut = malloc(BUFSIZE)) setvbuf(stdout,bufOut,_IOFBF,BUFSIZE);

  p = a[0]; i = sizeof(a);              /* set buffer to all spaces */
  while (i--) *p++ = ' ';


while (more) {                          /* process input */
    while(curLine < PAGELEN) {          /* test page length */
      if ( (c = getchar()) == EOF) {    /* test EOF */
        more = FALSE;
        break;
      }
      if (c == '\n') {                  /* convert return to spaces */
        while (curChar < LINELEN)
          a[curLine][curCol+curChar++] = ' ';
        curChar = 0; curLine++;
        SpinCursor(4);
        continue;
      }
      if (c == '\t') {                  /* expand a tab to spaces */
        tab = TABWIDTH;
        while (tab-- && curChar < LINELEN)
          a[curLine][curCol+curChar++] = ' ';
        continue;
      }
      if (curChar < LINELEN) {          /* test line length */
        a[curLine][curCol+curChar] = c; /* add to array */
        curChar++;
        continue;
      }
    }
```

```
    if (more && curCol == 0) {          /* start 2nd column */
      curCol = COLWIDTH;
    }
    else {
      curCol = LINELEN + COLWIDTH;
      for (i = 0; i < PAGELEN; i++)      /* put returns on each line */
        a[i][curCol] = '\n';
      for (p = a[0], i = sizeof(a); i; i--) {
        putchar(*p);                     /* write array to stdout */
        *p++ = ' ';
      }
      if (more) putchar('\f');           /* write page break */
      curCol = 0;
    }
    curLine = curChar = 0;
    if (!more) break;
  }
  return 0;
}
```

Conclusion

This chapter looked at how MPW came to be and examined the MPW Shell, the command language, and the tools provided with MPW.

Listings for many MPW scripts were presented in this chapter to demonstrate several important techniques for writing scripts. The source code for an MPW tool served to illustrate how simple it is to write tools. The final project described how to create a library of useful routines, in this case a set of callback routines that is useful for writing XCMDs to be used with HyperCard.

Recommended Reading

The MPW manuals document the MPW Shell and its tools. They are not just recommended reading, but essential reading. Do not forget to use the on-line help and Commando, as these features contain a lot of useful reference information that you will need on a daily basis.

MPW is similar to UNIX, so many of the books about UNIX actually give good insights into neat things that can be done with MPW. For example, Anderson and Anderson's *Unix C Shell Field Guide* documents the UNIX C Shell, which is fairly similar to the MPW Shell—or is it the other way around? Anyway, Kernighan and Pike's *The UNIX Programming Environment* is another UNIX text that is still very applicable to MPW programming.

The best books that convey the philosophy of creating tools in the UNIX and MPW style are *Software Tools* and *Software Tools in Pascal*, two similar versions of the same book by Kernighan and Plauger. Source code is presented in these books for many tools, including some for filters, files, sorting, text patterns, editing, formatting, and macro processing. The first version has sources in Ratfor—a preprocessed version of Fortran that looks suspiciously like C—and the Pascal version deals quite well with Pascal's I/O problems. Considering that Kernighan coauthored the C programming language (as well as "the White Book"), it is strange that a C version of *Software Tools* does not exist.

Another good pair of books is *Programming Pearls* and *More Programming Pearls: Confessions of a Coder* by Bentley. Bentley's books are enjoyable reading. The latter work uses awk in many examples; awk is further documented in another great little book that even non-awk users will find interesting, *The AWK Programming Language*, authored by Aho, Kernighan, and Weinberger.

If you want to write a sizable tool, try writing a compiler. The classic text in this field is the "dragon book," now in its second edition. Entitled *Compilers: Principles, Techniques, and Tools,* by Aho, Sethi, and Ullman, this book is heavy wading in places, but it is all in there. If you are writing a compiler, you will need this book.

If you want a gentler introduction to compiler theory, Wirth does a nice job of building up to a small compiler in *Algorithms + Data Structures = Programs*. Terry's *Programming Language Translation* is a good text that is similar in nature to Wirth's but that concentrates more on compiler issues than on general techniques of searching and sorting.

If you are considering using lex and yacc to build your compiler, Pyster's *Compiler Design and Construction* is for you. It is also highly recommended for users who do not plan to use lex and yacc.

## CHAPTER 7

ASSEMBLY
LANGUAGE

This chapter looks at assembly language and at the MPW Assembler, Asm. Understanding assembly language is important for two reasons. First, despite improvements in compilers, hand-crafted assembly language written by a skilled programmer is still more efficient than almost all code generated by compilers. Second, even if your application will not require any assembly code, you will still need a reading knowledge of assembly language. Why? Finding subtle bugs usually requires debugging at the assembly language level. In addition, compilers are not perfect, and sometimes bad code generation is the source of the bug. All the source-level debugging in the world will not find code-generation errors. A knowledge of assembly language will help you find such bugs.

One note about terminology: the language is called *assembly language,* and the tool is called an *assembler*. Many people erroneously say that they are "writing assembler," which is akin to saying that they are "writing compiler": neither makes any sense. It is possible to "write an assembler," which means actually writing an assembly language translator (which usually is done in C or Pascal), or to "write assembly language code," meaning to write in assembly language, but "writing assembler code" is just a grammatical error.

The MPW Assembler

MPW includes as its premier language tool an all-new assembler written by Ira Ruben. Asm generates code for the entire 68xxx family of processors, including the 68000, 68010, 68020, 68030, 68851, 68881, and 68882 processors. And Asm is fast: it assembles instructions at rates greater than 40,000 lines per minute on a Mac II.

Included with MPW is a full set of equates files that support the Toolbox as well as sample programs in assembly language for an application, a desk accessory, and an MPW tool. One volume of the documentation that comes with MPW is devoted to the many features and options found in Asm.

A highlight of Asm is its powerful macro processor, written by Fred Forsman. Using macros lets you operate at a higher level of abstraction than is normally available when using assembly language. Included with MPW is a set of structured macros (written by Ira Ruben) that implement many of the structured constructs that are available to C and

Pascal programmers. When you are using the structured macros, your assembly language code looks similar to Pascal, but it retains assembly's efficiency.

Another interesting use of Asm's macro processor is illustrated by a set of macros implementing Object assembly language. These object macros were written by Ken Doyle, who also wrote the object extensions to MPW Pascal. Object assembly language is 68xxx assembly code that can be called from Object Pascal programs. These object macros are also included with MPW, and they allow time-critical portions of object-oriented programs to be recoded in assembly language for greater speed.

The 95-percent / 5-percent Rule

For most applications, a high-level language such as C or Pascal has many advantages over assembly language. It is therefore wise to write most applications in a high-level language, resorting to assembly when needed. This is exactly what Bill Atkinson did, for example, with HyperCard: 95 percent of HyperCard's object code came from Pascal, with the remaining 5 percent being derived from assembly language.

How do you decide which 5 percent to rewrite in assembly language? Another rule is used to determine this: *measure first, then optimize*. First, you need to find out where the time is being spent. Often code is optimized unnecessarily when it accounts for only a small percentage of the running time. Several tools can be used to help measure performance. MPW includes a set of performance tools that can profile code, or you can write your own simple profiling code into your application, using conditional compilation to include the code for special debug versions of your application. For example, a basic count of how many times a procedure is called can be installed by simply incrementing a counter as the first line of each procedure.

One of my favorite methods is to use MacsBug and the AT command to flash the names of the traps on the screen as they are called. This can be done at any time without any recompiling of the sources, and you can quickly get a feel for where the time is being spent. This technique often shows that a particular A-trap is being called hundreds of times in a row for some strange reason. If this is the case, fixing the bug may solve the speed problem, with no assembly language coding required. If you break into MacsBug during a slow operation, the odds are that the break will occur right in the middle of the problematic code.

Once a procedure has been identified and verified as the problem area, and once you have determined that an assembly language routine is the best solution, you can write an assembly routine and declare it external (Pascal) or extern (C) in the high-level sources. The linker will take care of hooking everything together properly. Even global variables declared in the C or Pascal files can be imported and used in assembly routines.

Learning Assembly Language

One of the best ways of learning about assembly language is to disassemble already-compiled code and to read the resulting assembly language code. Here's how to do it. Write a simple, short program in C or Pascal. Then use DumpObj to look at the generated code of a single procedure. (Use the -m option to specify a single module rather than a whole file's worth of code.) Can you figure out the translation between the high-level language and assembly language? It is like breaking a code.

Next, try writing the same simple procedure yourself in assembly language, and link it in with the main C or Pascal program. Test it. If it works, write more and more assembly code. If you are stuck, fall back to the high-level language and disassembly trick again. Hang in there: assembly language programming has great rewards in the end.

The other way to learn assembly language is to study working assembly language source code. This chapter concludes by presenting a few examples of assembly language programming. The first is a desk accessory called Memory. This provides an example of how to implement a desk accessory (or driver!) in assembly language. The second is an application shell. You can take this code and turn it into your own assembly language application. Finally, the source code to an MPW tool written in C is listed. This tool uses a disassembler routine that is shipped as part of MPW version 3. Several other smaller assembly language examples can be found in Chapter 2 as well.

Memory — Assembly Language Desk Accessory

This simple desk accessory was one of the first things I wrote for the Macintosh. It later became a sample piece of code for the first release of MPW. The desk accessory simply shows how much memory is available on the disk, in the system heap, and in the current application heap.

```
****************************************************************************
****
****    MEMORY DESK ACCESSORY - A sample DA written in MPW 68000 Assembly
****
****    Copyright Apple Computer, Inc. 1985-1987
****    All rights reserved.
****
****************************************************************************

;   Asm Memory.a
;   Link Memory.a.o -o Memory -da -t DFIL -c DMOV -rt DRVR=12 -sg Memory

        STRING  PASCAL

        MAIN

        INCLUDE 'QuickEqu.a'
        INCLUDE 'ToolEqu.a'
        INCLUDE 'SysEqu.a'
        INCLUDE 'Traps.a'

; Desk accessories (drivers) cannot use global variables in the normal sense.
; Usually, a handle is allocated and stuffed into dCtlStorage and global
; variables are stored in this handle.  However, in this example, the globals
; are allocated at the end of the desk accessory's window record.  Since the
; window record is nonrelocatable storage, the variables will never move.
; This record structure below defines the layout of our "global variables."

GlobalVars  RECORD  windowSize            ; Put vars at end of window rec
aString     DS.B    28                    ; vol names must be < 28 char
aNumStr     DS.B    10                    ; sufficient for 10 GB of space
GlobalSize  EQU     *-GlobalVars          ; size of my globals
            ENDR

    WITH GlobalVars

aPBPtr  EQU     D7
```

```
**************************** DESK ACCESSORY ENTRY ***************************

DAEntry                                                 ; See Device Manager IM:2
    DC.B    (1<<dCtlEnable) + (1<<dNeedTime)            ; periodic,control flags set
    DC.B    0                                           ; Lower byte is unused
    DC.W    2*60                                        ; 2 sec periodic update
    DC.W    (1<<updatEvt)                               ; Handle only update events
    DC.W    0                                           ; No menu for this accessory

    DC.W    DAOpen-DAEntry                              ; Open routine
    DC.W    DADone-DAEntry                              ; Prime - unused
    DC.W    DACtl-DAEntry                               ; Control
    DC.W    DADone-DAEntry                              ; Status - unused
    DC.W    DAClose-DAEntry                             ; Close

DATitle
    DC.B    'Free Memory'                               ; DA Name (& Window Title)
    ALIGN   2                                           ; Word align


*********************** DESK ACCESSORY OPEN ROUTINE ***********************

DAOpen
    MOVEM.L     A1-A4,-(SP)                             ; preserve A1-A4
    MOVE.L      A1,A4                                   ; MOVE DCE pointer to a reg

    SUBQ.L      #4,SP                                   ; FUNCTION = GrafPtr
    MOVE.L      SP,-(SP)                                ; push a pointer to it
    _GetPort                                            ; push it on top of stack
    TST.L       DCtlWindow(A4)                          ; do we have a window?
    BNE.S       StdReturn                               ; If so, return, Else…

***************************** NEW WINDOW ROUTINE ***********************
    MOVE.L      #windowSize+GlobalSize,D0
    _NewPtr                                             ; allocate space for record

    SUBQ        #4,SP                                   ; FUNCTION = windowPtr
    MOVE.L      A0,-(SP)                                ; address of storage
    PEA         theWindow                               ; boundsRect
    PEA         DATitle                                 ; title
    CLR.W       -(SP)                                   ; visible flag FALSE
    MOVE.W      #noGrowDocProc,-(SP)                    ; window proc
    MOVE.L      #-1,-(SP)                               ; window in front
    MOVE.B      #1,-(SP)                                ; goAway box TRUE
    CLR.L       -(SP)                                   ; refCon is 0
    _NewWindow
```

```
        MOVE.L      (SP)+,A0
        MOVE.L      A0,DCtlWindow(A4)               ; save windowPtr
        MOVE.W      DCtlRefNum(A4),WindowKind(A0)   ; system window

        MOVE.L      maxSize,D0
        _CompactMem SYS
        MOVE.L      maxSize,D0
        _CompactMem

StdReturn
        _SetPort                                   ; old port on stack
        MOVEM.L     (SP)+,A1-A4                    ; restore regs



*********************** DESK ACCESSORY DONE ROUTINE ***********************

DADone
        MOVEQ       #0,D0                          ; return no error
        RTS                                        ; all done, exit



*********************** DESK ACCESSORY CLOSE ROUTINE ***********************

DAClose
        MOVEM.L     A1-A4,-(SP)                    ; preserve A1-A4
        MOVE.L      A1,A4                          ; MOVE DCE ptr to A4

        SUBQ.L      #4,SP                          ; FUNCTION = GrafPtr
        MOVE.L      SP,-(SP)                       ; push a pointer to it
        _GetPort                                   ; get it, now it's on TOS

        MOVE.L      DCtlWindow(A4),-(SP)           ; push the window
        _DisposWindow                              ; dispose of the window

        CLR.L       DCtlWindow(A4)                 ; mark DCE properly
        BRA.S       StdReturn                      ; all done with close, exit



*********************** DESK ACCESSORY CONTROL ROUTINE ***********************

DACtl
        MOVE.L      A4,-(SP)                       ; preserve reg
        MOVE.L      A1,A4                          ; move DCE ptr to A4
        MOVE.W      CSCode(A0),D0                  ; get the control opCode
        SUB.W       #accEvent,D0                   ; = 64? (event)
        BEQ.S       DoCtlEvent
        SUB.W       #1,D0                          ; = 65? (periodic)
        BEQ.S       DoPeriodic
```

```
CtlDone
    MOVE.L      A4,A1                       ; put DCE ptr back in A1
    MOVE.L      (SP)+,A4                    ; restore reg
    MOVEQ       #0,D0                       ; return no error
    MOVE.L      JIODone,-(SP)               ; jump to IODone
    RTS


************************** EVENT HANDLING ROUTINE **************************

DoCtlEvent
    MOVE.L      A3,-(SP)                    ; save reg
    MOVE.L      CSParam(A0),A3              ; get the event pointer
    MOVE.W      EvtNum(A3),D0               ; get the event number
    SUBQ        #updatEvt,D0                ; is it an update?
    BNE.S       CtlEvtDone                  ; If not, exit

    MOVE.L      EvtMessage(A3),-(SP)        ; push windowPtr
    _BeginUpdate                            ; begin the update operation

    MOVE.L      EvtMessage(A3),-(SP)        ; push windowPtr again
    _SetPort
    BSR.S       DrawWindow                  ; draw our items

    MOVE.L      EvtMessage(A3),-(SP)        ; one more time
    _EndUpdate                              ; end of update

CtlEvtDone
    MOVE.L      (SP)+,A3                    ; restore reg
    BRA.S       CtlDone                     ; exit


************************** PERIODIC ROUTINE **************************

DoPeriodic
    MOVE.L      DCtlWindow(A4),-(SP)        ; set the port
    _SetPort

    BSR.S       DrawWindow                  ; draw our window every 5s
    BRA.S       CtlDone
```

```
*************************** FONT METRICS ****************************

DrawWindow
    MOVE.W      #SrcCopy,-(SP)                  ; source mode
    _TextMode
    MOVE.W      #Monaco,-(SP)                   ; Monaco
    _TextFont
    MOVE.W      #9,-(SP)                        ; 9 point
    _TextSize
    MOVE.W      #1,-(SP)                        ; bold
    _TextFace


********************* WRITE APPLICATION HEAP FREEMEM *********************

    MOVE.W      #6,-(SP)
    MOVE.W      #10,-(SP)
    _MoveTo
    PEA         #'AppHeap: '
    _DrawString
    _FreeMem                                    ; free memory -> D0
    JSR         PrintNum                        ; draw our free mem

*********************** WRITE SYSTEM HEAP FREEMEM ***********************

    PEA         #' SysHeap: '
    _DrawString
    _FreeMem SYS                                ; free memory -> D0
    JSR         PrintNum                        ; draw our free sys mem

*************************** WRITELN VOL INFO ***************************

    PEA         #' Disk: '
    _DrawString

    MOVE.L      #ioHVQElSize,D0                 ; size of HFS ParamBlock
    _NewPtr CLEAR                               ; NewPtr -> A0
    BNE.S       Exit                            ; IF Error THEN Exit
    MOVE.L      A0,aPBPtr                       ; save PBPtr in D7
    MOVE.L      DCtlWindow(A4),A1               ; get window rec pointer
    LEA         aString(A1),A1                  ; address of string buffer
    MOVE.L      A1,ioVNPtr(A0)                  ; ioVNPtr = Volume Name
    _HGetVInfo                                  ; _GetVolInfo   info -> A0^
```

```
        MOVE.L      aPBPtr,A0
        MOVE.L      ioVAlBlkSiz(A0),D1      ; block size in D1
        MOVE.W      ioVFrBlk(A0),D2         ; free blocks in D2
        MOVE.W      D1,D0                   ; 32 bit * 16 bit multiply
        MULU.W      D2,D0                   ; right half of size
        SWAP        D1
        MOVE.W      D1,D3
        MULU.W      D2,D3                   ; left half of size
        SWAP        D3
        ADD.L       D3,D0                   ; total bytes free on vol
        JSR         PrintNum                ; write # bytes free

        PEA         #' free on '
        _DrawString
        MOVE.L      aPBPtr,A0
        MOVE.L      ioVNPtr(A0),-(SP)       ; offset for volName
        _DrawString

        PEA         #'    '
        _DrawString
        MOVE.L      aPBPtr,A0               ; free the memory
        _DisposPtr

Exit
    RTS


**************************** SUBROUTINES ****************************

PrintNum

    ; Binary integer to be drawn at CurPenPos in D0 on entry
    ; number drawn in plain text, bolding restored afterwords

        MOVE.L      D0,D6                   ; for safe keeping
        CLR.W       -(SP)                   ; plain text
        _TextFace
        MOVE.L      D6,D0                   ; and back again
        MOVE.L      DCtlWindow(A4),A0       ; get window rec pointer
        LEA         aNumStr(A0),A0          ; get buffer address
        CLR.W       -(SP)                   ; selector for NumToString
        _Pack7                              ; Binary-Decimal Package
        MOVE.L      A0,-(SP)                ; push the pointer to the str
        _DrawString
        MOVE.W      #1,-(SP)                ; bold text restored
        _TextFace
        RTS
```

```
****************************** DATA AREA ********************************

theWindow   DC.W    322,10,338,500           ; window top,left,bottom,right

    ENDWITH
    END
```

DKAD — Assembly Language Application Shell

The name DKAD is short for "Daniel Knight Allen's Development system," to be resumed real soon now. This application is presented as a starting point for applications written in assembly language. It puts up a window and menus and handles events. In addition, it demonstrates the conventions of how to reference global data and include MacsBug symbols. Getting this basic structure right is hard for beginning assembly language programmers; hence the need for this otherwise simplistic example.

Improving DKAD

Here is one suggestion for improving DKAD: The hierarchical menus were put into this program when they were first brand new. Since that time I have decided I do not like hierarchical menus because they are hard to use. Remove the hierarchical menus and implement a better way of accessing lots of information.

Here is the Makefile:

```
Includes =   "{AIncludes}Traps.a" ∂
             "{AIncludes}SysEqu.a" ∂
             "{AIncludes}QuickEqu.a" ∂
             "{AIncludes}ToolEqu.a"

DKAD  ƒƒ DKAD.a.o
    Link -o DKAD DKAD.a.o
DKAD  ƒƒ DKAD.r
    Rez -a -o DKAD DKAD.r
DKAD  ƒƒ {Worksheet}
    Setfile -d . -m . DKAD
    DKAD

DKAD.a.o  ƒ {AIncludes}Toolbox.d
```

```
{AIncludes}Toolbox.d     ƒ    {Includes}
    Echo ∂t ∂
        INCLUDE      ∂'Traps.a∂'       ∂n ∂
        INCLUDE      ∂'ToolEqu.a∂'     ∂n ∂
        INCLUDE      ∂'QuickEqu.a∂'    ∂n ∂
        INCLUDE      ∂'SysEqu.a∂'      ∂n ∂
        DUMP ∂'{AIncludes}Toolbox.d∂' ∂n ∂
        END | Asm -o dev:null
```

Here is the MPW assembly language code. MPW assembler directives are in all caps.

```
*    DKAD.a, by Dan Allen 6/23/87
*    Hierarchical Menus added 9/13/87
*    MenuJmp table added 11/10/87

                PRINT    DATA,NOHDR,NOPAGE,SYM
                STRING   ASIS
                LOAD     'ToolBox.d'

QDGlobals    RECORD   0,DECREMENT
thePort      ds.l     1
white        ds.b     8
black        ds.b     8
gray         ds.b     8
ltGray       ds.b     8
dkGray       ds.b     8
arrow        ds.b     cursRec
screenBits   ds.b     bitmapRec
randSeed     ds.l     1
             ORG      -grafSize
             ENDR

EventRecord  RECORD   0
what         ds.w     1
message      ds.l     1
when         ds.l     1
where        ds.l     1
modifiers    ds.w     1
             ENDR
```

```
MenuRecord  RECORD  0
Apple       ds.l    1
File        ds.l    1
Edit        ds.l    1
Info        ds.l    1
Tools       ds.l    1
Window      ds.l    1
View        ds.l    1       ; Hierarchical sub-menus of the Tools menu
Find        ds.l    1
Font        ds.l    1
Size        ds.l    1
Style       ds.l    1
Definitions ds.l    1
Language    ds.l    1       ; Hierarchical sub-sub-menus of the Definitions menu
Toolbox     ds.l    1
OS          ds.l    1
Machine     ds.l    1
            ENDR


g           RECORD  ,MAIN
qd          ds.b    QDGlobals
myEvent     ds.b    EventRecord
myWindow    ds.l    1
menuHandles ds.b    MenuRecord
quitApp     ds.b    1
            ENDR


            SEG 'Init'
InitWorld   PROC
            IMPORT  MakeWind

            link    a6,#-8
            _MaxApplZone
            pea     g.qd.thePort
            _InitGraf
            _InitFonts
            _InitWindows
            _InitMenus
            _TEInit
            clr.l   -(sp)
            _InitDialogs
            move.l  #$FFFF0000,-(sp)
            _FlushEvents
            sf      g.quitApp
            bsr.s   SetupMenus
            jsr     MakeWind
            _InitCursor
            unlk    a6
            rts
            dc.b    'INITWORL'
```

```
                STRING PASCAL
SetupMenus      link     a6,#0
                lea      g.menuHandles.Apple,a3
                move.w   #1,d3
@0              sub.l    #4,sp
                move.w   d3,-(sp)
                _GetRMenu
                move.l   (sp)+,(a3)+
                tst.l    -4(a3)
                bne.s    @01
                _ExitToShell
@01             add.w    #1,d3
                cmp.w    #16,d3
                ble.s    @0
                move.l   g.menuHandles.Apple,-(sp)
                move.l   #'DRVR',-(sp)
                _AddResMenu
                move.l   g.menuHandles.Font,-(sp)
                move.l   #'FONT',-(sp)
                _AddResMenu
                lea      g.menuHandles.Apple,a3
                move.l   #4,d3              ; insert regular menus
@1              move.l   (a3)+,-(sp)
                clr.w    -(sp)
                _InsertMenu
                dbra     d3,@1
                move.l   #10,d3             ; insert hierarchical menus
@2              move.l   (a3)+,-(sp)
                move.w   #-1,-(sp)
                _InsertMenu
                dbra     d3,@2
                _DrawMenuBar
                STRING ASIS
                unlk     a6
                rts
                dc.b     'SETUPMEN'
                ENDPROC


                SEG      'Main'
Main            MAIN
                IMPORT  InitWorld, DoEvent
```

```
                link    a6,#0
                jsr     InitWorld
                pea     InitWorld
                _UnLoadSeg
@0              bsr.s   DoEvent
                _SystemTask
                tst.b   g.quitApp
                beq.s   @0
                _ExitToShell
                unlk    a6
                rts
                dc.b    'MAIN    '
                ENDMAIN


DoEvent         PROC
                link    a6,#0
                sub.w   #2,a7
                move.w  #everyEvent,-(a7)
                pea     g.myEvent
                _GetNextEvent
                move.w  (a7)+,d0
                beq.s   @9                          ; exit if null event
                move.l  g.myWindow,-(sp)
                _SetPort
                cmp.w   #mButUpEvt,g.myEvent.what
                bgt.s   @1   ; includes mButDwnEvt
                bsr.s   DoMouse
                bra.s   @9
@1              cmp.w   #autoKeyEvt,g.myEvent.what
                bgt.s   @2   ; includes keyDwnEvt, keyUpEvt
                bsr     DoKey
                bra.s   @9
@2              cmp.w   #updatEvt,g.myEvent.what
                bne.s   @3
                bsr     DoUpdate
                bra.s   @9
@3              cmp.w   #activateEvt,g.myEvent.what
                bne.s   @9
                bsr     DoActivate
@9              unlk    a6
                rts
                dc.b    'DOEVENT '
```

```
DoMouse     link    a6,#-4
            sub.w   #2,sp
            move.l  g.myEvent.where,-(sp)
            pea     -4(a6)
            _FindWindow
            move.w  (sp)+,d0
            cmp.w   #inMenuBar,d0
            bne.s   @1
            bsr.s   DoMenu
@1          unlk    a6
            rts
            dc.b    'DOMOUSE '


DoMenu      link    a6,#0
            sub.w   #4,sp
            move.l  g.myEvent.where,-(sp)
            _MenuSelect
            move.l  (sp)+,d0
            move.l  d0,d1
            clr.w   d1                  ; clear item
            swap    d1                  ; keep menu in low word
            ext.l   d0                  ; keep item in low word
            cmp.w   #0,d1               ; check for bad menu numbers
            ble.s   @9
            cmp.w   #16,d1
            bgt.s   @9                  ; exit if bad menu number
            lea     MenuJmp,a0
            sub.w   #1,d1               ; to get jmp right
            asl.w   #1,d1               ; multiply by two
            add.w   0(a0,d1),a0         ; add table offset
            jsr     (a0)
            clr.w   -(sp)
            _HiliteMenu
@9          unlk    a6
            rts
            dc.b    'DOMENU  '
```

```
MenuJmp      dc.w      DoApple-MenuJmp       ; a jump table for fast case stmts
             dc.w      DoFile-MenuJmp
             dc.w      DoEdit-MenuJmp
             dc.w      DoInfo-MenuJmp
             dc.w      DoTools-MenuJmp
             dc.w      DoWind-MenuJmp
             dc.w      DoView-MenuJmp
             dc.w      DoFind-MenuJmp
             dc.w      DoFont-MenuJmp
             dc.w      DoSize-MenuJmp
             dc.w      DoStyle-MenuJmp
             dc.w      DoDefs-MenuJmp
             dc.w      DoLang-MenuJmp
             dc.w      DoToolbox-MenuJmp
             dc.w      DoOS MenuJmp
             dc.w      DoMachine-MenuJmp


DoApple      link      a6,#0
             nop
             unlk      a6
             rts
             dc.b      'DOAPPLE '


DoFile       link      a6,#0
             cmp.w     #14,d0        ; Quit Item ?
             bne.s     @1
             st        g.quitApp
@1           unlk      a6
             rts
             dc.b      'DOFILE  '

DoEdit       link      a6,#0
             nop
             unlk      a6
             rts
             dc.b      'DOEDIT  '

DoInfo       link      a6,#0
             nop
             unlk      a6
             rts
             dc.b      'DOINFO  '

DoTools      link      a6,#0
             nop
             unlk      a6
             rts
             dc.b      'DOTOOLS '
```

```
DoWind      link    a6,#0
            nop
            unlk    a6
            rts
            dc.b    'DOWIND  '

DoView      link    a6,#0
            nop
            unlk    a6
            rts
            dc.b    'DOVIEW  '

DoFind      link    a6,#0
            nop
            unlk    a6
            rts
            dc.b    'DOFIND  '

DoFont      link    a6,#-258
            move.l  g.menuHandles.Font,-(sp)
            move.w  d0,-(sp)
            pea     -256(a6)
            _GetItem
            pea     -256(a6)
            pea     -258(a6)
            _GetFNum
            move.w  -258(a6),-(sp)
            _TextFont
            move.l  g.myWindow,a0
            move.l  portRect(a0),-(sp)
            move.l  portRect+4(a0),-(sp)
            _InvalRect
            unlk    a6
            rts
            dc.b    'DOFONT  '

DoSize      link    a6,#0
            nop
            unlk    a6
            rts
            dc.b    'DOSIZE  '

DoStyle     link    a6,#0
            nop
            unlk    a6
            rts
            dc.b    'DOSTYLE '
```

```
DoDefs      link    a6,#0
            nop
            unlk    a6
            rts
            dc.b    'DODEFS  '

DoLang      link    a6,#0
            nop
            unlk    a6
            rts
            dc.b    'DOLANG  '

DoToolbox   link    a6,#0
            nop
            unlk    a6
            rts
            dc.b    'DOTOOLBO'

DoOS        link    a6,#0
            nop
            unlk    a6
            rts
            dc.b    'DOOS    '

DoMachine   link    a6,#0
            nop
            unlk    a6
            rts
            dc.b    'DOMACHIN'

DoKey       link    a6,#0
            move.l  g.myEvent.message,d0
            and.l   #charCodeMask,d0
            move.w  g.myEvent.modifiers,d1
            btst    #cmdKey,d1
            beq.s   @1
            cmp.b   #'q',d0
            bne.s   @1
            st      g.quitApp
@1          unlk    a6
            rts
            dc.b    'DOKEY   '
```

```
DoUpdate    link    a6,#0
            move.l  g.myWindow,-(sp)
            _BeginUpdate
            move.l  g.myWindow,a0
            move.l  portRect(a0),-(sp)
            move.l  portRect+4(a0),-(sp)
            _EraseRect
            move.l  #$00320032,-(sp)            ; move to (50,50)
            _MoveTo
            string pascal
            pea     #'DKAD: An Integrated Environment'
            _DrawString
            string asis
            move.l  g.myWindow,-(sp)
            _EndUpdate
            unlk    a6
            rts
            dc.b    'DOUPDATE'

DoActivate  link    a6,#0
            nop
            unlk    a6
            rts
            dc.b    'DOACTIVA'
            ENDPROC

MakeWind    proc
            link    a6,#-8
            move.l  g.qd.screenBits+6,-8(a6)
            move.l  g.qd.screenBits+10,-4(a6)
            pea     -8(a6)
            move.l  #$00300020,-(sp)
            _InsetRect
            sub.w   #4,sp
            move.l  #0,-(sp)                 ; on heap
            pea     -8(a6)                  ; rect
            STRING  PASCAL
            pea     #'Untitled'
            STRING  ASIS
            st      -(sp)                   ; visible
            move.w  #0,-(sp)                ; procID
            move.l  #-1,-(sp)               ; frontmost
            st      -(sp)                   ; goAway
            move.l  #0,-(sp)                ; refCon
            _NewWindow
            move.l  (sp),g.myWindow
            _SetPort
            unlk    a6
            rts
            dc.b    'MAKEWIND'
            ENDPROC
            END
```

DKAD.r—Rez Source Code for DKAD Resources

```
/*  DKAD.r, by Dan Allen 6/23/87    */
/*  Hierarchical Menus added 9/13/87  */
/*  Size added 11/10/87 */

#include "Types.r";

resource 'SIZE' (-1) {
  dontSaveScreen,
  acceptSuspendResumeEvents,
  enableOptionSwitch,
  canBackground,
  multiFinderAware,
  backgroundAndForeground,
  dontGetFrontClicks,
  ignoreChildDiedEvents,
  not32BitCompatible,
  reserved,reserved,reserved,reserved,reserved,reserved,reserved,
  128*1024,
  90*1024
};


resource 'MENU' (1, preload) {
  1,
  textMenuProc,
  0x7FFFEFFD,
  enabled,
  "\0x14",/* Apple Menu */ {
    "About DKAD…", noIcon, "", "", plain,
    "-", noIcon, "", "", plain
  }
};
```

```
resource 'MENU' (2, preload) {
  2,
  textMenuProc,
  0x7FFFEDF7,
  enabled,
  "File", {
    "New", noIcon, "N", "", plain,
    "Open…", noIcon, "O", "", plain,
    "Open Selection", noIcon, "D", "", plain,
    "-", noIcon, "", "", plain,
    "Close", noIcon, "W", "", plain,
    "Save", noIcon, "S", "", plain,
    "Save as…", noIcon, "", "", plain,
    "Save a Copy…", noIcon, "", "", plain,
    "Revert to Saved", noIcon, "", "", plain,
    "-", noIcon, "", "", plain,
    "Page Setup…", noIcon, "", "", plain,
    "Print…", noIcon, "P", "", plain,
    "-", noIcon, "", "", plain,
    "Quit", noIcon, "Q", "", plain
  }
};

resource 'MENU' (3, preload) {
  3,
  textMenuProc,
  0x7FFFFDBD,
  enabled,
  "Edit", {
    "Undo", noIcon, "Z", "", plain,
    "-", noIcon, "", "", plain,
    "Cut", noIcon, "X", "", plain,
    "Copy", noIcon, "C", "", plain,
    "Paste", noIcon, "V", "", plain,
    "Clear", noIcon, "", "", plain,
    "-", noIcon, "", "", plain,
    "Select All", noIcon, "A", "", plain,
    "Duplicate", noIcon, "D", "", plain,
    "-", noIcon, "", "", plain,
    "Show Clipboard", noIcon, "", "", plain
  }
};
```

```
resource 'MENU' (4, preload) {
  4,
  textMenuProc,
  0x7FFFFFFB,
  enabled,
  "Info", {
    "Document", noIcon, "", "", plain,
    "Index", noIcon, "", "", plain,
    "-", noIcon, "", "", plain,
    "Proc", noIcon, "", "", plain,
    "Library", noIcon, "", "", plain,
    "File", noIcon, "", "", plain,
    "Project", noIcon, "", "", plain
  }
};

resource 'MENU' (5, preload) {
  5,
  textMenuProc,
  0x7FFFFFBB,
  enabled,
  "Tools", {
    "View", noIcon, "\0x1B", "\0x07", plain,          /* 7 */
    "Find", noIcon, "\0x1B", "\0x08", plain,          /* 8 */
    "-", noIcon, "", "", plain,
    "Font", noIcon, "\0x1B", "\0x09", plain,          /* 9 */
    "Size", noIcon, "\0x1B", "\0x0A", plain,          /* 10 */
    "Style", noIcon, "\0x1B", "\0x0B", plain,         /* 11 */
    "-", noIcon, "", "", plain,
    "Definitions",noIcon,"\0x1B","\0x0C",plain        /* 12 */
  }
};

resource 'MENU' (6, preload) {
  6,
  textMenuProc,
  0x7FFFFFFD,
  enabled,
  "Window", {
    "Arrange…", noIcon, "", "", plain,
    "-", noIcon, "", "", plain
  }
};
```

```
resource 'MENU' (7, preload) {
  7,
  textMenuProc,
  0x7FFFFFAF,
  enabled,
  "View", {
    "By Document", noIcon, "", "", plain,
    "By Outline", noIcon, "", "", plain,
    "By Graph", noIcon, "", "", plain,
    "By Tree", noIcon, "", "", plain,
    "-", noIcon, "", "", plain,
    "By Code", noIcon, "", "", plain,
    "-", noIcon, "", "", plain,
    "By Name", noIcon, "", "", plain,
    "By Date", noIcon, "", "", plain,
    "By Size", noIcon, "", "", plain
  }
};

resource 'MENU' (8, preload) {
  8,
  textMenuProc,
  0x7FFFFFFB,
  enabled,
  "Find", {
    "Find…", noIcon, "F", "", plain,
    "Find Same", noIcon, "G", "", plain,
    "-", noIcon, "", "", plain,
    "Replace…", noIcon, "", "", plain,
    "Replace Same", noIcon, "", "", plain
  }
};

resource 'MENU' (9, preload) {
  9,
  textMenuProc,
  0x7FFFFFEF,
  enabled,
  "Font", {}
};
```

```
resource 'MENU' (10, preload) {
  10,
  textMenuProc,
  0x7FFFFFFF,
  enabled,
  "Size", {
    "7", noIcon, "", "", plain,
    "9", noIcon, "", "", outline,
    "10", noIcon, "", "", outline,
    "12", noIcon, "", "", outline,
    "14", noIcon, "", "", outline,
    "18", noIcon, "", "", outline,
    "24", noIcon, "", "", outline,
    "36", noIcon, "", "", plain
  }
};

resource 'MENU' (11, preload) {
  11,
  textMenuProc,
  0x7FFFFFFF,
  enabled,
  "Style", {
    "Plain", noIcon, "", noMark, plain,
    "Bold", noIcon, "", noMark, bold,
    "Italic", noIcon, "", noMark, italic,
    "Underline", noIcon, "", noMark, underline,
    "Outline", noIcon, "", noMark, outline,
    "Shadow", noIcon, "", noMark, shadow,
    "Condense", noIcon, "", noMark, condense,
    "Extend", noIcon, "", noMark, extend
  }
};

resource 'MENU' (12, preload) {
  12,
  textMenuProc,
  0x7FFFFFFF,
  enabled,
  "Definitions", {
    "Language", noIcon, "\0x1B", "\0x0D", plain,   /* 13 */
    "Toolbox", noIcon, "\0x1B", "\0x0E", plain,   /* 14 */
    "OS", noIcon, "\0x1B", "\0x0F", plain,   /* 15 */
    "Machine", noIcon, "\0x1B", "\0x10", plain   /* 16 */
  }
};
```

```
resource 'MENU' (13, preload) {
  13,
  textMenuProc,
  0x7FFFFFFF,
  enabled,
  "Language", {
    "ASCII Table", noIcon, "", noMark, plain,
    "Lexical", noIcon, "", noMark, plain,
    "Syntax", noIcon, "", noMark, plain,
    "Declarations", noIcon, "", noMark, plain,
    "Data Types", noIcon, "", noMark, plain,
    "Operators", noIcon, "", noMark, plain,
    "Expressions", noIcon, "", noMark, plain,
    "Functions", noIcon, "", noMark, plain,
    "Statements", noIcon, "", noMark, plain,
    "Input/Output", noIcon, "", noMark, plain
  }
};

resource 'MENU' (14, preload) {
  14,
  textMenuProc,
  0x7FFFFFFF,
  enabled,
  "Toolbox", {
    "Resources", noIcon, "", noMark, plain,
    "QuickDraw", noIcon, "", noMark, plain,
    "Fonts", noIcon, "", noMark, plain,
    "Events", noIcon, "", noMark, plain,
    "Windows", noIcon, "", noMark, plain,
    "Controls", noIcon, "", noMark, plain,
    "Menus", noIcon, "", noMark, plain,
    "Text Edit", noIcon, "", noMark, plain,
    "Dialogs", noIcon, "", noMark, plain,
    "Clipboard", noIcon, "", noMark, plain
  }
};
```

```
resource 'MENU' (15, preload) {
  15,
  textMenuProc,
  0x7FFFFFFF,
  enabled,
  "OS", {
    "Memory", noIcon, "", noMark, plain,
    "Files", noIcon, "", noMark, plain,
    "Processes", noIcon, "", noMark, plain,
    "Segments", noIcon, "", noMark, plain,
    "Devices", noIcon, "", noMark, plain,
    "Disks", noIcon, "", noMark, plain,
    "Networks", noIcon, "", noMark, plain,
    "Serial", noIcon, "", noMark, plain,
    "Sound", noIcon, "", noMark, plain,
    "Printing", noIcon, "", noMark, plain,
    "Errors", noIcon, "", noMark, plain,
    "Numerics", noIcon, "", noMark, plain
  }
};

resource 'MENU' (16, preload) {
  16,
  textMenuProc,
  0x7FFFFFFF,
  enabled,
  "Machine", {
    "Instructions", noIcon, "", noMark, plain,
    "Condition Codes", noIcon, "", noMark, plain,
    "Opcodes", noIcon, "", noMark, plain,
    "Timing", noIcon, "", noMark, plain,
    "Exceptions", noIcon, "", noMark, plain
  }
};
```

DisAsm — C Tool

This tool allows data forks and individual resources to be disassembled such that the resulting disassembly can be reassembled later. It is useful for exploring static code modules; MacsBug is the tool to use for exploring running code. In fact, to get the source code to MacsBug—with no comments—disassemble MacsBug's data fork with this tool.

The disassembler this tool uses is shipped in the `ToolLib.o` file as part of MPW version 3. Ira Ruben wrote the disassembler, which has been used in MacsBug, `DumpObj`, and `DumpCode`. Now you can use it in your favorite tool.

```c
/*
 *  DisAsm.c  - Object code disassmbler
 *            - Written by Dan Allen 4/2/88
 *            - Greatly enhanced on 8/17/88
 *            - Works on running Shell 1/2/89
 *            - Trap names & cursors added 2/1/89
 */

#include  <CursorCtl.h>
#include  <DisAsmLookup.h>
#include  <FCntl.h>
#include  <IOCtl.h>
#include  <Memory.h>
#include  <Resources.h>
#include  <StdIO.h>
#include  <StdLib.h>
#include  <Types.h>

#define fsRdPerm   1
#define BUFSIZE    32*1024

#ifdef ghs /* check for MPW C 2.0 */
#define openrfperm   OpenRFPerm
#endif

static  char   *bufin,*bufout;
static  long   fileSize;
void    GetRsrcFork(),GetDataFork();

main(int argc,char *argv[])
{
  char   *p, *q;
  char   opCode[256],operand[256],comment[256];
  short  bytesUsed;
  long   i,len,offset,pos = 0,lines = 0;
```

```
  if (argc < 2) {
    fprintf(stderr,"DisAsm [type id] file > stdout\n");
    return 1;
  }
  InitCursorCtl(nil);
  if (argc > 2) GetRsrcFork(argc,argv); else GetDataFork(argv[argc-1]);

  bufout = malloc(BUFSIZE);
  if (bufout) setvbuf(stdout, bufout, _IOFBF, BUFSIZE);

  printf("\tMAIN\t\t\t; %s\n",argv[argc-1]);
  p = bufin; q = p + fileSize; offset = - (long) p;
  while (p < q) {
    Disassembler(offset,&bytesUsed,p,opCode,operand,comment,nil);
    ModifyOperand(operand);
    printf("\n@%X\t%s\t",pos,&opCode[1]); pos += bytesUsed;
    SpinCursor(1);

    if (strchr(&comment[1],';') &&      /* from comment field */
        sscanf(&comment[2],"%X",&i) && /* get hex offset */
        opCode[1] == 'B' ||             /* and if Bnn or Bsr */
        (opCode[1] == 'J' &&            /* or Jsr or Jmp */
        !strchr(operand,'(')))          /* if PC relative */
      printf("@%X\t\t; %s\t = ",i,&operand[1]); /* convert */
    else {
      len = strlen(&operand[1]);
      if (len < 10) {
        if (!strcmp("DC.W",&opCode[1]) && operand[2] == 'A') {
          LookupTrapName(*((short *) p),comment);
          printf("%s\t\t; A-Trap\t = %P\t",&operand[1],comment);
        } else
          printf("%s\t\t;\t = ",&operand[1]);
      } else if (len < 20)
        printf("%s\t;\t = ",&operand[1]);
      else
        printf("%s;\t = ",&operand[1]);
    }
    while(bytesUsed--) {
      i = *p++;
      printf("%2.2X", i & 0x000000FF);
    }
    lines++;
  }
  printf("\n\n\tEND\n\n");
  printf("* Object size = %d bytes\n",pos);
  printf("* Source size = %d lines\n\n",lines);
  ioctl(1,FIOFNAME,(long *)comment);
  faccess(comment,F_STABINFO,(long *) 10);
  return 0;
}
```

```
static void GetDataFork(char *fileName)
{
  FILE   *input;

  input = fopen(fileName,"r");
  if (!input) {
    fprintf(stderr,"# Cannot open data fork of file %s\n",fileName);
    exit(1);
  }

  fseek(input,0,2);
  fileSize = ftell(input);
  if (!fileSize) {
    fprintf(stderr,"# Empty data fork\n");
    exit(0);
  }

  bufin = malloc(fileSize);
  if (!bufin) {
    fprintf(stderr,"# Not enough heapspace: %d bytes needed\n",fileSize);
    exit(2);
  }

  fseek(input,0,0);
  fread(bufin,1,fileSize,input);
  fclose(input);
}

static void GetRsrcFork(int argc, char *argv[])
{
  Boolean purgeFlag;
  char    oldState;
  short   refNum,oldResFile;
  Handle  h;
  ResType rt;

  oldResFile = CurResFile();
  SetResLoad(false);
  refNum = openrfperm(argv[argc-1],0,fsRdPerm);
  SetResLoad(true);
  if (refNum == -1) {
    UseResFile(oldResFile);
    fprintf(stderr,"# OpenRFPerm failed for file: %s\n",argv[argc-1]);
    exit(1);
  }
```

```
  rt = *((ResType *) argv[1]);
  SetResLoad(false);
  h = Get1Resource(rt,atoi(argv[2]));
  SetResLoad(true);
  if (!h) {
    UseResFile(oldResFile);
    fprintf(stderr,"# GetResource failed: #%d\n",ResError());
    exit(2);
  }

  fileSize = SizeResource(h);
  bufin = malloc(fileSize);
  if (!bufin) {
    UseResFile(oldResFile);
    fprintf(stderr,"# Not enough heapspace: %d bytes needed.\n",fileSize);
    exit(2);
  }

  purgeFlag = *h ? false : true;
  oldState = HGetState(h);
  LoadResource(h);
  if (ResError()) {
    UseResFile(oldResFile);
    fprintf(stderr,"# LoadResource failed.\n");
    exit(2);
  }

  HLock(h);
  if (rt == 'CODE') BlockMove(*h+4,bufin,fileSize-4);
  else BlockMove(*h,bufin,fileSize);
  HUnlock(h);
  HSetState(h,oldState);
  if (purgeFlag) EmptyHandle(h);
  UseResFile(oldResFile);
}
```

Conclusion

In this chapter, assembly language and the MPW assembler were examined. Assembly language is useful even for the dedicated Pascal programmer. The two most common reasons for needing an understanding of assembly language are for optimization and for tracking down bugs.

Three examples of assembly language code were presented. The first was a desk accessory that can be used as the basis for your desk accessories. The second was an application that can be used as the basis for your own assembly language applications. The last was an MPW tool written in C that disassembles code using a disassembler shipped with MPW version 3.

Recommended Reading

The Motorola reference manuals are absolutely essential when you are writing assembly code, but they provide no tutorial information. There really is no book of choice on the subject of assembly language programming for the Macintosh. Leventhal and Kane's *68000 Assembly Language Programming* is pretty good, but it makes no mention of the Macintosh, while many of the Macintosh assembly language books are simply inaccurate.

## CHAPTER 8

THE C LANGUAGE

C is becoming more and more popular in the Macintosh development community, as it is in the UNIX and MS-DOS worlds. As you read this chapter, however, keep in mind that even die-hard C programmers in the Macintosh world need to read Pascal at least, because the Macintosh operating system and Toolbox were written with Pascal in mind.

This chapter presents a series of MPW C tools for processing text. C is an excellent language for text processing. These tools will demonstrate various techniques of using C and writing MPW tools. Here is a short summary of the tools that will be presented in this chapter:

- `DeCom`, a tool to remove C comments using a state machine
- `FastCat`, a faster version of MPW's built-in `Catenate` command
- `Substitute`, a literal text-replacement tool designed for streams
- `Reduce`, a tool for replacing runs of specified characters with a single string
- `Sign`, a tool that implements the front pass of an anagram pipeline
- `Squash`, the last pass of an anagram pipeline
- `WordText`, which extracts ASCII text and page breaks from files created with MS Word 4.0
- `TextTool`, a Swiss Army knife for manipulating text
- `Sort`, a memory-based sorting tool with some specialized options
- `Index`, an indexing tool for sources and text files

For an example of a stand-alone application written in C, look at the `MacQ` program found in Chapter 5.

History of C

C was created by Brian W. Kernighan and Dennis M. Ritchie at Bell Labs in the late 1960s and early 1970s. It was created as a tool for system programming of the UNIX operating system. C was based on the language B, which in turn was based on the language BCPL, both of which were typeless languages.

The American National Standard for Information Systems (ANSI) standardized the C language in 1989, and MPW C 3.0 is an almost-conforming implementation. The main feature added by the 1989 standard to the classic version of C is more rigid type checking through function prototypes.

Building C Tools

For convenience, the Make file from Chapter 6 is duplicated here, with one small addition. Three of the tools from this chapter—Index, Sort, and TextTool—have Commando interfaces. Additional Make targets at the end of this Makefile will cause Rez to build the appropriate resources for these tools. This file will work with both MPW 2.0 and 3.0 versions of Make. Further explanation and details about Make and Makefiles can be found in Chapter 6.

This generic Makefile can be used to build any of the C tools given in this chapter. If you want to write your own new C tools, this will build those as well. Using this file is simple. For example, to make the FastCat tool presented below, just type Make FastCat. Select the resulting lines, press the Enter key, and the tool will be built. The following text would be found in a file called Makefile that should be located in the same directory (folder) that the sources are. Remember to set the current directory to this folder as well.

```
### C Tool Generic Makefile by Dan Allen 3/27/88

COptions  = -mbg ch8   # -g if using MPW C 2.0
LOptions  = -w -sg Main=STDIO,INTENV,SADEV,SACONSOL,CSANELib
SFOptions = -d . -m . -c "MPS " -t MPST

CLibs = "{Libraries}Stubs.o" ∂
        "{Libraries}Interface.o" ∂
        "{CLibraries}CInterface.o" ∂
        "{CLibraries}CRuntime.o" ∂
        "{CLibraries}StdClib.o" ∂
        "{CLibraries}CSANELib.o" ∂
        "{CLibraries}Math.o" ∂
        "{Libraries}ToolLibs.o"

     ƒ  .c.o
  Link -o {Default} {LOptions} {Default}.c.o {CLibs}
  Setfile {SFOptions} {Default}
  Delete {Default}.c.o
  Move -y {Default} {Tools}

Index   ƒƒ  Index.r
  Rez -o Index Index.r
```

```
Sort     ff  Sort.r
  Rez -o Sort Sort.r

TextTool ff  TextTool.r
  Rez -o TextTool TextTool.r
```

A Note For MPW C 2.0 Users

Several standard library functions are used in the various tools presented in this chapter. Many of the sources include a file named stdlib.h that gives the definitions of these routines. This file comes with MPW 3.0 but did not ship with MPW 2.0. Therefore, if you are using MPW C 2.0, you should create the following short header file and put it into the CIncludes folder.

Other changes between versions 2.0 and 3.0 are handled by using the #ifdef mechanism. All of these tools have been built successfully using both MPW C 2.0 and C 3.0.

```
/* stdlib.h for MPW C 2.0 */

#define RAND_MAX 32767
double atof ();
int atoi ();
int rand (void);
void srand (unsigned int seed);
void *malloc();
void *calloc();
void free();
void *realloc();
void abort();
int atexit();
void exit();
char *getenv();
void *bsearch();
void qsort();
int abs();
```

DeCom — C Tool

This tool has the task of removing comments from a C source file. As with many of the MPW tools that follow, two 32 KB buffers are allocated for increased speed. MPW tools should also call the rotating cursor routines to be good citizens. Doing so also allows background operation of MPW with post-2.0 versions of the MPW Shell. This tool uses the standard input and output streams so that pipelines are supported.

```c
/*
 *  DeCom.c - Removes all C comments
 *          - Written by Dan Allen 2/16/88
 *          - Rewritten using finite state machine 11/23/88
 */

#include <CursorCtl.h>
#include <StdIO.h>
#include <StdLib.h>

#define BUFSIZE 32*1024

enum {NOCOM,OPENSLASH,OPENSTAR,CLOSESTAR,CLOSESLASH} state = NOCOM;

main()     /* stdin --> stdout */
{
  char  *bufIn,*bufOut;
  int   c;

  InitCursorCtl(0);
  if (bufIn = malloc(BUFSIZE)) setvbuf(stdin,bufIn,_IOFBF,BUFSIZE);
  if (bufOut = malloc(BUFSIZE)) setvbuf(stdout,bufOut,_IOFBF,BUFSIZE);

  while ((c = getchar()) != EOF) {
    SpinCursor(1);
    if (c == '/' && state == NOCOM) {
      state = OPENSLASH; continue;
    }
    if (c == '*' && state == OPENSLASH) {
      state = OPENSTAR; continue;
    }
    if (c == '*' && state == OPENSTAR) {
      state = CLOSESTAR; continue;
    }
    if (c == '/' && state == CLOSESTAR) {
      state = NOCOM; continue;
    }
    if (state == OPENSLASH && c != '*') {
      putchar('/'); state = NOCOM;
    }
```

```
    if (state == CLOSESTAR && c != '*') {
      state = OPENSTAR; continue;
    }
    if (state == NOCOM) putchar(c);
  }
  return 0;
}
```

FastCat — C Tool

When large text files—actually the data forks of any Mac files—need to be copied quickly, this tool is perfect for the job. Because a common operation is to concatenate several files, this tool takes a list of files rather than using standard input. The result, however, is still sent to standard output. Note, too, that this particular tool uses the `open`, `read`, and `write` commands, which are not part of the ANSI standard but which are standard UNIX system calls supported by MPW C.

Using 256 KB for a buffer is overkill for most average-sized files, but the buffer size pays off when you are dealing with files in the megabytes. In fact, this tool was written in order to massage just one month's worth of bibliographic information, which was contained in a single text file almost 5 MB in size.

Another feature of this tool is that it inquires about the size of the sectors of the default volume and uses a buffer that is an integral multiple of this sector size. This gives a signficant boost to throughput.

As an example of the increased performance of this tool, copying a 256 KB text file on a Mac II with an Apple 80 MB SCSI hard disk takes 24 seconds with the built-in MPW Shell command `Catenate`, but the same operation takes only 2 seconds with `FastCat`! It is all in the buffers. . . .

Improving FastCat

Here are some suggestions for improving `FastCat`:

- Extend the argument processing so that standard input is also supported.
- Replace the UNIX-like system calls with ANSI standard library calls. Compare performance.
- Experiment with different buffer sizes. What relationship is there between disk allocation block size and buffer size? What is the optimal buffer size for floppy disks? For a 20 MB hard disk with 1K sectors? For a 160 MB hard disk with 2.5K sectors?

```
/*
 *  fcat.c  - Copies contents of data forks of specified files to stdout
 *          - Uses 256K buffer (if possible)
 *          - Written by Dan Allen 11/23/87
 *          - Revised on 11/23/88
 *          - Progress & auto added on 6/23/89
 *          - Buffer set to power of 2*allocBlockSize 6/24/89
 */

#include <CursorCtl.h>
#include <FCntl.h>
#include <Files.h>
#include <StdIO.h>
#include <StdLib.h>

pascal  long  TickCount() extern 0xA975;

static char *buffer,measureFlag,progFlag;
static unsigned bufSize,maxBuf,total,ticks;
static VolumeParam  pb;

main(int argc,char *argv[])    /* files… --> stdout */
{
  OSErr err;

  InitCursorCtl(0);

  err = PBGetVol((ParmBlkPtr) &pb,false);
  pb.ioCompletion = nil;
  err = PBGetVInfo((ParmBlkPtr)&pb,false);
  maxBuf = bufSize = pb.ioVAlBlkSiz * 512;

  if (argv[1][0] == '-') {
    progFlag = 1;
    if (argv[1][1] == 'm') measureFlag = 1;
    else {
      bufSize = atoi(&argv[1][1]);
      buffer = malloc(bufSize);
      if (!buffer) {
        fprintf(stderr,"# Cannot allocate a %d byte buffer\n",bufSize);
        return 2;
      }
    }
  }
  else do {
    bufSize >>= 1;
    buffer = malloc(bufSize);
  } while (!buffer);
```

```
   if (measureFlag)
     for (bufSize = pb.ioVAlBlkSiz; bufSize <= maxBuf; bufSize <<= 1) {
       buffer = malloc(bufSize);
       if (!buffer) exit(2);
       total = 0;
       Catenate(argc,argv);
       fprintf(stderr,"BufSize: %7d  Ticks: %7d  Bytes: %7d  Bytes/Sec: %7d\n",
                     bufSize,ticks,total,total*60/ticks);
       free(buffer);
     }
   else {
     Catenate(argc,argv);
     if (progFlag)
       fprintf(stderr,"BufSize: %7d  Ticks: %7d  Bytes: %7d  Bytes/Sec: %7d\n",
                     bufSize,ticks,total,total*60/ticks);
     free(buffer);
   }
   return 0;
}

Catenate(int argc,char *argv[])
{
  int count,i,input;

  ticks = TickCount();
  for (i = 1 + progFlag; i < argc; i++) {
    input = open(argv[i], O_RDONLY);
    if (input == -1) {
      fprintf(stderr, "# Cannot open: %s\n", argv[i]);
      exit(1);
    }
    while ( (count = read(input, buffer, bufSize)) > 0) {
      total += count;
      SpinCursor(2);
      if (count == -1) return 2;
      if (write(1, buffer, count) != count) exit(2);
      SpinCursor(-2);
    }
    if (close(input) == -1) exit(3);
  }
  ticks = TickCount() - ticks;
}
```

Substitute — C Tool

The next step of complexity beyond simply copying a file's contents, as we did with `FastCat`, is to process the text in some way. Tools that take text from an input stream, perform some set of transformations, and then output the changed text are often called *filters*. This filter, called `Substitute`, looks for occurrences of any string and replaces them with another string. All other text is passed through unchanged. `Substitute` uses standard input and output, and is always case-sensitive.

`Substitute` was written because the built-in command `Replace` was too slow for large open windows. For example, if you were to change a list of 31,155 words separated by spaces to a list with each word on a separate line, `Replace -c / / ∂n` takes hours, yet `Substitute " " ∂n` takes just 13 seconds. Although `Substitute` does not support regular expressions as `Replace` does, that is not why `Substitute` is so much faster: the speed increase is the result of not overloading the Macintosh Memory Manager. The built-in `Replace` routine calls `NewPtr` for each little chunk of text replaced, which eventually creates thousands of objects in the heap, and the Memory Manager chugs to a near halt.

The find-and-replace arguments can be of different sizes. If this transformation were to be done "in place," this fact would require a much more complex solution to the problem. Using a stream approach to the problem, however, allows the input to be scanned and passed through until the find string is found. At that point the replace string is ejected into the stream, and then the search continues. Simple!

Improving Substitute

Here are some suggestions for improving `Substitute`:

- Modify `Substitute` to look for wildcard patterns (regular expressions) as does the built-in `Replace` command.
- Add the ability to search and replace across multiple files. Should the output go to different files or all to one file?

```
/*
 *   Substitute.c - changes occurances of argv[1] to argv[2] via stdin, stdout
 *              - Written by Dan Allen 3/27/88
 *
 */

#include  <CursorCtl.h>
#include  <StdIO.h>
#include  <StdLib.h>
#include  <String.h>
```

```
#define BUFSIZE 1024*32

main(int argc, char *argv[])      /* stdin --> stdout */
{
  char       c,*bufIn,*bufOut;
  unsigned   count = 0,i,findLen,repLen;

  if (argc != 3) {
    fprintf(stderr,"Substitute findStr replaceStr <stdin >stdout\n");
    return 1;
  }
  findLen = strlen(argv[1]); repLen = strlen(argv[2]);

  InitCursorCtl(0);
  if (bufIn = malloc(BUFSIZE)) setvbuf(stdin,bufIn,_IOFBF,BUFSIZE);
  if (bufOut = malloc(BUFSIZE)) setvbuf(stdout,bufOut,_IOFBF,BUFSIZE);

  while ((c = getchar()) != EOF) {
    if (c == '\n') SpinCursor(1);
tryagain:
    if (c == argv[1][count]) {
      count++;
      if (count == findLen) {
        printf("%s",argv[2]);
        count = 0;
      }
      continue;
    }
    if (count) {
      for (i = 0; i < count; i++) putchar(argv[1][i]);
      count = 0; goto tryagain;
    }
    putchar(c);
  }
  for (i = 0; i < count; i++) putchar(argv[1][i]);
  return 0;
}
```

Reduce — C Tool

Reduce—like Substitute—takes two arguments that specify a text transformation. The replace argument is the same as Substitute, but the find argument is interpreted not as a string but as a set of characters. If the supplied input text contains a run of more than one of the characters of this set, the specified replace string is output. All other text is passed through unchanged.

This tool was originally hardcoded to reduce runs of spaces and tabs to a single tab character. Tabs and spaces occurring by themselves were passed through unchanged. Why such a tool? Often TTY output uses many spaces as padding to simulate columns of text. Using Reduce on such text allows the text to be pasted into a spreadsheet easily, for example, because tabs are often used as column or field delimiters. Another use is to reduce the number of white-space characters in source files, thus reducing the lexical scanning time of a compiler.

In the tool's current implementation, you could specify the following to reduce runs of spaces and tabs.

```
Reduce " ∂t" ∂t < old > new # Reduce runs of spaces & tabs to 1 tab
```

This version of Reduce will reduce any set of characters to any single character or string. Thus Reduce '0123456789.' $ would take any number that was made up of more than one character and reduce it to a single dollar sign. The name Reduce is somewhat of a misnomer, as the tool can also expand a source under the right circumstances: Reduce " ." ".∂n∂n" could be used on average prose to expand a paragraph's sentences each into their own paragraphs, separated by lines. Reduce is limited only by your imagination in the number of ways that it can manipulate text.

Improving Reduce

Here are some suggestions for improving Reduce:

- Add a count option for specifying how many characters from the set constitute a match. What would a count of 1 do?
- This version of Reduce will reduce within quoted strings, so careful use is recommended for source code. Extend the tool to skip quoted literals and strings. What about comments? Should a separate language-beautifier tool be written instead? Write such a tool for your favorite language.

```
/*
 *  Reduce.c  - Reduces runs of spaces and tabs to a single tab
 *            - Written by Dan Allen 3/27/88
 *            - Options added to reduce any string 12/11/88
 *
 */

#include  <CursorCtl.h>
#include  <StdIO.h>
#include  <StdLib.h>

#define BUFSIZE   32*1024
typedef unsigned char byte;

static byte array[256];
```

```
main(int argc,byte *argv[])   /* stdin --> stdout */
{
  byte   *bufIn,*bufOut,lastChar;
  int    c,count;

  InitCursorCtl(0);
  if (bufIn = malloc(BUFSIZE)) setvbuf(stdin,bufIn,_IOFBF,BUFSIZE);
  if (bufOut = malloc(BUFSIZE)) setvbuf(stdout,bufOut,_IOFBF,BUFSIZE);

  if (argc != 3) {
    fprintf(stderr,"Reduce inChars outString < stdin > stdout\n");
    return 1;
  }

  while (c = *(argv[1])++)
    array[c]++;

  count = 0;
  while ((c = getchar()) != EOF) {
    if (c == '\n') SpinCursor(2);
    if (array[c]) {
      count++;
      lastChar = c;
      continue;
    }
    if (count > 1) printf("%s",argv[2]);
    if (count == 1) putchar(lastChar);
    count = 0;
    putchar(c);
  }
  return 0;
}
```

Sign — C Tool

This tool is rather specialized. It is the first step of a pipeline of tools used to generate *anagrams*. Anagrams are words (or sentences) that contain the same characters, but in a different order. For example, "integral" and "triangle" are anagrams of each other, as are "algorithmic" and "logarithmic"; "evil," "live," and "veil" are all anagrams of one another.

The motivation for this problem comes from Bentley's *Programming Pearls*, a delightful book that is highly recommended reading. Given a file called words, one word per line, Sign < words | Sort | Squash will output to standard output a list of all the possible anagram combinations. This marvelously simple solution easily reduces an otherwise combinatoric nightmare to a tractable problem. Squash and Sort follow.

Sign demonstrates ways of using C's excellent set of standard library routines to do the dirty work: in this case, scanf, strcpy, qsort, and printf do it all.

```
/*
 *  Sign.c  - Sorts the characters of each word of each line of the input file
 *          - Step one of a pipeline to produce anagrams
 *          - Written by Dan Allen 11/6/88
 */

#include  <CursorCtl.h>
#include  <StdIO.h>
#include  <StdLib.h>
#include  <String.h>

#define    LINELEN    4096
#define    BUFSIZE    32*1024

static char in[LINELEN],out[LINELEN];

main()  /* stdin --> stdout */
{
  char    *bufIn,*bufOut;
  int     compChar();

  InitCursorCtl(0);
  if (bufIn = malloc(BUFSIZE)) setvbuf(stdin,bufIn,_IOFBF,BUFSIZE);
  if (bufOut = malloc(BUFSIZE)) setvbuf(stdout,bufOut,_IOFBF,BUFSIZE);

  while(scanf("%4096[^\n]\n",&in) == 1) {
    strcpy(out,in);
    qsort(out,strlen(out),1,compChar);
    printf("%s\t%s\n",out,in);
    SpinCursor(1);
  }
  return 0;
}

int compChar(char *i,char *j)
{
  if (*i < *j) return -1;
  else if (*i > *j) return 1;
  else return 0;
}
```

Squash — C Tool

This tool was originally written as the final portion of an anagram pipeline, but it has since become quite useful for many other text processing tasks. Given an input stream containing sorted lines of text, Squash will condense into a single line multiple lines whose first fields are the same. Further examples of using Squash will be found below in the section on the text tool called TextTool.

```
/*
 *   Squash.c   - Squashes sorted lines with same first fields into one line
 *              - Written by Dan Allen 10/30/88
 *              - Last step of an anagram pipeline
 *              - Options added 11/30/88
 *
 *   Sample Anagram Pipelines:
 *
 *   FastCat dictionary | TextTool -l | Sign | Sort -u |
 *                    Squash | TextTool -t | Sort
 *
 *   ATrap | TextTool -t -l | Sign | Sort | Squash | TextTool -t | Sort
 *
 */

#include   <CType.h>
#include   <CursorCtl.h>
#include   <StdIO.h>
#include   <StdLib.h>
#include   <String.h>

#define    FALSE      0
#define    TRUE       1
#define    LINELEN    4096
#define    BUFSIZE    32*1024

static char *useage = "Squash [-c][-l sep] < stdin > stdout\n";
static char f1[LINELEN],f2[LINELEN],g1[LINELEN],g2[LINELEN];
static char *listSep = "\t",*format = "%4096[^\t]\t%4096[^\n]\n";
static char countFlag;
```

```
main(int argc,char *argv[])
{
  char        *bufIn,*bufOut,sameKey = 0;
  unsigned   i,count;

  for(i = 1; i < argc; i++) {
    if (argv[i][0] == '-' && argv[i][2] == '\0')
      switch(tolower(argv[i][1])) {
        case 'c': countFlag = TRUE; break;
        case 'l': listSep = argv[++i]; break;
        default:  fprintf(stderr,"%s",useage); return 1;
      }
  }

  InitCursorCtl(0);
  if (bufIn = malloc(BUFSIZE)) setvbuf(stdin,bufIn,_IOFBF,BUFSIZE);
  if (bufOut = malloc(BUFSIZE)) setvbuf(stdout,bufOut,_IOFBF,BUFSIZE);

  if (scanf(format,f1,f2) != 2) return 2;
  while(scanf(format,g1,g2) == 2) {
    SpinCursor(1);
    if (!strcmp(f1,g1)) {
      if (!sameKey) {
        if (countFlag) {
          count = 2;
          printf("%s",f1);
        }
        else printf("%s\t%s%s%s",f1,f2,listSep,g2);
      }
      else {
        if (countFlag) count++;
        else printf("%s%s",listSep,g2);
      }
      sameKey = 1;
      continue;
    }
    if (sameKey) {
      sameKey = 0;
      if (countFlag) printf("\t%u\n",count);
      else putchar('\n');
    }
    if (scanf(format,f1,f2) != 2) break;
```

```
    if (!strcmp(f1,g1)) {
      if (!sameKey) {
        if (countFlag) {
          count = 2;
          printf("%s",g1);
        }
        else printf("%s\t%s%s%s",g1,g2,listSep,f2);
      }
      else {
        if (countFlag) count++;
        else printf("%s%s",listSep,f2);
      }
      sameKey = 1;
      continue;
    }
  }
  if (sameKey)
    if (countFlag) printf("\t%u\n",count);
    else putchar('\n');
  return 0;
}
```

WordText — C Tool

WordText extracts the text and page break information from a Microsoft Word 4.0 document in an *ad hoc* manner. Because WordText takes a list of files, a whole folder of files can be processed easily. The actual text of the Word documents is sent to standard output, with page breaks being interjected into the text as form feed characters (ASCII 12). Style information and pictures are not output. The motivation behind this tool was to help generate an index for this book using Index, another C tool presented later in this chapter. The -x option of Index uses the form feed character to recognize page breaks.

The format of Word 4.0 files was ascertained by the experimental method using Fedit, so this tool does not deal with the full file format. Word places accurate page break information in a fixed spot only after doing a non-fast save of a document. The best way to force Word to place accurate page breaks in a fixed spot is to open the Word file of interest, hold down the shift key, and select Repaginate from the Document menu. Immediately select Close from the File menu and save the changes. Before you run WordText, do this in MS Word for all of the files you wish to process.

Interesting stats about document sizes will be sent to standard diagnostic if you use -p, with increased detail about page sizes available through -P. Either progress option lists a count of how many times each character is used over all of the files input.

Improving `WordText`

Here are some suggestions for improving `WordText`:

- Argument processing for this tool is somewhat lazy: the progress option is not recognized unless it is the first argument given. Fix this.

- `WordText` currently reads only the text and page information. Extend it to extract styles, footnotes, and graphics. What destination formats would hold this information? Write a tool to translate a MS Word file into a ASCII text description language such as RTF, TeX or PostScript. Sell the tool to a major software vendor.

```
/*
 *  wordtext.c  - Extracts text and page breaks from a MS Word document
 *              - Written by Dan Allen 8/3/88
 *              - Working moderately well with 3.0 files 10/29/88
 *              - Added progress options 12/19/88
 *              - Added letter freq & totals 2/20/89
 *              - Updated for Word 4.0 files 6/12/89
 */

#include <CursorCtl.h>
#include <StdIO.h>
#include <StdLib.h>

#define    BUFSIZE    32768
#define    MAXPAGES   1000

static long progress,totalBytes,totalChars,totalPages,pageStarts[MAXPAGES];
static unsigned count[256];

main(int argc,char *argv[])
{
  char   c,*p,*buffer;
  short  pageGuess;
  long   i,j,length,size,total,*pgBrkPtr;
  FILE   *input;

  /* check args */
  InitCursorCtl(0);
  if (argc < 2) {
    fprintf(stderr,"WordText [-p] files… > stdout\n");
    return 1;
  }
  if (argv[1][0] == '-') progress++;
  if (argv[1][1] == 'P') progress++;
```

```
/* make buffer */
buffer = malloc(BUFSIZE);
if (!buffer) {
  fprintf(stderr,"# Not enough mem to create a %d byte buffer.\n",BUFSIZE);
  return 2;
}

for (i = progress ? 2 : 1; i < argc; i++) {
  input = fopen(argv[i],"r");
  if (!input) {
    fprintf(stderr,"# Cannot open file: %s\n",argv[i]);
    return 2;
  }
  if (progress) fprintf(stderr,"File: %-19s\n",argv[i]);

  /* clear the slate */
  total = 0;
  for (j = 0; j < MAXPAGES; j++) pageStarts[j] = 0;

  /* find ptrs and approximate # pages */
  fseek(input,0x5E,0);
  fread(&pgBrkPtr,sizeof(pgBrkPtr),1,input);
  fread(&pageGuess,sizeof(pageGuess),1,input);
  pageGuess = pageGuess/8;

  /* seek to page break table */
  fseek(input,(long)pgBrkPtr,0);
  if (pageGuess >= MAXPAGES) pageGuess = MAXPAGES - 1;
  fread(&pageStarts[0],sizeof(long *),pageGuess,input);


  /* read text */
  fseek(input,0x100,0);
  for (j = 1; j <= pageGuess; j++) {
    size = pageStarts[j] - pageStarts[j-1];
    if (size < 0 | size > BUFSIZE) break;
    total += size;
    if (progress > 1)
      fprintf(stderr," Page %3d: %5d chars, total of %7d chars\n",
              j,size,total);
    fread(buffer,sizeof(char),size,input);
    p = buffer;
    while (size--) {
      c = *p++;
      if (c > 7 && c != 31) putchar(c); /* 1-7 used by Word */
      if (c == '\n') SpinCursor(1);
      count[(unsigned char)c]++; /* COMPILER BUG: should not have to cast */
    }
    printf("\n\f\n");
  }
```

```
      fseek(input,0,2);
      length = ftell(input);
      fclose(input);
      totalBytes += length; totalChars += total; totalPages += j-1;
   }
   if (progress) {
      fprintf(stderr,"%s %7d chars   %7d bytes   %4d pages\n\n",
              " TOTAL: ",totalChars,totalBytes,totalPages);
      fprintf(stderr,"Graphics: %-8u  Footnotes: %-8u  Formulas: %-8u\n",
                     count[1],count[5],count[6]);
      fprintf(stderr,"Spaces:   %-8u  Tabs:      %-8u  Returns:  %-8u\n",
                     count[32],count[9],count[13]);
      for (i = 33; i < 127; i++) {
         fprintf(stderr,"%6u %c  ",count[i],i);
         if (i % 8 == 0) fprintf(stderr,"\n");
      }
      fprintf(stderr,"\n");
   }
   return 0;
}
```

TextTool — **C Tool**

The main purpose of `TextTool` is to extract text from an input stream. This general text tool began as several different little tools that were used together so often that the tool has become like a Swiss Army knife: a collection of highly useful tools brought together under one roof. Because you can use the sixteen available options in different ways, the tool gives you literally thousands of different ways of manipulating text.

The defaults consider each line separated by a carriage return to be a record, which is further composed of fields separated by tabs. `TextTool` gets input from standard input one line at a time, breaking each line into fields. The output of `TextTool` is sent to standard output. The default behavior on output also uses tabs and returns as field and record separators, so using `TextTool` without any options is just a slow way to concatenate a file. However, the input and output field and record delimiters are customizable, which allows for very flexible processing of text.

The real usefulness of `TextTool` appears when only a certain field of a record is desired, or when field delimiters need to be changed from tabs to spaces, or when the positions of two fields need to be swapped. Fields to be output are selected with the `-s` option, which can be used as many times as there are fields. The order of the `-s` options is the order in which the fields will be output. If all of the fields but the first are desired, the `-t` (tail) option is a fast LISP-like shorthand.

Suppose you had a file called `books` that contained one book per line in the following format: `DDC# tab Author tab Title return`, where DDC# is the Dewey Decimal number in ASCII and tab and return are their respective ASCII control characters. Now suppose that with this subject, author, and title information you wanted various top ten lists. Using the text tools provided here you could get some interesting information quickly, through the following pipelines:

```
# Top Ten Authors by number of titles
TextTool -s 2 -s 3 < books | Sort -d | Squash -c | TextTool -s 2 -s 1 |
Sort -n -r | TextTool -a 10 -s 2 -s 1

# Top Ten Subject Categories by number of titles
TextTool -s 1 -s 3 < books | Sort -n | Squash -c | TextTool -s 2 -s 1 |
Sort -n -r | TextTool -a 10 -s 2 -s 1
```

On my library, these pipelines yield the two lists shown in the tables that follow.

Author	# of Books in Collection
Asimov, Isaac	16
Apple Computer	13
Durant, Will	12
Nibley, Hugh	11
LDS Church	9
Knuth, Donald E.	8
Brautigan, Richard	7
Kierkegaard, Soren	7
Madsen, Truman G.	7
Motorola	7

Dewey Decimal Number	# of Books in Collection
1.6424	35
289.3	22
1.6425	20
500.2	17
515.63	13
530.11	13
5.133	12
901	12
289.322	11
509	11

Another capability of TextTool is to assign each book a nearly unique ID number based on a hash of its author and title. The pipeline

```
TextTool -s 2 -s 3 < books -f " " | TextTool -k 1 | Sort -n
```

will output a list sorted by hash number. Running Squash on this output list will catch duplicate ID numbers: if Squash returns nothing, there are no duplicates; if duplicates do exist, it will list them. In my collection of 850 different titles, no duplicate IDs are generated when hashing modulo the default HASHNUM.

Another use of `TextTool` would be to list the files on a disk that have the same name. The following lines will generate a list of the full path names of those files which have the same leaf file names:

```
Files -f -s -r {Boot} > names
   TextTool -e -d ∂: -j names < names |
   TextTool -s 2 -s 1 | Sort -f | Squash
```

Improving `TextTool`

Here are some suggestions for improving `TextTool`:

- `TextTool` is record-based. Does it make any sense to write a version of `TextTool` that is stream-based? Which options would still apply? What new options could be added?

- `TextTool` does a simple version of joining two files: it blindly appends each line of file 2 to the end of each line of the primary input stream when the -j option is used. Implement a relational join so that `TextTool` can join on specific fields.

- How many other interesting options could be added for manipulating two files simultaneously?

Finally, here is the source code for `TextTool`:

```
/*
 *  tt.c  - TextTool by Dan Allen, begun 25 Nov 1988
 *         - Prime number generator added 30 Nov 1988
 *         - Output separators allowed to be strings 11 Dec 1988
 *         - Fixed bug in select, changed NextPrime 4 Jan 1989
 *         - End, join, proper options added, 6 May 1989
 */

#include <CType.h>
#include <CursorCtl.h>
#include <Math.h>
#include <StdIO.h>
#include <StdLib.h>
#include <String.h>
```

```
#define FALSE      0
#define TRUE       1
#define HASHNUM   33554393
#define MAXFIELDS 64
#define FIELDSIZE 4096
#define BUFSIZE   (32*1024)

typedef unsigned char byte;
typedef unsigned int  word;

byte   *fieldBufs[MAXFIELDS],joinBuf[FIELDSIZE],*p,*select;
byte   *beginStr,end,numerate,lowerCase,properCase,upperCase;
byte   fieldSep = '\t',recSep = '\n',*fieldOutSep,*recOutSep;
word   fieldNum,recNum,selectNum,order[MAXFIELDS+1];
word   firstRecs,firstChars,tailRec,hashNum,hashKey,Hash();
FILE   *joinFile;
void   Setup(),OutputRecord();

main(int argc,char *argv[])
{
  int c,fieldLen = 0;

  Setup(argc,argv);
  p = fieldBufs[0];

  while ((c = getchar()) != EOF) {
    if (c == fieldSep) {
      *p = '\0';
      p = fieldBufs[++fieldNum];
      if (fieldNum >= MAXFIELDS) {
        fprintf(stderr,"# Too many fields in record #%u\n",++recNum);
        return 2;
      }
      fieldLen = 0;
      SpinCursor(1);
      if (fieldSep != recSep) continue;
    }
    if (c == recSep) {
      *p = '\0';
      OutputRecord();
      p = fieldBufs[fieldNum = fieldLen = 0];
      SpinCursor(1);
      continue;
    }
```

```
      if (firstChars && fieldLen >= firstChars) continue;
      if (upperCase || properCase && !fieldLen) c = toupper(c);
      if (lowerCase || properCase && fieldLen) c = tolower(c);

      if (fieldLen++ == FIELDSIZE) {
        fprintf(stderr,"# Record %u, field %u: too long\n",++recNum,++fieldNum);
        return 2;
      }
      *p++ = c;
    }
  if (joinFile) fclose(joinFile);
  return 0;
}

void OutputRecord()
{
  word  i,thisField;

  recNum++;
  if (numerate) printf("%u%s",recNum,fieldOutSep);
  if (beginStr) printf("%s%s",beginStr,fieldOutSep);
  if (select) {
    if (hashKey) printf("%u%s",Hash(fieldBufs[hashKey-1]),fieldOutSep);
    for(i = 0; i < selectNum; i++) {
      thisField = order[i];
      if (thisField > fieldNum) fieldBufs[thisField][0] = '\0';
      if (i+1 < selectNum) {
        printf("%s%s",fieldBufs[thisField],fieldOutSep);
      } else {
        if (joinFile) {
          fscanf(joinFile,"%4096[^\n]\n",joinBuf);
          printf("%s%s",joinBuf,fieldOutSep);
        }
        printf("%s%s",fieldBufs[thisField],recOutSep);
      }
    }
  }
  else {
    if (hashKey) printf("%u%s",Hash(fieldBufs[hashKey-1]),fieldOutSep);
    for(i = 0; i < fieldNum; i++) {
      if (tailRec && !i || end) continue;
      printf("%s%s",fieldBufs[i],fieldOutSep);
    }
    if (joinFile) {
      fscanf(joinFile,"%4096[^\n]\n",joinBuf);
      printf("%s%s",joinBuf,fieldOutSep);
    }
    printf("%s%s",fieldBufs[i],recOutSep);
  }
  if (firstRecs && firstRecs == recNum) exit(0);
}
```

```c
word Hash(byte *s)
{
  word h = 0;

  while(*s) {
    h += *s++;
    h *= 255;
  }
  return h % hashNum;
}

word NextPrime(word n)
{
  word  i,max,factor;

  if (n > 0) {
    if (n % 2 == 0) n++;
    for ( ; n <= 0xFFFFFFFF; n += 2) {
      max = sqrt(n)+1;
      factor = 0;
      for (i = 3; i <= max; i += 2)
        if (n % i == 0) { factor = i; break; }
      if (!factor) return n;
    }
  }
  return HASHNUM;
}

void Setup(int argc,char *argv[])
{
  char  *bufIn,*bufOut;
  word  i;
```

```
    InitCursorCtl(0);
    for(i = 1; i < argc; i++)
      if (argv[i][0] == '-' && argv[i][2] == '\0')
        switch (tolower(argv[i][1])) {
          case 'a': firstRecs = atoi(argv[++i]); break;
          case 'b': beginStr = argv[++i]; break;
          case 'c': firstChars = atoi(argv[++i]); break;
          case 'd': fieldSep = argv[++i][0]; break;
          case 'e': end = TRUE; break;
          case 'f': fieldOutSep = argv[++i]; break;
          case 'h': hashNum = NextPrime(atoi(argv[++i]));
                    if (!hashKey) hashKey = select ? order[0]+1 : 1; break;
          case 'i': recSep = argv[++i][0]; break;
          case 'j': joinFile = fopen(argv[++i],"r");
                    if (!joinFile) {
                      fprintf(stderr,"# Cannot open join file: %s\n",
                          argv[i]);
                      exit(1);
                    }
                    break;
          case 'k': hashKey = atoi(argv[++i]);
                    if (!hashNum) hashNum = HASHNUM; break;
          case 'l': lowerCase = TRUE; break;
          case 'n': numerate = TRUE; break;
          case 'p': properCase = TRUE; break;
          case 'r': recOutSep = argv[++i]; break;
          case 's': select = argv[++i];
                    order[selectNum++] = atoi(select)-1; break;
          case 't': tailRec = TRUE; break;
          case 'u': upperCase = TRUE; break;
        }
      else {
        fprintf(stderr,"tt [options…] < stdin > stdout # Texttool\n");
        fprintf(stderr,"    [-a num][-c num][-t][-e][-l|-p|-u][-j file]\n");
        fprintf(stderr,"    [-n][-b str][-h num][-k fld][-s fld]\n");
        fprintf(stderr,"    [-d char][-f str] # default fieldSep is tab\n");
        fprintf(stderr,"    [-i char][-r str] # default recSep is return\n");
        exit(1);
      }
    if (!fieldOutSep) fieldOutSep = "\t";
    if (!recOutSep) recOutSep = "\n";

    for (i = 0; i < MAXFIELDS; i++)
      if (!(fieldBufs[i] = malloc(FIELDSIZE))) {
        fprintf(stderr,"# Out of memory (field buffer #%d)\n",i);
        exit(3);
      }

    if (bufIn = malloc(BUFSIZE)) setvbuf(stdin,bufIn,_IOFBF,BUFSIZE);
    if (bufOut = malloc(BUFSIZE)) setvbuf(stdout,bufOut,_IOFBF,BUFSIZE);
}
```

TextTool.r — Rez Source Code for a Commando Interface

TextTool offers so many options that it is helpful to have a Commando interface with explanatory text. Here is the Rez source for just such an interface:

```
/* tt.r - The Commando companion for TextTool, a tool by Dan Allen. */
/* Begun 1/4/89 */

#include "cmdo.r";            /* top, left, bottom, right */

resource 'cmdo' (128, "TextTool") {
  {
    300,
    "TextTool - A field/record oriented tool for munging textfiles. "
    "Up to 64 fields, each of 4096 characters, can be read in and output "
    "while undergoing various transformations.  Useful as a sort filter.",
    {
      NotDependent { }, RegularEntry {
        "Input Field Sep", {60, 12, 76, 120}, {59, 131, 75, 165},
        "", ignoreCase, "-d",
        "The default input field separator is a tab.  Use of this option "
        "allows a different single character to delimit fields."
      },
      NotDependent { }, RegularEntry {
        "Input Record Sep", {88, 12, 104, 128}, {87, 131, 103, 165},
        "", ignoreCase, "-i",
        "The default input record separator is a return.  Use this option "
        "to change this single record delimiter character."
      },

      NotDependent { }, RegularEntry {
        "Output Field Sep", {60, 182, 76, 296}, {59, 311, 75, 341},
        "", ignoreCase, "-f",
        "Fields are separated on output with tabs by default.  Use of this "
        "option allows any arbitrary string to be used instead."
      },
      NotDependent { }, RegularEntry {
        "Output Record Sep", {88, 182, 104, 308}, {87, 311, 103, 341},
        "", ignoreCase, "-r",
        "Records are separated on output with returns by default.  Use of "
        "this option allows any arbitrary string to be used instead."
      },
```

```
NotDependent { }, RadioButtons {
  {
    {130, 20, 144, 104}, "Std", "", Set,
      "Case is preserved.  The default.",
    {145, 20, 159, 104}, "Lower", "-l", NotSet,
      "All text is output in lower-case.",
    {160, 20, 174, 104}, "Proper", "-p", NotSet,
      "Each field's text begins capitalized, followed by lower case.",
    {175, 20, 189, 104}, "Upper", "-u", NotSet,
      "All text is output in upper-case.",
  }
},
NotDependent { }, CheckOption {
  NotSet, {131, 124, 147, 208}, "Number", "-n",
  "Each record is numbered, starting with the number 1.  This preceeds"
  " every other option, such as hash numbers and leading strings."
},
NotDependent { }, CheckOption {
  NotSet, {149, 124, 165, 208}, "End", "-e",
  "Only the last field of each record is output."
},
NotDependent { }, CheckOption {
  NotSet, {168, 124, 183, 208}, "Tail", "-t",
  "All fields EXCEPT the first field are output."
},
NotDependent { }, TextBox { gray, {125, 12, 191, 212}, "Options" },

NotDependent { }, RegularEntry {
  "Field", {25, 357, 41, 425}, {23, 432, 39, 462},
  "", ignoreCase, "-s",
  "Specifies field N to be output.  This option can be repeated "
  "for output of a selection of fields."
},
NotDependent { }, RegularEntry {
  "Hash Key", {47, 357, 63, 425}, {46, 432, 62, 462},
  "", ignoreCase, "-k",
  "Specifies that field N will be used to determine the hash value.  "
  "If the -h option is not specified, an implied hash value of 33554393 "
  "will be used. If a different hash number is desired, the -h option "
  "should follow this option."
},
NotDependent { }, RegularEntry {
  "1st Chars", {70, 357, 86, 425}, {69, 432, 85, 462},
  "", ignoreCase, "-c",
  "The first N characters of each field will be output."
},
NotDependent { }, RegularEntry {
  "1st Recs", {93, 357, 109, 425}, {92, 432, 108, 462},
  "", ignoreCase, "-a",
  "Outputs only the first N records, using the input def of a record."
},
NotDependent { }, TextBox { gray, {16, 352, 116, 471}, "Select" },
```

```
        NotDependent { }, RegularEntry {
          "String", {139, 228, 155, 280}, {138, 285, 154, 458},
          "", ignoreCase, "-b",
          "Begin each record with the specified text, separated by the "
          "current output field separator."
        },
        NotDependent {}, RegularEntry {
          "Hash #", {167, 228, 183, 280}, {166, 285, 182, 350},
          "", ignoreCase, "-h",
          "Hashing of the first field will be done modulo this number. The hash "
          "value preceeds the first output field. If N is zero, then a "
          "default value of 33554393 is used."
        },
        NotDependent{}, Files {
          InputFile,
          RequiredFile {
            {164, 368, 184, 460}, /* top, left, bottom, right */
            "Join File",
            "-j",
            "Specifies a file to be joined.  All of the specified fields from "
            "the main input file are output, then an output field specifier "
            "follows, then the next line from the join file, and then the "
            "output record specifier.",
          },
          Additional {"", "", "", "", {}}
        },
        NotDependent {}, TextBox {gray,{125,224,191,471},"Additional Text"},

        NotDependent { }, Redirection {
          StandardInput,
          {16, 14}
        },
        NotDependent { }, Box { gray, {16, 11, 116, 173} },

        NotDependent { }, Redirection {
          StandardOutput,
          {16, 182}
        },
        NotDependent { }, Box { gray, {16, 178, 116, 349} },

        NotDependent { }, VersionDialog {
          VersionString { "1.0 B2" },
          "TextTool 1.0 B2 - Created on November 25, 1988 by Dan Allen.\n"
          "Built on " $$Date " @ " $$Time ".\n"
          "Written using MPW C 3.0 for the book "On Macintosh Programming".",
          noDialog
        }
      }
    }
};
```

Sort — C Tool

Versions 1.0 and 2.0 of MPW did not include a `Sort` tool, so here is a RAM-based sorting tool with a few interesting options that even the MPW 3.0 `Sort` tool does not have.

The basic theory of this tool's operation is that it reads lines from standard input, copying lines with the standard library `malloc` routine and setting up pointers to the lines in an array. Then the library `qsort` routine is called to sort the lines; actually, it sorts only the pointers to the lines, thus saving a lot of unnecessary copying of the much larger text strings. Next, the lines are output in ascending, descending, or tree order, depending upon the option selected. If you want just the unique lines to be output, use the `-u` option.

You can select among several different sorting comparison routines. The default is case-sensitive sorting, and case-insensitive ordering or folding is selected by `-f`. Floating-point numbers are sorted with `-n`, and hex numbers are sorted with `-h`. A random option sorts in any order (`-a`).

Dictionary ordering is case-insensitive, but it allows some punctuation to be skipped while other punctuation is observed. This particular dictionary routine orders lines in the same way as a professional indexer would order them; the routine has been verified by passing the equivalent of Knuth's spectral test for indexes: `Sort -d` sorts the same way *Words into Type*, the *Chicago Manual of Style*, and *Webster's Dictionary* do.

The most esoteric option (`-g`) sorts according to the Greek alphabet (α, β, γ, δ . . .), properly handling accents and breathing marks. This works with the encoding used in the SuperGreek fonts made for the Macintosh, and to a lesser extent with the Symbol font built into the LaserWriter. Although the Symbol font is satisfactory for mathematical symbols, it is not aesthetically acceptable for use with the Greek language, even though it has Greek characters. Classical Greek looks like the characters found in the SuperGreek font and requires the diacriticals and breathing marks also present in that font.

Other fonts with special characters, punctuation, and orderings could be added to this tool by creating arrays indicating character classes as I have done for the SuperGreek font.

Improving Sort

Here are some suggestions for improving `Sort`:

- The slowest variant of sorting currently is the numeric sort, because it rescans strings to floating-point numbers at every comparison. Improve `Sort` to scan the strings only once and sort these numbers directly. Do not forget about the rest of the text following the numbers! Hint: try a `union`.

- The facility for unique lines works properly only with case-sensitive and case-insensitive sorts. Add the other types of orderings to the unique code.

- This `Sort` is RAM-based. Extend it to use an external sort and merge process using files on disk so that it can sort arbitrarily large files. Does performance suffer?

- How would you sort multiple files? Should the output go to multiple files or to a single file? Add the ability to sort a list of files to the basic standard input facility.

- Often it is useful to sort on fields of a line. `TextTool` can be used to change field ordering, or sort fields can be put directly into `Sort`. Which way seems best to you?

- Replace the library `qsort` (Quicksort) routine with your implementation of a favorite sort algorithm, such as a binary sort or your own version of Quicksort. If the comparison routine is hardcoded into your own algorithm—thus saving a procedure call— is there a noticeable performance improvement?

- What percentage of the program's run time is spent in these string-comparison routines? Try recoding some of the string-comparison routines in more efficient C or perhaps even in assembly language in order to improve performance. Was it worth the effort?

- Discover what algorithm `qsort` uses, using your favorite disassembler.

```
/*
 *  Sort.c   - RAM based sort tool
 *           - Written by Dan Allen, begun 10/27/87
 *           - Added random & numeric sorts 11/17/87
 *           - Added tree order output 12/30/87
 *           - Greek option added 4/10/88
 *           - Updated to MPW C 3.0 10/7/88
 *           - Started over again 10/30/88
 *           - Dynamic allocation of line array 11/23/88
 *           - Put it all together 11/24/88
 *           - Several fixes to dictionary ordering 12/26/88
 *           - Hex ordering added 1/4/89
 *           - Numeric & hex call strcmp if equal 1/4/89
 *           - Unique works for case-insensitive 5/6/89
 */

#include  <CType.h>
#include  <CursorCtl.h>
#include  <StdIO.h>
#include  <StdLib.h>
#include  <String.h>
#include  <Types.h>

pascal long TickCount() extern 0xA975;
```

```
typedef unsigned char byte;
typedef unsigned int  word;

#define BUFSIZE   (32*1024)
#define LINESIZE  4096
#define LINEINC   4096
#define RANDMIDPT (RAND_MAX / 2)
#define isdict(c) (isascii(c) ? (isspace(c) || ispinct(c)) : 1)

static char    *version = "# Sort 1.0 B3 - 6 May 1989";
static void    GetArgs(),WriteSort(),WriteTree();
static int     CaseCompare(),FoldCompare(),DictCompare();
static int     NumericCompare(),HexCompare(),AnyCompare(),GreekCompare();

static Boolean progress,reverseFlag,treeFlag,uniqueFlag;
static byte    *((*linePtrs)[]),line[LINESIZE];
static word    n,t;
enum {CASE,FOLD,DICT,NUMERIC,HEX,ANY,GREEK} sortType = CASE;

main(int argc,char *argv[])
{
  char  *buffer,*p;
  int    curSize = LINEINC;

  GetArgs(argc,argv);
  buffer = malloc(BUFSIZE);
  if (buffer) setvbuf(stdin,buffer,_IOFBF,BUFSIZE);

  linePtrs = malloc(curSize*sizeof(char *));
  while(fgets(line,LINESIZE,stdin)) {
    p = malloc(strlen(line)+1);
    if (!p) {
      fprintf(stderr,"# Out of memory for strings\n");
      return 2;
    }
    if (n == curSize) {
      curSize += LINEINC;
      linePtrs = realloc(linePtrs,curSize*sizeof(char *));
      if (!linePtrs) {
        fprintf(stderr,"# Out of memory for line pointers\n");
        return 2;
      }
    }
    strcpy(p,line);
    (*linePtrs)[n++] = p;
    SpinCursor(-1);
  }
```

```
    switch (sortType) {
      case CASE:    qsort(linePtrs,n,sizeof(byte *),CaseCompare); break;
      case FOLD:    qsort(linePtrs,n,sizeof(byte *),FoldCompare); break;
      case DICT:    qsort(linePtrs,n,sizeof(byte *),DictCompare); break;
      case NUMERIC: qsort(linePtrs,n,sizeof(byte *),NumericCompare); break;
      case HEX:     qsort(linePtrs,n,sizeof(byte *),HexCompare); break;
      case ANY:     qsort(linePtrs,n,sizeof(byte *),AnyCompare); break;
      case GREEK:   qsort(linePtrs,n,sizeof(byte *),GreekCompare); break;
    }

    if (progress) fprintf(stderr,"# Time to sort = %.2f sec\n",
                          (TickCount() - t)/60.0);
    if (buffer) setvbuf(stdout,buffer,_IOFBF,BUFSIZE);
    if (treeFlag) WriteTree(); else WriteSort();
    return 0;
}

void GetArgs(int argc,char *argv[])
{
    int i;

    t = TickCount();
    InitCursorCtl(0);
    for (i = 1; i < argc; i++) {
      if (argv[i][0] == '-' && argv[i][2] == '\0') {
        switch(tolower(argv[i][1])) {
          case 'a': sortType = ANY; srand(TickCount()); break;
          case 'd': sortType = DICT; break;
          case 'f': sortType = FOLD; break;
          case 'g': sortType = GREEK; break;
          case 'h': sortType = HEX; break;
          case 'n': sortType = NUMERIC; break;
          case 'p': progress = true; fprintf(stderr,"%s\n",version); break;
          case 'r': reverseFlag = true; break;
          case 't': treeFlag = true; break;
          case 'u': uniqueFlag = true; break;
          default:
            fprintf(stderr,
                "Sort [-a|-d|-f|-g|-h|-n] [-p] [-r] [-t|-u] < stdin > stdout\n");
            fprintf(stderr,
        "#    Any Dict Fold Greek Hex Numeric Progress Reverse Tree Unique\n");
            exit(1);
        }
      }
    }
}
```

```
void WriteSort()
{
  int    i;

  for(i = 0; i < n; i++) {
    if (uniqueFlag && i) {
      if (sortType == CASE) {
        if (!strcmp((*linePtrs)[i],(*linePtrs)[i-1])) continue;
      }
      else if (!strfold((*linePtrs)[i],(*linePtrs)[i-1])) continue;
    }
    printf("%s",(*linePtrs)[i]);
    SpinCursor(-1);
  }
}

/*  WriteTree prints sorted array in infix tree order */
/*  Example: 0 through 8 is printed as 4,2,6,1,3,5,7,0,8 */
/*  Useful for include/omit list input for Index tool */

static void WriteTree()
{
  byte  *((*p)[]),*((*max)[]);
  word  inc, offset, keysRemain;

  max = linePtrs + n*sizeof(byte *);
  inc = keysRemain = n;
  while (keysRemain > 0) {
    SpinCursor(-1);
    offset = inc*sizeof(byte *);
    p = linePtrs + (inc >> 1) * sizeof(byte *);
    while (p < max) {
      if (keysRemain == 0) return;
      if ((*p)[0]) {
        printf("%s",(*p)[0]);
        (*p)[0] = nil;
        --keysRemain;
      }
      p += offset ? offset : sizeof(byte *);
    }
    inc >>= 1;
  }
}

int CaseCompare(byte **i,byte **j)
{
  SpinCursor(1);
  if (reverseFlag) return -strcmp(*i,*j);
  else return strcmp(*i,*j);
}
```

```c
int FoldCompare(byte **i,byte **j)
{
  byte   a,b,*p,*q;

  SpinCursor(1);
  p = *i; q = *j;
  while ( (a = tolower(*p)) == (b = tolower(*q)) ) {
    if (*p == '\0') return 0;
    p++; q++;
  }
  if (reverseFlag) return (a < b) ? 1 : -1;
  else return (a < b) ? -1 : 1;
}

int DictCompare(byte **i,byte **j)
  /*
     This routine orders words like a dictionary or index
     would, ignoring most punctuation.  See "Words into Type",
     "The Chicago Manual of Style", and "Webster's New World
     Dictionary, Third College Edition" for more info & examples.
  */
{
  byte     a,b,*p,*q;
  Boolean flag = false;

  SpinCursor(1);
  p = *i; q = *j;
  while (true) {
    a = tolower(*p); b = tolower(*q);
    if (a == b) {
      if (!a) return 0;
      if (a == ',') flag = true;
      p++; q++; continue;
    }
    if (!a || a == '\n') return reverseFlag ? 1 : -1;
    if (!b || b == '\n') return reverseFlag ? -1 : 1;
    if (a == ',' || a == ':' || a == '.' && flag) return reverseFlag ? 1 : -1;
    if (b == ',' || b == ':' || b == '.' && flag) return reverseFlag ? -1 : 1;
    if (isdict(a)) { p++; continue; }
    if (isdict(b)) { q++; continue; }
    break;
  }
  if (reverseFlag) return (a < b) ? 1 : -1;
  else return (a < b) ? -1 : 1;
}
```

```c
int NumericCompare(byte **i,byte **j)
{
  extended  x,y;

  SpinCursor(1);
  x = atof(*i); y = atof(*j); /* this is slow! */
  if (x == y) return strcmp(*i,*j);
  if (reverseFlag) return (x > y) ? -1 : 1;
  else return (x > y) ? 1 : -1;
}

int HexCompare(byte **i,byte **j)
{
  int x,y;

  SpinCursor(1);
  x = strtol(*i,0,16); y = strtol(*j,0,16); /* this is slow! */
  if (x == y) return strcmp(*i,*j);
  if (reverseFlag) return (x > y) ? -1 : 1;
  else return (x > y) ? 1 : -1;
}

int AnyCompare()
{
  SpinCursor(1);
  return (rand() > RANDMIDPT) ? 1 : -1;
}

int strfold(byte *i,byte *j)
{
  byte  a,b;

  SpinCursor(1);
  while ( (a = tolower(*i)) == (b = tolower(*j)) ) {
    if (*i == '\0') return 0;
    i++; j++;
  }
  if (reverseFlag) return (a < b) ? 1 : -1;
  else return (a < b) ? -1 : 1;
}

static byte superGreekFold[256] = {
  0,0,0,0,0,0,0,0,0,0,0,0,0,0,0,0,0,0,0,0,0,0,0,0,0,0,0,0,0,0,0,0, /* 0-31 */
  0,0,114,0,0,0,0,1,0,0,0,1,0,0,0,1, /* 32 to 47 */
  0,0,0,0,0,0,0,0,0,0,0,0, /* 48 to 58 */
  1,0,0,0,0,0, /* 59 to 64 */

  65,66,86,68,69,85,67,71,73,1, /* 65 to 74 */
  74,75,76,77,78,79,72,81,82,83,84,1, /* 75 to 86 */
  88,78,87,70, /* 87 to 90 */
  1,1,1,1,0,0, /* 91 to 96 */
```

```
  65,66,86,68,69,85,67,71,73,1, /* 97 to 106 */
  74,75,76,77,78,79,72,81,82,83,84,1, /* 107 to 118 */
  88,78,87,70, /* 119 to 122 */
  1,1,1,1,0, /* 123 to 127 */

  0,0,0,0,0,0,0,0,0,0,0,0,0,0,0,0,0,0,0,0,0,0,0,0,0,0,0,0,0,0,0,0, /*128-159 */
  0,0,0,0,0,0,0,0,0,0,0,0,0,0,0,0,0,0,0,0,0,0,0,0,0,0,0,0,0,0,0,0, /*160-191 */
  1,0,0,0,0,0,1,1,1, /* 192 to 200 */
  0,0,0,0,0,0,0,1,0, /* 201 to 209 */
  1,1,1,1,1,0,1,1,    /* 210 to 217 */
  0,0,0,0,0,0,0,0,0,0,0,0,0,0,0,0,0,0,0,0,0, /* 218 to 238 */
  1
};

int GreekCompare(byte **i,byte **j)
{
  byte   a,b,*p,*q;

  SpinCursor(1);
  p = *i; q = *j;
  while (true) {
    while ((a = superGreekFold[*p++]) == 1)
      ;
    while ((b = superGreekFold[*q++]) == 1)
      ;
    if (a == b) {
      if (a == '\0') return 0;
      continue;
    } else
      break;
  }
  if (reverseFlag) return (a < b) ? 1 : -1;
  else return (a < b) ? -1 : 1;
}
```

Sort.r — Rez Source Code for a Commando Interface

```
/* Sort.r - The Commando companion for Sort, a tool by Dan Allen. */
/* Begun 2/10/88 */

#include "cmdo.r";                    /* top, left, bottom, right */

resource 'cmdo' (128, "Sort") {
{   300,
    "Sort - A general purpose RAM-based sort tool.",
    {

/* WORD DEFINITION */

NotDependent { }, RadioButtons {
    {
        {32, 200, 48, 291}, "Case", "", Set,
            "A case sensitive sort according to ASCII order.  Capital letters "
            "therefore come before lower case letters.  The default.",
        {54, 200, 70, 291}, "Fold", "-f", NotSet,
            "Specifies a case INsensitive ordering, folding upper and "
            "lower case together for sort comparisons.",
        {76, 200, 92, 291}, "Dictionary", "-d", NotSet,
            "Specifies a dictionary ordering for the sort comparisons.  "
            "Dictionary ordering is NOT case sensitive and ignores most "
            "punctuation characters.  The resultant ordering is "
            "like that found in a dictionary or index.",
        {98, 200, 114, 291}, "Numeric", "-n", NotSet,
            "Sort lines according to numeric order.  This assumes that each "
            "line begins with a number.  Also works with floating point.",
        {120, 200, 136, 292}, "Hex", "-h", NotSet,
            "Sort lines according to hexadecimal order."
            "  Hex numbers may also begin with 0x.",
        {142, 200, 158, 292}, "Any", "-a", NotSet,
            "Sort lines in a random order.  Any order may result.",
        {164, 200, 180, 292}, "Greek", "-g", NotSet,
            "Specifies a case insensitive sort using the SuperGreek font. "
            "Sorts according to the Greek alphabet, i.e., alpha, beta, gamma… "
            " Ignores Greek punctuation such as accents & breathing marks.",
    }
},
NotDependent { }, TextBox { gray, {20, 180, 184, 298}, "Sort Type" },
```

```
/* OUTPUT  */
NotDependent { }, RadioButtons {
    {
        {36, 344, 52, 428}, "Std", "", Set,
            "Standard output of all lines.  The default.",
        {60, 344, 76, 428}, "Tree", "-t", NotSet,
            "Outputs the sort in a binary tree in-order, with the middle node "
            "first.  This greatly increases performance with include or omit "
            "files and the Index tool.",
        {84, 344, 100, 428}, "Unique", "-u", NotSet,
            "Outputs only those lines that are unique, that is, only one "
            "occurance of multiple identical lines will be output.",
    }
},
NotDependent { }, TextBox { gray, {21, 320, 110, 434}, "Output" },

/* OPTIONS */
NotDependent { }, CheckOption {
    NotSet, {134, 344, 150, 428}, "Progress", "-p",
    "Outputs the version number of sort as well as the time it takes to sort."
},
NotDependent { }, CheckOption {
    NotSet, {158, 344, 174, 428}, "Reverse", "-r",
    "Sort in reverse or descending (z-a, Z to A, 9 to 0) order. "
    "The default is ascending (0-9, A to Z, a-z) order.",
},
NotDependent { }, TextBox { gray, {125, 328, 184, 434}, "Options" },

/* STANDARD IO */
NotDependent { }, Redirection {
    StandardInput, {20, 28}
},
NotDependent { }, Redirection {
    StandardOutput, {70, 28}
},
NotDependent { }, Redirection {
    DiagnosticOutput, {120, 28}
},
NotDependent { }, VersionDialog {
    VersionString { "1.0 B3" },
    "Sort 1.0 B3 - Created on October 27, 1987 by Dan Allen.\n"
    "Built on " $$Date " @ " $$Time ".\n"
    "Written using MPW C 3.0 for the book "On Macintosh Programming".",
    noDialog
},
} } };
```

Index —C Tool

`Index` is a tool that creates indexes, cross-references, concordances, and word-frequency lists from text files. The default output of `Index` is to generate a cross-reference, displaying an alphabetical list of all words followed by a full list of occurrences by file and line number. The following explanatory definitions are helpful when you are considering which type of an index you wish to generate.

A *word count* includes the number of characters, the number of words, and the number of lines of text. These statistics, along with summary totals of all of the input files, are always sent to the diagnostic output whenever `Index` is run, unless the quiet (`-q`) option is used.

A *unique word* list contains just the unique words found in the indexed text. A *word frequency* list additionally contains the number of occurrences of each unique word. These types of indexes can be obtained by `Index -u` and `Index -f`, respectively.

An *index* is an ordered list of words, and is a general term that can be applied to many different kinds of lists. The standard type of index (like those found in the back of many books) is usually a non-exhaustive alphabetical list of words listing the location of the main occurrences of each word (or topic). Such an index neither lists *all* of the words found in the document nor *all* of the occurrences of any given word from the document. Rather, a standard index usually lists only those occurrences that are important or notable. This type of index can be approximated by using `Index` in either of two ways. First, with the `-i` option, you can specify a list of all words to be included in the index. Or, if there are only a few words you do *not* want indexed (for example, a list of "noise" words or reserved words), you can use the `-o` option to create an index minus those words you want omitted.

A *cross reference* is an exhaustive index—that is, it lists all words found in the document and all instances of those words. Usually a cross-reference is an alphabetical list of words, where each word has associated with it a list of line numbers in ascending order. This is the default output of `Index`.

`Index` normally reads all of the characters found in a file (including words in quotes) and uses as its standard criteria for words the following definition: A word is a sequence of letters (A . . . Z, a . . . z), digits (0 . . . 9), and periods (.), but not beginning with a period. This definition allows basic words and numbers. The default string comparison routine is not case-sensitive and supports the international character set as well. By default, `Index` does an ascending sort.

The default rules are different for file names ending in .a, .c, .h, .p, and .r. If a file name ends in one of these suffixes, the appropriate language-specific rules are used for convenience in indexing 68xxx assembly language, C, C header, Pascal, and `Rez` files, respectively. This allows a set of different files to be indexed together. For a complete description of these automatic language-specific changes, see the appropriate language option. Note that for source files, reserved words are included in the indexes. If you do not want reserved words indexed, use the omit option and supply a file of the language-specific reserved words that you want omitted from the index.

By default, `Index` reads standard input, but a list of file names to be indexed may be provided instead. The created index is sent to standard output. Errors, progress information, and file statistics are all written to diagnostic output. Use of the `-q` (quiet) option suppresses the progress and statistics; errors, however, are still sent to diagnostic output. `Index` returns the status values described in the following table.

Status Value	Description
0	No errors
1	Syntax error (error in parameters)
2	OS Level error (file not found, etc.)
3	Not enough memory for operation

Options

`Index` supports the following options. See the syntax description above for possible option conflicts.

-a   Assembly language defaults. When you use this option, `Index` will use the following 68xxx assembly language defaults for all input files, regardless of file suffix: Words located in valid assembly comments are not indexed. The comment conventions used are those used by the MPW 68xxx Assembler: comments begin with a semicolon and continue to the end of the line; comments can also begin with an asterisk if it is the first character on a line. Comments may be continued by use of the backslash (\). `Index` is not case-sensitive while reading assembly files, and it uses the assembler's definition of identifiers for its definition of words to index, which is as follows: the first character of an identifier may be an upper- or lowercase letter (A . . . Z,a . . . z), an underscore (_), or an at symbol (@). Subsequent characters may be letters, digits (0 . . . 9), underscores (_), dollar signs ($), number signs (#), percent signs (%), or at symbols (@). Strings and character constants are delimited by single quotes and are skipped. Escaped quotes (two single quotes in succession) are also skipped.

-b   Blanks as separators. Any run of characters constitutes a word with the only word separators being some form of blank space: spaces, tabs, and carriage returns. This option is the opposite of the `-w` words-only option.

-c   C defaults. When you use this option, `Index` will use the following C language defaults for all input files, regardless of file suffix: Words located in valid C comments are not indexed. Valid C comments are separated by pairs of slashes and asterisks—for example, /* this is a C comment */. `Index` is case-sensitive when reading C files and uses as its definition for a word the definition of a legal C identifier, which is as follows: An identifier is a sequence of letters (A ... Z, a ... z), digits (0 . ..9), and underscores (_), not beginning with a digit. Strings in C are delimited by double quotes and character constants by single quotes. The contents in either case, as well as in the case of escaped quotes (quotes preceded by the backslash), are skipped.

-d   Dictionary ordering. This is not case-sensitive, and it orders words ignoring punctuation, thus producing the kind of ordering found in dictionaries and indexes. Specifically, when comparing two words, this option ignores all space and punctuation characters except commas, colons, and semicolons.

-f   Frequency count. This option specifies a word-frequency list that is alphabetically sorted and that includes the number of occurrences of each word.

-h   Huge file. This option automatically limits the number of occurrences of words three characters or shorter to only the first ten occurrences. All words four characters or longer will have all of their occurrences indexed. Use of this option will usually greatly reduce the amount of memory required when indexing a document.

-i filename   Include for indexing. This option allows you to give `Index` a list of words to be indexed; only those words will be indexed. Words are contained in the file `filename` and should be listed one word per line, where lines are separated by carriage returns. `Index` looks only in the current MPW directory for `filename`, but you may specify a full path name if desired.

-l length   Using this option gives you a way to specify the length of words to be included in the generated index, where `length` is an integer. If it is a positive integer, all words whose length is greater than or equal to `length` will be included in the index. If it is a negative integer, all words whose length is less than or equal to `length` will be included in the index.

-n count   Using this option gives you a way to specify the maximum number of occurrences to index for any given word. For example, using a count of ten will confine the output of the final index to just the first ten instances of each word. Use of this option will usually greatly reduce the amount of memory required when indexing a document.

-o filename   Omit from index. This option allows you to give Index a list of words to omit from its generated index. All words *not* found in this list will be indexed. The words are listed one word per line, where lines are separated by carriage returns. Index looks only in the current MPW directory for filename, but you may specify a full path name if desired.

-p   Pascal defaults. When you use this option, Index will use the following Pascal language defaults for all input files, regardless of file suffix: Words located in valid Pascal comments are not indexed. Valid Pascal comments are separated by braces ({ }). In addition, comments may also be separated by matching pairs of parentheses and asterisks—for example, (* this is a valid Pascal comment *). Index is case-insensitive when reading Pascal files, and it uses as its definition for a word the definition of a legal Pascal identifier, which is as follows: An identifier is a sequence of letters (A . . . Z, a . . . z), digits (0 . . . 9), and underscores (_), not beginning with a digit. Strings in Pascal are delimited by single quotes and are skipped. Escaped quotes (two single quotes in succession) are also skipped.

-q   Quiet output. The default is for Index to provide progress and statistical information while reading the input files. This option overrides this information: the only output that can occur when you use this option is error information.

-r   Reverse sort. By default, sorting is done in ascending order. If you use this option, the sort will be done in a descending order. All sorting is based on the ASCII collating sequence, modified by the case-sensitive option (which also affects the extended characters and international sorting).

-s   Case-sensitive comparisons. The default is to be case-insensitive and to provide for international sorting. If you use this option, all of the language defaults will be overridden, and all string comparisons will be case-sensitive. Performance increases markedly with this option.

-t   Text file defaults. This option turns off the language default rules that apply for file names ending in .a, .c, .h, .p, and .r and instead uses the normal default rules, which are described earlier in this section. All of the text contained in the files is indexed, including text in quoted strings.

-u   Unique words. This type of index is a simple list of all unique words found in the input file(s).

-w   Words only. Only alphabetic characters (A-Z, a-z) are allowed in words. This option specifies that the definition of a word excludes all numbers, spaces, and punctuation marks. This option is the opposite of the -b option, which uses blanks as separators to identify words.

-x   Words only with form feed characters separating pages rather than returns separating lines. This option is useful in conjunction with the WordText tool in indexing MS Word files. See the WordText tool description provided earlier in this chapter for more information.

-z   Rez defaults. When you use this option, Index will use the Rez language defaults for all input files, regardless of file suffix. The Rez defaults are identical to the C defaults described above, except that Rez is not case-sensitive.

Examples

```
Index {aincludes}≈.a > xref

Index sample.a sample.c sample.p > xref

Index -t -f sample.a sample.c sample.p > xref
```

The first example above creates a standard cross-reference of all of the assembler equates files, sorted alphabetically without case distinctions and omitting all comments. The second example properly handles the appropriate language-specific properties for comments, case, and word definition as it indexes three different types of files. The final example creates a word frequency list of all words—including comments and the contents of quoted strings.

Improving `Index`

Here are some suggestions for improving `Index`:

- Multi-character suffixes like `.ps` are not handled correctly by the automatic file-type-detection mechanism. Likewise, escaped characters like `\"` are not processed correctly. Fix these minor bugs.

- The size and number of files that `Index` can treat is limited by available RAM. Consider enhancing `Index` to work in a disk-based manner. How large an architectural change would this require?

- The contents of quoted strings and constants are always skipped when the language-specific defaults apply. One way to work around this problem is to use the `-t` option so that everything is indexed (including comments). Is there a simple fix to this?

- The sort is strictly by ASCII orderings. The dictionary sort is ASCII but ignores certain characters if they are found in a word. Add a provision for numeric sorting.

- `Index` does not automatically become case-sensitive while reading assembly language files if a CASE ON directive is found. All assembly source code is therefore treated as case-insensitive or case-sensitive if the `-s` option is specified. Should `Index` itself parse files for these directives, or should different language parsers be written as separate preprocessors for `Index`?

- How can `Index` help in preparing a table of contents, dictionary, lexicon, or glossary?

- A *key word in context* (KWIC) listing is an index along with some contextual information that pertains to each specific reference. It is arranged alphabetically by topic or key word. Each word entry consists of a line reference along with the line on which the word was used. This type of an index is sometimes also referred to as a *topical guide*. A *concordance* is an exhaustive KWIC listing. It lists all of the words from a given document or set of documents, along with each occurrence of every word. In addition, it provides a key word in context extract (the entire line) for every occurrence of every word. Add these types of indexing capabilities to `Index`.

- The prolific author of `Asm`, `Backup`, and many more tools once said at a warm Wednesday afternoon MPW meeting, "It's gotta have an option." Make Ira happy by adding more options to `Index` so that it competes with his `PasMat` in terms of the number of directives possible.

Here is the source code to the largest single program found in this book, Index.

```
/*
 *   Index.c - A general purpose indexing program
 *           - Written by Dan Allen
 *           - 23 Mar 1987 Started
 *           - 28 Jul 1987 Rewritten from scratch
 *           - 10 Sep 1987 Added indexing
 *           - 15 Sep 1987 Added language scanning
 *           - 17 Oct 1987 MultiFinder/cursor support
 *           - 17 Nov 1987 Added b & j options
 *           - 16 Dec 1987 Added huge option
 *           - 22 Dec 1987 Added i & o options
 *           - 23 Dec 1987 Added u option
 *           - 29 Dec 1987 Changed w to f, j to w
 *           - 30 Dec 1987 Added d option
 *           - 04 Jan 1988 Sets output tabs to 20
 *           - 24 Mar 1988 Fixed autofile recognition
 *           - 09 Apr 1988 Added greek ordering
 *           - 11 Apr 1988 Finally fixed m option
 *           - 14 Jun 1988 Changed RotateCursor to SpinCursor
 *           - 03 Aug 1988 Uses commas if 1 file; pg #
 *           - 11 Oct 1988 Brought forward to MPW C 3.0; x option added
 *           - 29 Oct 1988 Fixed -x option
 *           - 23 Nov 1988 Fixed comment scanning
 *           - 08 Dec 1988 Fixed omit file bug (NULL to p)
 *           - 12 Dec 1988 Include/omit files set by file suffix
 *           - 26 Dec 1988 Several fixes to dictionary ordering
 *           - 25 Mar 1989 Bug fix for -m & -o at the same time
 *
 */

/*  Includes  */
#include  <CType.h>
#include  <CursorCtl.h>
#include  <FCntl.h>
#include  <IOCtl.h>
#include  <StdIO.h>
#include  <StdLib.h>
#include  <String.h>
#include  <Types.h>

pascal  long  TickCount() extern 0xA975;
pascal  void  MacsBug() extern 0xA9FF;

void  OutPutIndex(),ReadList(),Search();
void  InitWorld(),IndexFile();
void  GetText(),GetAsm(),GetC(),GetPas(),GetGreek();
```

```
/*  Defines   */
#define CRSRSPEED 6
#define STRSIZE    256
#define FBUFSIZ    16*BUFSIZ
#define MAXCNT     0xFFFF
#define isdict(c) (isascii(c) ? (isspace(c) || ispunct(c)) : 1)

struct item {
  struct item   *next;
  unsigned int  fileNum : 10; /* 10 bits = 1,023 files maximum */
  unsigned int  filePos : 22; /* 22 bits = 4,194,303 lines per file max */
};

struct key {
  char          *keyStr;
  struct key    *left;
  struct key    *right;
  struct item   *first;
  struct item   *last;
  unsigned short count;      /* 16 bits = 65535 occurrences maximum */
};


/*  Global Variables  */
static char *version = "# Index 1.0 B3 - 25 Mar 1989";

/* State Globals */
enum  {ASM,C,PASCAL,REZ,GREEK,TEXT} fileType = TEXT;
enum  {INDEX,FREQ,UNIQ} indexType = INDEX;
static  struct key *root;
static  char caseSense,CRFlag,prelimFlag,sepChar = '\n';
static  FILE *input;

/* Options - Language, Index type, Independent options */
static char asmFlag,cFlag,pasFlag,rezFlag,greekFlag,textFlag;
static char freqFlag,maxFlag,uniqueFlag;
static char blanksFlag,dictFlag,wordFlag;
static char caseSenFlag,hugeFlag,quietFlag,reverseFlag;
static char *inclFile,*omitFile;
static short fFlagPos,lFlagPos,nFlagPos;
static unsigned short numCount = MAXCNT;
static unsigned int lenCount;
static int a,b,result;

/* Sizes */
static char fileBuffer[FBUFSIZ], theWord[STRSIZE];
static unsigned int wordLen,keyChars,refChars,occChars,t;
static unsigned int inChars,inWords,inLines,inFiles;
static unsigned int outChars,outWords,outLines;
static unsigned int sumChars,sumWords,sumLines;
```

```
/*  Main Program  */
main(int argc,char *argv[])
{
  int i;

  InitWorld(argc,argv);
  if (inclFile || omitFile) ReadList(argv);

  for (i = 1; argc--; i++) {
    if (argv[i][0] == '-') continue;
    if (lenCount && i == lFlagPos) continue;
    if (numCount && i == nFlagPos) continue;
    if ((inclFile || omitFile) && i == fFlagPos) continue;
    if (argc == 0) break; else inFiles++;
    if (indexType == INDEX) printf("File #%3d = %s\n",inFiles,argv[i]);
    IndexFile(argv[i]);
  }
  if (!inFiles) IndexFile("dev:stdin");
  OutPutIndex();
  return 0;
}

static void Munged(scriptErr,realErr)
  int scriptErr,realErr;
{
  switch(scriptErr) {
    case 1:
      fprintf(stderr,"Index [options] < stdin | files… > stdout\n");
      break;
    case 2:
      fprintf(stderr,"# Mac OS Error: %d\n",realErr);
      break;
    case 3:
      fprintf(stderr,"\n# Out of RAM. Try -h, -n, or -l options.\n");
      OutPutIndex();
      break;
    default:
      fprintf(stderr,"# Internal error #%d\n",realErr);
  }
  exit(scriptErr);
}
```

```c
static void InitWorld(int argc,char *argv[])
{
  char  c;
  int   i,opts = 0;

  InitCursorCtl(0);
  t = TickCount();
  for(i = 1; i <= argc; i++) {
    if (argv[i][0] != '-') continue;
    if (argv[i][2] != '\0') Munged(1);
    switch(c = tolower(argv[i][1])) {
      case 'a': asmFlag = true; fileType = ASM; break;
      case 'b': blanksFlag = true; fileType = TEXT; break;
      case 'c': cFlag = true; fileType = C; break;
      case 'd': dictFlag = true; break;
      case 'f': freqFlag = true; indexType = FREQ; break;
      case 'g': greekFlag = true; fileType = GREEK; break;
      case 'h': hugeFlag = true; break;
      case 'i': inclFile = argv[fFlagPos = i+1]; opts++; break;
      case 'l': lenCount = atoi(argv[lFlagPos = i+1]); opts++; break;
      case 'm': maxFlag = true; indexType = FREQ; break;
      case 'n': numCount = atoi(argv[nFlagPos = i+1]);
                if (numCount < 1) numCount = 1;
                opts++; break;
      case 'o': omitFile = argv[fFlagPos = i+1]; opts++; break;
      case 'p': pasFlag = true; fileType = PASCAL; break;
      case 'q': quietFlag = true; break;
      case 'r': reverseFlag = true; break;
      case 's': caseSenFlag = true; break;
      case 't': textFlag = true; fileType = TEXT; break;
      case 'u': uniqueFlag = true; indexType = UNIQ; break;
      case 'x': sepChar = '\f'; /* fall through */
      case 'w': wordFlag = true; fileType = TEXT; break;
      case 'z': rezFlag = true; fileType = REZ; break;
      default:  fprintf(stderr,"# -%c is not a valid option.\n",c); Munged(1);
    }
    opts++;
  }

  if (argc - opts == 1) quietFlag = true;
  if (!quietFlag) fprintf(stderr,"%s\n",version);
  if (asmFlag + cFlag + pasFlag + rezFlag + greekFlag +
      textFlag + blanksFlag + wordFlag > 1 ||
    caseSenFlag + dictFlag > 1 ||
    freqFlag + uniqueFlag + maxFlag > 1 ||
    inclFile != NULL && omitFile != NULL )
  {
    fprintf(stderr,"# Conflicting options specified.\n");
    Munged(1);
  }
}
```

```
static void OpenFile(char *fileName)
{
  char    c,*ptr;
  extern  short MacOSErr;

  if ((input = fopen(fileName,"r")))
    setvbuf(input,fileBuffer,_IOFBF,FBUFSIZ);
  else {
    fprintf(stderr,"# Cannot open file: %s \n",fileName);
    Munged(2,MacOSErr);
  }
  if (!quietFlag)
    fprintf(stderr,"# %-19s",
        (ptr = strrchr(fileName,':')) ? ptr+1 : fileName);
  fileType = TEXT; c = 't';
  if (!(textFlag || wordFlag || blanksFlag)) {
    if (ptr = strrchr(fileName,'.')) {
      c = tolower(*(ptr+1));
      if (*(ptr+2)) c = 't';
      if (c == 'h') c = 'c';
    }
    if (c != 'a' && c != 'c' && c != 'p' && c != 'r') {
      if (asmFlag) c = 'a';
      else if (cFlag) c = 'c';
      else if (pasFlag) c = 'p';
      else if (rezFlag) c = 'r';
      else if (greekFlag) c = 'g';
      else c = 't';
    }
    if (c == 'a') fileType = ASM;
    if (c == 'c') fileType = C;
    if (c == 'p') fileType = PASCAL;
    if (c == 'r') fileType = REZ;
    if (c == 'g') fileType = GREEK;
  }
  caseSense = (fileType == C) ? true : caseSenFlag;
  if (!quietFlag) fprintf(stderr,"(%c) ",toupper(c));
  fflush(stderr);
}
```

```c
static void IndexFile(char *fileName)
{
  inChars = inWords = inLines = 0;
  OpenFile(fileName);
  switch(fileType) {
    case ASM:      GetAsm(); break;
    case C:        GetC(); break;
    case PASCAL:   GetPas(); break;
    case REZ:      GetC(); break;
    case GREEK:    GetGreek(); break;
    default:       GetText(); break;
  }
  fclose(input);
  sumChars += inChars; sumWords += inWords; sumLines += inLines;
  if (!quietFlag)
    fprintf(stderr,"Chars: %8u  Words: %6u  Lines: %6u  (%uK)\n",
      inChars,inWords,inLines,keyChars+refChars+occChars+1024>>10);
}

static int ScanTillChar(char termChar)
{
  int c;

  do {
    if ((c = getc(input)) == EOF)
      return c;
    else {
      inChars++;
      if (c == '\n') inLines++;
    }
  } while (c != termChar);
  CRFlag = (termChar == '\n') ? true : false;
  return 0;
}

static int IsComment(char termChar)
{
  int   c,state = 0;

  if ( (c = getc(input)) != '*') {
    ungetc(c,input);
    return 0;
  }
  else
    inChars++;  /* comment begin */
```

```
  while ( (c = getc(input)) != EOF) {
    inChars++;
    if (c == '*' && state == 0) { state = 1; continue; }
    if (state == 1 && c == termChar) return 0;   /* comment end */
    if (state == 1 && c != '*') state = 0;
    if (c == '\n') inLines++;
  }
  return EOF;
}

static void GetTillBlank()  /* the only delimiter is white space */
{
  int c,d;

  while ((c = getc(input)) != EOF) {
    d = c; inChars++; wordLen = theWord[0] = 0;

    if(c > 32) {
      do {
        theWord[wordLen++] = c; inChars++;
      } while ((c = getc(input)) > 32);
    } else {
      if (c == sepChar) { inLines++; SpinCursor(CRSRSPEED); }
      continue;
    }

    inWords++; theWord[wordLen++] = '\0';
    if (wordLen > lenCount) Search(root);
    if (c == sepChar) { inLines++; SpinCursor(CRSRSPEED); }
  }
  if (inChars > 0 && d != '\n') inLines++;
}
```

```c
static void GetWords()
{
  int c,d;

  while ((c = getc(input)) != EOF) {
    d = c; inChars++; wordLen = theWord[0] = 0;
    if (isalpha(c)) {
      do {
        theWord[wordLen++] = c; inChars++;
      } while (isalpha(c = getc(input)));
    } else {
      if (c == sepChar) { inLines++; SpinCursor(CRSRSPEED); }
      continue;
    }
    inWords++; theWord[wordLen++] = '\0';
    if (wordLen > lenCount) Search(root);
    if (c == sepChar) { inLines++; SpinCursor(CRSRSPEED); }
  }
  if (inChars > 0 && d != '\n') inLines++;
}

static void GetText()
{
  int c,d;

  if (sepChar == '\f') inLines = 1; /* start with pg 1 */

  if (blanksFlag) { GetTillBlank(); return; }
  else if (wordFlag) { GetWords(); return; }
  while ((c = getc(input)) != EOF) {
    d = c; inChars++; wordLen = theWord[0] = 0;
    if (isalpha(c)) {
      do {
        theWord[wordLen++] = c; inChars++;
      } while (isalnum(c = getc(input)));
    } else if (isdigit(c)) {
      do {
        theWord[wordLen++] = c; inChars++;
      } while (isdigit(c = getc(input)) || c == '.');
    } else {
      if (c == sepChar) { inLines++; SpinCursor(CRSRSPEED); }
      continue;
    }

    inWords++; theWord[wordLen++] = '\0';
    if (wordLen > lenCount) Search(root);
    if (c == sepChar) { inLines++; SpinCursor(CRSRSPEED); }
  }
  if (inChars > 0 && d != '\n') inLines++;
}
```

```
static void GetAsm()
{
  int c,d;

  CRFlag = true;  /* for first line of file */
  while ((c = getc(input)) != EOF) {
    d = c; inChars++;
    if (c == '*' && CRFlag) {
      if (ScanTillChar('\n')) return; else continue;
    }
    else if (c == ';' && ScanTillChar('\n')) return;
    else if (c == '\"' && ScanTillChar('\"')) return;
    else if (c == '\'' && ScanTillChar('\'')) return;
    else if (isalpha(c) || c == '_'|| c == '@') {
      wordLen = theWord[0] = 0;
      do {
        theWord[wordLen++] = c; inChars++;
      } while (isalnum(c = getc(input)) || c == '_' || c == '@'
                    || c == '$' || c == '#' || c == '%');
      inWords++; theWord[wordLen++] = '\0';
      if (wordLen > lenCount) Search(root);
    }
    if (c == '\n') { inLines++; SpinCursor(CRSRSPEED); CRFlag = true; }
    else CRFlag = false;
  }
  if (inChars > 0 && d != '\n') inLines++;
}

static void GetC()
{
  int c,d;

  while ((c = getc(input)) != EOF) {
    d = c; inChars++;
    if (c == '/' && IsComment('/')) return;
    else if (c == '\"' && ScanTillChar('\"')) return;
    else if (c == '\'' && ScanTillChar('\'')) return;
    else if (isalpha(c) || c == '_') {
      wordLen = theWord[0] = 0;
      do {
        theWord[wordLen++] = c; inChars++;
      } while (isalnum(c = getc(input)) || c == '_');
      inWords++; theWord[wordLen++] = '\0';
      if (wordLen > lenCount) Search(root);
    }
    if (c == '\n') { inLines++; SpinCursor(CRSRSPEED); }
  }
  if (inChars > 0 && d != '\n') inLines++;
}
```

```c
static void GetPas()
{
  int c,d;

  while ((c = getc(input)) != EOF) {
    d = c; inChars++;
    if (c == '(' && IsComment(')')) return;
    else if (c == '{' && ScanTillChar('}')) return;
    else if (c == '\'' && ScanTillChar('\'')) return;
    else if (isalpha(c) || c == '_') {
      wordLen = theWord[0] = 0;
      do {
        theWord[wordLen++] = c; inChars++;
      } while (isalnum(c = getc(input)) || c == '_');
      inWords++; theWord[wordLen++] = '\0';
      if (wordLen > lenCount) Search(root);
    }
    if (c == '\n') { inLines++; SpinCursor(CRSRSPEED); }
  }
  if (inChars > 0 && d != '\n') inLines++;
}

static struct key *NewKey()
{
  struct key  *p;
  struct item *occur;

  if (inclFile && !prelimFlag) return NULL;
  p = malloc(sizeof(struct key));
  if (p && (p->keyStr = malloc(wordLen))) {
    strcpy(p->keyStr,theWord);
    keyChars += wordLen;
    refChars += sizeof(struct key);
  } else Munged(3);

  p->left = p->right = NULL;
  if (prelimFlag) {
    p->count = 0;
    p->first = p->last = NULL;
    return p;
  } else p->count = 1;
```

```
    if (indexType == INDEX) {
      occur = p->first = p->last = malloc(sizeof(struct item));
      if (occur) {
        occur->next = NULL;
        occur->fileNum = inFiles;
        occur->filePos = inLines+1;
        occChars += sizeof(struct item);
      }
      else Munged(3);
    }
    return p;
}

static void NewOccur(struct key *p)
{
  struct item *occur,*q;

  if (omitFile && p->count == NULL) return;
  if (hugeFlag && wordLen <= 4 && p->count == 10) return;
  if (p->count != MAXCNT) p->count++;
  if (p->count > numCount) return;
  if (indexType > INDEX) return;

  q = p->last;
  if (q && q->fileNum == inFiles && q->filePos == inLines+1) return;
  if (occur = malloc(sizeof(struct item))) {
    if (!p->first) p->first = occur;
    p->last = q->next = occur;
    occur->next = NULL;
    occur->fileNum = inFiles;
    occur->filePos = inLines+1;
    occChars += sizeof(struct item);
  } else Munged(3);
}

static void Search(struct key *p)
{
  struct key  *q;
  int      cond;

  if (!p) { root = NewKey(); return; }
  while (p) {
    if (caseSense) cond = StrictCompare(theWord,p->keyStr);
    else if (dictFlag) cond = DictCompare(theWord,p->keyStr);
    else cond = Compare(theWord,p->keyStr);

    q = p;
```

```
      if (cond < 0) { p = p->left; continue; }
      else if (cond > 0) { p = p->right; continue; }
      else { NewOccur(p); return; }
    }
    if (cond > 0) q->right = NewKey();
    else q->left = NewKey();
}

static int StrictCompare(unsigned char *i,unsigned char *j)
{
  while (*i == *j) {
    if (*i == '\0') return 0;
    i++; j++;
  }
  if (reverseFlag) return *i < *j ? 1 : -1;
  else return *i < *j ? -1 : 1;
}

static int Compare(unsigned char *i,unsigned char *j)
{
  while ( (a = tolower(*i)) == (b = tolower(*j)) ) {
    if (*i == '\0') return 0;
    i++; j++;
  }
  if (reverseFlag) return a < b ? 1 : -1;
  else return a < b ? -1 : 1;
}

static int DictCompare(unsigned char *i,unsigned char *j)
{
  Boolean flag = false;

  /*
    This is a highly specialized ordering that indexes use.
    See "Words into Type" and "The Chicago Manual of Style"
    for examples of the proper order of an index.
  */
```

```
  while (true) {
    a = tolower(*i); b = tolower(*j);
    if (a == b) {
      if (!a) return 0;
      i++; j++; continue;
    }
    if (!a) return reverseFlag ? 1 : -1;
    if (!b) return reverseFlag ? -1 : 1;
    if (a == ',' || a == ':' || a == '.' && flag) return reverseFlag ? 1 : -1;
    if (b == ',' || b == ':' || b == '.' && flag) return reverseFlag ? -1 : 1;
    if (isdict(a)) { i++; continue; }
    if (isdict(b)) { j++; continue; }
    break;
  }
  result = (a < b) ? -1 : 1;
  return reverseFlag ? -result : result;
}

static void ReadList(char *argv[])
{
  int c;

  prelimFlag = true;
  OpenFile(argv[fFlagPos]);
  while ( (c = getc(input)) != EOF) {
    inChars++;
    if (c != '\n')
      theWord[wordLen++] = c;
    else {
      theWord[wordLen++] = '\0';
      Search(root); wordLen = 0; SpinCursor(-CRSRSPEED);
      inWords++; inLines++;
    }
  }
  fclose(input);
  prelimFlag = false;
  if (!quietFlag)
    fprintf(stderr,"Chars: %8u  Words: %6u  Lines: %6u  (%uK)\n",
      inChars,inWords,inLines,keyChars+refChars+occChars+1024>>10);
}
```

```c
static void ListOccur(struct item *p)
{
  int i = 0;

  while(p) {
    if (inFiles < 2) {
      if (i) printf(", ");
      printf("%u",p->filePos);
    }
    else printf("%u:%u ",p->fileNum,p->filePos);
    p = p->next; i++;
    if (p && i == 10) {
      printf("\n\t"); i = 0;
    }
  }
  printf("\n");
}

static void DoIndex(struct key *p)
{
  if (p != NULL) {
    DoIndex(p->left);
    if (p->count) {
      outWords += p->count; outLines++; SpinCursor(-CRSRSPEED);
      printf("%s\t",p->keyStr);
      ListOccur(p->first);
    }
    DoIndex(p->right);
  }
}

/* DESCENDING FREQUENCY CODE */
typedef struct {
  struct key  *kp;
  unsigned  order;
} hack;
static hack      *ka;
static unsigned kaCount;

static void DoFreqDesc(struct key *p)
{
  if (p) {
    DoFreqDesc(p->left);
    ka->kp = p;
    ka->order = kaCount++;
    ka++;
    DoFreqDesc(p->right);
  }
}
```

```
static int SpecialCompare(hack *i,hack *j)
{
  unsigned  a,b;

  a = i->kp->count; b = j->kp->count;
  if (a == b && i->order < j->order) return -1;
  else if (a > b) return -1;
  else return 1;
}

static void SortDown(struct key *p)
{
  hack  *k;
  int    bytes,n;

  outLines = n = refChars / sizeof(struct key);
  bytes = n * 8;
  k = ka = malloc(bytes);
  if (!k) {
    fprintf(stderr,"# Cannot get %d bytes needed for key array\n",bytes);
    exit(2);
  }
  if (!quietFlag)
    fprintf(stderr,"# Sorting frequencies with temporary %dK buffer...\n",
        bytes+1024>>10);
  DoFreqDesc(p);
  qsort(ka = k,n,8,SpecialCompare);
  while (n--) {
    if (k->kp->count) printf("%u\t%s\n",k->kp->count,k->kp->keyStr);
    k++; SpinCursor(-CRSRSPEED);
  }
  free(ka);
}
static void DoFreq(struct key *p)
{
  if (p) {
    DoFreq(p->left);
    if (p->count) {
      printf("%u\t%s\n",p->count,p->keyStr);
      outWords += p->count; outLines++; SpinCursor(-CRSRSPEED);
    }
    DoFreq(p->right);
  }
}
```

```
static void DoUnique(struct key *p)
{
  if (p) {
    DoUnique(p->left);
    if (p->count) {
      printf("%s\n",p->keyStr);
      outWords += p->count; outLines++; SpinCursor(-CRSRSPEED);
    }
    DoUnique(p->right);
  }
}

static void OutPutIndex()
{
  char  fileName[256];

  if (!quietFlag)
    fprintf(stderr,"# %22s Chars: %8u  Words: %6u  Lines: %6u  (%uK)\n",
      "Input Totals:",sumChars,sumWords,sumLines,
        keyChars+refChars+occChars+1024>>10);

  fflush(stdout); setvbuf(stdout,fileBuffer,_IOFBF,FBUFSIZ);
  if (indexType == INDEX) {
    if (sepChar == '\f') printf("(Indexed by page number)\n");
    printf("\n");
  }
  switch (indexType) {
    case INDEX: DoIndex(root); break;
    case FREQ:  if (maxFlag) SortDown(root); else DoFreq(root); break;
    case UNIQ:  DoUnique(root); break;
  }
  if (indexType < UNIQ) {
    ioctl(1,FIOFNAME,(long *) fileName);
    faccess(fileName,F_STABINFO,(long *) 20);
  }
  t = TickCount() - t;
  if (!quietFlag) {
    fprintf(stderr,
        "# %22s Chars: %8u   Keys: %6u   Time: %6.1f sec   (%.2f MB/hr)\n",
        "Index Totals:",ftell(stdout),outLines,t/60.0,
        sumChars/t*60.0*3600/1048576);
  }
}
```

```
/* GREEK CODE */
static unsigned char superGreek[256] = {
  0,0,0,0,0,0,0,0,0,0,0,0,0,0,0,0,0,0,0,0,0,0,0,0,0,0,0,0,0,0,0,0, /* 0-31 */
  0,0,114,0,0,0,0,1,0,0,0,1,0,0,0,1, /* 32 to 47 */
  0,0,0,0,0,0,0,0,0,0,0,0, /* 48 to 58 */
  1,0,0,0,0,0, /* 59 to 64 */
  65,66,86,68,69,85,67,71,73,1, /* 65 to 74 */
  74,75,76,77,78,79,72,81,82,83,84,1, /* 75 to 86 */
  88,78,87,70, /* 87 to 90 */
  1,1,1,1,0,0, /* 91 to 96 */
  97,98,118,100,101,117,99,103,105,1, /* 97 to 106 */
  106,107,108,109,111,112,104,113,114,115,116,1, /* 107 to 118 */
  120,110,119,102, /* 119 to 122 */
  1,1,1,1,0, /* 123 to 127 */
  0,0,0,0,0,0,0,0,0,0,0,0,0,0,0,0,0,0,0,0,0,0,0,0,0,0,0,0,0,0,0,0, /*128-159*/
  0,0,0,0,0,0,0,0,0,0,0,0,0,0,0,0,0,0,0,0,0,0,0,0,0,0,0,0,0,0,0,0, /*160-191*/
  1,0,0,0,0,0,1,1,1, /* 192 to 200 */
  0,0,0,0,0,0,0,0,0, /* 201 to 209 */
  1,1,1,1,1,0,1,1,   /* 210 to 217 */
  0,0,0,0,0,0,0,0,0,0,0,0,0,0,0,0,0,0,0,0,0, /* 218 to 238 */
  1
};

static unsigned char superGreekFold[256] = {
  0,0,0,0,0,0,0,0,0,0,0,0,0,0,0,0,0,0,0,0,0,0,0,0,0,0,0,0,0,0,0,0, /* 0-31 */
  0,0,114,0,0,0,0,1,0,0,0,1,0,0,0,1, /* 32 to 47 */
  0,0,0,0,0,0,0,0,0,0,0,0, /* 48 to 58 */
  1,0,0,0,0,0, /* 59 to 64 */
  65,66,86,68,69,85,67,71,73,1, /* 65 to 74 */
  74,75,76,77,78,79,72,81,82,83,84,1, /* 75 to 86 */
  88,78,87,70, /* 87 to 90 */
  1,1,1,1,0,0, /* 91 to 96 */
  65,66,86,68,69,85,67,71,73,1, /* 97 to 106 */
  74,75,76,77,78,79,72,81,82,83,84,1, /* 107 to 118 */
  88,78,87,70, /* 119 to 122 */
  1,1,1,1,0, /* 123 to 127 */
  0,0,0,0,0,0,0,0,0,0,0,0,0,0,0,0,0,0,0,0,0,0,0,0,0,0,0,0,0,0,0,0, /*128-159*/
  0,0,0,0,0,0,0,0,0,0,0,0,0,0,0,0,0,0,0,0,0,0,0,0,0,0,0,0,0,0,0,0, /*160-191*/
  1,0,0,0,0,0,1,1,1, /* 192 to 200 */
  0,0,0,0,0,0,0,0,0, /* 201 to 209 */
  1,1,1,1,1,0,1,1,   /* 210 to 217 */
  0,0,0,0,0,0,0,0,0,0,0,0,0,0,0,0,0,0,0,0,0, /* 218 to 238 */
  1
};
```

```c
static int GreekStrictCompare(unsigned char *i,unsigned char *j)
{
  while (true) {
    while ((a = superGreek[*i++]) == 1) ;
    while ((b = superGreek[*j++]) == 1) ;
    if (a == b) {
      if (a == '\0') return 0;
      continue;
    } else break;
  }
  if (reverseFlag) return a < b ? 1 : -1;
  else return a < b ? -1 : 1;
}

static int GreekCompare(unsigned char *i,unsigned char *j)
{
  while (true) {
    while ((a = superGreekFold[*i++]) == 1) ;
    while ((b = superGreekFold[*j++]) == 1) ;
    if (a == b) {
      if (a == '\0') return 0;
      continue;
    } else break;
  }
  if (reverseFlag) return a < b ? 1 : -1;
  else return a < b ? -1 : 1;
}

static void GreekSearch(struct key *p)
{
  struct key   *q;
  int          cond;

  if (!p) { root = NewKey(); return; }
  while (p) {
    if (caseSense) cond = GreekStrictCompare(theWord,p->keyStr);
    else cond = GreekCompare(theWord,p->keyStr);
    q = p;
    if (cond < 0) { p = p->left; continue; }
    else if (cond > 0) { p = p->right; continue; }
    else { NewOccur(p); return; }
  }
  if (cond > 0) q->right = NewKey();
  else q->left = NewKey();
}
```

```
static void GetGreek()
{
  int    c,d;

  while ((c = getc(input)) != EOF) {
    d = c; inChars++; wordLen = theWord[0] = 0;
    if (superGreek[c]) {
      do {
        theWord[wordLen++] = c; inChars++;
      } while (superGreek[c = getc(input)]);
    } else {
      if (c == '\n') { inLines++; SpinCursor(CRSRSPEED); }
      continue;
    }
    inWords++; theWord[wordLen++] = '\0';
    if (wordLen > lenCount) GreekSearch(root);
    if (c == '\n') { inLines++; SpinCursor(CRSRSPEED); }
  }
  if (inChars > 0 && d != '\n') inLines++;
}
```

Index.r—Rez Source Code for a **Commando** Interface

```
/* Index.r - The Commando companion for Index, a tool by Dan Allen. */
/* Begun April 11, 1987 */

#include "cmdo.r";          /* rects: top, left, bottom, right */

resource 'cmdo' (128, "Index") {
{ 300,
  "Index - General purpose indexing and cross-referencing tool.\n"
  "Supports indexing Asm, C, Pascal, Rez, and Greek languages.\n"
  "Also indexes & analyzes word frequencies of any text files.",
  {

/* FILE TYPES */
NotDependent { }, RadioButtons {
  {
    {30, 145, 45, 205}, "Auto", "", Set,
      "Automatically parses files according to their filename suffix,"
      " i.e., files ending in .c are treated as if the -c option was "
      "set, files ending in .a turn on the -a option, etc.  Files w/o "
      "a suffix are text files.",
    {50, 145, 65, 205}, "Asm", "-a", NotSet,
      "Treat files as MPW Assembly files.  Comments started by ; and "
      "* are skipped until EOL; quoted strings are skipped; case "
      "insensitive; words starts: [A-Za-z_@], word continuation: "
      "[A-Za-z0-9_@$#%].",
```

```
    {70, 145, 85, 205}, "C", "-c", NotSet,
      "Treat files as MPW C files.  Comments spanned by /* and */ "
      "are skipped; quoted strings are skipped; case sensitive; "
      "words starts: [A-Za-z_], word continuation: [A-Za-z0-9_].",
    {90, 145, 105, 205}, "Pascal", "-p", NotSet,
      "Treat files as MPW Pascal files.  Comments spanned by { and } "
      "or by (* and *) are skipped; quoted strings are skipped; "
      "case insensitive; words starts: [A-Za-z_], word continuation:"
      "[A-Za-z0-9_].",
    {110, 145, 125, 205}, "Rez", "-z", NotSet,
      "Treat files as MPW Rez files.  Comments spanned by /* and */ "
      "are skipped; quoted strings are skipped; case insensitive; "
      "words starts: [A-Za-z_], word continuation: [A-Za-z0-9_].",

    {30, 210, 45, 285}, "Text", "-t", NotSet,
      "Scans textfiles for words and numbers.  Contents of "
      "strings are included; case insensitive; words are either a)"
      " start: [A-Za-z], continuation: [A-Za-z0-9] or b) start [0-9]"
      ", continuation [0-9.].",
    {50, 210, 65, 285}, "Words", "-w", NotSet,
      "Scans textfiles for just words: no numbers or punctuation "
      "are allowed.  Contents of strings are included; case "
      "insensitive; words: [A-Za-z].  Results in fewer keys, more "
      "occurrences.",
    {70, 210, 85, 285}, "Blanks", "-b", NotSet,
      "Anything delimited by white space is a word.  Contents of "
      "strings are included; case insensitive; words are delimited "
      "by tabs, spaces, and returns.  "
      "Results in more keys, fewer occurrences.",
    {90, 210, 105, 285}, "Greek", "-g", NotSet,
      "Files of Greek words in the SuperGreek font are indexed in a "
      "Greek lexicon ordering, i.e., alpha, beta, gamma,… "
      "(See Liddel & Scott's Greek-English Lexicon)  Case-insensitive; "
      "contents of strings & breathing marks included.",
    {110, 210, 125, 285}, "MS Word", "-x", NotSet,
      "This option implies the -w option and is to be used with "
      "files preprocessed by the WordText tool for indexing MS "
      "Word files.  It causes the index to be done on a page "
      "(using the formfeed character) rather than line basis.",
  }
},
NotDependent { }, TextBox { gray, {20, 135, 135, 290}, "File Type" },
```

```
/* INDEX TYPES */
NotDependent { }, RadioButtons {
  {
    {30, 305, 45, 375}, "Std", "", Set,
      "A standard alphabetical index with 10 refs/line is generated."
      "\nMultiple lines are used when needed for an entry."
      "\nOUTPUT FORMAT: word TAB file:line file:line... CR",
    {50, 305, 65, 375}, "Max", "-m", NotSet,
      "A word frequency list sorted numerically in descending "
      "order from max to min.\nOUTPUT FORMAT: wordFreq TAB word CR",
    {70, 305, 85, 375}, "Freq", "-f", NotSet,
      "A word frequency list sorted alphabetically."
      "\nOUTPUT FORMAT: wordFreq TAB word CR",
    {90, 305, 105, 375}, "Unique", "-u", NotSet,
      "A list of unique words sorted alphabetically."
      "\nOUTPUT FORMAT: word CR",
  }
},
NotDependent { }, TextBox { gray, {20, 295, 111, 379}, "Index" },

/* WORD DEFINITION */
NotDependent { }, RadioButtons {
  {
    {145, 302, 160, 340}, "Std", "", Set,
      "All words are indexed.",
    {145, 346, 160, 396}, "Omit", "-o", NotSet,
      "Omit all words listed in the specified file. Words are "
      "listed in the file one word per line, separated by returns.",
    {145, 400, 160, 470}, "Include", "-i", NotSet,
      "Include in the generated index only those words listed in a "
      "specified include file.  Each line of this file contains one "
      "word to be included, thus returns separate entries.",
  }
},
Or{ { (2<<12) + 5, (3<<12) + 5} }, Files {
  InputFile,
  RequiredFile {
    {166, 315, 186, 445}, /* top, left, bottom, right */
    "Include/Omit File",
    "",
    "Specifies the file containing the include or omit file.  "
    "Speed is SLOWEST if this file is already in sorted order, "
    "as index creates a binary tree.  For FASTEST results use "
    "Sort -t on this file first to create an inorder list.",
  },
  Additional {"", "", "", "", {}}
},
NotDependent { }, TextBox { gray, {137, 295, 192, 471}, "Words" },
```

```
/* OPTIONS */
NotDependent { }, CheckOption {
  NotSet, {30, 390, 45, 465}, "Dict", "-d",
  "Specifies dictionary ordering for the sorted index.  Dictionary "
  "ordering is NOT case sensitive and ignores most punctuation "
  "characters.  The resultant ordering is like that found in a "
  "dictionary or index.",
},
NotDependent { }, CheckOption {
  NotSet, {50, 390, 65, 465}, "Case On", "-s",
  "Specifies a case sensitive ordering.  This is useful in "
  "distinguishing upper and lower case words and abbreviations.  "
  "The default is to not be case sensitive.",
},
NotDependent { }, CheckOption {
  NotSet, {70, 390, 85, 465}, "Reverse", "-r",
  "Sort in reverse or descending (z-a, Z to A, 9 to 0) order. "
  "The default is ascending (0-9, A to Z, a-z) order.",
},
NotDependent { }, CheckOption {
  NotSet, {90, 390, 105, 465}, "Huge", "-h",
  "Useful for huge text files, this option will only index "
  "the first ten entries of words three characters or shorter, but "
  "WILL index all occurrences of words greater than 3 characters "
  "in length; saves memory.",
},
NotDependent { }, CheckOption {
  NotSet, {110, 390, 125, 465}, "Quiet", "-q",
  "The default is to list to stderr various statistical measures "
  "when parsing the files. Using this option restricts output to "
  "stderr to just error messages.",
},
NotDependent { }, TextBox { gray, {20, 385, 135, 470}, "Options" },
```

```
/* WORD LENGTH  */
NotDependent { }, RegularEntry {
  "Word Length",
  {170,145,185,235},     /* title */
  {170,240,185,270},     /* TEBox */
  "", ignoreCase, "-l",
  "By default all words are indexed.  By defining a length you "
  "can specify the minumum length of a word in order to be indexed. "
  "Use of this option allows ignoring small noise "
  "words and also reduces the memory used."
},
NotDependent { }, RegularEntry {
  "Word Count",
  {144,145,160,235},     /* title */
  {144,240,160,270},     /* TEBox */
  "", ignoreCase, "-n",
  "By default all occurrences of a word are indexed.  By stating a "
  "count one can specify the maximum number of word occurrences that "
  "will be listed. Use of this option will also reduce memory requirements."
},

/* FILES AND STANDARD IO */
NotDependent { }, MultiFiles {
  "Files…",
  "A list of files to index.\n"
  "LIMITS: 1023 files, 4M lines/file, 65535 occurences/word,"
  " 255 chars/word",
  {22, 15, 42, 127}, /* top, left, bottom, right */
  "File(s) to index:",
  "",
  MultiInputFiles { { text }, "", "","", }
},
NotDependent { }, Redirection {
  StandardInput, {50, 15}
},
NotDependent { }, Redirection {
  StandardOutput, {90, 15}
},
NotDependent { }, Redirection {
  DiagnosticOutput, {130, 15}
},
NotDependent { }, VersionDialog {
  VersionString { "1.0 B3" },
  "Index 1.0 B3 - Begun March 23, 1987 by Dan Allen.\n"
  "Built on " $$Date " @ " $$Time ".\nWritten using "
  "MPW C 3.0 for the book "On Macintosh Programming".",
  noDialog
},
} } };
```

Conclusion

This chapter provided numerous examples of using C on the Macintosh. The source code for a series of text processing tools has illustrated various techniques for using C and its standard libraries. These tools included:

- `DeCom`, a tool to remove C comments using a state machine
- `FastCat`, a faster version of MPW's built-in `Catenate` command
- `Substitute`, a literal text replacement tool designed for streams
- `Reduce`, a tool for replacing runs of specified characters with a single string
- `Sign`, a tool that implements the front pass of an anagram pipeline
- `Squash`, the last pass of an anagram pipeline
- `WordText`, which extracts ASCII text and page breaks from files created with MS Word 4.0
- `TextTool`, a Swiss Army knife for manipulating text
- `Sort`, a memory-based sorting tool with some specialized options
- `Index`, an indexing tool for sources and text files

Recommended Reading

The C Programming Language (also called The White Book or K&R), by Kernighan and Ritchie, is the classic work about the C language and is absolutely essential reading for beginners or experts. The first edition described the "classic" version of C, and the second edition describes the ANSI standard version of C. The book contains both tutorial and reference material. Its 275 pages are packed with information.

When you are learning the language—and when is it ever fully learned?—Bolsky's *The C Programmer's Handbook* is a handy book, as is Barkakati's *The Waite Group's Essential Guide to ANSI C*. The Microsoft Quick Reference series has an ANSI C quick reference guide called *Standard C* that was written by the knowledgeable pair of Plauger and Brodie, but the presentation is somewhat confusing.

The X3J11 committee's document *American National Standard for Information Systems—Programming Language C* is the definitive document on C. The *de facto* reference manual for language implementors over the past few years has been Harbison and Steele's *A C Reference Manual,* and with its second edition covering ANSI C it is still highly recommended for those implementing the C language and libraries.

## CHAPTER 9

THE PASCAL LANGUAGE

Pascal is an important language in the Macintosh world. Almost all documentation from Apple about the Macintosh is written using Pascal examples. Whether you prefer C or Pascal, you will need a reading knowledge of Pascal.

This chapter will examine the history of Pascal at Apple, which will help explain how Pascal came to be so important in the Macintosh world. Following this, the chapter will look at the Object Pascal language extensions and the MacApp framework written in Object Pascal. Next, the source code for two Pascal applications will be presented. The first, `StyleTest`, is a text editor that uses the new version of TextEdit. `StyleTest` supports multiple fonts, sizes, styles, printing, and even colored text. The second application, `GraphSort`, graphically demonstrates several different sorting algorithms.

History of Pascal

Pascal was originally designed by Niklaus Wirth in 1970 as a language for teaching programming to students at the university level. Since then, it has gained great popularity as a mainstream programming language. In the mid- to late 1970s, UCSD Pascal provided an implementation of Pascal based on an intermediate P-code that allowed it to be widely ported to various machines. Pascal further grew in popularity in 1983 with Borland's Turbo Pascal, first available for CP/M machines, then for MS-DOS, and finally for the Macintosh in 1986.

One problem with Pascal has been the non-uniformity across implementations, because of major limitations in the language. Many implementors extended the language, each in their own direction. As Pascal originally had a very small set of standard library routines, most Pascals have implemented and extended library routines in different ways. In 1983, an ANSI X3.97-1983/IEEE 770 standard for Pascal was formally completed, and Apple's MPW Pascal complies quite well with the standard, although it has many extensions.

As mentioned, Pascal was originally designed as a tool for students learning to program. It is excellent for such purposes, but as more and more people learned Pascal, they began to use it for system and general-purpose programming. These tasks showed up Pascal's weaknesses, with various individuals attacking the problems of Pascal. Examples include the infamous, somewhat tongue-in-cheek article by Ed Pest in the July

1983 issue of *Datamation* entitled "Real Programmers Don't Use Pascal," and the decidedly more serious Bell Labs internal memo authored by Brian Kernighan in 1981 entitled *Why Pascal Is Not My Favorite Programming Language*. His memo criticized Pascal for the following reasons:

- The size of an array is part of its type, which makes string handling difficult
- There are no static variables and no data initialization
- Related program components must be kept separate
- There is no separate compilation
- There are some miscellaneous problems of type and scope
- There is no escape from the type mechanism
- There is no guaranteed order of evaluation of logical operators
- There are no statements for exiting or continuing loops
- There are no statements for exiting procedures or the entire program
- There is no default clause for the case statement
- The run-time environment and I/O facilities are poor
- Use of the semicolon is irregular
- There are no bit operators
- There is no facility for writing non-printing characters in a string
- There is no macro processor
- Expressions are not allowed to define a constant

Apple's Pascals

It was about the same time that Kernighan wrote his memo that Apple was choosing Pascal as a major language for its work on Lisa and Macintosh. Many of the engineers knew Pascal well and had extended the language to suit their needs and to solve many of the problems listed above. They evolved UCSD Pascal into Lisa Pascal, the ancestor of MPW Pascal. Lisa Pascal was originally done by Silicon Valley Software (SVS) for Apple in 1981, although Apple has maintained it for years now. It supported Units, a concept that originated with UCSD Pascal. Units provided a method of separate compilation that provides an `Interface` as well as an `Implementation` section for each module of code, thus providing similar facilities to Wirth's later language Modula-2.

In addition to Units, with their facility for separate compilation, Lisa (and hence MPW) Pascal were extended to support conditional compilation and compile-time variables, bit operators, short-circuit Boolean operators, `Leave` and `Cycle` statements (similar to `break` and `continue` in C), type coercion, and many other concepts. Thus, Apple's Pascal overcomes most of Kernighan's smaller objections to Pascal, but it still does not have conformant arrays, static variables, a full macro processor, or data initialization. For some of these reasons, C is currently becoming increasingly used at Apple.

Apple's Object-oriented Pascals

Another extension to Pascal took place when some early explorations into object-oriented programming created a language called Clascal. Clascal was begun in 1983 when Larry Tesler (formerly of Xerox PARC and since 1980 with Apple Computer) asked Chris Franklin to implement classes. Clascal was later enhanced by Al Hoffman and then by Ira Ruben. Clascal was designed to implement the Lisa Toolkit, the predecessor to MacApp.

Early in 1985, Larry Tesler and Niklaus Wirth created Object Pascal as a superset of Pascal and a successor to Clascal. Object Pascal supported the concepts of objects, classes, and inheritance, but in a simpler and clearer way than Clascal did. Ken Doyle finished things up by writing the Object Pascal extensions to the MPW Pascal compiler. MPW Pascal is thus a full Object Pascal compiler. (More on object-oriented programming can be found later in this chapter.)

Pascal on Macintosh Today

After the Pascal compiler was moved from Lisa to MPW, new features continued to be added. New in 1987 for MPW 2.0 was the additional facility for the Pascal compiler to generate 68020 and 68881 code. New for MPW 3.0 Pascal was an automatic load/dump mechanism that greatly speeds up compile times.

Two other Pascals for the Macintosh are noteworthy: Borland's Turbo Pascal and Think's Lightspeed Pascal. Each is about 90-percent compatible with MPW Pascal, but that 10-percent difference is big enough that large software projects, such as HyperCard, cannot be built with them. Nevertheless, Turbo and Lightspeed are good for prototyping and quick builds. I usually start Pascal projects in Turbo Pascal because of its quick turn-around time and then move the finished code to MPW Pascal for final builds. The MPW code size is smaller, but this is mainly because the linker removes dead code. The Turbo Pascal code generator is remarkably good, especially considering the fact that the entire Pascal compiler is only a single 24 KB code segment! Turbo Pascal has not been updated for several years, which is a shame. It is a remarkable product.

Think's Pascal has a nice integrated debugging environment, much like its predecessor Macintosh Pascal. Version 2 of Think's Pascal offers 68020 and 68881 code generation and many other new features. For someone learning Pascal, Think's Pascal is hard to beat.

Object Pascal

The MPW Pascal compiler supports object-oriented programming. It actually implements Object Pascal, a language that is a superset of Pascal. To a first approximation, the following equation derived by Peter Wegner defines object-oriented languages:

object-oriented = objects + classes + inheritance

Objects are the atomic entities of object-oriented programming and can be viewed as consisting of a data structure and its related methods (procedures), which can manipulate objects. Objects are specific instances of a class. Classes are arranged hierarchically, with descendant objects referred to as *subclasses* and ancestor objects referred to as *superclasses*. Objects of a subclass inherit properties from their ancestor objects. Objects can send, receive, and respond to messages sent by other objects.

Simula 67 was the first object-oriented language. Since then, several other object-oriented languages have been developed: SmallTalk (circa 1972), C++ (1983), and Object Pascal (1985). Ada, C, and Modula-2—contrary to the many popular articles that mention the buzzword "object-oriented programming"—are *not* object-oriented.

It should be noted that data abstraction is an orthogonal language attribute from object-orientedness. An abstract data type as supported in Ada or C++ is a data structure and a set of associated operations that are the only way to access the private data structure. An object-oriented language like Object Pascal, however, can access or modify any field of known objects—in other words, there are no private members of objects. C++ is interesting because it allows for fully private members of an object—thus supporting data abstraction—as well as allowing for public members, thus supporting the object-oriented style of programming. Ada and Modula-2 are not object-oriented, as they do not support objects or inheritance. Too many people are confusing data-abstraction with object-orientedness.

MacApp

MacApp, short for generic "Macintosh application," is a toolkit sold as an add-on part of MPW. It is essentially a huge library of routines, consisting of some 29,000+ lines of Object Pascal and 1,600+ lines of Object Assembly. MacApp is a separately sold product built upon Object Pascal, so use of MacApp requires MPW and MPW Pascal.

MacApp's seeds came out of the Lisa Toolkit, done by Larry Tesler, Larry Rosenstein, and Pete Young. The Lisa Toolkit was written using Clascal, Apple's first object-oriented Pascal. MacApp was a completely new system designed by Larry Rosenstein, Larry Tesler, Scott Wallace, and Ken Doyle and implemented by Larry Rosenstein and Scott Wallace. Early development versions ran in the Lisa Workshop, but versions 1, 2, and all subsequent releases are for MPW.

MacApp fully implements the standard Macintosh User Interface in a generic Macintosh application on which you build your own application. This technique greatly reduces the amount of code you need to write without reducing the ensuing quality. For example, you would need to write only routines to draw items in windows, write files to the disk, and things of that sort. The MacApp libraries support such standard features of the Macintosh interface as desk accessories, menus, multiple documents, error-handling, the clipboard, printing, and scrolling, moving, resizing, and zooming windows.

With the help of MacApp, significant Macintosh applications can be built in a few weeks rather than in several months. Even more important, they comply with the recommended guidelines for developing applications and therefore are more robust to changes in system software. Users also benefit from applications that are consistent with the Mac interface and hence are easier to use.

MacApp includes the full source code to the MacApp libraries, as well as many sample programs illustrating object-oriented Macintosh programming. Also included is a "Cookbook" of tips and routines that you may find useful when you are creating Macintosh applications.

StyleTest — Pascal Application

This application is a simple text editor that uses the new Styled TextEdit to support multiple fonts, sizes, styles, and colored text. This application also supports printing. It is a good shell from which to begin a programming project because it has the basic main event loop and event-handling procedures in place.

Here is the Makefile:

```
POptions    = -mbg ch8 -r
PLibs =      "{PLibraries}PasLib.o" ∂
             "{PLibraries}SaneLib.o" ∂
             "{Libraries}Interface.o" ∂
             "{Libraries}Runtime.o"

StyleTest    ff  StyleTest.r
    Rez -a -o StyleTest StyleTest.r -c STYT
StyleTest    ff  StyleTest.p.o {PLibs}
    Link -w -o StyleTest -sg Main StyleTest.p.o {PLibs}
StyleTest    ff  {Worksheet}
    Setfile -a B -t APPL -c STYT -d . -m . StyleTest
    StyleTest
```

and here is the code:

```
{$D+} {$R-}

PROGRAM StyleTest;

USES
  Memtypes,Quickdraw,OSIntf,ToolIntf,PackIntf,PrintTraps;

VAR
  quit:       Boolean;
  shiftDown:  Boolean;
  theChar:    Char;
  templ:      LongInt;

  mousePt:    Point;
  dragRect:   Rect;
  txRect:     Rect;
  myEvent:    EventRecord;
  wRecord:    WindowRecord;
  myWindow:   WindowPtr;
  theWindow:  WindowPtr;

  iBeamHdl:   CursHandle;
  menuDA:     MenuHandle;
  menuFile:   MenuHandle;
  menuEdit:   MenuHandle;
  menuFont:   MenuHandle;
  menuSize:   MenuHandle;
  menuStyle:  MenuHandle;
  menuColor:  MenuHandle;
  textH:      TEHandle;
  printH:     THPrint;
  fontArray:  ARRAY[1..64] OF Integer;
  sizeArray:  ARRAY[1..32] OF Integer;

PROCEDURE AboutDialog;                        FORWARD;
PROCEDURE CheckMenus;                         FORWARD;
PROCEDURE DoActivate;                         FORWARD;
PROCEDURE DoKey;                              FORWARD;
PROCEDURE DoMenu(result: LongInt);            FORWARD;
PROCEDURE DoUpdate;                           FORWARD;
PROCEDURE InitWorld;                          FORWARD;
FUNCTION  LongToHex(long: LongInt) : Str255;  FORWARD;
PROCEDURE PrintDoc;                           FORWARD;
PROCEDURE SetupMenus;                         FORWARD;
PROCEDURE UpdateActive;                       FORWARD;
PROCEDURE UpdateRects;                        FORWARD;
```

```
PROCEDURE AboutDialog;
VAR
  aRect:    Rect;
  oldPort:  GrafPtr;
  aWindow:  WindowPtr;
BEGIN
  GetPort(oldPort);
  WITH aRect DO
    BEGIN
      left := (screenbits.bounds.right - screenbits.bounds.left) DIV 2 - 100;
      right := left + 200;
      top := (screenbits.bounds.bottom - screenbits.bounds.top) DIV 2 - 50;
      bottom := top + 100;
    END;
  aWindow := NewWindow(NIL,aRect,'',TRUE,dBoxProc,Pointer(-1),TRUE,0);
  SetPort(aWindow);
  TextFont(systemFont);
  MoveTo(10,40); DrawString('Welcome To The About Box');
  MoveTo(24,70); DrawString(Concat('TEHandle is ',LongToHex(ORD(textH))));
  REPEAT SystemTask UNTIL Button;
  DisposeWindow(aWindow);
  SetPort(oldPort);
  FlushEvents(mUpMask+mDownMask,0);
END;


PROCEDURE CheckMenus;
VAR
  flag:       Boolean;
  i:          Integer;
  lineHeight: Integer;
  fontAscent: Integer;
  n:          LongInt;
  curStyle:   TextStyle;
  name:       Str255;
  item:       StyleItem;
BEGIN
  TEGetStyle(textH^^.selStart,curStyle,lineHeight,fontAscent,textH);

  { clear check marks from the text menus }
  FOR i := 1 TO CountMItems(menuFont) DO CheckItem(menuFont,i,FALSE);
  FOR i := 1 TO CountMItems(menuSize) DO CheckItem(menuSize,i,FALSE);
  FOR i := 1 TO CountMItems(menuStyle) DO CheckItem(menuStyle,i,FALSE);
  FOR i := 1 TO CountMItems(menuColor) DO CheckItem(menuColor,i,FALSE);

  { make the current font size show up outlined in the menu }
  FOR i := 1 TO CountMItems(menuSize) DO
    IF RealFont(curStyle.tsFont,sizeArray[i])
    THEN SetItemStyle(menuSize,i,[outline])
    ELSE SetItemStyle(menuSize,i,[]);
```

```
{ checkmark which font is being used }
i := 1; WHILE fontArray[i] <> curStyle.tsFont DO i := i+1;
CheckItem(menuFont,i,TRUE);

{ checkmark the size of the current selection }
i := 1; WHILE sizeArray[i] <> curStyle.tsSize DO i := i+1;
CheckItem(menuSize,i,TRUE);

{ checkmark the style attributes of the selection }
IF curStyle.tsFace = [] THEN CheckItem(menuStyle,1,TRUE);
FOR item := bold TO extend DO
  BEGIN
    IF item IN curStyle.tsFace THEN flag := TRUE
    ELSE flag := FALSE;
    CheckItem(menuStyle,ORD(item)+2,flag);
  END;
  CheckItem(menuStyle,9,BitTst(@curStyle.tsFace,0));
END;


PROCEDURE DoActivate;
BEGIN
  IF WindowPtr(myEvent.message) = myWindow THEN
    BEGIN
      IF BAND(myEvent.modifiers,activeFlag) <> 0 THEN
        BEGIN
          TEActivate(textH);
          DisableItem(menuEdit,1);
        END
      ELSE
        BEGIN
          TEDeactivate(textH);
          EnableItem(menuEdit,1);
        END;
    END;
END;
```

```
PROCEDURE DoKey;
BEGIN
  IF myWindow = FrontWindow THEN
    BEGIN
      theChar := CHR(BAND(myEvent.message,charCodeMask));
      IF (BAND(myEvent.modifiers,cmdKey) = 0) THEN
        TEKey(theChar,textH)
      ELSE
        IF BAND(myEvent.modifiers,shiftKey) = 0 THEN
          DoMenu(MenuKey(theChar))
        ELSE
          BEGIN
            CASE theChar OF { cmd shift keys for styles }
              CHR(30):  TESetSelect(0,0,textH);
              CHR(31):  TESetSelect(32767,32767,textH);
              'b':      DoMenu($60002);
              'i':      DoMenu($60003);
              'u':      DoMenu($60004);
              'o':      DoMenu($60005);
              's':      DoMenu($60006);
              'c':      DoMenu($60007);
              'e':      DoMenu($60008);
              'h':      DoMenu($60009);
              OTHERWISE DoMenu($60001);
            END;
          END;
    END;
END;

PROCEDURE DoMenu(result: LongInt);
CONST
  doToggle = 32; { requires System 6.0 }
VAR
  bool:     Boolean;
  theItem:  Integer;
  theMenu:  Integer;
  temp:     Integer;
  name:     Str255;
  theStyle: TextStyle;
  ht,ascnt: Integer;
  hack:     ^Integer;
BEGIN
  theItem := LoWord(result);
  theMenu := HiWord(result);
  InitCursor;
```

```pascal
CASE theMenu OF
  1: { Apple menu }
    IF (theItem = 1) THEN
      AboutDialog
    ELSE
      BEGIN
        GetItem(menuDA, theItem, name);
        temp := OpenDeskAcc(name);
        SetPort(myWindow);
      END;
  2: { File menu }
    CASE theItem OF
      1:  BEGIN { a quick way to insert a bunch of text to play with }
            name := 'This is a test of the emergency broadcasting system. ';
            TEInsert(Pointer(ORD(@name)+1),Length(name),textH);
            TESelView(textH);
          END;
      2:  DebugStr(LongToHex(ORD(textH))); { go into MacsBug for debugging }
      4:  bool := PrStlDialog(printH);
      5:  IF PrJobDialog(printH) THEN PrintDoc;
      7:  quit := TRUE;
    END;
  3: { Edit menu }
    BEGIN
      IF NOT SystemEdit(theItem - 1) THEN
        CASE theItem OF
          3:  BEGIN { Cut }
                templ := ZeroScrap;
                TECut(textH);
              END;
          4:  BEGIN { Copy }
                templ := ZeroScrap;
                TECopy(textH);
              END;
          5:  TEStylPaste(textH); { Paste }
          6:  TEDelete(textH); { Clear }
          8:  TESetSelect(0,32767,textH); { Select All }
        END;
    END;
  4: { Font menu }
    BEGIN
      GetItem(menuFont,theItem,name);
      GetFNum(name,temp);
      theStyle.tsFont := temp;
      TESetStyle(doFont,theStyle,TRUE,textH);
    END;
```

```
5: { Size menu }
  BEGIN
    GetItem(menuSize,theItem,name);
    StringToNum(name,templ);
    theStyle.tsSize := templ;
    TESetStyle(doSize,theStyle,TRUE,textH);
  END;
6: { Style menu }
  BEGIN
    HiliteMenu(6);
    IF theItem = 1 THEN
      BEGIN
        theStyle.tsFace := [];
        TESetStyle(doFace,theStyle,TRUE,textH);
      END
    ELSE
      BEGIN
        theStyle.tsFace := [];
        BitSet(@theStyle.tsFace,9 - theItem);
        TESetStyle(doFace+doToggle,theStyle,TRUE,textH);
      END;
  END;
7: { Color menu }
  BEGIN
    CASE theItem OF
      1:  BEGIN
            theStyle.tsColor.red := 0;
            theStyle.tsColor.green := 0;
            theStyle.tsColor.blue := 0;
          END;
      2:  BEGIN
            theStyle.tsColor.red := $FFFF;
            theStyle.tsColor.green := 0;
            theStyle.tsColor.blue := 0;
          END;
      3:  BEGIN
            theStyle.tsColor.red := 0;
            theStyle.tsColor.green := $FFFF;
            theStyle.tsColor.blue := 0;
          END;
      4:  BEGIN
            theStyle.tsColor.red := 0;
            theStyle.tsColor.green := 0;
            theStyle.tsColor.blue := $FFFF;
          END;
      5:  BEGIN
            theStyle.tsColor.red := $FFFF;
            theStyle.tsColor.green := $FFFF;
            theStyle.tsColor.blue := 0;
          END;
```

```
        6:   BEGIN
               theStyle.tsColor.red := 0;
               theStyle.tsColor.green := $FFFF;
               theStyle.tsColor.blue := $FFFF;
             END;
        7:   BEGIN
               theStyle.tsColor.red := $FFFF;
               theStyle.tsColor.green := 0;
               theStyle.tsColor.blue := $FFFF;
             END;
      END;
      TESetStyle(doColor,theStyle,TRUE,textH);
    END;
  END;
  HiliteMenu(0);
END;


PROCEDURE DoMouse;
VAR
  thePart:  Integer;
BEGIN
  thePart := FindWindow(myEvent.where,theWindow);
  CASE thePart OF
    inMenuBar:
      BEGIN
        CheckMenus;
        DoMenu(MenuSelect(myEvent.where));
      END;
    inSysWindow:
      SystemClick(myEvent,theWindow);
    inContent:
      BEGIN
        IF theWindow <> FrontWindow THEN
          SelectWindow(theWindow)
        ELSE
          IF theWindow = myWindow THEN
            BEGIN
              GlobalToLocal(myEvent.where);
              shiftDown := BAND(myEvent.modifiers,shiftKey) <> 0;
              TEClick(myEvent.where,shiftDown,textH);
            END;
      END;
    inDrag:
      DragWindow(theWindow,myEvent.where,dragRect);
```

```
     inGrow:
       BEGIN
         templ := GrowWindow(theWindow,myEvent.where,screenBits.bounds);
         InvalRect(theWindow^.portRect);
         SizeWindow(theWindow,LoWord(templ),HiWord(templ),FALSE);
         UpdateActive;
       END;
     inGoAway:
       IF TrackGoAway(theWindow,myEvent.where) THEN quit := TRUE;
     inZoomIn,inZoomOut:
       IF TrackBox(theWindow, myEvent.where, thePart) THEN
         BEGIN
           ZoomWindow(theWindow, thePart, FALSE);
           UpdateActive;
         END;
   END;
END;


PROCEDURE DoPeriodic; { give time to DAs, set cursor, flash idle cursor }
BEGIN
  SystemTask;
  IF (myWindow = FrontWindow) THEN
    BEGIN
      GetMouse(mousePt);
      IF PtInRect(mousePt, txRect)
      THEN SetCursor(iBeamHdl^^)
      ELSE SetCursor(arrow);
      TEIdle(textH);
    END;
END;


PROCEDURE DoUpdate;
BEGIN
  theWindow := WindowPtr(myEvent.message);
  IF theWindow = myWindow THEN
    BEGIN
      SetPort(theWindow);
      BeginUpdate(theWindow);
      EraseRect(theWindow^.portRect);
      TEUpdate(theWindow^.portRect,textH); { actually draws the text }
      DrawGrowIcon(theWindow);
      EndUpdate(theWindow);
    END;
END;
```

```
PROCEDURE InitWorld;
BEGIN
  MaxApplZone;
  FlushEvents(everyEvent,0);
  InitGraf(@thePort);
  InitFonts;
  InitWindows;
  InitMenus;
  TEInit;
  InitDialogs(NIL);
  InitCursor;
  PrOpen;
  printH := THPrint(NewHandle(SizeOf(TPrint)));
  IF printH = NIL THEN DebugStr('Not enough memory for print record.');
  PrintDefault(printH);

  SetupMenus;
  SetRect(dragRect,-32767,-32767,32767,32767);
  WITH screenBits.bounds DO SetRect(txRect,4,24,right-4,bottom-4);
  InsetRect(txRect,5,20);
  myWindow := NewWindow(NIL,txRect,'StyleTest',TRUE,zoomDocProc,
                        Pointer(-1),TRUE,0);
  SetPort(myWindow);

  UpdateRects; TextFont(times); TextSize(18);
  textH := TEStylNew(txRect,txRect);
  TEAutoView(TRUE,textH);
  iBeamHdl := GetCursor(iBeamCursor);

  quit := FALSE;
END;

FUNCTION IntToHex(word: Integer) : Str255;
VAR
  i,d:      Integer;
  hexStr:   Str255;
BEGIN
  hexStr := '0000';
  FOR i := 1 TO 4 DO
    BEGIN
      d := BAND(BSR(word,((4-i)*4)),$000F);
      IF d < 10 THEN hexStr[i] := CHR(ORD('0')+d)
      ELSE hexStr[i] := CHR(ORD('A')+d-10);
    END;
  IntToHex := hexStr;
END;

FUNCTION LongToHex(long: LongInt) : Str255;
BEGIN
  LongToHex := Concat(IntToHex(HiWord(long)),IntToHex(LoWord(long)));
END;
```

```
PROCEDURE PrintDoc; { print 1 page of text with its styles }
VAR
  aRect:      Rect;
  printTE:    TEHandle;
  printPort:  TPPrPort;
  status:     TPrStatus;
BEGIN
  aRect := printH^^.rPaper;
  InsetRect(aRect,72,72);

  printPort := PrOpenDoc(printH,NIL,NIL);
  printTE := TEStylNew(aRect,aRect);
  IF printTE = NIL THEN DebugStr('Not enough memory for print TERec.');
  printTE^^.inPort := GrafPtr(printPort);

  { Print Mgr needs its own TERec, so we'll copy & paste our text & styles }
  TESetSelect(0,32767,textH);
  TECopy(textH);
  TESetSelect(0,0,textH);
  TESetSelect(0,0,printTE);
  TEStylPaste(printTE);

  PrOpenPage(printPort,NIL);
  TEUpdate(aRect,printTE); { this actually draws the text on the printer }
  PrClosePage(printPort);
  PrCloseDoc(printPort);
  TEDispose(printTE);
  IF printH^^.prJob.bJDocLoop = bSpoolLoop
  THEN PrPicFile(printH,NIL,NIL,NIL,status);
END;

PROCEDURE SetupMenus;
VAR
  i,n: Integer;
  l:   LongInt;
  s:   Str255;
BEGIN
  menuDA := NewMenu(1,Concat(CHR(20)));
  AppendMenu(menuDA,'About StyleTest…;(-');
  AddResMenu(menuDA,'DRVR');
  InsertMenu(menuDA,0);

  menuFile := NewMenu(2,'File');
  AppendMenu(menuFile,'Text/T;MacsBug/D;(-;Page Setup…;Print…;(-;Quit/Q');
  InsertMenu(menuFile,0);

  menuEdit := NewMenu(3,'Edit');
  AppendMenu(menuEdit,Concat('Undo/Z;(-;Cut/X;Copy/C;Paste/V;Clear/B;',
                        '(-;Select All/A'));
  InsertMenu(menuEdit,0);
```

```pascal
    menuFont := NewMenu(4,'Font');
    AddResMenu(menuFont,'FONT');
    InsertMenu(menuFont,0);

    menuSize := NewMenu(5,'Size');
    AppendMenu(menuSize,'6;7;8;9;10;12;14;18;20;24;27;30;36;');
    AppendMenu(menuSize,'42;48;54;60;72;96;144;216;288;360;432;504');
    InsertMenu(menuSize,0);

    menuStyle := NewMenu(6,'Style');
    AppendMenu(menuStyle,'Plain;Bold<B;Italic<I;Underline<U;Outline<O;');
    AppendMenu(menuStyle,'Shadow<S;Condense;Extend;Hot Text');
    InsertMenu(menuStyle,0);

    menuColor := NewMenu(7,'Color');
    AppendMenu(menuColor,'Black;Red;Green;Blue;Yellow;Aqua;Magenta');
    InsertMenu(menuColor,0);

    DrawMenuBar;
    FOR i := 1 to CountMItems(menuFont) DO
      BEGIN
        GetItem(menuFont,i,s);
        GetFNum(s,n);
        fontArray[i] := n;
      END;
    FOR i := 1 to CountMItems(menuSize) DO
      BEGIN
        GetItem(menuSize,i,s);
        StringToNum(s,l);
        sizeArray[i] := l;
      END;
END;


PROCEDURE UpdateActive;
BEGIN
  InvalRect(myWindow^.portRect);
  UpdateRects;
  WITH textH^^ DO
    BEGIN
      destRect := txRect;
      viewRect := txRect;
    END;
  TECalText(textH);
END;
```

```
PROCEDURE UpdateRects;
BEGIN
  txRect := thePort^.portRect;
  WITH txRect DO
    BEGIN
      left := left + 4;
      right := right - 20;
      bottom := bottom - 20;
    END;
END;

BEGIN { Main }
  InitWorld;
  REPEAT
    DoPeriodic;
    IF GetNextEvent(everyEvent,myEvent) THEN
      CASE myEvent.what OF
        mouseDown:    DoMouse;
        keyDown:      DoKey;
        autoKey:      DoKey;
        activateEvt:  DoActivate;
        updateEvt:    DoUpdate;
      END;
  UNTIL quit;
  PrClose;
END.
```

StyleTest.r — Rez Source Code for StyleTest Resources

```
/* StyleTest.r - By Dan Allen */

#include "Types.r";

type 'STYT' { pstring; };

resource 'STYT' (0) {
  "StyleTest 1.0 B1 by Dan Allen\n";
};
```

```
resource 'SIZE' (-1) {
  dontSaveScreen,
  acceptSuspendResumeEvents,
  enableOptionSwitch,
  canBackground,
  multiFinderAware,
  backgroundAndForeground,
  dontGetFrontClicks,
  ignoreChildDiedEvents,
  not32BitCompatible,
  reserved, reserved, reserved, reserved, reserved, reserved, reserved,
  96*1024,
  64*1024
};

resource 'FREF' (128) { 'APPL', 0, "" };

resource 'BNDL' (128) {
  'STYT', 0, { 'ICN#', { 0, 128 }; 'FREF', { 0, 128 } }
};

resource 'ICN#' (128, purgeable, preload) {
  { /* array: 2 elements */
    /* [1] */
    $"00 01 00 00 00 02 80 00 00 04 40 00 00 09 20 00 00 12 10 00"
    $"00 24 48 00 00 48 84 00 00 90 12 00 01 02 21 00 02 44 44 80"
    $"04 88 88 40 09 11 11 20 10 20 00 10 24 04 40 48 48 88 BF 04"
    $"91 11 40 92 42 22 80 41 24 05 30 22 10 83 C8 14 09 1E 7F 0F"
    $"04 22 30 07 02 41 00 07 01 08 80 07 00 90 60 07 00 42 1F E7"
    $"00 24 42 1F 00 10 84 07 00 09 08 00 00 04 10 00 00 02 20 00"
    $"00 01 40 00 00 00 80",
    /* [2] */
    $"00 01 00 00 00 03 80 00 00 07 C0 00 00 0F E0 00 00 1F F0 00"
    $"00 3F F8 00 00 7F FC 00 00 FF FE 00 01 FF FF 00 03 FF FF 80"
    $"07 FF FF C0 0F FF FF E0 1F FF FF F0 3F FF FF F8 7F FF FF FC"
    $"FF FF FF FE 7F FF FF FF 3F FF FF FE 1F FF FF FC 0F FF FF FF"
    $"07 FF FF FF 03 FF FF FF 01 FF FF FF 00 FF FF FF 00 7F FF FF"
    $"00 3F FE 1F 00 1F FC 07 00 0F F8 00 00 07 F0 00 00 03 E0 00"
    $"00 01 C0 00 00 00 80"
  }
};
```

GraphSort — Pascal Application

This small application graphically displays different types of sorting algorithms at work. It was developed to give users a better understanding of some of the popular sorting algorithms. It has a single resizable window, uses menus to specify options, and uses the classic color calls so that output will show up in color if a color monitor is around.

The original idea for such an application can be attributed to Robert Sedgewick and Marc Brown, who have done a lot of work with graphically displaying algorithms. (See Sedgewick's text, *Algorithms*.) The algorithms used for sorting in this application are primarily from Gaston Gonnet's *Handbook of Algorithms and Data Structures* and Wirth's *Algorithms + Data Structures = Programs*.

Improving GraphSort

Here are some suggestions for improving GraphSort:

- The larger number of bars are only partially shown on screen. Revise the program so that sorts of thousands of items can be shown. Because the standard Macintosh screen is 512 pixels wide, how will you represent thousands of bars? What methods of selection are appropriate?

- Add more extensive colorization to the program, perhaps showing through color which bars are moved the most.

- Add other sorting algorithms, or rewrite these algorithms in assembly language for speed.

```
(*
 *   GraphSort - Written by Dan Allen
 *            - Begun 6/3/89
 *
 *   Select the following lines to build with MPW:

     Pascal GraphSort.p -mbg ch8
     Link -o GraphSort GraphSort.p.o {PLibraries}PasLib.o ∂
       {Libraries}Runtime.o {Libraries}Interface.o
 *)

PROGRAM GraphSort;

USES
  MemTypes,QuickDraw,OSIntf,ToolIntf,PackIntf,SANE;
```

```
CONST
  maxArray    = 5000;

  appleID     = 1;
  fileID      = 2;
    ascndItem = 1;
    dscndItem = 2;
    randItem  = 3;
    size10    = 5;
    size25    = 6;
    size50    = 7;
    size100   = 8;
    size250   = 9;
    size500   = 10;
    size1000  = 11;
    size2500  = 12;
    size5000  = 13;
    quitItem  = 15;
  editID      = 3;
    undoItem  = 1;
    cutItem   = 3;
    copyItem  = 4;
    pasteItem = 5;
  sortID      = 4;
    insrtItem = 1;
    selctItem = 2;
    exchgItem = 3;
    shellItem = 5;
    heapItem  = 6;
    quickItem = 7;
    quick2Itm = 8;
    quick3Itm = 9;

TYPE
  SortOrder   = (ascending,descending,randomSort);
```

```
VAR
  quit:       Boolean;
  sorted:     Boolean;
  lastSort:   Integer;
  numBars:    Integer;
  barWidth:   Integer;
  windHeight: Integer;
  windWidth:  Integer;
  numMoves:   LongInt;
  numCmp:     LongInt;
  theTicks:   LongInt;
  theEvent:   EventRecord;
  theWindow:  WindowPtr;
  appleMenu:  MenuHandle;
  fileMenu:   MenuHandle;
  editMenu:   MenuHandle;
  sortMenu:   MenuHandle;
  dragRect:   Rect;
  a,b:        ARRAY[0..maxArray] OF Integer;
  curOrder:   SortOrder;

PROCEDURE MacsBug; INLINE $A9FF;

PROCEDURE CalcBars;
VAR i:   Integer;
    bar: Extended;
BEGIN
  WITH theWindow^.portRect DO
    BEGIN
      windHeight := bottom - top;
      windWidth := right - left;
    END;
  barWidth := windWidth DIV numBars;
  IF barWidth < 1 THEN barWidth := 1;
  bar := windHeight / numBars;
  CASE curOrder OF
    ascending:
      FOR i := 1 TO numBars DO
        a[i] := Round(i*bar);
    descending:
      FOR i := 1 TO numBars DO
        a[i] := Round((numBars-i)*bar);
    randomSort:
      FOR i := 1 TO numBars DO
        a[i] := Abs(Random) MOD windHeight;
  END;
  FOR i := 1 to numBars DO b[i] := a[i];
  sorted := FALSE;
END;
```

```pascal
PROCEDURE DrawStats;
VAR str:  Str255;
BEGIN
  ForeColor(blackColor);
  MoveTo(5,12);
  NumToString(theTicks,str);
  DrawString(Concat('Sort ticks  = ',str));

  MoveTo(5,24);
  NumToString(numCmp,str);
  DrawString(Concat('Comparisons = ',str));

  MoveTo(5,36);
  NumToString(numMoves,str);
  DrawString(Concat('Assignments = ',str));
END;

PROCEDURE SetColor(i: Integer);
VAR value:  Integer;
BEGIN
  value := a[i];
  IF value < 50 THEN ForeColor(blackColor)
  ELSE IF value < 100 THEN ForeColor(magentaColor)
  ELSE IF value < 150 THEN ForeColor(redColor)
  ELSE IF value < 200 THEN ForeColor(greenColor)
  ELSE IF value < 250 THEN ForeColor(cyanColor)
  ELSE IF value < 300 THEN ForeColor(yellowColor)
  ELSE ForeColor(blueColor);
END;

PROCEDURE DrawBars;
VAR i:  Integer;
    x:  Integer;
    r:  Rect;
BEGIN
  SetPort(theWindow);
  EraseRect(theWindow^.portRect);
  FOR i := 1 TO numBars DO
    BEGIN
      x := barWidth*(i-1);
      SetRect(r,x,windHeight-a[i],x+barWidth,windHeight);
      SetColor(i);
      FillRect(r,black);
    END;
  IF sorted THEN DrawStats;
END;
```

```
PROCEDURE Draw1Bar(i: Integer);
VAR x: Integer;
    r: Rect;
BEGIN
  x := barWidth*(i-1);
  SetRect(r,x,0,x+barWidth,windHeight);
  FillRect(r,white);
  SetRect(r,x,windHeight-a[i],x+barWidth,windHeight);
  SetColor(i);
  FillRect(r,black);
  numMoves := numMoves + 1;
END;

PROCEDURE DrawSwap(i,j: Integer);
VAR x: Integer;
    r: Rect;
BEGIN
  x := barWidth*(i-1);
  SetRect(r,x,0,x+barWidth,windHeight);
  FillRect(r,white);
  SetRect(r,x,windHeight-a[j],x+barWidth,windHeight);
  SetColor(j);
  FillRect(r,black);

  x := barWidth*(j-1);
  SetRect(r,x,0,x+barWidth,windHeight);
  FillRect(r,white);
  SetRect(r,x,windHeight-a[i],x+barWidth,windHeight);
  SetColor(i);
  FillRect(r,black);
  numMoves := numMoves + 2;
END;
```

```pascal
PROCEDURE Insertion;
VAR i,j,x:  Integer;
BEGIN
  FOR i := 2 TO numBars DO
    BEGIN
      IF Button THEN EXIT(Insertion);
      x := a[i]; a[0] := x;
      j := i - 1;
      numCmp := numCmp + 1;
      WHILE x < a[j] DO
        BEGIN
          numCmp := numCmp + 1;
          DrawSwap(j+1,j);
          a[j+1] := a[j];
          j := j - 1;
        END;
      DrawSwap(j+1,0);
      a[j+1] := x;
    END;
END;

PROCEDURE Selection;
VAR i,j,k,x:  Integer;
BEGIN
  FOR i := 1 TO numBars - 1 DO
    BEGIN
      IF Button THEN Exit(Selection);
      k := i; x := a[i];
      FOR j := i+1 TO numBars DO
        BEGIN
          numCmp := numCmp + 1;
          IF a[j] < x THEN
            BEGIN
              k := j; x := a[j];
            END;
        END;
      DrawSwap(i,k);
      a[k] := a[i]; a[i] := x;
    END;
END;
```

```
PROCEDURE Exchange; { Bubblesort }
VAR i,j,x: Integer;
BEGIN
  FOR i := 2 TO numBars DO
    BEGIN
      IF Button THEN EXIT(Exchange);
      FOR j := numBars DOWNTO i DO
        BEGIN
          numCmp := numCmp + 1;
          IF a[j-1] > a[j] THEN
            BEGIN
              DrawSwap(j-1,j);
              x := a[j-1]; a[j-1] := a[j]; a[j] := x;
            END;
        END;
    END;
END;


PROCEDURE Shellsort;  { G.H. Gonnet, Diminishing Increment using .45454 }
VAR d,i,j,x: Integer;
BEGIN
  d := numBars;
  WHILE d > 1 DO
    BEGIN
      IF Button THEN EXIT(Shellsort);
      IF d < 5 THEN d := 1 ELSE d := (5*d-1) DIV 11;
      FOR i := numBars - d DOWNTO 1 DO
        BEGIN
          x := a[i]; j := i+d;
          numCmp := numCmp + 1;
          WHILE (j <= numBars) AND (x > a[j]) DO
            BEGIN
              numCmp := numCmp + 1;
              a[j-d] := a[j];
              Draw1Bar(j-d);
              j := j + d;
            END;
          a[j-d] := x;
          Draw1Bar(j-d);
        END;
    END;
END;
```

```pascal
PROCEDURE Heapsort; { G.H. Gonnet }
VAR i,x:  Integer;
  PROCEDURE SiftUp(i,n: Integer);
  VAR j,x:  Integer;
  BEGIN
    WHILE 2*i <= n DO
      BEGIN
        IF Button THEN EXIT(Heapsort);
        j := 2*i;
        IF j < n THEN
          BEGIN
            numCmp := numCmp + 1;
            IF a[j] < a[j+1] THEN j := j + 1;
          END;
        numCmp := numCmp + 1;
        IF a[i] < a[j] THEN
          BEGIN
            DrawSwap(i,j);
            x := a[j]; a[j] := a[i]; a[i] := x;
            i := j;
          END
        ELSE i := n + 1;
      END;
  END;
BEGIN
  FOR i := numBars DIV 2 DOWNTO 2 DO SiftUp(i,numBars);
  FOR i := numBars DOWNTO 2 DO
    BEGIN
      Siftup(1,i);
      DrawSwap(1,i);
      x := a[1]; a[1] := a[i]; a[i] := x;
    END;
END;
```

```
PROCEDURE Quicksort(lo,hi: Integer); { G.H. Gonnet }
VAR i,j,x: Integer;
BEGIN
  WHILE hi > lo DO
    BEGIN
      i := lo; j := hi; x := a[lo];
      WHILE i < j DO
        BEGIN
          numCmp := numCmp + 1;
          WHILE a[j] > x DO
            BEGIN
              numCmp := numCmp + 1;
              j := j - 1;
            END;
          a[i] := a[j];
          Draw1Bar(i);
          numCmp := numCmp + 1;
          WHILE (i < j) AND (a[i] <= x) DO
            BEGIN
              numCmp := numCmp + 1;
              i := i + 1;
            END;
          a[j] := a[i];
          Draw1Bar(j);
        END;
      a[i] := x;
      Draw1Bar(i);
      IF i-lo < hi-i THEN
        BEGIN
          QuickSort(lo,i-1);
          lo := i + 1;
        END
      ELSE
        BEGIN
          QuickSort(i+1,hi);
          hi := i - 1;
        END;
    END;
END;
```

```pascal
PROCEDURE QuickSort2(l,r: Integer); { N. Wirth }
VAR i,j,x,w: Integer;
BEGIN
  i := l; j := r;
  x := a[(l+r) DIV 2];
  REPEAT
    numCmp := numCmp + 1;
    WHILE a[i] < x DO
      BEGIN
        i := i + 1;
        numCmp := numCmp + 1;
      END;
    numCmp := numCmp + 1;
    WHILE x < a[j] DO
      BEGIN
        j := j - 1;
        numCmp := numCmp + 1;
      END;
    IF i <= j THEN
      BEGIN
        DrawSwap(i,j);
        w := a[i]; a[i] := a[j]; a[j] := w;
        i := i + 1; j := j -1;
      END;
  UNTIL i > j;
  IF l < j THEN QuickSort2(l,j);
  IF i < r THEN QuickSort2(i,r);
END;

PROCEDURE QuickSort3; { N. Wirth - non-recursive version }
CONST m = 12;
VAR i,j,l,r,s,x,w: Integer;
    stack:  ARRAY[1..m] OF RECORD l,r: Integer END;
```

```
BEGIN
  s := 1; stack[1].l := 1; stack[1].r := numBars;
  REPEAT
    l := stack[s].l; r := stack[s].r; s := s - 1;
    REPEAT
      i := l; j := r; x := a[(l+r) DIV 2];
      REPEAT
        numCmp := numCmp + 1;
        WHILE a[i] < x DO
          BEGIN
            i := i + 1;
            numCmp := numCmp + 1;
          END;
        numCmp := numCmp + 1;
        WHILE x < a[j] DO
          BEGIN
            j := j - 1;
            numCmp := numCmp + 1;
          END;
        IF i <= j THEN
          BEGIN
            DrawSwap(i,j);
            w := a[i]; a[i] := a[j]; a[j] := w;
            i := i + 1; j := j - 1;
          END;
      UNTIL i > j;
      IF j - l < r - i THEN
        BEGIN
          IF i < r THEN
            BEGIN
              s := s + 1; stack[s].l := i; stack[s].r := r;
            END;
          r := j;
        END
      ELSE
        BEGIN
          IF l < j THEN
            BEGIN
              s := s + 1; stack[s].l := l; stack[s].r := j;
            END;
          l := i;
        END;
    UNTIL l >= r;
  UNTIL s = 0;
END;
```

```
PROCEDURE InitWorld;
VAR i,n:    LongInt;
    myRect: Rect;
BEGIN
  MaxApplZone;
  InitGraf(@thePort);
  InitFonts;
  InitWindows;
  InitMenus;
  TEInit;
  InitDialogs(NIL);
  InitCursor;
  FlushEvents(everyEvent,0);

  SetRect(dragRect,-32767,-32767,32767,32767);
  myRect := screenBits.bounds;
  InsetRect(myRect,50,50);
  theWindow := NewWindow(NIL,myRect,'GraphSort by Dan Allen',
                            TRUE,8,Pointer(-1),TRUE,0);
  SetPort(theWindow);
  TextFont(monaco);
  TextSize(9);

  appleMenu := NewMenu(appleID,Concat(CHR(20)));
  AppendMenu(appleMenu,'(GraphSort 1.0;(-');
  AddResMenu(appleMenu,'DRVR');
  InsertMenu(appleMenu,0);

  fileMenu := NewMenu(fileID,'File');
  AppendMenu(fileMenu,'Ascending/A;Descending/D;Random/R;(-');
  AppendMenu(fileMenu,'10 Bars/1;25 Bars/2;50 Bars/3;100 Bars/4');
  AppendMenu(fileMenu,'250 Bars/5;500 Bars/6;1000 Bars/7');
  AppendMenu(fileMenu,'2500 Bars/8;5000 Bars/9;(-;Quit/Q');
  InsertMenu(fileMenu,0);

  editMenu := NewMenu(editID,'Edit');
  AppendMenu(editMenu,'Undo/Z;(-;Cut/X;Copy/C;Paste/V');
  InsertMenu(editMenu,0);

  sortMenu := NewMenu(sortID,'Sort');
  AppendMenu(sortMenu,'Straight Insertion/I;Straight Selection/S');
  AppendMenu(sortMenu,'Straight Exchange/B;(-;Shellsort/T');
  AppendMenu(sortMenu,'Heapsort/H;Quicksort/E;Quicksort2;Quicksort3'
  InsertMenu(sortMenu,0);
  DrawMenuBar;
```

```
    quit := FALSE;
    lastSort := 0;
    numBars := 25;
    curOrder := randomSort;
    randSeed := TickCount;
    CalcBars;
END;

PROCEDURE SetupMenus;
VAR i:  Integer;
BEGIN
  CheckItem(fileMenu,1,curOrder = ascending);
  CheckItem(fileMenu,2,curOrder = descending);
  CheckItem(fileMenu,3,curOrder = randomSort);
  CheckItem(fileMenu,5,numBars = 10);
  CheckItem(fileMenu,6,numBars = 25);
  CheckItem(fileMenu,7,numBars = 50);
  CheckItem(fileMenu,8,numBars = 100);
  CheckItem(fileMenu,9,numBars = 250);
  CheckItem(fileMenu,10,numBars = 500);
  CheckItem(fileMenu,11,numBars = 1000);
  CheckItem(fileMenu,12,numBars = 2500);
  CheckItem(fileMenu,13,numBars = 5000);

  FOR i := 1 TO CountMItems(sortMenu) DO
    CheckItem(sortMenu,i,i = lastSort);
END;

PROCEDURE DoMenu(menu,item: Integer);
VAR i,t:  LongInt;
    pic:  PicHandle;
    str:  Str255;
BEGIN
  HiliteMenu(menu);
  Delay(5,i);
  CASE menu OF
    appleID:
      IF item > 1 THEN
        BEGIN
          GetItem(appleMenu,item,str);
          i := OpenDeskAcc(str);
        END;
```

```pascal
fileID:
  BEGIN
    CASE item OF
      ascndItem:  curOrder := ascending;
      dscndItem:  curOrder := descending;
      randItem:   curOrder := randomSort;
      size10:     numBars := 10;
      size25:     numBars := 25;
      size50:     numBars := 50;
      size100:    numBars := 100;
      size250:    numBars := 250;
      size500:    numBars := 500;
      size1000:   numBars := 1000;
      size2500:   numBars := 2500;
      size5000:   numBars := 5000;
      quitItem:   quit := TRUE;
    END;
    IF item <> quitItem THEN
      BEGIN
        CalcBars;
        DrawBars;
      END;
  END;
editID:
  IF NOT SystemEdit(item - 1) THEN
    CASE item OF
      undoItem:
        BEGIN
          FOR i := 1 TO numBars DO a[i] := b[i];
          sorted := FALSE;
          DrawBars;
        END;
      cutItem:
        BEGIN
          FOR i := 1 TO numBars DO a[i] := 1;
          FOR i := 1 TO numBars DO b[i] := 1;
          sorted := FALSE;
          DrawBars;
        END;
      copyItem:
        BEGIN
          t := ZeroScrap;
          pic := OpenPicture(theWindow^.portRect);
          DrawBars;
          ClosePicture;
          i := GetHandleSize(Handle(pic));
          t := PutScrap(i,'PICT',Handle(pic)^);
          DisposHandle(Handle(pic));
        END;
      pasteItem:  ;
    END;
```

```
      sortID:
        BEGIN
          FOR i := 1 TO numBars DO a[i] := b[i];
          sorted := FALSE;
          DrawBars;
          numMoves := 0;
          numCmp := 0;
          lastSort := item;
          theTicks := TickCount;
          CASE item OF
            insrtItem:  Insertion;
            selctItem:  Selection;
            exchgItem:  Exchange;
            shellItem:  Shellsort;
            heapItem:   Heapsort;
            quickItem:  Quicksort(1,numBars);
            quick2Itm:  Quicksort2(1,numBars);
            quick3Itm:  Quicksort3;
          END;
          theTicks := TickCount - theTicks;
          sorted := TRUE;
          DrawStats;
        END;
  END;
  HiliteMenu(0);
END;


PROCEDURE DoKey;
VAR result: LongInt;
BEGIN
  IF BitAnd(theEvent.modifiers,cmdKey) > 0 THEN
    BEGIN
      result := MenuKey(Char(theEvent.message));
      DoMenu(HiWord(result),LoWord(result));
    END;
END;
```

```pascal
PROCEDURE DoMouse;
VAR i,location:   Integer;
    result:       LongInt;
    whichWindow:  WindowPtr;
    pt:           Point;
BEGIN
  location := FindWindow(theEvent.where,whichWindow);
  CASE location OF
    inMenuBar:
      BEGIN
        SetupMenus;
        result := MenuSelect(theEvent.where);
        DoMenu(HiWord(result),LoWord(result));
      END;
    inSysWindow:
      SystemClick(theEvent,whichWindow);
    inContent:
      REPEAT
        GetMouse(pt);
        i := Abs(pt.h) DIV barWidth + 1;
        a[i] := windHeight - pt.v;
        b[i] := a[i];
        Draw1Bar(i);
      UNTIL NOT StillDown;
    inDrag:
      BEGIN
        DragWindow(whichWindow,theEvent.where,dragRect);
      END;
    inGrow:
      BEGIN
        result := GrowWindow(whichWindow,theEvent.where,dragRect);
        SizeWindow(whichWindow,LoWord(result),HiWord(result),FALSE);
        CalcBars;
        DrawBars;
      END;
    inGoAway:
      BEGIN
        quit := TrackGoAway(whichWindow,theEvent.where);
      END;
    inZoomIn,inZoomOut:
      IF TrackBox(whichWindow,theEvent.where,location) THEN
        BEGIN
          ZoomWindow(whichWindow,location,TRUE);
          CalcBars;
        END;
  END;
END;
```

```
PROCEDURE DoUpdate;
BEGIN
  IF WIndowPtr(theEvent.message) = theWindow THEN
    BEGIN
      BeginUpdate(theWindow);
      DrawBars;
      EndUpdate(theWindow);
    END;
END;

PROCEDURE MainEvent;
BEGIN
  WHILE NOT GetNextEvent(everyEvent,theEvent) DO SystemTask;
  CASE theEvent.what OF
    mouseDown:  DoMouse;
    mouseUp:    DoMouse;
    keyDown:    DoKey;
    keyUp:      DoKey;
    autoKey:    DoKey;
    updateEvt:  DoUpdate;
    diskEvt:      ;
    activateEvt:;
  END;
END;

BEGIN
  InitWorld;
  REPEAT MainEvent UNTIL quit;
END.
```

Conclusion

This chapter looked at the Pascal language and its history on the Macintosh. A reading knowledge of Pascal is essential to all Macintosh programmers because most Apple documentation uses examples written in Pascal.

Two applications written in Pascal were also presented. The first, StyleText, illustrates the use of TextEdit as well as demonstrating an application written in Pascal. The second, GraphSort, illustrates the use of QuickDraw while exploring the interesting world of sort algorithms.

Recommended Reading

The main reference manual for Pascal is Jensen and Wirth's *Pascal User Manual and Report*. It contains a modest tutorial as well as the definitive language reference manual for Pascal. I prefer Wirth's *Algorithms + Data Structures = Programs*, however, for its excellent examples of using Pascal to solve problems in sorting, searching, and compiler construction. Do not confuse this excellent work with Wirth's later work entitled *Algorithms and Data Structures*, which uses Modula-2 instead of Pascal, is not as nicely typeset, is more expensive, and omits much of the material of the earlier work.

The Pascal compiler manuals are also good resources. Apple's MPW Pascal manual includes syntax charts of the language; Borland's Turbo Pascal manual is a great course in Pascal and in the basics of Macintosh programming; Think's manual has the nicest presentation of them all, with good information about this version of Pascal, although not as much information about Mac programming as Borland's manual.

Additional works that use Pascal extensively in their examples are Sedgewick's *Algorithms* and Kernighan and Plauger's *Software Tools in Pascal*, both of which were used as references for the sorting program.

## CHAPTER 10

HYPERCARD

This chapter begins by taking a look at the object-oriented background of HyperCard. Next, it examines several different scripts written in HyperTalk, including:

- `HomeStack`—My customized version of the Home stack
- `DrawRandom`—A script that illustrates how to use the painting tools from a script
- `DuplicateBackground`—A script that copies and pastes backgrounds, a feature not included in HyperCard
- `CImport`—A script that will import C header files into a HyperCard stack
- `Calendar`—Produces a small calendar displaying two months at a glance
- `Books`—Provides an example of a more complex stack that catalogs books

Following these scripts, the chapter discusses how you can extend HyperCard by writing XCMDs and XFCNs. Numerous examples are provided, with source code in both C and Pascal.

History of HyperCard

HyperCard is the creation of Bill Atkinson. Bill actually laid the groundwork for HyperCard years earlier when he wrote QuickDraw, the graphics routines found on the Lisa and Macintosh. Later, he wrote MacPaint to show off QuickDraw's abilities. These events all happened prior to the unveiling of the original Macintosh in January of 1984.

Not too long after the Macintosh shipped, Bill Atkinson wrote a public domain program called Rolodex, which displayed a series of fixed-size note cards, each of which could hold a name and address or some other small amount of text. Rolodex opened only one file, whose contents were read into memory; this allowed cards to be searched very quickly. This small, handy program was only about 8 KB in size. It was later renamed QuickFile because of legal issues.

Late in 1985, Bill began work on a new program he called WildCard. He described his new project to me at that time as "a cross between MacPaint, QuickFile, and an adventure game." All of these elements did not come together at first, however. In its early versions, WildCard had the look and feel of QuickFile, with only a single ever-growing file called a stack. Most of the development releases—which had a very small distribution within Apple—were designed so that Switcher was used with MacPaint to create graphics that were then pasted into WildCard. The influence and results of Bill's work on MacPaint finally began to make their appearance when WildCard got its own set of paint tools. The adventure game aspects surfaced in the form of hot regions called buttons that, when clicked on, could display another card in the stack.

Later versions of WildCard allowed multiple stacks to be accessed instead of a single monolithic stack, and stacks could be compacted to reclaim empty space in files. Because stacks could be quite large, the memory-based searching of QuickFile was not appropriate, so Bill came up with an entirely different scheme for fast text searching of disk-based data. Early users had to negotiate seven different interim file formats, but each new release usually could read and convert the previous format, so data usually made it forward into the new version.

By October 1986, after almost a year of development, it was realized that small scripts were needed to express what happened when a user clicked on a button. Dan Winkler joined the WildCard project to create and implement a language that came to be known as WildTalk. The power of WildCard expanded greatly when this English-like programming language was added. In April of 1987, XCMDs were added as Dan continued to evolve the language's extensibility.

Everyone was planning on calling the product WildCard, but legal problems again required a name change. Because the program had become more hypertext-like, HyperCard was begrudgingly accepted as its new name. However, HyperCard's creator signature to this day reflects its original name: `WILD`.

What Is HyperCard?

When HyperCard was introduced in August of 1987, everyone thought it was neat, but no one knew quite what it was. Applications have traditionally fit into one of five categories: word processors, spreadsheets, databases, graphics, and communications. HyperCard is an example of a new type of application that does not fit neatly into one of the Big Five Categories of software, because it actually incorporates elements of all of them.

HyperCard's inventor, Bill Atkinson, likes to refer to HyperCard as a "software erector set"—a way of getting people into programming the Macintosh. This he has accomplished. Early expectations were that 10 percent of the users of HyperCard would delve into HyperTalk, but actually more than 50 percent of HyperCard users have written HyperTalk scripts!

Others at Apple refer to HyperCard as an "information toolkit." Indeed, because of its customizable user interface, HyperTalk, XCMDs, and ease of use, HyperCard has become used increasingly as a front-end to relational databases, mainframe computers, networks, bulletin boards, mail systems, and even to artificial intelligence inference engines. It provides the tools to access information.

HyperCard has been bundled with every Macintosh sold since the fall of 1987. HyperCard versions 1 through 1.2.5 require 750 KB of memory to run under MultiFinder, and the application occupies about 400 KB of disk space.

HyperCard and Object-oriented Programming

The basic paradigm of HyperCard is as follows: Related information is kept in a stack. Each stack contains a variable number of cards and backgrounds. Every card belongs to exactly one background. A background can contain fields, buttons, and a bit map of 512 by 342 pixels. Cards can also have their own specific fields, buttons, and bit maps. The screen displays a superimposition of these two layers—card and background—with the card layer being "on top."

Each of these five fundamental objects—stacks, backgrounds, cards, fields, and buttons—can have its own HyperTalk script. Messages are sent by the system, and optionally by scripts, to indicate actions and events. Messages are responded to by handlers (procedures and functions) contained in scripts or by commands built into HyperTalk.

Because of the way HyperTalk handles objects and messages, HyperTalk is considered an object-oriented language. As was mentioned in chapter 9, object-oriented languages can be described by the following equation:

$$\textbf{object oriented = objects + classes + inheritance}$$

HyperTalk follows the object-oriented programming tradition, with its own flavor of objects, classes, and inheritance. HyperCard's classes are stacks, backgrounds, cards, fields, and buttons. Users can create many new instances of objects, although they cannot create new classes. In other words, users can create all of the buttons and cards they want, but they currently cannot create a spreadsheet class.

Each individual object can be associated with a script. Each HyperTalk script can contain many handlers (methods) that can send, receive, and service messages. Handlers are similar to procedures in that they can be passed parameters and can be called recursively, but handler definitions cannot be nested. Handlers support local and global variables.

Object-oriented languages support inheritance; HyperTalk's inheritance path allows messages to be dealt with by handlers at various points in the system. In HyperTalk, this means that a message, such as `mouseUp`, can be handled by the stack, background, card, or part (button or field), depending on the situation. When a message is passed to a HyperCard object, the script of that object is checked for a corresponding handler of the same name. If one is found, it is dealt with; if one is not found, the current card's script is checked, then the background script, then the stack's script, then the stack script of the home stack, and finally HyperCard itself. Most of HyperTalk's messages are handled by HyperCard.

Actually, the inheritance path is slightly more complicated when the currently executing script goes to a different card or stack during its execution. In that situation, the current script's card and stack are searched as well as the current visible card and stack.

HyperCard commands are simply messages handled by HyperCard and thus can be redefined by the user through this inheritance path. Objects can subvert the standard hierarchy by use of the keyword `send`.

`HomeStack` — HyperTalk Script

HyperCard uses a special stack named "Home" to allow users to customize HyperCard to their own taste. The script presented here shows my Home stack. Here is a brief description of a few useful handlers that I have added to the standard Apple scripts.

The `on ControlKey` handler allows ADB keyboards (found on Mac SEs and later machines) to use the Control key for additional functionality. The keys A to Z are mapped to the numbers 1 to 26, so Control-A selects all of the text of the currently active field, for example. Other Control handlers allow you to cut and duplicate cards and to manipulate text with the Replace and Strip XCMDs presented later in this chapter.

The `WriteScripts` handler is useful for exporting all of the scripts of a stack to a text file, perhaps to be printed or indexed or archived with the help of MPW or a word processor. It lists the sizes and properties of all background fields and buttons, along with their scripts, as well as the stack and background scripts themselves. You could easily add ways of handling card-specific fields, buttons, and scripts, if desired. This script uses the `SetCreator` XCMD, presented later in this chapter, to set the file type for MPW. Obviously, other creators could be used. (See Chapter 2 for a list of popular creator signatures.)

```
on ControlKey num
  if n = 1 then select text of the selectedField
  else if n = 4 then
    doMenu "Copy Card"
    doMenu "Paste Card"
  else if n = 18 then
    put replace(return,space,the selection) into the selection
  else if n = 19 then
    put strip(the selection) into the selection
  else if n = 24 then doMenu "Cut Card"
  else pass ControlKey
end ControlKey
```

```
on WriteScripts stackName -- write scripts of a stack into a file
  push this card
  put "*****" into delimit
  repeat 4 times
    put delimit after delimit
  end repeat
  put return into last char of delimit
  if stackName is not empty then go to stack stackName
  get the long name of this stack
  delete char 1 to 7 of it -- label & quote before name
  delete last char of it -- trailing quote
  put ".ht" after it
  put it into fullpath
  open file fullpath
  get the script of this stack
  write delimit to file fullpath
  write the long name of this stack & return to file fullpath
  write delimit to file fullpath
  write it & return & return to file fullpath
  repeat with i = 1 to the number of bkgnds
    go to card 1 of bkgnd i
    get the script of this bkgnd
    write delimit to file fullpath
    write the long name of this bkgnd & return to file fullpath
    write delimit to file fullpath
    write it & return & return to file fullpath
    repeat with j = 1 to the number of bkgnd buttons
      get the script of bkgnd button j
      write delimit to file fullpath
      write GetPartInfo(name of bkgnd btn j) to file fullpath
      write delimit to file fullpath
      write it & return & return to file fullpath
    end repeat
    repeat with j = 1 to the number of fields
      get the script of field j
      write delimit to file fullpath
      write GetPartInfo(name of field j) to file fullpath
      write delimit to file fullpath
      write it & return & return to file fullpath
    end repeat
  end repeat
  close file fullpath
  SetCreator fullpath,"MPS "
  pop card
end writeScripts
```

```
function GetPartInfo part
  set cursor to busy
  put part & return into info
  put "Font:" && the textFont of part after info
  put "  Size:" && the textSize of part after info
  put "  Style:" && the textStyle of part after info
  put "  Align:" && the textAlign of part & return after info
  put "Rect:" && the rect of part after info
  put "  Loc:" && the loc of part after info
  put "  Visible:" && the visible of part after info
  put "  Style:" && the style of part & return after info
  if word two of part is "field" then
    put "Locktext:" && the lockText of part after info
    put "  Showlines:" && the showLines of part after info
    put "  Widemargins:" && the wideMargins of part & return after info
  else
    put "Icon:" && the icon of part after info
    put "  Hilite:" && the hilite of part after info
    put "  Autohilite:" && the autoHilite of part after info
    put "  Showname:" && the showName of part & return after info
  end if
  return info
end GetPartInfo

-- Apple's standard scripts follow:

on xy
  repeat until the mouse is down
    put the mouseLoc
  end repeat
end xy

on c
  choose browse tool
  doMenu "Card Info..."
end c

on b
  choose browse tool
  doMenu "Bkgnd Info..."
end b

on s
  choose browse tool
  doMenu "Stack Info..."
end s

on startUp
  getHomeInfo
  pass startUp
end startUp
```

```
on resume
  getHomeInfo
  pass resume
end resume

on getHomeInfo
  global stacks,applications,documents,userName
  set lockScreen to true
  set lockMessages to true
  push this card
  go to card "User Preferences" of stack "Home"
  put card field "User Name" into userName
  set userLevel to card field "User Level"
  set powerKeys to the hilite of button "Power Keys"
  set textArrows to the hilite of button "Text Arrows"
  set blindTyping to the hilite of button "Blind Typing"
  put field "paths" of card "stacks" into stacks
  put field "paths" of card "applications" into applications
  put field "paths" of card "documents" into documents
  pop card
  set lockScreen to false
  set lockMessages to false
end getHomeInfo
```

DrawRandom — HyperTalk Script

This simple HyperTalk script will draw random regular polygons on the screen. It is not very useful, except perhaps as a tool for mesmerizing someone. It is shown here as an example of driving the paint tools from a script. The script could be placed in a button, card, background, or stack script and will randomly paint polygons on the current card's picture.

```
on mouseUp
  if item 3 of the screenRect = 512 then hide menubar
  reset paint
  choose reg poly tool
  doMenu "Select All"
  doMenu "Clear Picture"
  set filled to true
  repeat until the mouse is down
    set polysides to random(5)+2
    set pattern to random(12)
    drag from random(512),random(342) to random(512),random(342)
  end repeat
  choose browse tool
end mouseUp
```

DuplicateBackground — HyperTalk Script

Not every useful piece of functionality is directly built into HyperCard; that is why there is a HyperTalk language. The most common and useful operations are built into the language, and somewhat obscure operations are left to ingenious scripts.

Here is an example: HyperTalk allows cards and pictures and text to be cut, copied, and pasted, but there is no simple way to copy and paste a background. This HyperTalk script duplicates a background—that's a copy and paste in one operation. The resulting two backgrounds found in the same stack will have the same pictures, buttons, fields, and scripts. Only their internal IDs and names will be different. Card-specific information is not copied. (Incidentally, it is because of this that HyperCard does not make this a built-in command: many people would create identical-looking backgrounds accidentally.)

```
on duplicateBackground
  lock screen
  put the id of this card into old
  doMenu "New Background"
  put the id of this card into new
  go old
  choose field tool
  repeat with i = 1 to the number of fields
    select field i
    doMenu "Copy Field"
    go new
    doMenu "Paste Field"
    go old
  end repeat
  choose button tool
  repeat with i = 1 to the number of bg btns
    select bg btn i
    doMenu "Copy Button"
    go new
    doMenu "Paste Button"
    go old
  end repeat
  choose select tool
  doMenu "Background"
  doMenu "Select All"
  doMenu "Copy Picture"
  go new
  doMenu "Paste Picture"
  go old
  choose browse tool
  get the script of this bg
  go new
  set the script of this bg to it
end duplicateBackground
```

`CImport` — **HyperTalk Script**

This script will import all of the MPW C and C++ interface files into a HyperCard stack. It then deletes everything that has to do with C++, strips out various `#ifdef` lines to make reading the interfaces easier on the eyes, and compacts the stack. This script requires the `NthFileName` and `Strip` XFCNs presented later in this chapter, and it illustrates how these are useful for importing text from many text files.

The actual importing of text is quite fast, but the stripping operations take a while in HyperTalk. Such text massaging is probably better done in MPW. In fact, MPW and HyperCard often complement each other when you are dealing with large quantities of text. If you have at least 2.5 MB of memory and are running MultiFinder, you can have HyperCard running with this stack open while you are also programming in MPW—this creates a nice composite development environment.

This script requires a background with fields named `Name`, `Version`, and `Text` in which the information can be put.

```
on mouseUp
  answer "Import CIncludes ?" with "OK" or "Cancel"
  if it is "Cancel" then exit mouseUp
  put "HD:MPW:Interfaces:CIncludes:" into path -- your pathname goes here
  repeat with i = 1 to NthFilename(path,0)
    if i ≠ 1 then doMenu "New Card"
    put NthFilename(path,i) into fileName
    put fileName into field "Name"
    put path before fileName
    put empty into text
    open file fileName
    repeat
      read from file fileName for 16384
      if it is empty then exit repeat else put it after text
    end repeat
    close file fileName
    put Strip(text) into field "Text"
  end repeat
  cleanImport
end mouseUp

on cleanImport
  go first card
  set lockScreen to true
  go first card
  removeCPlusPlus
  go first card
  removeSafeLink
  go first card
  removeHeaders
  go first card
  doMenu "Compact Stack"
end cleanImport
```

```
on removeHeaders
  go first card
  repeat for the number of cards
    set cursor to busy
    get field "text"
    repeat until "*/" is in line 1 of it
      if line 1 of it contains "Created:"
      then put line 1 of it into field "Version"
      delete line 1 of it
    end repeat
    delete line 1 of it
    repeat while line 1 of it is empty
      delete line 1 of it
      if it is empty then exit repeat
    end repeat
    repeat while line 1 of it contains "#ifndef __"
      delete line 1 to 3 of it
      repeat while line 1 of it is empty
        delete line 1 of it
        if it is empty then exit repeat
      end repeat
    end repeat
    if last line of it contains "#endif" then delete last line of it
    put it into field "Text"
    go next card
  end repeat
end removeHeaders

on removeCPlusPlus
  repeat
    set cursor to busy
    find whole "#ifndef __cplusplus"
    if the result is "not found" then exit repeat
    get the foundLine
    delete it
    subtract 1 from word two of it
    if the value of it is empty then delete it
    find whole "#endif"
    delete the foundLine
  end repeat
end removeCPlusPlus
```

```
on removeSafeLink
  repeat
    set cursor to busy
    find whole "#ifdef __safe_link"
    if the result is "not found" then exit repeat
    put the foundLine into temp
    find whole "#endif"
    put the foundLine into temp2
    put " to" && word 2 of temp2 after word 2 of temp
    delete temp
  end repeat
end removeSafeLink
```

Calendar — HyperTalk Script

This sample HyperTalk script is a handler that could be placed in a locked field that looks similar to the one shown in Figure 10–1. (The field must be locked so that `mouseUp` messages are sent to it.) Clicking on the upper portion of the calendar backs up a month; clicking on the lower portion moves ahead one month. This field is on the first card of my main Home stack. Another handler checks the current date when the stack is opened and updates the calendar appropriately so the current month is always at the top of this card field named "Calendar."

```
March 1989
Su  Mo  Tu  We  Th  Fr  Sa
                1   2   3   4
 5   6   7   8   9  10  11
12  13  14  15  16  17  18
19  20  21  22  23  24  25
26  27  28  29  30  31

April 1989
Su  Mo  Tu  We  Th  Fr  Sa
                            1
 2   3   4   5   6   7   8
 9  10  11  12  13  14  15
16  17  18  19  20  21  22
23  24  25  26  27  28  29
30
```

Figure 10–1: My "Calendar" Card Field

```
on mouseUp
  if me is empty then
    get the long date
    convert it to dateItems
    put 1 into item 3 of it
    convert it to long date
  else
    get the clickLoc
    if item 2 of it > (the height of me / 2 + the top of me)
    then put 1 into offset
    else put -1 into offset

    get line 1 of me
    put " 1, " after word 1 of it
    convert it to dateItems
    add offset to item 2 of it
    if item 2 of it = 0 then
      add offset to item 1 of it
      put 12 into item 2 of it
    end if
    convert it to long date
  end if
  Make2Months it
end mouseUp

on Make2Months theDate -- long date of first day of a month
  -- print first month
  get theDate
  put DaysInMonth(word 2 of it,item 3 of it) into n

  put word 2 of it && word 4 of it & return into me
  convert it to dateItems
  put item 7 of it into dayNum
  put MakeMonth(dayNum,n) after me

  -- print next month
  add 1 to item 2 of it
  convert it to long date
  put word 2 of it && word 4 of it & return after me
  put DaysInMonth(word 2 of it,item 3 of it) into n
  convert it to dateItems
  put item 7 of it into dayNum
  put MakeMonth(dayNum,n) after me
end Make2Months
```

```
function DaysInMonth month,year
  if month is in "April,June,August,October"
  then return 30
  else if month is "February" then
    if year mod 4 = 0 then return 29
    else return 28
  else return 31
end DaysInMonth

function MakeMonth dayNum,n
  put "Su  Mo  Tu  We  Th  Fr  Sa" & return into temp
  put 1 into column
  repeat while column < dayNum
    put "    " after temp -- 4 spaces
    add 1 to column
  end repeat
  repeat with i = 1 to n
    set cursor to busy
    if i < 10 then put space & i after temp
    else put i after temp
    if column < 7 then
      put space & space after temp
      add 1 to column
    else
      put return after temp
      put 1 into column
    end if
  end repeat
  if last char of temp ≠ return then put return after temp
  return temp & return
end MakeMonth
```

Books — HyperTalk Script

Here is a stack for cataloging books. It will sort by various criteria, total values of some or all of the books, allows easy export of information to MS Word and MS Excel, and even create a formatted bibliography at the touch of a button. In fact, this stack was used to create the bibliography of this book. Figure 10–2 shows what the stack looks like.

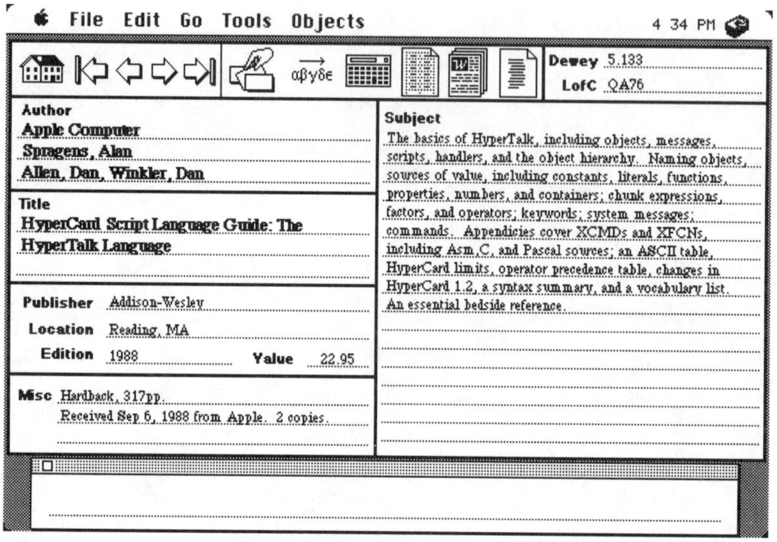

Figure 10–2: The Books Stack

Here is the documentation for the stack, including a listing of the various fields, buttons, and all of the scripts contained in the stack. This listing of its scripts, fields, and buttons was created with the `WriteScripts` handler described above in my custom `HomeStack` script. This information will allow you to recreate most aspects of the stack if desired, with background art and custom icons as exceptions.

```
*************************************************************************
stack "SR71:Docs:DKA:DKA/Books"
*************************************************************************
on openStack
  show msg at 19,305
end openStack

on closeStack
  hide msg
end closeStack
```

```
on closeCard
  if field "Dewey" is empty then
    ask "Enter Dewey Decimal number for this book:"
    if it is not empty then put it into field "Dewey"
  end if
end closeCard


*****************************************************************************
bkgnd "DKA Books" of stack "SR71:Docs:DKA:DKA/Books"
*****************************************************************************
on newCard
  tabKey
end newCard

on doMenu what
  if what is "Delete Card" or what is "Cut Card" then
    answer "Really delete this book?" with "Cancel" or "OK"
    if it is "Cancel" then exit doMenu
  end if
  pass doMenu
end doMenu what

on GetStats searchString
  push this card
  set lockScreen to true
  go first card
  find whole searchString
  if the result is "not found" then
    answer quote & searchString & quote && "not found." with "OK"
    pop card
    exit GetStats
  end if
  put one into count
  put field "Value" into total
  put the number of this card into firstCard
  repeat
    set cursor to busy
    go next card
    find whole searchString
    if the number of this card is firstCard then exit repeat
    add one to count
    add line one of field "Value" to total
  end repeat
  pop card
  set numberFormat to "0"
  put "n =" && count into temp
  set numberFormat to "0.00"
  put "  sum = $" & total & "  avg = $" & total/count after temp
  answer temp with "OK"
end GetStats
```

```
on browseStack
  if the commandKey is down then
    show cards -- show forever
  else if the optionKey is down then
    set cursor to watch
    set lockScreen to true
    show all cards -- prewarm
  else
    repeat until the mouse is down
      visual dissolve very fast
      go next card
    end repeat
  end if
end browseStack
```

```
*************************************************************************
bkgnd button "Prev"
Font: Chicago  Size: 12  Style: plain  Align: center
Rect: 69,30,94,55  Loc: 81,42  Visible: true  Style: transparent
Icon: 1014  Hilite: false  Autohilite: false  Showname: false
*************************************************************************
on mouseDown
  if the cmdKey is down then browseStack
  repeat
    visual wipe down
    go prev card
    if the mouse is up then exit repeat
  end repeat
end mouseDown
```

```
*************************************************************************
bkgnd button "Next"
Font: Chicago  Size: 12  Style: plain  Align: center
Rect: 93,30,117,55  Loc: 105,42  Visible: true  Style: transparent
Icon: 1013  Hilite: false  Autohilite: false  Showname: false
*************************************************************************
on mouseDown
  repeat
    visual wipe down
    go next card
    if the mouse is up then exit repeat
  end repeat
end mouseDown
```

```
*************************************************************************
bkgnd button "Go Home"
Font: Chicago  Size: 12  Style: plain  Align: center
Rect: 6,30,42,55  Loc: 24,42  Visible: true  Style: transparent
Icon: 1011  Hilite: false  Autohilite: false  Showname: false
*************************************************************************
on mouseUp
  visual barn door close
  go "Home"
end mouseUp


*************************************************************************
bkgnd button "Export Excel"
Font: Chicago  Size: 12  Style: plain  Align: center
Rect: 263,25,293,59  Loc: 278,42  Visible: true  Style: transparent
Icon: 17303  Hilite: false  Autohilite: true  Showname: false
*************************************************************************
on mouseUp
  put the short name of this stack & ".xl" into defaultName
  ask "Export DDC,author,title to Excel:" with defaultName
  if it is empty then exit mouseUp
  put it into fileName
  open file fileName
  go to first card
  set lockScreen to true
  repeat for the number of cards
    write line 1 of field "dewey" & tab &¬
    line 1 of field "author" & tab &¬
    line 1 of field "title" & return to file fileName
    go to next card
    set cursor to busy
  end repeat
  close file fileName
  SetCreator fileName,"XCEL"
end mouseUp


*************************************************************************
bkgnd button "Dewey"
Font: Helvetica  Size: 9  Style: bold  Align: center
Rect: 361,26,399,41  Loc: 380,33  Visible: true  Style: transparent
Icon: 0  Hilite: false  Autohilite: true  Showname: true
*************************************************************************
on mouseUp
  answer "Sort by Dewey Decimal # ?" with "Cancel" or "Sort"
  if it is "Cancel" then exit mouseUp
  push card
  sort numeric by field "Dewey"
  pop card
end mouseUp
```

```
******************************************************************************
bkgnd button "LofC"
Font: Helvetica  Size: 9  Style: bold  Align: center
Rect: 370,42,399,57  Loc: 384,49  Visible: true  Style: transparent
Icon: 0  Hilite: false  Autohilite: true  Showname: true
******************************************************************************
on mouseUp
  answer "Sort by Library of Congress Card Catalog # ?" ¬
  with "Cancel" or "OK"
  if it is "Cancel" then exit mouseUp
  sort by field "LOfC"
end mouseUp


******************************************************************************
bkgnd button "Author"
Font: Helvetica  Size: 9  Style: bold  Align: center
Rect: 8,61,47,75  Loc: 27,68  Visible: true  Style: transparent
Icon: 0  Hilite: false  Autohilite: true  Showname: true
******************************************************************************
on mouseUp
  answer "Sort by Author?" with "Cancel" or "OK"
  if it is "Cancel" then exit mouseUp
  sort by field "Author"
end mouseUp


******************************************************************************
bkgnd button "Title"
Font: Helvetica  Size: 9  Style: bold  Align: center
Rect: 7,121,33,137  Loc: 20,129  Visible: true  Style: transparent
Icon: 0  Hilite: false  Autohilite: true  Showname: true
******************************************************************************
on mouseUp
  answer "Sort by Title?" with "Cancel" or "OK"
  if it is "Cancel" then exit mouseUp
  sort by field "Title"
end mouseUp


******************************************************************************
bkgnd button "Subject"
Font: Helvetica  Size: 9  Style: bold  Align: center
Rect: 253,63,296,79  Loc: 274,71  Visible: true  Style: transparent
Icon: 0  Hilite: false  Autohilite: true  Showname: true
******************************************************************************
on mouseUp
  answer "Sort by Subject?" with "Cancel" or "OK"
  if it is "Cancel" then exit mouseUp
  sort by field "Subject"
end mouseUp
```

```
****************************************************************************
bkgnd button "Edition"
Font: Helvetica  Size: 9  Style: bold  Align: center
Rect: 21,219,63,234  Loc: 42,226  Visible: true  Style: transparent
Icon: 0  Hilite: false  Autohilite: true  Showname: true
****************************************************************************
on mouseUp
  answer "Sort by Edition" with "Cancel" or "First" or "Current"
  if it is "Cancel" then exit mouseUp
  if it is "First" then sort numeric by item 1 of field "Edition"
  if it is "Current" then sort numeric by last item of field "Edition"
end mouseUp


****************************************************************************
bkgnd button "Value"
Font: Helvetica  Size: 9  Style: bold  Align: center
Rect: 164,221,199,235  Loc: 181,228  Visible: true  Style: transparent
Icon: 0  Hilite: false  Autohilite: true  Showname: true
****************************************************************************
on mouseUp
  answer "Sort by current Value ?" with "Cancel" or "OK"
  if it is "Cancel" then exit mouseUp
  sort descending numeric by field "Value"
end mouseUp


****************************************************************************
bkgnd button "Publisher"
Font: Helvetica  Size: 9  Style: bold  Align: center
Rect: 7,185,63,201  Loc: 35,193  Visible: true  Style: transparent
Icon: 0  Hilite: false  Autohilite: true  Showname: true
****************************************************************************
on mouseUp
  answer "Sort by Publisher?" with "Cancel" or "OK"
  if it is "Cancel" then exit mouseUp
  sort by field "Publisher"
end mouseUp


****************************************************************************
bkgnd button "Location"
Font: Helvetica  Size: 9  Style: bold  Align: center
Rect: 13,202,63,218  Loc: 38,210  Visible: true  Style: transparent
Icon: 0  Hilite: false  Autohilite: true  Showname: true
****************************************************************************
on mouseUp
  answer "Sort by Location?" with "Cancel" or "OK"
  if it is "Cancel" then exit mouseUp
  sort by field "Location"
end mouseUp
```

```
*************************************************************************
bkgnd button "First"
Font: Chicago  Size: 12  Style: plain  Align: center
Rect: 45,30,70,55  Loc: 57,42  Visible: true  Style: transparent
Icon: 30557  Hilite: false  Autohilite: false  Showname: false
*************************************************************************
on mouseUp
  if the cmdKey is down then
    set cursor to watch
    set lockScreen to true
    show all cards -- prewarm
  end if
  go first card
end mouseUp


*************************************************************************
bkgnd button "Last"
Font: Chicago  Size: 12  Style: plain  Align: center
Rect: 116,30,142,55  Loc: 129,42  Visible: true  Style: transparent
Icon: 26865  Hilite: false  Autohilite: false  Showname: false
*************************************************************************
on mouseUp
  if the cmdKey is down then show cards
  go last card
end mouseUp


*************************************************************************
bkgnd button "DoMsgBox"
Font: Chicago  Size: 12  Style: plain  Align: center
Rect: 0,294,512,342  Loc: 256,318  Visible: true  Style: transparent
Icon: 0  Hilite: false  Autohilite: false  Showname: false
*************************************************************************
on mouseUp
  set lockScreen to true
  go next
  do msg box
  if the result is "not found" then go prev
  else unlock screen with dissolve fast
end mouseUp


*************************************************************************
bkgnd button id 69
Font: Chicago  Size: 12  Style: plain  Align: center
Rect: 146,25,185,59  Loc: 165,42  Visible: true  Style: transparent
Icon: 20186  Hilite: false  Autohilite: true  Showname: false
*************************************************************************
on mouseUp
  visual barn door close fast to gray
  visual barn door open fast to card
  go any card
end mouseUp
```

```
*************************************************************************
bkgnd button id 80
Font: Chicago  Size: 12  Style: plain  Align: center
Rect: 225,26,264,59  Loc: 244,42  Visible: true  Style: transparent
Icon: 12121  Hilite: false  Autohilite: false  Showname: false
*************************************************************************
on mouseUp
  answer "Compute total value of books:" ¬
  with "All" or "Criteria" or "Cancel"
  if it is "Criteria" then
    ask "Total the values of cards with this text: "
    if it is empty then exit mouseUp
    GetStats it
  else if it is "All" then
    push this card
    set lockScreen to true
    go first
    put 0 into total
    repeat for the number of cards
      add line 1 of field "Value" to total
      go next
      set cursor to busy
    end repeat
    pop card
    set numberFormat to "0.00"
    answer "Total value = $" & total with "OK"
  end if
end mouseUp
```

```
*************************************************************************
bkgnd button "Bibliography"
Font: Chicago  Size: 12  Style: plain  Align: center
Rect: 295,25,326,59  Loc: 310,42  Visible: true  Style: transparent
Icon: 16566  Hilite: false  Autohilite: true  Showname: false
*************************************************************************
on mouseUp
  put the short name of this stack & ".wd" into defaultName
  ask "Write RTF bibliography to file:" with defaultName
  if it is empty then exit mouseUp
  put it into fileName
  open file fileName
  go to first card
  lock screen
  write RTFHeader() to file fileName
  repeat for the number of cards
    get field "Dewey"
    if it < 2 or (it >=4 and it < 7) or (it >= 510 and it < 520) then
      write authors() & title() to file fileName
      write field "subject" && "\par" & return to file fileName
    end if
    go to next card
    set cursor to busy
  end repeat
  write "}" to file fileName -- RTF end
  close file fileName
  SetCreator fileName,"MSWD"
end mouseUp


function RTFHeader -- Microsoft's Rich Text Format
  -- write version number, font info, AW book format
  return "{\rtf0\mac {\fonttbl{\f4\fmodern Monaco;}" &¬
  "{\f20\froman Times;}{\f21\fswiss Helvetica;}" &¬
  "{\f22\fmodern Courier;}{\f23ftech Symbol;}}" &¬
  "{\stylesheet{\qj\fi-540\li540\sl240 \f20\fs20 " &¬
  "\sbasedon222\snext0 Normal;}}" &¬
  "\margl2347\margr2347\margt2707\margb2707" &¬
  "\facingp\gutter907" &¬
  "\pard\plain\qj\fi-540\li540\sl240 \f20\fs20 "
end RTFHeader
```

```
function authors
  get line 1 of field "Author"
  repeat with i = 2 to 3
    if line i of field "Author" = empty then exit repeat
    put the number of items of line i of field "Author" into num
    put ", " after it
    if num = 1 then put line i of field "Author" after it
    if num = 2 then
      put item 2 of line i of field "Author" && item 1 of line i¬
      of field "Author" after it
    end if
  end repeat
  if last char of it ≠ "." then put "." after it
  return it && " "
end authors

function title
  return "{\i" && line 1 of field "title" & "}." &&¬
  item 1 of line 1 of field "location" & ":" &&¬
  line 1 of field "Publisher" & "," &&¬
  line 1 of field "Edition" & ".  "
end title

*************************************************************************
bkgnd button "Export MPW"
Font: Chicago  Size: 12  Style: plain  Align: center
Rect: 328,25,358,60  Loc: 343,42  Visible: true  Style: transparent
Icon: 11044  Hilite: false  Autohilite: true  Showname: false
*************************************************************************
on mouseUp
  put the short name of this stack & ".tx" into defaultName
  ask "Export text to MPW:" with defaultName
  if it is empty then exit mouseUp
  put it into fileName
  answer "How much information should be exported ?" ¬
  with "All" or "Basic" or "Cancel"
  if it is "Cancel" then exit mouseUp
  if it is "All" then put true into flag else put false into flag
  open file fileName
  go to first card
  set lockScreen to true
```

```
    if flag then
      repeat for the number of cards
        put empty into temp
        repeat with i = 1 to the number of fields
          put field i & tab after temp
        end repeat
        put replace(return,space,temp) into it
        put return into last char of it
        write it to file fileName
        go to next card
        set cursor to busy
      end repeat
    else
      repeat for the number of cards
        write line 1 of field "dewey" & tab &¬
        line 1 of field "author" & tab &¬
        line 1 of field "title" & tab &¬
        line 1 of field "subject" & return to file fileName
        go to next card
        set cursor to busy
      end repeat
    end if
    close file fileName
    SetCreator fileName,"MPS "
end mouseUp
```

```
*************************************************************************
bkgnd button "Misc"
Font: Helvetica  Size: 9  Style: bold  Align: center
Rect: 8,247,34,260  Loc: 21,253  Visible: true  Style: transparent
Icon: 0  Hilite: false  Autohilite: true  Showname: true
*************************************************************************
```

```
*************************************************************************
bkgnd button "Sort Stack"
Font: Chicago  Size: 12  Style: plain  Align: center
Rect: 186,25,224,59  Loc: 205,42  Visible: true  Style: transparent
Icon: 11716  Hilite: false  Autohilite: false  Showname: false
*************************************************************************
on mouseUp
  answer "Compact stack:" ¬
  with "Cancel" or "Compact" or "& Sort"
  if it is "Cancel" then exit mouseUp
  push card
  if it contains "&" then sort numeric by field "Dewey"
  pop card
  doMenu "Compact Stack"
end mouseUp
```

```
****************************************************************************
bkgnd field "Author"
Font: Times  Size: 12  Style: bold,condense  Align: left
Rect: 7,73,247,118  Loc: 127,95  Visible: true  Style: transparent
Locktext: false  Showlines: true  Widemargins: false
****************************************************************************


****************************************************************************
bkgnd field "Title"
Font: Times  Size: 12  Style: bold,condense  Align: left
Rect: 7,134,247,179  Loc: 127,156  Visible: true  Style: transparent
Locktext: false  Showlines: true  Widemargins: false
****************************************************************************
on closeField
  repeat
    get offset(return,me)
    if it > 0 then put space into char it of me
    else exit repeat
  end repeat
  repeat
    if last char of me is space or last char of me is return
    then delete last char of me
    else exit repeat
  end repeat
end closeField

****************************************************************************
bkgnd field "Publisher"
Font: Times  Size: 10  Style: plain  Align: left
Rect: 66,185,247,201  Loc: 156,193  Visible: true  Style: transparent
Locktext: false  Showlines: true  Widemargins: false
****************************************************************************


****************************************************************************
bkgnd field "Location"
Font: Times  Size: 10  Style: plain  Align: left
Rect: 66,203,247,219  Loc: 156,211  Visible: true  Style: transparent
Locktext: false  Showlines: true  Widemargins: false
****************************************************************************


****************************************************************************
bkgnd field "Edition"
Font: Times  Size: 10  Style: plain  Align: left
Rect: 66,221,154,236  Loc: 110,228  Visible: true  Style: transparent
Locktext: false  Showlines: true  Widemargins: false
****************************************************************************
```

```
****************************************************************************
bkgnd field "Value"
Font: Times  Size: 10  Style: plain  Align: center
Rect: 203,221,247,237  Loc: 225,229  Visible: true  Style: transparent
Locktext: false  Showlines: true  Widemargins: false
****************************************************************************


****************************************************************************
bkgnd field "Misc"
Font: Times  Size: 10  Style: plain  Align: left
Rect: 34,246,247,288  Loc: 140,267  Visible: true  Style: transparent
Locktext: false  Showlines: true  Widemargins: false
****************************************************************************


****************************************************************************
bkgnd field "Dewey"
Font: Times  Size: 10  Style: plain  Align: left
Rect: 399,25,507,41  Loc: 453,33  Visible: true  Style: transparent
Locktext: false  Showlines: true  Widemargins: false
****************************************************************************


****************************************************************************
bkgnd field "LofC"
Font: Times  Size: 10  Style: plain  Align: left
Rect: 399,41,507,57  Loc: 453,49  Visible: true  Style: transparent
Locktext: false  Showlines: true  Widemargins: false
****************************************************************************


****************************************************************************
bkgnd field "Subject"
Font: Times  Size: 10  Style: plain  Align: left
Rect: 253,78,506,286  Loc: 379,182  Visible: true  Style: transparent
Locktext: false  Showlines: true  Widemargins: false
****************************************************************************
on closeField
  repeat
    get offset(return,me)
    if it > 0 then put space into char it of me
    else exit repeat
  end repeat
  repeat
    if last char of me is space or last char of me is return
    then delete last char of me
    else exit repeat
  end repeat
end closeField
```

External Commands and Functions (XCMDs)

When HyperTalk runs out of speed or functionality, a couple of trap doors can be used: XCMDs and XFCNs. An XCMD or XFCN is compiled code, and writing such code is a task for programmers, *not* for end users. The only difference between an XFCN and an XCMD is that an XFCN returns a result. This difference is much like the difference between a procedure and a function in Pascal. We refer to them collectively as XCMDs for the sake of convenience. If you use MPW, you can write XCMDs in assembly language, C, or Pascal.

Anyone competent with HyperTalk can easily use an XCMD once it is written. XCMDs are called as if they were built-in HyperTalk commands; they are invoked by HyperTalk through its inheritance mechanism. As a message ascends the hierarchy, the resource forks of several files (the script's stack, the current stack, the home stack, and HyperCard) are checked to see if they have an XCMD or XFCN resource of that name to handle the message. If the appropriate resource name is found, the resource is loaded into memory and HyperCard jumps to the start of it. After the XCMD has executed, control returns to HyperCard.

XCMDs can be installed and moved between files easily with ResEdit, or better yet, with ResCopy, which itself is an XCMD. ResCopy, written by Steve Maller, imitates the Font/DA Mover interface for moving resources between stacks.

Several different reasons exist for using an XCMD:

- As an interface to drivers, thus allowing HyperCard to control external devices, such as video disk players and CD-ROM drives
- As a means of accessing the Macintosh OS and Toolbox routines
- As a means of accessing some of HyperCard's own internal routines
- As a means of speeding up execution of time-critical code

XCMDs and Drivers

HyperCard has an outstanding user interface. It is easy to use and especially amiable to customization. HyperCard is therefore a great "front end" for the Macintosh to talk to other devices.

An example of using HyperCard in this manner is hooking up a video disk player to a Macintosh. A video disk player can be easily controlled through the built-in RS-232 ports of the Mac. XCMDs can be the glue that cements together the video disk player and HyperCard.

In this example, three pieces of code would need to be written. The driver for the video disk player would be a standard Macintosh driver, which really knows nothing about HyperCard. These specialized pieces of code have been around since the beginning of Macintosh, and many people have become proficient in writing drivers because desk accessory is a driver. For more information on writing drivers, see *Inside Macintosh*, Volume II, Chapter 6.

The second piece of code is the XCMD. It would be small, and its purpose would be simply to convert HyperTalk messages to the appropriate driver calls.

The third piece of code would be the HyperTalk scripts that call the XCMD with various parameters, asking it to ask the driver to ask the laser disk player to go to a certain frame, or to back up, or whatever.

Using XCMDs as an interface to traditional drivers is a simple but powerful proposition. If an XCMD gets too big, think about writing a driver.

XCMDs and the Toolbox

HyperTalk embodies a lot of functionality, but if you need something it does not have, the Macintosh OS and Toolbox might have it. Indeed, Macintosh programming sometimes seems like an endless series of calls to the Mac ROMs.

Most Toolbox traps and routines can be called from XCMDs, with certain restrictions and limitations, which are outlined below. Such routines are not allowed to do everything that an application is allowed to do, as they are guests in HyperCard's heap. XCMDs are more like desk accessories than applications in this regard.

Here are a few guidelines for writings XCMDs:

- Do not initialize any of the Macintosh managers by calling their init traps—that is, do not call `InitGraf`, `InitFonts`, `InitWindows`, etc.

- Do not assume that you will have lots of memory available for your code. There is some extra space in HyperCard's heap, but if HyperCard is running in 750K under MultiFinder, for example, your XCMDs should not be bigger than about 32K each.

- Do not use register A5 of the 68xxx processor. The value in A5 is HyperCard's and points to HyperCard's global data, jump table, and other things that constitute an A5 World. XCMDs do not currently have their own A5 World.

- No A5 World means no global data for XCMDs.

- No global data means no use of string literals with MPW C, as MPW C makes string literals into global data. (To work around this problem, use STR resources or put the strings in a short assembly glue file.)

- No A5 World means no jump table. No jump table means no code segments. No code segments means a 32K limit on code size for 68000-based machines. (The 68020 supports longer branches.)

- XCMDs can, however, allocate small chunks of memory using standard calls to `NewHandle` (and if you really must do it, `NewPtr`).

- If your code allocated some memory in the heap, it must deallocate the memory. HyperCard does not automatically clean up after an XCMD like the MPW Shell does with its tools.

- If your XCMD allocates a handle to save state information between invocations of the XCMD, you must also use HyperTalk to store the handle somewhere in the current stack, perhaps in a hidden field. You will need to convert the handle from a `LongInt` to a string because everything is treated as a string on the HyperTalk end of things.

- Because HyperTalk blindly jumps to the start of an XCMD piece of code, it is important that the `main` routine actually ends up at the start of the XCMD. Thus, the link order is very important.

XCMDs and HyperTalk Callback Routines

HyperTalk allows XCMDs to call many useful internal routines, both conversion routines and stack access routines. The header files and sources for the library that is used to access the callback routines can be found in chapter 6, which discusses MPW.

The conversion routines provide support for converting among various styles of strings and numbers. For example, there are routines to convert C-style strings (zero-terminated) to Pascal-style strings (length byte followed by string) and back again. There are also routines to convert strings to integers and vice versa. The stack access routines allow an XCMD to call back into HyperTalk and send messages to the current card or to HyperCard itself. In addition, you can recall and store values of variables, and contents of fields can be examined.

`Make` — Shell Script

The following MPW Shell script imitates the action of the `Make` tool, with the restriction that only one make target file can be given to it at a time. This Makefile will build all of the XCMDs and XFCNs given in the remainder of this chapter; you can extend it easily to build your own XCMDs.

The reason that the `Make` tool cannot be used for this purpose is that XCMDs each have a unique resource ID that must be incorporated into the build instructions, and the `Make` tool has no easy facility to assign IDs generically when the default build rules are used. To solve this problem, we wrote our own customized Make script using MPW's Shell language. MPW usually looks in the current directory before using its search paths, so whenever this file—named `Make`—exists in the folder containing XCMD sources, it will be called instead of the `Make` tool.

This script works with both C and Pascal source code. The major shortcoming of the script is that each XCMD needs to be "registered" by name so that resource IDs do not collide, a problem attributable to the Resource Manager.

To use this script to build the `replace.c` and `strip.p` XFCNs, for example, just type the following line:

```
make replace.c strip.p
```

Next, select the resulting output lines and press Enter.

```
# Make, a build script for XCMDs
# Written by Dan Allen 10/14/88

Set Dest      "{SystemFolder}Home"       # Location of stack to build XCMDs into
Set Debug     '-mbg off'                  # Or your favorite incantation
Set Libs      "{Libraries}HyperXLib.o {Libraries}Interface.o "

If {1} =~ /cprint.≈/
    Set 2 'XCMD=12'
Else If {1} =~ /NthFileName.≈/
    Set 2 'XFCN=9'
Else If {1} =~ /Replace.≈/
    Set 2 'XFCN=11'
Else If {1} =~ /DateDMY.≈/
    Set 2 'XFCN=71'
Else If {1} =~ /SetCreator.≈/
    Set 2 'XCMD=9'
Else If {1} =~ /Strip.≈/
    Set 2 'XFCN=12'
End

If {1} =~ /(≈)®1.p/
    Set Lang Pascal
    Set LOpts "-w -rt {2} -m ENTRYPOINT -sg {®1}"
    Set Libs "{Libs} {PLibraries}PasLib.o"
Else If {1} =~ /(≈)®1.c/
    Set Lang C
    Set LOpts "-w -rt {2} -m ENTRYPOINT -sg {®1}"
    Set Libs "{Libs} {CLibraries}CRuntime.o"
Else
    Alert "Only C and Pascal sources are currently allowed."
    Exit 1
End

If `Newer {1} {1}.o`         # This is the "Make-like" line
    Echo {Lang} {1} {Debug}
End

Echo Link  {LOpts} -o {Dest} {1}.o {Libs}
```

NthFileName — C XFCN

This XFCN will return the name of the *N*th file in a specified directory. By repeatedly calling this, you can enumerate all of the files in a given directory. Asking for the name of the zeroth file will return the number of files in the directory. This XFCN is useful for importing multiple text files into HyperCard. It is used, for example, in the CInterfaces stack described earlier.

The build information is in the Makefile given previously; a Pascal version follows this C version.

```
/*
 *  NthFileName.c - A HyperCard XFCN to return the Nth file in a directory
 *                - Written by Dan Allen 7/20/88
 *                - Fully MPW 3.0 compatible
 *
 */

#include <Types.h>
#include <Memory.h>
#include <Files.h>
#include <HyperXCmd.h>

pascal void EntryPoint(XCmdPtr paramPtr)
{
  char          *p,*q,str[256];
  short         err;
  long          n;
  Handle        h;
  CInfoPBRec    pbRec;
  ParamBlockRec pbVol;

  if (paramPtr->paramCount != 2) return;
  ZeroToPas(paramPtr,*(paramPtr->params[0]),str); /* a callback to HC */
  pbVol.volumeParam.ioNamePtr = str;
  pbVol.volumeParam.ioVolIndex = -1;
  pbVol.volumeParam.ioVRefNum = 0x8000;
  pbVol.volumeParam.ioCompletion = nil;
  err = PBGetVInfo(&pbVol,false);

  ZeroToPas(paramPtr,*(paramPtr->params[0]),str);
  pbRec.dirInfo.ioNamePtr = str;
  pbRec.dirInfo.ioFDirIndex = 0;
  pbRec.dirInfo.ioDrDirID = 0;
  pbRec.dirInfo.ioCompletion = nil;
  pbRec.dirInfo.ioVRefNum = err ? 0 : pbVol.volumeParam.ioVRefNum;
  err = PBGetCatInfo(&pbRec,false);
  if(err) return;
```

```
ZeroToPas(paramPtr,*(paramPtr->params[1]),str);
n = StrToNum(paramPtr,str);
if (!n) {
  NumToStr(paramPtr,pbRec.dirInfo.ioDrNmFls,str);
  paramPtr->returnValue = PasToZero(paramPtr,str);
  return;
}
pbRec.dirInfo.ioFDirIndex = n;
pbRec.dirInfo.ioCompletion = nil;
err = PBGetCatInfo(&pbRec,false);
if(err) return;

n = pbRec.dirInfo.ioNamePtr[0];
p = &(pbRec.dirInfo.ioNamePtr[1]);
h = NewHandle(n+3);
if (h) q = *h; else return;

if(pbRec.dirInfo.ioFlAttrib & 0x10) *q++ = ':';
while (n--) *q++ = *p++;
if(pbRec.dirInfo.ioFlAttrib & 0x10) *q++ = ':';
*q = '\0';

paramPtr->returnValue = h;
return;
}
```

NthFileName — Pascal XFCN

```
(*
 *  NthFileName.p - A HyperCard XFCN to return the Nth file in a directory
 *                - Written by Dan Allen 7/20/88
 *                - Fully MPW 3.0 compatible
 *)

{$R-}
{$Z+}

UNIT DummyUnit;

INTERFACE

USES MemTypes, QuickDraw, OSIntf, ToolIntf, HyperXCmd;

IMPLEMENTATION
```

```
PROCEDURE EntryPoint(paramPtr: XCmdPtr);
VAR
  err:        OSErr;
  n:          LongInt;
  str:        Str255;
  pbRec:      CInfoPBRec;
  pbVol:      ParamBlockRec;
BEGIN
  WITH paramPtr^ DO
    BEGIN
      IF paramCount <> 2 THEN
        BEGIN
          returnValue := '';
          EXIT(EntryPoint);
        END;

      ZeroToPas(paramPtr,params[1]^,str);
      WITH pbVol DO
        BEGIN
          ioNamePtr := @str;
          ioVolIndex := -1;
          ioVRefNum := $8000;              { illegal vRefNum }
          ioCompletion := nil;
        END;
      err := PBGetVInfo(@pbVol,FALSE);     { in order to get vRefNum }

      ZeroToPas(paramPtr,params[1]^,str); { get pathname again }
      WITH pbRec DO
        BEGIN
          ioNamePtr := @str;
          ioFDirIndex := 0;
          ioDirID := 0;
          ioCompletion := nil;
          IF err = 0
          THEN ioVRefNum := pbVol.ioVRefNum
          ELSE ioVRefNum := 0;             { default volume }
        END;
      err := PBGetCatInfo(@pbRec,FALSE);  { in order to get dirID }
      IF err <> 0 THEN
        BEGIN
          NumToStr(paramPtr,err,str);
          returnValue := PasToZero(paramPtr,Concat('Error:: Bad path; #',str));
          EXIT(EntryPoint);
        END;
```

```
      ZeroToPas(paramPtr,params[2]^,str);
      n := StrToNum(paramPtr,str);
      IF n = 0 THEN
        BEGIN
          NumToStr(paramPtr,pbRec.ioDrNmFls,str);
          returnValue := PasToZero(paramPtr,str);
          EXIT(EntryPoint);
        END;

      WITH pbRec DO
        BEGIN
          ioFDirIndex := n;
          ioCompletion := nil;
        END;
      err := PBGetCatInfo(@pbRec,FALSE);   { to get Nth file/dir Name }
      IF err <> 0 THEN
        BEGIN
          NumToStr(paramPtr,err,str);
          returnValue := PasToZero(paramPtr,Concat('Error:: Bad info; #',str));
          EXIT(EntryPoint);
        END;

      n := Ptr(pbRec.ioNamePtr)^;
      BlockMove(Pointer(pbRec.ioNamePtr),@str,n+1); { copy to str }
      IF BitTst(@pbRec.ioFlAttrib,3) THEN str := Concat(':',str,':');
      returnValue := PasToZero(paramPtr,str);
    END;
END;

END.
```

SetCreator — C XCMD

This XCMD is simple: it sets the file creator of a given file to whatever you wish. A list of popular file types and creators can be found in chapter 4. HyperTalk can write only files of type TEXT, so a SetFileType command is rarely needed. Here is the C version, followed by a Pascal version:

```c
/*
 *  SetCreator.c  - A HyperCard XCMD to set the file creator
 *                - Written by Dan Allen 10/16/88
 *                - MPW 3.0 compatible 10/19/88
 *
 */

#include <Types.h>
#include <Files.h>
#include <HyperXCmd.h>

pascal void EntryPoint(XCmdPtr paramPtr)
{
    char            str[256];
    short           err;
    OSType          rt;
    ParamBlockRec pb;

    if (paramPtr->paramCount != 2) return;

    ZeroToPas(paramPtr,*(paramPtr->params[0]),str);
    rt = *( (OSType *) *(paramPtr->params[1]));
    pb.fileParam.ioNamePtr = str;
    pb.fileParam.ioFDirIndex = 0;
    pb.fileParam.ioVRefNum = 0;
    pb.fileParam.ioCompletion = nil;
    err = PBGetFInfo(&pb,false);

    pb.fileParam.ioFlFndrInfo.fdCreator = rt;
    err = PBSetFInfo(&pb,false);
    return;
}
```

SetCreator — Pascal XCMD

```
(*
 *  SetCreator.p  - A HyperCard XCMD to set the file creator
 *                - Written by Dan Allen 10/16/88
 *                - MPW 3.0 compatible 10/19/88
 *
 *)

{$R-}
{$Z+}

UNIT DummyUnit;

INTERFACE

USES MemTypes, QuickDraw, OSIntf, HyperXCmd;

IMPLEMENTATION

PROCEDURE EntryPoint(paramPtr: XCmdPtr);
TYPE
  OSPtr = ^OSType;
VAR
  str:    Str255;
  err:    OSErr;
  rt:     OSType;
  pb:     ParamBlockRec;
BEGIN
  WITH paramPtr^ DO
    BEGIN
      IF paramCount <> 2 THEN EXIT(EntryPoint);
      ZeroToPas(paramPtr,params[1]^,str);
      rt := OSPtr(params[2]^)^;
      pb.ioNamePtr := @str;
      pb.ioFDirIndex := 0;
      pb.ioVRefNum := 0;
      pb.ioCompletion := NIL;
      err := PBGetFInfo(@pb,FALSE);
      pb.ioFlFndrInfo.fdCreator := rt;
      err := PBSetFInfo(@pb,FALSE);
    END;
END;

END.
```

Strip — C XFCN

This XFCN is useful for importing into HyperCard text that contains runs of spaces and tabs. Strip replaces such a sequence of characters with a single space. (Tabs are deleted by HyperCard as a field containing them is edited.) Again, C and Pascal versions are presented.

```c
/*
 *  Strip - XFCN to reduce runs of spaces and tabs to a space
 *        - Written by Dan Allen in MPW C 10/19/88
 *        - Fully MPW 3.0 compatible 10/19/88
 *
 *  Sample HyperTalk line:
 *
 *  put strip(field 1) into field 1 -- reduce tabs & spaces
 *
 */

#include <HyperXCmd.h>
#include <Memory.h>
#include <Types.h>

pascal void MoveHHiTrap(Handle h) = { 0x205F, 0xA064 };

pascal void EntryPoint(XCmdPtr paramPtr)
{
  char    *p,*q;
  Handle  h;

  if(paramPtr->paramCount != 1) return;
  MoveHHiTrap(paramPtr->params[0]);
  h = NewHandle(GetHandleSize(paramPtr->params[0]));
  if (!h) return;
  p = *(paramPtr->params[0]);
  q = *h;
  while(*p) {
    if (*p == '\t' || *p == ' ') {
      do
        p++;
      while (*p == '\t' || *p == ' ');
      *q++ = ' ';
    } else
      *q++ = *p++;
  }
  *q = '\0';
  paramPtr->returnValue = h;
}
```

Strip — Pascal XFCN

```
(*
 *   Strip - XFCN to reduce runs of spaces and tabs to a space
 *        - Written by Dan Allen in MPW Pascal 10/19/88
 *        - Fully MPW 3.0 compatible 10/19/88
 *
 *   Sample HyperTalk line:
 *
 *   put strip(field 1) into field 1 -- reduce tabs & spaces
 *
 *)

{$R-}
{$Z+}

UNIT DummyUnit;

INTERFACE

USES MemTypes, QuickDraw, OSIntf, HyperXCmd;

IMPLEMENTATION

PROCEDURE MoveHHiTrap(h: Handle); INLINE $205F, $A064;

PROCEDURE EntryPoint(paramPtr: XCmdPtr);
CONST
  tab = 9;
  space = 32;
VAR
  h:     Handle;
  p,q:   Ptr;
BEGIN
  WITH paramPtr^ DO
    BEGIN
      IF paramCount <> 1 THEN EXIT(EntryPoint);
      MoveHHiTrap(params[1]);
      h := NewHandle(GetHandleSize(params[1]));
      IF h = NIL THEN EXIT(EntryPoint);
      p := params[1]^;
      q := h^;
      WHILE p^ <> 0 DO
        IF (p^ = tab) OR (p^ = space) THEN
          BEGIN
            REPEAT
              p := POINTER(ORD(p)+1);
            UNTIL (p^ <> tab) AND (p^ <> space);
            q^ := space;
            q := Pointer(ORD(q)+1);
          END
```

```
         ELSE
           BEGIN
             q^ := p^;
             p := POINTER(ORD(p)+1);
             q := Pointer(ORD(q)+1);
           END;
         q^ := 0;
         returnValue := h;
      END; { with }
END; { procedure }
END. { unit }
```

Replace — C XFCN

Replace is yet another XCMD that allows text to be imported and exported cleanly. For example, text downloaded from Usenet contains a carriage return character at the end of every line. In order to transfer such text into HyperCard nicely, you can call Replace(return,space,the selection) on a paragraph of selected text; this will allow TextEdit to treat the text as a single line, doing appropriate word wrap, rather than as a bunch of lines. Again, C and Pascal versions are presented.

```
/*
 *   Replace - XFCN to replace any char by any other char
 *           - Written by Dan Allen in MPW Pascal 7/20/88
 *           - Rewritten in C/Asm 9/22/88
 *           - Fully MPW 3.0 compatible 10/19/88
 *
 *   Sample HyperTalk lines:
 *
 *   put replace(tab,space,field 1) into field 1 -- change tabs to spaces
 *   put replace("®",empty,it) -- delegalize the container it
 *
 */

#include <Types.h>
#include <Memory.h>
#include <HyperXCmd.h>

pascal void MoveHHiTrap(Handle h) = { 0x205F, 0xA064 };

pascal void EntryPoint(XCmdPtr paramPtr)
{
   char    a,b,*p,*q;
   Handle  h;
```

```
  if(paramPtr->paramCount != 3) return;
  a = **(paramPtr->params[0]);
  b = **(paramPtr->params[1]);
  MoveHHiTrap(paramPtr->params[2]);
  h = NewHandle(GetHandleSize(paramPtr->params[2]));
  if (!h) return;
  p = *(paramPtr->params[2]);
  q = *h;
  while(*p) {
    *q = (*p == a) ? b : *p;
    p++; if (*q) q++;
  }
  *q = '\0';
  paramPtr->returnValue = h;
}
```

Replace — Pascal XFCN

```
(*
 *  Replace - XFCN to replace any char by any other char
 *          - Written by Dan Allen 7/20/88
 *          - Fully MPW 3.0 compatible 10/19/88
 *
 *  Sample HyperTalk lines:
 *
 *    put replace(tab,space,field 1) into field 1 -- replace all tabs w/spaces
 *    put replace("®",empty,it) -- delegalize the container it
 *
 *)

{$R-}
{$Z+}

UNIT DummyUnit;

INTERFACE

USES MemTypes, QuickDraw, OSIntf, HyperXCmd;

IMPLEMENTATION

PROCEDURE MoveHHiTrap(h: Handle); INLINE $205F, $A064;
```

```
PROCEDURE EntryPoint(paramPtr: XCmdPtr);
VAR a,b:   SignedByte;
    h:     Handle;
    p,q:   Ptr;
BEGIN
  WITH paramPtr^ DO
    BEGIN
      IF paramCount <> 3 THEN EXIT(EntryPoint);
      a := params[1]^^;
      b := params[2]^^;
      MoveHHiTrap(params[3]);
      h := NewHandle(GetHandleSize(params[3]));
      IF h = NIL THEN EXIT(EntryPoint);
      p := params[3]^;
      q := h^;
      WHILE p^ <> 0 DO
        BEGIN
          IF p^ = a THEN q^ := b ELSE q^ := p^;
          p := Pointer(ORD(p)+1);
          IF q^ <> 0 THEN q := Pointer(ORD(q)+1);
        END;
      q^ := 0;
      returnValue := h;
    END; { with }
END; { procedure }
END. { unit }
```

CPrint — C XCMD

CPrint stands for "container print." It allows you to print a scrolling field's contents, or perhaps the contents of a large HyperTalk variable. CPrint allows a choice of fonts, sizes, line heights, and optionally will put up the standard print dialogs. This XCMD is given here only in C.

CPrint takes advantage of HyperTalk's ability to accept a variable number of parameters. Given only the actual text to print, this XCMD uses Times 12, automatically computing the line height to use. If more options are given, they override the defaults. This XCMD is optimized for LaserWriter use, so some of these defaults should be changed for ImageWriter use.

```
/*
 *   CPrint.c  - XCMD to print any container
 *             - Written by Dan Allen in MPW C 10/1/88
 *             - MPW 3.0 compatible 10/19/88
 *             - added dialog flag 3/3/89
 *
 *   Sample HyperTalk lines:
 *
 *   CPrint it -- Prints the container "it" in the default of Times 12
 *   CPrint field "foo",21,9,11 -- Prints field in Helvetica 9 on 11 pt spacing
 *
 */

#include <HyperXCmd.h>
#include <Memory.h>
#include <PrintTraps.h>
#include <TextEdit.h>
#include <Types.h>

pascal void MoveHHiTrap(Handle h) = { 0x205F, 0xA064 };

pascal void EntryPoint(XCmdPtr paramPtr)
{
  char       dialogFlag;
  short      fontNum,fontSize,lnHt,lines,lpp,pgHt,pages;
  long       size;
  TEPtr      tep;
  TEHandle   te;
  THPrint    h;
  TPPrPort   pp;
  TPrStatus  status;
  Rect       rect;
  Str31      str;

  InitCursor();
  if (paramPtr->paramCount < 1) return;
  MoveHHiTrap(paramPtr->params[0]);
  HLock(paramPtr->params[0]);

  if (paramPtr->paramCount >= 2) {
    ZeroToPas(paramPtr,*(paramPtr->params[1]),str);
    fontNum = StrToNum(paramPtr,str);
  } else fontNum = 20;

  if (paramPtr->paramCount >= 3) {
    ZeroToPas(paramPtr,*(paramPtr->params[2]),str);
    fontSize = StrToNum(paramPtr,str);
  } else fontSize = 12;
```

```
if (paramPtr->paramCount >= 4) {
  ZeroToPas(paramPtr,*(paramPtr->params[3]),str);
  lnHt = StrToNum(paramPtr,str);
} else lnHt = fontSize + fontSize/3;
if (lnHt < fontSize) lnHt = fontSize;

dialogFlag = (paramPtr->paramCount == 5) ? 1 : 0;
size = StringLength(paramPtr,*(paramPtr->params[0]));
if (size > 32765) return;

h = (THPrint) NewHandle(sizeof(TPrint));
if (!h) return;
PrOpen();
PrintDefault(h);
if (!dialogFlag || PrStlDialog(h) && PrJobDialog(h)) {
  rect = (**h).rPaper;
  InsetRect(&rect,72,72);
  pgHt = (rect.bottom - rect.top);
  lpp = pgHt/lnHt;
  pgHt = lpp*lnHt;
  rect.bottom = rect.top + pgHt;

  te = TENew(&rect,&rect);
  if (!te) return;
  tep = *te;
  tep->txFont = fontNum;
  tep->txSize = fontSize;
  tep->lineHeight = lnHt;
  tep->fontAscent = lnHt - lnHt/4;
  TESetText(*(paramPtr->params[0]),size,te);
  lines = (**te).nLines;
  pages = lines*lnHt/pgHt;
  if (lnHt*lines > pgHt*pages) pages++;
```

```
    pp = PrOpenDoc(h,nil,nil);
    (**te).inPort = (GrafPtr) pp;
    while (pages--) {
      PrOpenPage(pp,nil);
      TextFont(fontNum);
      TextSize(fontSize);
      TEUpdate(&rect,te);
      PrClosePage(pp);
      TEScroll(0,-pgHt,te);
    }
    PrCloseDoc(pp);
    TEDispose(te);
    if ((**h).prJob.bJDocLoop == bSpoolLoop)
      PrPicFile(h,nil,nil,nil,&status);
  }
  PrClose();
  DisposHandle((Handle) h);
  HUnlock(paramPtr->params[0]);
}
```

DateDMY — Pascal XFCN

This XFCN is provided only in Pascal. It returns the current (or specified) date in what is sometimes known as the military date format—that is, 29 Mar 1989.

```
(*
 *  DateDMY.p - A HyperCard XFCN to return the date in DD MMM YYYY format
 *            - Written by Dan Allen 8/16/88
 *            - Fully MPW 3.0 compatible
 *)

{$R-}
{$Z+}

UNIT DummyUnit;

INTERFACE

USES
  Memtypes, Quickdraw, OSIntf, HyperXCmd;

IMPLEMENTATION
```

```
PROCEDURE EntryPoint(paramPtr: XCmdPtr);
VAR
  i,secs:      LongInt;
  monthName:   STRING[3];
  str,str2:    Str255;
  date:        DateTimeRec;
BEGIN
  WITH paramPtr^ DO
    BEGIN
      IF paramCount <> 1 THEN
        GetDateTime(secs)
      ELSE
        BEGIN
          ZeroToPas(paramPtr,params[1]^,str);
          secs := StrToNum(paramPtr,str);
        END;

      Secs2Date(secs,date);
      i := date.day;
      LongToStr(paramPtr,i DIV 10,str);
      LongToStr(paramPtr,i MOD 10,str2);
      str := Concat(str,str2);

      CASE date.month OF
         1: monthName := 'Jan';
         2: monthName := 'Feb';
         3: monthName := 'Mar';
         4: monthName := 'Apr';
         5: monthName := 'May';
         6: monthName := 'Jun';
         7: monthName := 'Jul';
         8: monthName := 'Aug';
         9: monthName := 'Sep';
        10: monthName := 'Oct';
        11: monthName := 'Nov';
        12: monthName := 'Dec'
      END;
      LongToStr(paramPtr,date.year,str2);
      returnValue := PasToZero(paramPtr,Concat(str,' ',monthName,' ',str2));
    END; { with }
  END; { procedure }
END. { unit }
```

Conclusion

This chapter looked briefly at HyperCard and its object-oriented language, HyperTalk. Next, it presented a series of scripts and stacks that demonstrated various features of HyperCard and HyperTalk.

Finally, the chapter looked at how you can extend HyperTalk by writing XCMDs and XFCNs. Numerous examples were given. Although it takes a programmer to write XCMDs and XFCNs, anyone fluent in HyperTalk can use them.

Recommended Reading

As of this writing, the definitive language reference manual for HyperTalk is the Apple publication entitled the *HyperCard Script Language Guide*. This is the only one of the many books on HyperTalk that was personally reviewed by the engineers who created HyperCard and HyperTalk. (Dan Winkler and I were the main two reviewers.)

Many of the HyperTalk books on the market are worthless, but a few bear mentioning. First, there are Danny Goodman's *Complete HyperCard Handbook* and *HyperCard Developers Guide*. These books are a bit lengthy, but they are appropriate choices if you are new to scripting and XCMDs. A good introduction to XCMD writing—with lots of examples—can be found in Gary Bond's *XCMDs for HyperCard*.

My personal favorite is Lon Poole's excellent quick reference guide entitled simply *HyperTalk*, from Microsoft Press. It is small, easy to use, complete, accurate, and affordable. Once you know the basics of HyperTalk, this is the book you will use the most.

Two other books are soon to be released by the author of HyperTalk, Dan Winkler. These should become definitive works on the subject.

MACINTOSH CHARACTER SET

Decimal	Meaning	Decimal	Meaning
0	NUL - Null	16	DLE - Data Link Escape
1	SOH - Start of Heading	17	DC1 - Device Control 1
2	STX - Start of Text	18	DC2 - Device Control 2
3	ETX - End of Text	19	DC3 - Device Control 3
4	EOT - End of Transmission	20	DC4 - Device Control 4
5	ENQ - Enquiry	21	NAK - Negative Acknowledge
6	ACK - Acknowledge	22	SYN - Synchronous Idle
7	BEL - Bell	23	ETB - End of Transmission Block
8	BS - Backspace	24	CAN - Cancel
9	HT - Horizontal Tab	25	EM - End of Medium
10	LF - Line Feed	26	SUB - Substitute
11	VT - Vertical Tab	27	ESC - Escape
12	FF - Form Feed	28	FS - File Separator
13	CR - Carriage Return	29	GS - Group Separator
14	SO - Shift Out	30	RS - Record Separator
15	SI - Shift In	31	US - Unit Separator

32		77	M	122	z	167	ß	212	'
33	!	78	N	123	{	168	®	213	'
34	"	79	O	124	|	169	©	214	÷
35	#	80	P	125	}	170	™	215	◊
36	$	81	Q	126	~	171	´	216	ÿ
37	%	82	R	127		172	¨	217	Ÿ
38	&	83	S	128	Ä	173	≠	218	/
39	'	84	T	129	Å	174	Æ	219	¤
40	(	85	U	130	Ç	175	Ø	220	‹
41	)	86	V	131	É	176	∞	221	›
42	*	87	W	132	Ñ	177	±	222	fi
43	+	88	X	133	Ö	178	≤	223	fl
44	,	89	Y	134	Ü	179	≥	224	‡
45	-	90	Z	135	á	180	¥	225	·
46	.	91	[	136	à	181	μ	226	,
47	/	92	\	137	â	182	∂	227	,,
48	0	93	]	138	ä	183	Σ	228	‰
49	1	94	^	139	ã	184	Π	229	Â
50	2	95	_	140	å	185	π	230	Ê
51	3	96	`	141	ç	186	∫	231	Á
52	4	97	a	142	é	187	ª	232	Ë
53	5	98	b	143	è	188	º	233	È
54	6	99	c	144	ê	189	Ω	234	Í
55	7	100	d	145	ë	190	æ	235	Î
56	8	101	e	146	í	191	ø	236	Ï
57	9	102	f	147	ì	192	¿	237	Ì
58	:	103	g	148	î	193	¡	238	Ó
59	;	104	h	149	ï	194	¬	239	Ô
60	<	105	i	150	ñ	195	√	240	
61	=	106	j	151	ó	196	ƒ	241	Ò
62	>	107	k	152	ò	197	≈	242	Ú
63	?	108	l	153	ô	198	Δ	243	Û
64	@	109	m	154	ö	199	«	244	Ù
65	A	110	n	155	õ	200	»	245	ı
66	B	111	o	156	ú	201	…	246	^
67	C	112	p	157	ù	202		247	~
68	D	113	q	158	û	203	À	248	‾
69	E	114	r	159	ü	204	Ã	249	˘
70	F	115	s	160	†	205	Õ	250	˙
71	G	116	t	161	°	206	Œ	251	°
72	H	117	u	162	¢	207	œ	252	¸
73	I	118	v	163	£	208	–	253	˝
74	J	119	w	164	§	209	—	254	
75	K	120	x	165	•	210	"	255	ˇ
76	L	121	y	166	¶	211	"		

BIBLIOGRAPHY

This annotated bibliography contains works I used in preparing this book as well as other books I have found useful over the years. If more than one edition of a work was published, you will see the first year it was published and the year in which the most recent edition was published. My notes may include a listing of the topics covered, and, in some cases, my opinion concerning what areas of the book are particularly useful.

The bibliography is divided into the following areas:

- Algorithms
- The C programming language
- Compiler construction and computer languages
- Desktop publishing and graphics
- Handbooks
- Hardware
- History of computers
- HyperCard and HyperTalk
- Information theory
- Logic
- Macintosh
- Mathematics
- Object-oriented programming
- Operating systems
- The Pascal language
- Physics and astronomy
- Software engineering
- Software tools
- Symbolic algebra
- Symbolic manipulation and artificial intelligence

Algorithms

Aho, Alfred V., John E. Hopcroft, Jeffrey D. Ullman. *Data Structures and Algorithms*. Reading, MA: Addison-Wesley, 1983, 1985. Algorithm analysis and design techniques; running time of programs; lists, stacks, queues, mappings, recursive procedures; trees; abstract data types (ADT); basic operations on sets, including dictionaries, hash tables, priority queues; tries; directed graphs; sorting; external storage; memory management. Examples use Pascal.

Baase, Sara. *Computer Algorithms: Introduction to Design and Analysis*. Reading, MA: Addison-Wesley, 1988. Sorting; selection and adversary arguments; graphs and digraphs; string matching; dynamic programming; polynomials, matrices, and FFT; transitive closure, Boolean matrices, and equivalence relations; NP-Complete problems; parallel algorithms. Algorithms are presented in a language similar to Modula-2.

Chartrand, Gary. *Introductory Graph Theory*. New York: Dover, 1977. Mathematical models, graphs, networks; elementary concepts of graph theory. Transportation problems, including the Königsberg Bridge Problem (introduction to Eulerian graphs) and the Salesman's Problem (introduction to Hamiltonian graphs). Connection problems, including the Minimal Connector Problem (introduction to trees), and PERT and the Critical Path Method. Party problems, including the Problem of the Eccentric Hosts (introduction to Ramsey numbers) and the Dancing Problem (introduction to matching). Games and puzzles, including Knight's Tour, Tower of Hanoi, Cannibals and Missionaries Problem. Digraphs, including a Traffic System Problem and Tournaments. Planar graphs, coloring problems (Four Color Problem), Scheduling Problem (introduction to chromatic numbers). Appendix on sets, relations, functions, and proofs.

Folk, Michael J., Bill Zoellick. *File Structures: A Conceptual Toolkit*. Reading, MA: Addison-Wesley, 1987. File structures as opposed to data structures. Information retrieval; sorting and searching; indexing; cosequential processing; tree access methods, B-trees, B* and B+ trees; hashing. Examples in C and Pascal. Appendices on string functions in Pascal and on the C programming language.

Gonnet, Gaston H. *Handbook of Algorithms and Data Structures*. London: Addison-Wesley, 1984. This wonderful volume contains the important algorithms of computer science. It covers searching, sorting, selection, and arithmetic algorithms. Particular detail is given to hashing. The algorithms are given in appendices in C and Pascal. A highly recommended reference handbook.

Graham, Ronald L., Donald E. Knuth, Oren Patashnik. *Concrete Mathematics*. Reading, MA: Addison-Wesley, 1989. A book about CONtinuous as well as disCRETE mathematics. Chapters cover recurrent problems, sums, integer functions, number theory, binomial coefficients, special numbers, generating functions, discrete probability, and asymptotics. Interesting subtopics include primes, mod, hashing, and big O manipulation. The book's formulas are typeset in AMS Euler, a new font. Humorous sidebars. Excellent compendium of information never gathered together before. Recommended.

Gries, David. *The Science of Programming*. New York: Springer-Verlag, 1981. Proving programs correct, logic, programming language semantics.

Knuth, Donald E. *Art of Computer Programming—Fundamental Algorithms*. Reading, MA: Addison-Wesley, 1968, 1973. This remarkable volume is advanced, historical, and a classic. It contains a good introduction to the mathematics needed for algorithm analysis and introduces a hypothetical assembly language called MIX, in which information structures are then presented. Knuth's style is readable, his scope is encyclopedic, and his subject is at the core of all programming. An absolute must-have reference for every computer scientist.

Knuth, Donald E. *Art of Computer Programming—Seminumerical Algorithms*. Reading, MA: Addison-Wesley, 1969, 1981. This second volume in Knuth's set is the definitive reference on random numbers and the basis of computer arithmetic. The latter portion of the book provides information that is useful for implementing symbolic manipulation packages.

Knuth, Donald E. *Art of Computer Programming—Sorting and Searching*. Reading, MA: Addison-Wesley, 1973. This third volume of the unfinished seven-volume set is the definitive reference on sorting and searching. Knuth clearly presents and analyzes many different algorithms in a way that makes this book a classic and that leaves the reader wanting the final four volumes of the set.

Purdom, Paul W., Cynthia A. Brown. *The Analysis of Algorithms*. New York: Holt, Rinehart & Winston, 1985. Recurrence relations, NP Completeness, statistics, math.

Sedgewick, Robert. *Algorithms*. Reading, MA: Addison-Wesley, 1983, 1988. Fundamentals, including Pascal, data structures, trees, recursion, analysis and implementation of algorithms; sorting, quicksort, priority queues, mergesort, radix and external sorting; searching, binary and balanced trees, hashing, radix and external searching; string processing, Knuth-Morris-Pratt, Boyer-Moore, Rabin-Karp algorithms, pattern matching, parsing, file compression, and cryptology; geometric algorithms, finding convex hull, range-searching, geometric intersection, closest-point problems; graph algorithms, connectivity, weighted and directed graphs, network flow; math algorithms, random numbers, arithmetic, Gaussian elimination, curve-fitting, integration; parallel algorithms, Fast Fourier Transform (FFT), dynamic and linear programming, exhaustive search, NP-Complete problems. Algorithms in Pascal.

Tucker, Alan. *Applied Combinatorics*. New York: Wiley, 1980. Pigeonhole Principle; Mastermind; binomial coefficients; generating functions; recurrence relations, graph theory, network algorithms, Traveling Salesman problem.

Van Wyk, Christopher J. *Data Structures and C Programs*. Reading, MA: Addison-Wesley, 1988. Part 1 covers the complexity of algorithms, pointers and dynamic storage, stacks and queues, linked lists, and memory organization. Part 2 covers searching, hashing, sorted lists, priority queues, sorting, and applying data structures. Part 3 covers acyclic and regular graphs. Appendices summarize C and library functions.

Wirth, Niklaus. *Algorithms and Data Structures*. Englewood Cliffs, NJ: Prentice-Hall, 1983. Sorting, searching, recursion, lists, trees. Examples are given in Modula-2. Not as good as his original Pascal text.

Wirth, Niklaus. *Algorithms + Data Structures = Programs*. Englewood Cliffs, NJ: Prentice-Hall, 1976. Sorting, searching, recursion, lists, trees, compiler construction. A well-written text that shows algorithm development using Pascal. The book's chapters build upon one another and culminate in full Pascal source code to a PL/O compiler, a subset of PL/1. Highly recommended.

The C Programming Language

Barkakati, Naba. *The Waite Group's Essential Guide to ANSI C.* Indianapolis: Howard W. Sams, 1988. A quick reference guide to ANSI C. Includes an overview of ANSI C, the C preprocessor, the C language, and the C library. Details the 146 functions found in the C standard libraries. Very readable.

Bolsky, M.I. *The C Programmer's Handbook.* Englewood Cliffs, NJ: Prentice-Hall, 1985. Syntax, data types, operators, and expressions; statements; functions; declaration; preprocessor; program structure; I/O library; other libraries; formatted input/output; portable C programs; character set. A handy reference to the C programming language, although it has not yet been revised to cover ANSI C.

Dr. Dobbs. *Dr. Dobbs' Toolbook of C.* New York: Prentice-Hall, 1986. The C programming language; how compilers work; full C source code is given for The Small-C Compiler, a macro assembler, Getargs, Cross-Reference Generator, and Small-Tools: Programs for Text Processing; CP/M BDOS and BIOS calls; Grep.c; optimizing strings in C.

Feuer, Alan R. *The C Puzzle Book.* Englewood Cliffs, NJ: Prentice-Hall, 1982. Puzzles for the C programming language, with solutions.

Harbison, Samuel P., Guy L. Steele. *A C Reference Manual.* Englewood Cliffs, NJ: Prentice-Hall, 1984, 1987. Lexical elements; C preprocessor; declarations; types; conversions; expressions; statements; functions; program structure; ANSI C; the C libraries; character processing; string processing; memory functions; input/output facilities; storage allocation; math functions; time/date functions; control functions. Appendices on the ASCII character set and syntax of the C language. This is a good book for implementors of the C language.

Hogan, Thom. *The C Programmer's Handbook.* Bowie, NJ: Brady, Prentice-Hall, 1984. A description of the C language. Appendices include a bibliography of books on C and an ASCII character chart.

Holub, Allen I. *The C Companion.* Englewood Cliffs, NJ: Prentice-Hall, 1987. This book explains some of the more esoteric concepts of the programming language C. Chapters cover the C compiler; binary arithmetic; assembly language; code generation and subroutine linkage; structured programming and stepwise refinement; pointers; recursion and compiler design; the anatomy of Printf(); debugging.

Kernighan, Brian W., Dennis M. Ritchie. *The C Programming Language.* Englewood Cliffs, NJ: Prentice-Hall, 1978, 1988. The C reference manual and language report, written by the authors of the C language. The second edition includes an updated reference manual for proposed ANSI C. The book's programs have been rewritten in the new style and include many interesting examples. Appendices include the reference manual, a full summary of the standard C libraries, and a description of the changes between the first and second editions of this book. Highly recommended. An essential bedside reference.

Koenig, Andrew. *C Traps and Pitfalls.* Reading, MA: Addison-Wesley, 1989. Lexical pitfalls, syntactic pitfalls, semantic pitfalls, linkage, library functions, the preprocessor, portability pitfalls, advice and answers. Includes an appendix on printf.

Plauger, P. J., Jim Brodie. *Standard C: Programmer's Quick Reference*. Redmond, WA: Microsoft Press, 1989. A quick reference guide to ANSI/ISO C. The language sections include characters, preprocessing, syntax, types, declarations, functions, and expressions. The standard C libraries include assert.h, ctype.h, errno.h, float.h, limits.h, locale.h, math.h, setjmp.h, signal.h, stdarg.h, stddef.h, stdio.h, stdlib.h, string.h, time.h. Two appendices detail portability issues and names. Unfortunately, the presentation is hard to follow (too many diagrams and type styles), which makes getting the information harder than it should be.

Tondo, Clovis L., Scott E. Gimpel. *The C Answer Book*. Englewood Cliffs, NJ: Prentice Hall, 1985. Solutions to the exercises found in The White book, *The C Programming Language*.

Compiler Construction and Computer Languages

Aho, Alfred V., Jeffrey D. Ullman. *Principles of Compiler Design*. Reading, MA: Addison-Wesley, 1977, 1979. This is the original "dragon book" about writing compilers. Topics include programming languages, finite automata and lexical analysis; parsing techniques, automatic construction of efficient parsers; syntax-directed translation; symbol tables; error detection; code and loop optimization; data-flow analysis. A look at some compilers and a compiler project. Examples use Pascal.

Aho, Alfred V., Ravi Sethi, Jeffrey D. Ullman. *Compilers: Principles, Techniques, and Tools*. Reading, MA: Addison-Wesley, 1986. Referred to as the "new dragon book," this mainly theoretical classic covers syntax-directed translation, parsing, lexical analysis, symbol tables, finite automata, syntax analysis, type checking, run-time environments, intermediate code generation, code optimization. Studies of EQN, Pascal, C, Fortran H, Bliss/11, and Modula-2 compilers. The appendix contains the details of a compiler construction project. Examples in C and Pascal. The opening chapters present C source code for a simple syntax-directed infix-to-postfix translator. An essential bedside reference.

Fischer, Charles N. *Crafting a Compiler*. Menlo Park, CA: Benjamin Cummings, 1988. Compiler construction using Ada/CS. Scanning, grammars and parsing, LL(1) grammars, LR parsing, semantic processing, symbol tables, run-time storage organization, processing declarations, processing expressions and data structure references, translating control structures, translating procedures and functions, attribute grammars and multipass translation, code generation and local code optimization, global optimization, parsing in the real world. Six appendices.

Ghezzi, Carlo, Mehdi Jazayeri. *Programming Language Concepts*. New York: John Wiley & Sons, 1982, 1987. Software development process; computer architecture and programming languages; historical perspective; preview: evolution of concepts in programming languages; the structure of programming languages; data types; control structures; programming in the large; functional and logic programming.

Hopcroft, John E., Jeffrey D. Ullman. *Introduction to Automata Theory, Languages, and Computation*. Reading, MA: Addison-Wesley, 1979. Finite automata and regular expressions; properties of regular sets; context-free grammars and languages; Turing machines; undecidability; Chomsky hierarchy; deterministic context-free languages; closure properties of families of languages; computational complexity theory; intractable problems.

Horowitz, Ellis. *Fundamentals of Programming Languages*. Rockville, MD: CS Press, 1983. An overview of the history of programming languages and their variety.

Kane, Gerry, Doug Hawkins, Lance Leventhal. *68000 Assembly Language Programming*. Berkeley, CA: Osborne/McGraw Hill, 1981, 1986.

Pyster, Arthur B. *Compiler Design and Construction*. New York: Van Nostrand Reinhold, 1980, 1988. This is the most practical of the compiler texts. Chapters include compiler overview; lexical analysis; recursive descent parsing; LL(1) parsing; LR(1) parsing; syntax-directed translation; run-time environments; datatypes and intermediate code; code optimization; code generation. Includes C sources for Ginevra, a C mini-preprocessor; Cecilia, an expression compiler; Gioconda, a lexical analyzer generator; Express, a language of arithmetic expressions; and Marli, an LL(1) parser generator. Includes lex code for lexical analyzers for both Pascal and C, as well as yacc code for a full Pascal grammar. A useful book that gives a good head start on writing a compiler. Highly recommended. An essential bed-side reference.

Schreiner, Friedman Jr. *Introduction to Compiler Construction with Unix*. Englewood Cliffs, NJ: Prentice Hall. A good practical introduction to using lex and yacc to make a simple version of a C compiler.

Terry, Patrick D. *Programming Language Translation*. Wokingham, England: Addison-Wesley, 1986. This book gives lots of sources to recursive descent parsers. Chapters cover translators and interpreters; simple assemblers; advanced assembler features; languages and grammars; top-down parsing; a simple compiler; block structure and storage management; concurrent programming; data abstraction. Appendices include cross-references for the macro-assembler and the CLANG compiler, as well as a CLANG specification. Includes twelve listings of programs written in Pascal. Highly recommended.

Tremblay, Sorenson. *An Implementation Guide to Compiler Writing*. New York: McGraw Hill, 1982. A companion volume to *The Theory and Practice of Compiler Writing,* this volume provides full PL/1 source code to a GAUSS compiler, GAUSS being a string-oriented Algol-like block structured language.

Tremblay, Sorenson. *The Theory and Practice of Compiler Writing*. New York: McGraw Hill, 1985. A theoretical look at compiler construction. Includes an interesting chapter on programming language design, with a look at the design of the Ada language.

Tucker, Allen B. *Programming Languages*. New York: McGraw-Hill, 1977, 1986. A systematic and in-depth study of eleven programming languages: Ada, APL, C, COBOL, FORTRAN, LISP, Pascal, PL/1, Prolog, Snobol, and Modula-2. Also includes chapters related to language design on semantics, syntax, and pragmatics. Languages are compared and evaluated against nine criteria: expressivity, well-definedness, data types and structures, modularity, input/output facilities, portability, efficiency, pedagogy, and generality.

Desktop Publishing and Graphics

Adobe Systems. *PostScript Language Reference Manual*. Reading, MA: Addison-Wesley, 1985. Raster output devices; scan conversion; page description languages; interpreter; syntax; data types and objects; stacks; execution; virtual memory; operator overview; graphics; path construction, coordinate systems and transformations; painting; images; colors and halftones; fonts; character encoding; font metric information; font cache. List of operators. Appendix on the Apple LaserWriter.

Adobe Systems. *PostScript Language Tutorial and Cookbook*. Reading, MA: Addison-Wesley, 1985. PostScript as a page description language (PDL). Stack and arithmetic; beginning graphics; procedures and variables; printing text; loops and conditionals; arrays; more fonts; clipping and line details; images; PostScript printers (Apple LaserWriter). This cookbook includes 21 example PostScript programs.

Foley, James D., Andries Van Dam. *Fundamentals of Interactive Computer Graphics*. Reading, MA: Addison-Wesley, 1982, 1983. Geometrical transformations, hidden line algorithms, and shading.

Holzmann, Gerard J. *Beyond Photography: The Digital Darkroom*. Englewood Cliffs, NJ: Prentice Hall, 1988. Image processing, digital photos and cameras, scanners; transformations, Cartesian and polar coordinates; point and area processes; altered images. Full sources in C for a portable picture editor (popi) are given, including a lexical analyzer, parser, file handler, and interpreter. Catalogs various image transformations, including making a negative, logarithmic correction, simulated solarization, contrast expansion and normalization, focus restoration, blurring, enlarging and reducing by a factor, mirroring, flipping and rotating, relief, grid transforms, oil transfer, picture shear, slicing, tiling, melting, and making a matte. A good practical introduction to the topic.

Jain, Anil K. *Fundamentals of Digital Image Processing*. Englewood Cliffs, NJ: Prentice Hall, 1989. An advanced highly mathematical text covering image representation, modeling, enhancement, restoration, analysis, reconstruction, and data compression. A math introduction details Fourier and Z transformations, MTF, matrices, random signals. Sampling theory; image transformation, including unitary, DFT, cosine, sine, Hadamard, Haar, slant, and KL. Stochastic modeling, image filtering, Bayesian methods, PCM coding, and many more topics.

Knuth, Donald E. *Computers and Typesetting—The T$_E$Xbook*. Reading, MA: Addison-Wesley, 1986. This is the user manual of a document preparation language called T$_E$X. Chapters cover book printing versus ordinary typing; controlling T$_E$X; fonts of type; grouping; dimensions; boxes; glue; modes; typing math formulas; displayed equations; definitions; making boxes; alignment; breaking paragraphs into lines; making lines into pages.

Knuth, Donald E. *Computers and Typesetting—T$_E$X: The Program*. Reading, MA: Addison-Wesley, 1986. This book contains the full source code to T$_E$X. It is written in a literate form of Pascal called Web. Interesting sections detail the algorithms of T$_E$X, including dynamic memory allocation, the semantic nest, hash tables, token lists, syntactic routines, scanning routines, typesetting math formulas, breaking paragraphs into lines, hyphenation, building pages, etc.

Knuth, Donald E. *Computers and Typesetting—The Metafont Book*. Reading, MA: Addison-Wesley, 1986. The user manual for an interesting font-description language called Metafont. Chapters cover using Metafont, coordinates, curves, pens, variables, algebraic expressions, equations, assignments, magnification and resolution, boxes, drawing, filling, erasing, paths, transformations, calligraphic effects, grouping, definitions (macros), conditions and loops, random numbers, strings, and font metric information.

Knuth, Donald E. *Computers and Typesetting—Metafont: The Program*. Reading, MA: Addison-Wesley, 1986. This book contains the full source code to Metafont. It is written in a literate form of Pascal called Web. Interesting sections detail the algorithms of Metafont, including arithmetic, algebraic and transcendental functions, hash tables, token lists, path and edge structures, filling contours and envelopes, polygonal and elliptical pens, dynamic linear and nonlinear equations, macro processing, parsing, and command interpretation.

Knuth, Donald E. *Computers and Typesetting—Computer Modern Typefaces*. Reading, MA: Addison-Wesley, 1986. An introduction to the parameters of the Computer Modern typeface family; 62 parameters are described and then varied, with the resulting fonts displayed.

Letraset. *Graphic Materials Handbook*. Paramus, NJ: Letraset, 1962, 1987. This is a catalog of fonts, PANTONE color-matching system, various patterns, and other materials used in graphic arts design. Includes Times, Helvetica, and Zapf fonts.

McLean, Ruari. *The Thames and Hudson Manual of Typography*. London: Thames and Hudson, 1980, 1988. The art and skill of designing printed matter is treated as follows: historical outline; studio and equipment; legibility; lettering and calligraphy; letters for printing, classification of typefaces, sans-serif type, a font of type, the point system and measurement of letters; methods of composition, hot-metal machine and cold-metal setting, filmsetting, computers; paper, watermarks, paper kinds and terms, paper sizes, the weight of paper; cast-off and layout; book design, margins, paper size and shape, grids, bleeds; the parts of a book, prelims, main text, captions, appendices, bibliography, index, end-papers, case, jackets; jobbing typography, letterheads, tables, calendars, ambiguity, posters; newspaper and magazine typography.

Skillin, Marjorie. *Words Into Type*. Englewood Cliffs, NJ: Prentice-Hall, 1974, 1978. The classic work in the field of publishing. Chapters cover authorship and printing; manuscripts, footnotes, tables, bibliographies, copyright law, copy and proof, layout, indexes, abbreviations, capitalization, punctuation, typographical style, composition of foreign languages, grammar, verbs, nouns, use of words, wordiness, spelling, typography, illustration, mechanics of composition, type measurement, points, the em, typefaces, photocomposition, paper, book sizes, and binding.

Ulichney, Robert. *Digital Halftoning*. Cambridge, MA: MIT Press, 1987. Physical reconstruction functions, grid geometries; tools for Fourier analysis; dithering with white noise; clustered-dot ordered dither; dispersed-dot ordered dither, recursive tessellation; ordered dither on asymmetric grids; dithering with blue noise.

University of Chicago Press. *The Chicago Manual of Style*. Chicago: University of Chicago Press, 1906, 1982. The classic work from the field of document style. Chapters cover bookmaking, manuscript preparation and copyediting, proofs, rights and permissions, style, punctuation, spelling, names and terms, numbers, foreign languages in type, quotations, illustrations, captions, legends, tables, mathematics in type, abbreviations, documentation, references, notes, bibliographies, indexes, production and printing, design and typography, composition, and binding.

Handbooks

Abramowitz, Milton, Irene A. Stegun. *Handbook of Mathematical Functions*. New York: Dover, 1964, 1972. With formulas, graphs, and tables. Mathematical and physical constants; analytical methods; elementary transcendental functions; special functions; combinatorial analysis; numerical interpolation, differentiation and integration; probability functions; Laplace transformations. The standard reference book for values of mathematical functions.

Aland, Kurt, Eberhard Nestle. *Greek-English New Testament*. Stuttgart: Deutsche Bibelgesellschaft, 1981, 1986. Combined edition of Greek and English New Testaments. Uses the 26th edition of the Nestle Greek text and the 2nd edition of the Revised Standard Version (RSV) English text. Includes four appendices on codices, citations, textual differences between different Greek and English versions, and abbreviations. Clothbound, approximately 1,500 pages.

Allen, C. W. *Astrophysical Quantities*. London: William Clowes, 1973. Tables listing all known weights and measurements of the planets, stars, and universe. An essential reference work, although a bit dated now.

Ballou, Glen, editor. *Handbook for Sound Engineers: The New Audio Cyclopedia*. Indianapolis: Howard W. Sams, 1987. The classic work in the field of audio engineering. Chapters cover fundamentals of sound and acoustics; acoustical design of audio rooms for speech, music; electronic components for sound engineering, including resistors, capacitors, inductors, transformers, tubes, discrete solid-state devices, integrated circuits, heat sinks, wire, and relays; electroacoustic devices, including microphones, loudspeakers, enclosures and headphones; audio electronic circuits and equipment, including amplifiers, attenuators, filters, equalizers, delay, power supplies, constant and variable speed devices, consoles; disk, magnetic, and digital recording and playback; sound system design; the broadcast chain; image projection; audio measurements, fundamentals, and units. An essential reference.

Berkow, Robert. M.D., editor. *The Merck Manual of Diagnosis and Therapy*. Rahway, NJ: Merck, 1947, 1987. The classic work in the field of medical diagnosis. Covers infectious and parasitic diseases, immunology; allergic, hematologic, cardiovascular, respiratory, genitourinary, gastrointestinal, hepatic disorders; gynecology, child care, ear, nose, and throat disorders; dental, opthalmic, nutritional, endocrine, musculoskeletal, neurologic, psychiatric, and dermatologic disorders; venereal diseases; poisoning; prescriptions.

Beyer, William H. *CRC Standard Mathematical Tables*. Boca Raton, FL: CRC Press, 1964, 1974. Constants, conversion factors; algebra; combinatorial analysis; geometry; trigonometry; logarithmic, exponential and hyperbolic functions; analytic geometry; calculus; differential equations; special functions; numerical methods; probability and statistics; financial tables; mathematical symbols and abbreviations. This useful perennial seems to have a few errors in the integral tables these days.

Chemical Rubber Co. *The CRC Handbook of Chemistry and Physics*. Boca Raton, FL: CRC Press, 1973. Physics, chemistry, mathematical tables.

Diem, K., C. Lentner. *Scientific Tables*. Basle, Switzerland: Ciba-Geigy, 1970. Mathematics, statistics, physics, physical chemistry, biochemistry, nutrition, composition and functions of the body, body fluids, body measurements, hormones.

Hoffman, Mark S., editor. *World Almanac and Book of Facts 1988*. New York: Pharos Books, 1868, 1988. Lists and tables about countries, history, sports, education, employment, health, medicine, population, etc.

Jordan, Edward C., editor in chief. *Reference Data for Engineers: Radio, Electronics, Computer, and Communications*. Indianapolis: Howard W. Sams, 1943, 1986. The classic work in the field of radio engineering, this work has recently been renamed and expanded to include post-radio technology. Chapters cover frequency data; units, constants, conversion factors; properties of materials; networks, Fourier waveform analysis; transformers, rectifiers, filters, power supplies; semiconductors, transistors, circuits; optical, analog, satellite, space, and digital communications and signal processing; information theory, computers; broadcasting, recording standards; electroacoustics; lasers; logic design; mathematical tables, data, and equations. An essential reference.

Liddell, Scott. *Greek-English Lexicon*. Oxford, England: Oxford University Press, 1983. The canonical Greek-English dictionary.

Menzel, Donald H. *Fundamental Formulas of Physics*. New York: Dover, 1955, 1960. A good compilation of essential mathematical and physics formulas, in two volumes.

Oxford. *Oxford English Dictionary*. Oxford, England: Oxford University Press, 1930. A massive small-print dictionary of English word usage—the compact version of the OED includes a magnifying glass! Differs from most dictionaries by giving actual usage of a word by quoting passages from historical documents taken from literature, history, and science. The epic tome on the English language.

Pearson, Carl E. *Handbook of Applied Mathematics*. New York: Van Nostrand Reinhold, 1974, 1983. Formulas from algebra, trigonometry, analytic geometry; elements of analysis; vector and tensor analysis; complex variables; differential equations; special functions; PDEs; integral equations; transform methods; asymptotic methods; oscillations; perturbation methods; wave propagation; matrices and linear algebra; functional approximation; numerical analysis; mathematical models and their formulation; optimization techniques; probability and statistics.

Sennitt, Andrew G., editor. *World Radio TV Handbook*. New York: Billboard Publications, 1964, 1988. World radio and television stations by country and frequency. Includes SW, MW, LW, AM, FM, and TV. Lists broadcast times. Includes receiver specifications, world maps, reference sections on band selection, reception conditions, solar activity, and world time.

Tuma, Jan J. *Handbook of Physical Calculations*. New York: McGraw-Hill, 1976. A good source book of physics and engineering formulas, including statics and dynamics of rigid bodies; mechanics of deformable bodies, fluids, heat, and gases; electrostatics and electric current; magnetism and electrodynamics; vibration and acoustics; geometrical and wave optics. Dozens of appendices, including physical tables and unit conversions. Recommended.

Tuma, Jan J. *Technology Mathematics Handbook*. New York: McGraw-Hill, 1975. Another source book, this time covering the mathematics used in science and engineering. Includes basic arithmetic; algebra; plane, space, and plane analytic geometry; differential and integral calculus; scalars, vectors, matrices; series and numerical procedures. Appendices include units, numerical tables, and metric conversions. Recommended.

Webster, Daniel. *Webster's New World Dictionary of American English, Third College Edition*. New York: Simon & Schuster, 1988. All dictionaries are not alike. After a long search, I have decided that this is the best one-volume dictionary around. It has excellent word etymologies, many Americanisms, and a good selection of older words otherwise found only in the Oxford English Dictionary. Make sure you do not get a "student's" version, as it is abbreviated.

Hardware

Kane, Gerry, Doug Hawkins, Lance Leventhal. *68000 Assembly Language Programming*. Berkeley, CA: Osborne / McGraw-Hill, 1981, 1986. Many examples of simple assembly routines; I/O with 6820 and 6850 chips.

Keyes, Robert W. *The Physics of VLSI Systems*. Wokingham, England: Addison-Wesley, 1987. Microelectronics and integration; semiconductors and semiconductor devices; physical representation of information; energy and voltage; information storage; IC fabrication; limits to miniaturization; large systems; performance; alternative logic technologies.

Motorola. *MC68000 8/16/32-Bit Microprocessors Programmer's Reference Manual*. Englewood Cliffs, NJ: Prentice-Hall, 1979, 1986. Architectural description; data organization and addressing capabilities; instruction set summary; exception processing. Appendices cover condition codes computation; instruction set details; instruction format summary; MC68000 instruction execution times; MC68008 instruction execution times; MC68010/MC68012 instruction execution times; MC68010/MC68012 loop mode operation.

Motorola. *MC68020 32-Bit Microprocessor User's Manual*. Englewood Cliffs, NJ: Prentice-Hall, 1984, 1985. Data organization and addressing capabilities; instruction set summary; signal description; bus operation; processing states; on-chip cache memory; coprocessor interface description; instruction execution timing; electrical specifications; ordering information and mechanical data. Appendices cover condition codes computation, instruction set, instruction format survey, advanced topics, MC68020 extensions to M68000 family.

Motorola. *MC68030 Enhanced 32-Bit Microprocessor User's Manual*. Englewood Cliffs, NJ: Prentice-Hall, 1987. Data organization and addressing capabilities; instruction set; processing states; signal description; on-chip cache memories; bus operation; exception processing; memory management unit; coprocessor interface description; instruction execution timing; applications information; electrical specifications; ordering information and mechanical data.

Motorola. *MC68851 Paged Memory Management Unit User's Manual*. Englewood Cliffs, NJ: Prentice-Hall, 1986. Overview of system operation; signal description; bus operation description; address translation; instruction set processor; protection; breakpoints; coprocessor interface; access level control interface; operation timings; electrical specifications; ordering information and mechanical data. Appendices cover the instruction set; hardware considerations; software considerations.

Motorola. *MC68881/MC68882 Floating-Point Coprocessor User's Manual*. Englewood Cliffs, NJ: Prentice-Hall, 1985, 1987. General description; programming model; instruction set; exception processing; coprocessor interface; instruction execution timing; functional signal descriptions; bus operation; interfacing methods; electrical specifications; ordering information and mechanical data. Appendices provide a glossary of terms, abbreviations and acronyms. The text details conformance with the IEEE 754 standard.

Motorola. *MC88100 Risc Microprocessor User's Manual*. Austin, TX: Motorola, 1988. A description of Motorola's first reduced instruction set computer (RISC) microprocessor. Includes a full description of its IEEE-754 floating-point arithmetic. The programming model, addressing modes, and instruction set are all described in this reference document.

History of Computers

ACM Press. *ACM Turing Award Lectures: The First Twenty Years*. New York: Addison-Wesley, 1987. Various lectures on programming languages, AI, logic, algorithms and systems by Edsger W. Dijkstra, Donald E. Knuth, John Backus, CAR Hoare, Dennis M. Ritche, Ken Thompson, Niklaus Wirth, Hamming, Marvin Minsky, Wilkinson, John McCarthy, Codd, and others. Wonderful reading.

Freiberger, Paul, Michael Swaine. *Fire in the Valley*. Berkeley, CA: Osborne/McGraw-Hill, 1984. A history of personal computers, focusing on Apple Computer.

Goldberg, Adele, editor. *A History of Personal Workstations*. Reading, MA: Addison-Wesley, 1988. A collection of papers presented January 9–10, 1986, in Palo Alto, CA. Authors include Gordon Bell, Doug Engelbart, Vannevar Bush, Alan Kay, Bert Sutherland, Peter Denning. Includes a history of Arpanet, Dynabook, Xerox Alto, Ethernet, and Hewlett-Packard calculators.

Levy, Steven. *Hackers*. New York: Dell Publishing, 1984. History of personal computer revolution, with coverage of MIT hackers and early Apple Computer.

Moritz, Michael. *The Little Kingdom*. New York: Morrow, 1984. Another history of Apple Computer.

Young, Jeffrey S. *Steve Jobs: The Journey Is the Reward*. New York: Lynx Books, 1987, 1988. A biography of Steven Paul Jobs, born February 24, 1955. Details the history of Apple Computer and the beginnings of NeXT. Although not an authorized biography, it is not bad.

HyperCard and HyperTalk

Apple Computer. *HyperCard Script Language Guide: The HyperTalk Language*. Reading, MA: Addison-Wesley, 1988. The basics of HyperTalk, including objects, messages, scripts, handlers, and the object hierarchy. Naming objects, sources of value, including constants, literals, functions, properties, numbers, and containers; chunk expressions, factors, and operators; keywords; system messages; commands. Appendices cover XCMDs and XFCNs, including assembly language, C, and Pascal sources; an ASCII table, HyperCard limits, operator precedence table, changes in HyperCard 1.2, a syntax summary, and a vocabulary list. This is the current definitive work about HyperTalk, being reviewed thoroughly by Dan Winkler and Dan Allen of the HyperCard team.

Bond, Gary. *XCMD's for HyperCard*. Portland, OR: MIS Press, 1988. Designing XCMDs and XFCNs for HyperTalk on the Apple Macintosh. Uses MPW Pascal and LightSpeed C. Discusses XCmdBlock records and glue routines. Includes source code (in both C and Pascal) for 20 different XCMDs, including HardCopy, EjectDisk, SetGlobal, NewMenuBar, RestoreMenuBar, PopMenu, AddMenu, ResMenu, ClearMenu, ModifyMenuItem, SmartSum, GetEvent, QuickSort, CopyRes, GetDiskVol, TalkString, GetPathName, SetWindowName, FontReal, DeleteFile. A good introduction to the world of XCMDing.

Goodman, Danny. *The Complete HyperCard Handbook*. New York: Bantam Books, 1987, 1988. An introduction to Apple's HyperCard. Includes an interview with Bill Atkinson. Browsing, painting, authoring, and scripting are described, as are inheritance and the properties of fields, buttons, cards, and stacks. Sample HyperCard stacks are provided for a corporate directory, a telephone logbook, a time sheet, a to-do list, a conversion calculator, and a visual outliner. Importing and exporting data. Includes information on the HyperTalk language. Providing lots of good reading for beginners, this work has been updated to cover more recent versions of HyperCard. Recommended.

Goodman, Danny. *HyperCard Developer's Guide*. New York: Bantam Books, 1988. Stack development issues, including designing for all models of Macintosh; user interface; screen aesthetics; stack structure; importing; stack protection; HyperTalk scripts; the object hierarchy; system messages; control structures; linking cards; searching and sorting; resources for stack developers; making icons; writing XCMDs using Turbo Pascal, LightSpeed C and LightSpeed Pascal; using ResEdit. Includes sources to three XCMDs: AboutBox, PopUpMenu, SerialPort. Appendices include source code and interfaces for the various XCMDs as well as an article on interactive sound by Tim Oren.

Poole, Lon. *HyperTalk*. Redmond, WA: Microsoft Press, 1988. An alphabetical listing of the vocabulary found in HyperTalk as of version 1.2.1. This quick reference also includes appendices on the inheritance path, operators, and sources of value. An essential bedside reference, this is my favorite reference work on HyperTalk.

Winkler, Dan, Scot Kamins. *HyperTalk—The Book*. New York: Bantam Books, 1989. This forthcoming language reference work could become the new definitive work on HyperTalk, as it is written by the authors of HyperTalk.

Winkler, Dan, Scott Knaster. *Cooking with HyperTalk*. New York: Bantam Books, 1989. A book full of helpful scripts, XCMDs, and hints by the author of HyperTalk.

Information Theory

Kahn, David. *The Codebreakers.* New York: MacMillan, 1967. The definitive work on the history of stenography, codes, cyphers, cryptography, cryptoanalysis, and cryptology. Includes material from the time of the Egyptians until the modern era, with special details regarding World War II, Pearl Harbor, etc. Excellent.

Pierce, John R. *An Introduction to Information Theory: Symbols, Signals and Noise.* New York: Dover, 1961, 1980. The world and theories; origins of information theory; a mathematical model; encoding and binary digits; entropy; language and meaning; efficient encoding; the noisy channel; many dimensions; information theory and physics; cybernetics; information theory, psychology, and art. Appendix on mathematical notation. An essential bedside reference.

Shannon, Claude E., Warren Weaver. *The Mathematical Theory of Communication.* Urbana, IL: University of Illinois, 1949. The original paper that created information theory by Bell Lab's famous Shannon. Subsections cover discrete noiseless systems, the discrete channel with noise, continuous information, the continuous channel, and the rate for a continuous source. An advanced mathematical treatment; highly recommended.

Von Neumann, John. *The Computer and the Brain.* New Haven: Yale, 1958. A study about computation and cybernetics.

Welsh, Dominic. *Codes and Cryptography.* Oxford, England: Oxford University Press, 1988. An excellent text on communications theory from a mathematical standpoint, this work covers entropy, Shannon's noiseless coding theorem for memoryless sources, communication through noisy channels; error-correcting codes, including Hamming, cyclic, and Reed-Muller codes; Markov sources; the structure of natural languages, the entropy of English, Zipf's law, and word entropy, and the redundancy of a language; cryptosystems using a one-time pad and linear shift-register sequences; computational complexity and NP Complete algorithms; one-way functions, including the Data Encryption Standard (DES) and the discrete logarithm; public key cryptosystems (RSA); authentication and digital signatures; randomized encryption. An appendix includes letter frequencies of English. Highly recommended reading.

Logic

Carnap, Rudolf. *Introduction to Symbolic Logic and Its Applications.* New York: Dover, 1954, 1958. The simple language A (sentential connectives, truth tables, L-concepts, tautologies, definitions, identity); the language B (semantical and syntactical systems, proofs, derivations); the extended language C (compound predicate expressions, extensionality, relative products, relations, heredity). Forms and methods of the construction of languages. Axiom systems for set theory, arithmetic, geometry, physics, biology.

Hofstadter, Douglas R. *Gödel, Escher, Bach: An Eternal Golden Braid.* New York: Random House, 1979, 1980. One of the classic works that has influenced my thought, this Pulitzer prize winner discusses what constitutes intelligence. Three themes are interwoven: the math of Kurt Gödel, the paintings of M. C. Escher, and the music of J. S. Bach. Technical chapters alternate with original dialogs between the tortoise and the hare. The dialogs themselves contain deep insights into the following chapter. The book covers such topics as computers, recursion, levels of description, propositional calculus, self-replication, AI, and DNA. Highly recommended. An essential bedside companion.

Hofstadter, Douglas R. *Metamagical Themas*. New York: Basic Books, 1985. More fun from Hofstadter, with topics covering AI, the self, metamathematics, LISP, DNA, Prisoner's Dilemma, Metafont, and creativity. Do you know what constitutes the essence of the letter A? Read Hofstadter.

Manna, Zohar, Richard Waldinger. *The Logical Basis of Computer Programming*. Volume 1. Reading, MA: Addison-Wesley, 1985. Deductive reasoning (logic: the calculus of computer science), mathematical logic, propositional logic, truth tables, semantic trees, predicate logic, theories with induction: nonnegative integers, strings, trees, lists, sets, bags, tuples.

Northrop, F.S.C. *Science and First Principles*. Woodbridge, CT: Yale, 1932, 1979. A philosophical look at the history of science from the Greeks to quantum mechanics. Propounds the macroatomic theory of matter, with three qualities of matter: the physical, the formal, and the psychical. One of the most influential books on my thought. Highly recommended. An essential bedside reference.

Popper, Karl R. *Conjectures and Refutations: The Growth of Scientific Knowledge*. New York: Harper & Row, 1963, 1965. Popper's philosophy of science is developed further as he convinces the reader that science progresses by conjectures and refutations rather than by the so-called scientific method. The implications for software development are massive.

Popper, Karl R. *The Logic of Scientific Discovery*. New York: Harper & Row, 1959. Popper's philosophy of science directly applies to the task of creating computer software. His studies into the degrees of testability, verifiability, and falsifiability are fascinating.

Quine, Willard Van Orman. *Mathematical Logic*. Cambridge, MA: Harvard University Press, 1940, 1981. A technical volume on logic. Chapters cover statements, quantification, terms, extended theory of classes, relations, number, and syntax. Includes material on tautologies, stratification, the ancestral, real numbers, protosyntax, incompleteness. Includes an appendix on theorem versus metatheorem, as well as lists of definitions and theorems. Requires concentration, but has a good reward.

Russell, Bertrand. *Principles of Mathematics*. New York: Norton, 1903, 1938. Indefinables, number, quantity, order, infinity and continuity, space, matter, and motion. Symbolic logic, the propositional calculus, implication, denoting, classes, relations, the contradiction, cardinal numbers, finite and infinite, whole and part, infinite wholes, ratios and fractions, quantities, zero, order, progressions, Dedekind's theory of number, real numbers, Cantor, transfinite ordinals and cardinals.

Smullyan, Raymond. *Forever Undecided, a Puzzle Guide to Gödel*. New York: Alfred A. Knopf, 1987. A host of puzzles about liars and truth tellers (knaves and knights), interspersed with an introductory account of symbolic logic and Gödel's Incompleteness Theorem. Later chapters detail self-fulfilling beliefs, Löb's theorem, and possible world semantics. Mathematics, logic, computer science (and artificial intelligence), and philosophy are all intertwined in this book of recreational games. Recommended.

Macintosh

Apple Computer. *Apple Numerics Manual*. Reading, MA: Addison-Wesley, 1986, 1988. IEEE arithmetic detailed, with an emphasis on Apple's Standard Apple Numerics Environment (SANE). Includes information on data types, conversions, expression evaluation, infinities, NaNs, denormalized numbers, arithmetic operations and comparisons, and ways of controlling the SANE environment. Elementary functions and examples. Part II describes SANE for the 65C816 and 6502 microprocessors used in the Apple II family of computers, and Part III describes software SANE as implemented for the 68xxx family of processors used in the Macintosh. Part IV describes 68881 SANE as used by the Macintosh II. Appendices cover SANE in high-level languages (C and Pascal) and provide quick reference tables.

Apple Computer. *AppleTalk Network System Overview*. Reading, MA: Addison-Wesley, 1989. An overview of the AppleTalk system that serves as a good introduction for programmers.

Apple Computer. *Designing Cards and Drivers for Macintosh II and Macintosh SE*. Reading, MA: Addison-Wesley, 1987. The Macintosh II architecture, including NuBus, data transfers, access to address spaces, arbitration, card electrical design guidelines, physical design guidelines, firmware and card driver design. Includes as examples the NuBus Test Card, SCSI-NuBus Test Card, and the Mac II Video Card. The Macintosh SE architecture, electrical and physical design, and the design of a disk controller for the Mac SE.

Apple Computer. *Human Interface Guidelines: The Apple Desktop Interface*. Reading, MA: Addison-Wesley, 1987. The philosophy, elements, and specifications of the Apple Desktop Interface are presented. (This is a revised and expanded edition of a chapter from *Inside Macintosh*.) This document gives good guidelines on most things, other than placement of dialog buttons.

Apple Computer. *Inside Macintosh Volumes I, II, and III*. Reading, MA: Addison-Wesley, 1984, 1986. Programming the Apple Macintosh is detailed. Volume 1 covers the ToolBox, volume 2 covers the operating system, and volume 3 covers hardware and provides summaries. *Inside Macintosh* is essential reading for anyone working on the Macintosh. It should be memorized. It is well written and amazingly correct for a work of its scope. We are lucky to have such a treasure.

Apple Computer. *Inside Macintosh, Volume IV*. Reading, MA: Addison-Wesley, 1986. Routines new to the Macintosh Plus 128 KB ROMs are detailed.

Apple Computer. *Inside Macintosh, Volume V*. Reading, MA: Addison-Wesley, 1988. Routines new to the Macintosh 256 KB ROMs are detailed.

Apple Computer. *Inside Macintosh, X-Ref*. Reading, MA: Addison-Wesley, 1988. A general index to all five volumes of *Inside Macintosh*.

Apple Computer. *LaserWriter Reference*. Reading, MA: Addison-Wesley, 1988. About the LaserWriter, LW Plus, IISC, IINT, and IINTX. All about fonts, including naming and downloading. Working in the printing environment, using AppleTalk, Diablo emulation, and LaserJet emulation. A functional overview of PostScript is provided, as are specifications for serial port communication.

Apple Computer. *Macintosh Family Hardware Reference*. Reading, MA: Addison-Wesley, 1988. Classic Macintosh hardware overview; processor, control, memory, mouse, keyboard, I/O ports, video, sound, and power supply. Similar topics for the Mac SE and Mac II, including Apple Desktop Bus (ADB), the SE Expansion slot, and NuBus. Appendices detail specifications and differences between the various members of the family.

Apple Computer. *Programmer's Introduction to the Macintosh Family*. Reading, MA: Addison-Wesley, 1988. Introduces the topics of event-driven programming, memory management, file I/O, resources, MPW, MacApp, and QuickDraw graphics.

Apple Computer. *Technical Introduction to the Macintosh Family*. Reading, MA: Addison-Wesley, 1987. An overview of the Macintosh. Includes information on its software, including the toolbox, resources, graphics, memory, operating system, and UNIX operating system, as well as its hardware.

Apple Computer. *Understanding Computer Networks*. Reading, MA: Addison-Wesley, 1989. A simple guide to networking for end users. Good illustrations, but low technical content.

Apple Computer, Gursharan S. Sidhu, Richard F. Andrews, Alan B. Oppenheimer. *Inside AppleTalk*. Reading, MA: Addison-Wesley, 1989. A detailed look at AppleTalk that is suitable for programmers implementing network software. Covers all levels of AppleTalk protocols including LLAP, ELAP, DDP, RTMP, AEP, ATP, NBP, ADSP, ZIP, ASP, PAP, AFP, and PostScript. An appendix contains detailed information about the LocalTalk hardware.

Bove, Tony, Fred Davis, Cheryl Rhodes. *Adobe Illustrator: The Official Handbook for Designers*. New York: Bantam Books, 1987. Introduction to Adobe Illustrator, a page description tool for the Apple Macintosh, LaserWriter, and Postscript. Maps, charts, clip art; graphic design and illustration; technical illustrations; reference manual for Illustrator; EPS and Illustrator file formats described; Postscript tutorial.

Chernicoff, Steve. *Macintosh Revealed*. Volumes 1, 2, and 3. Hasbrook Heights, NJ: Hayden, 1985, 1987. The basics of programming the Macintosh. An interesting supplement to—but not a replacement for—*Inside Macintosh*.

Cobb, Douglas, Judy Mynhier, Steven Cobb. *Excel in Business*. Louisville, KY: The Cobb Group, 1985. The definitive guide to Microsoft Excel for the Apple Macintosh.

Hoffman, Paul E. *Microsoft Word 4.0 for the Macintosh*. Reading, MA: Addison-Wesley, 1989. A dictionary of Word's commands. Includes a useful quick reference guide.

Knaster, Scott. *How To Write Macintosh Software*. Hasbrook Heights, NJ: Hayden, 1986. A useful book of tips and pointers on programming the Apple Macintosh. Concentrates on debugging, memory management, and machine compatibility issues.

Knaster, Scott. *Macintosh Programming Secrets*. Reading, MA: Addison-Wesley, 1988. Concepts and ideas about Macintosh computers. Use of color with the Mac II. Sending Postscript to a LaserWriter. Compatibility across the various Macintosh computers is discussed.

Mynhier, Judy, Gena B. Cobb. *Word Companion*. Louisville, KY: The Cobb Group, 1987. The definitive guide to Microsoft Word 3.0 for the Apple Macintosh.

Mathematics

Barnett, Stephen. *Matrix Methods for Engineers & Scientists*. London: McGraw-Hill, 1979. Algebra of matrices, linear equations, determinants, inverses, Kronecker products, eigenvalues, least squares, quadratic and hermitian forms, matrix functions.

Beiler, Albert H. *Recreations in the Theory of Numbers*. New York: Dover, 1964, 1966. Number theory is presented from a recreational point of view, including prime and perfect numbers.

Braun, M. *Differential Equations and Their Applications*. New York: Springer Verlag, 1983. Systems of differential equations, mathematical modeling including L. F. Richardson's theory of conflict, Lanchester's combat models and the battle of Iwo Jima, qualitative properties of orbits, predator-prey problems, the Threshold Theorem of epidemiology, and a model for the spread of gonorrhea; also includes an introduction to APL.

Buck, R. Creighton. *Advanced Calculus*. New York: McGraw-Hill, 1956, 1978. Sets, functions, continuity, differentiation, integration, series, uniform convergence, differentiation of transformations, applications to geometry and analysis, differential geometry and vector calculus, numerical methods, logic and set theory, quaternions, differential forms, extremal problems.

Burdon, Richard L., J. Douglas Faires, Albert C. Reynolds. *Numerical Analysis*. Boston: Prendle, Weber & Schmidt, 1978, 1981. Structured numerical algorithms are presented in a readable manner. This is an excellent intermediate- level text on numerical analysis.

Crowe, Michael J. *A History of Vector Analysis*. New York: Dover, 1967, 1985. Beginning with October 16, 1843, and Sir William Rowan Hamilton, this work traces the rise of vectorial systems from the discovery of quaternions until the final acceptance of vectors in about 1910.

Gill, Philip E., Walter Murray, Margaret H. Wright. *Practical Optimization*. New York: Academic Press, 1981. Excellent introductory chapter on numerical analysis and especially on matrix math. Covers linear and non-linear optimization.

Hamming, R. W. *Numerical Methods for Scientists and Engineers*. New York: Dover, 1973. Theme: The purpose of computing is insight, not numbers. Contents: fundamentals and algorithms, polynomial approximation—classical theory; Fourier approximation—modern theory; exponential approximation; eigenvalues.

Hildebrand, F. B. *Introduction to Numerical Analysis*. New York: Dover, 1956, 1974. Approximation, interpolation, Lagrangian methods, finite-difference interpolation, numerical solution of differential equations, least-squares polynomial approximation, Gaussian quadrature, splines, numerical solutions of equations (Gauss and Crout reduction).

Householder, Alston. *The Theory of Matrices in Numerical Analysis*. New York: Dover, 1964, 1975. Norms, localization theorems, eigenvectors, numerical analysis, and matrices.

Howard, James C. *Mathematical Modeling of Diverse Phenomena*. Washington, D.C.: Government Printing Office, 1979. Scalars, vectors, tensors, aeronautics, particle dynamics, fluid mechanics, general relativity and cosmological applications, symbolic manipulation with Macsyma and Reduce.

Peitgen, Richter. *The Beauty of Fractals*. Berlin: Springer Verlag, 1983. Mandlebrot fractals are illustrated in beautiful color photos.

Press, William H., Brian P. Flannery, *et al. Numerical Recipes: The Art of Scientific Computing*. Cambridge: Cambridge University Press, 1986. Preliminaries; solution of linear algebraic equations; interpolation and extrapolation; integration of functions; evaluation of functions; special functions; random numbers; sorting; root finding and nonlinear sets of equations; minimization or maximization of functions; eigensystems; Fourier transform spectral methods; statistical description of data; modeling of data; integration of ordinal differential equations; two-point boundary value problems; partial differential equations. Includes about 200 algorithms, both in Fortran and Pascal.

Press, William H., Brian P. Flannery, *et al. Numerical Recipes in C: The Art of Scientific Computing*. Cambridge: Cambridge University Press, 1988. A good cookbook of numerical analysis techniques. Topics include preliminaries; solution of linear algebraic equations; interpolation and extrapolation; integration of functions; evaluation of functions; special functions; random numbers; sorting; root finding and nonlinear sets of equations; minimization or maximization of functions; eigensystems; Fourier transform spectral methods; statistical description of data; modeling of data; integration of ordinal differential equations; two-point boundary value problems; partial differential equations. Includes about 200 algorithms in standard and in ANSI C. Highly recommended.

Ralston, Anthony, Philip Rabinowitz. *A First Course in Numerical Analysis*. New York: McGraw-Hill, 1965, 1978. Interpolation, approximation, quadrature, matrices, solutions of equations, DEQ. An excellent advanced text on numerical analysis.

Saff, E. B., A. D. Snider. *Fundamentals of Complex Analysis for Mathematics, Science & Engineering*. Englewood Cliffs, NJ: Prentice-Hall, 1976. Complex numbers, analytic functions, complex integration, series representations for analytic functions, residue theory, conformal mapping.

Wells, David. *The Penguin Dictionary of Curious and Interesting Numbers*. London: Penguin Books, 1986, 1987. This book is categorized by number. Each entry tells you all about the properties of any given number. Most parts of number theory are presented, including prime, Mersenne, Fermat, and Fibonacci numbers. Very enjoyable reading.

Object-oriented Programming

Kaehler, Ted, Dave Patterson. *A Taste of Smalltalk*. New York: W. W. Norton, 1986. An introduction to Smalltalk-80. Chapters cover the Tower of Hanoi example; a Rosetta Stone: Pascal, C, LISP, and Smalltalk; messages and objects everywhere; running the example; defining a class; animating the program; and an algorithm for the rest of us.

Pinson, Lewis J., Richard S. Wiener. *An Introduction to Object-Oriented Programming and Smalltalk*. Reading, MA: Addison-Wesley, 1988. Object-oriented programming is defined to be the collection of abstraction, encapsulation, inheritance, and polymorphism. Classes, subclasses, superclasses, instances, methods, objects, and messages are discussed. The model-view-controller (MVC) concept is presented with examples. The book uses Smalltalk-80 throughout. Appendices cover Smalltalk syntax, the Smalltalk image, and protocol summaries for selected classes.

Schmucker, Kurt. *Object-oriented Programming for the Macintosh*. Hasbrook Heights, NJ: Hayden, 1986. An introduction to MacApp and Object Pascal on the Macintosh, this work deals with MacApp version 1, so it is somewhat outdated.

Stroustrup, Bjarne. *The C++ Programming Language*. Reading, MA: Addison-Wesley, 1986. Declarations and constants; expressions and statements; functions and files; classes; operator overloading; derived classes; streams; reference manual. Includes an overview of C++ and a comparison with K&R C. This is the definitive work on the language, but it sure is hard to read. This edition deals with C++ version 1; a new and much improved edition covering version 2 is rumored to be in the works.

Wiener, Richard S., Lewis J. Pinson. *An Introduction to Object-oriented Programming and C++*. Reading, MA: Addison-Wesley, 1988. Classes, objects, encapsulation; subclasses, inheritance, polymorphism. The differences between C and C++. Abstract data types and data hiding using C++. Three case studies: spelling checker, bank teller discrete event simulation, and an interactive function evaluator. This book does not contain correct definitions of object-oriented concepts.

Operating Systems

Bach, Maurice J. *The Design of the UNIX Operating System*. Englewood Cliffs, NJ: Prentice-Hall, 1986. Introduction to the kernel; architecture of the UNIX operating system; the buffer cache; internal representation of files; system calls for the file system; the structure of processes; process control; process scheduling and time; memory management policies (swapping, demand paging); I/O subsystem (drivers, streams); interprocess communication (networks, sockets); multiprocessor and distributed systems. An appendix lists the UNIX system calls. Includes C fragments to illustrate algorithms.

Comer, Douglas. *Internetworking with TCP/IP: Principles, Protocols, and Architecture*. Englewood Cliffs, NJ: Prentice-Hall, 1988. Long haul and local area networks; the Internet; Ethernet, ProNet, Arpanet, X25Net, Cypress; Internet addresses, ARP, RARP; routing IP datagrams; error and control messages (ICMP); protocol layering, the ISO model; user datagram protocol; reliable stream transport service (TCP); core gateway system (GGP); autonomous systems and confederations (EGP); interior gateway protocols (RIP, HELLO, GATED); transparent gateways and subnet addressing; client-server model of interaction; the domain name system; application level services, FTP, electronic mail, rlogin. Appendices detail the 4.3 BSD UNIX interface to Internet protocols; guide to RFCs; official DARPA Internet protocols.

Comer, Douglas, Steven Munson. *Operating System Design, Volume 1: The Xinu Approach (Macintosh Edition)*. Englewood Cliffs, NJ: Prentice-Hall, 1989. This book provides complete C and assembly source code for a UNIX work-alike operating system that runs as a Macintosh application. Topics covered include: introduction and overview of the Macintosh; list and queue manipulation; scheduling and context switching; process management; process coordination; memory management; interrupt processing; real-time clock management; message passing; process-based hardware event handling; device- independent input and output; an example device driver; window management using devices; system initialization; high-level memory management and message passing; a disk driver; file systems; a syntactic namespace; user interface design; an example user interface: the Xinu Shell; an example set of shell commands; exception handling and support routines; system configuration. Appendices include a quick introduction to C and the Xinu programmer's manual.

Hoare, C. A. R. *Communicating Sequential Processes*. Englewood Cliffs, NJ: Prentice-Hall, 1985. Parallel processing. Processes, laws, traces; concurrency, the "Dining Philosophers," deadlock, mathematical theory of deterministic processes; nondeterminism, interleaving; communication, pipes; interrupts; shared resources; Occam; a calculus of communicating systems. An interesting book about modern operating system design issues.

Tanenbaum, Andrew S. *Operating Systems: Design and Implementation*. Englewood Cliffs, NJ: Prentice-Hall, 1987. History of operating systems; concepts and system calls; processes, IPC, process scheduling; input/output, deadlocks, RAM disks, disks, clocks, terminals; memory management, swapping, virtual memory, page replacement algorithms; file systems, file servers, security, protection mechanisms. Includes full source code in C to Minix, a UNIX-compatible operating system described, designed, and implemented in this book. Excellent reading showing how an operating system really works.

Tanenbaum, Andrew S. *Structured Computer Organization*. Englewood Cliffs, NJ: Prentice-Hall, 1984. Multilevel machines, digital logic, microprogramming, OS, assembly language. A good introduction to hardware for software people.

The Pascal Language

Borland International. *Turbo Pascal for the Mac: User's Guide and Reference Manual*. Scotts Valley, CA: Borland International, 1986. Includes two diskettes of software for the Macintosh. Documents the Pascal language, writing Macintosh applications, and writing Macintosh desk accessories. Appendices describe differences between Turbo Pascal and other Pascals, error messages, compiler directives, the Macintosh Interface Units, the Macintosh character set, and Turtlegraphics. An amazing compiler and succinct manual make this a great starter's programming package.

Wirth, Niklaus. *Programming In Modula-2*. Berlin: Springer Verlag, 1982, 1983. The successor to Pascal is detailed by example and in a Modula-2 language report. Searching, sorting, and a cross-reference program are explored along the way.

Wirth, Niklaus, Kathleen Jensen. *Pascal User Manual & Report*. New York: Springer-Verlag, 1974, 1978. The offical Pascal language report as well as a tutorial on its use, by its author.

Physics and Astronomy

Barrow, John D., Frank J. Tipler. *The Anthropic Cosmological Principle*. Oxford: Oxford University Press, 1986. Design arguments for the existence of God; modern teleology; the weak anthropic principle in physics and astrophysics; physical constants; anthropic principles in classical cosmology; quantum mechanics; biochemistry; space-travel argument against the existence of extraterrestrial life; future of the universe. Excellent synthesis of science, philosophy, and religion.

Bate, Roger R., Donald D. Mueller, Jerry E. White. *Fundamentals of Astrodynamics*. New York: Dover, 1971. Orbital mechanics, orbit determination, trajectories.

Cowan, Henry J., Peter R. Smith. *The Science and Technology of Building Materials*. New York: Van Nostrand Reinhold, 1988. Historical introduction; strength and deformation; dimensional stability and joints; exclusion of water and water vapor; transmission, reflection, and absorption of visible light and radiant heat; thermal insulation and inertia; effect of fires on building materials; durability; acoustic properties; iron and steel; nonferrous metals; natural stone; lime, gypsum, and cement; concrete; clay products; wood; glass; plastics and carpets; paints, adhesives, and sealants; criteria for choice of building materials. Contains good chemistry and physics formulas.

Davies, P. C. W. *The Accidental Universe*. Cambridge: Cambridge University Press, 1982. The fundamental ingredients of nature; scales of structure; the delicate balance; cosmic coincidences; the anthropic principle. Big number theory, astronomy and cosmology are all detailed in this outstanding little book. A highly recommended introduction to the field. An essential bedside reference.

Duffett-Smith, Peter. *Practical Astronomy with Your Calculator*. Cambridge: Cambridge University Press, 1979. A handy little book of algorithms for determining the positions of the sun, moon, and planets.

Feynman, Richard, Robert B. Leighton, Matthew Sands. *The Feynman Lectures on Physics*. 3 volumes. Reading, MA: Addison-Wesley, 1963. A wonderful introductory set on physics. The three volumes generally are concerned with mechanics, electromagnetism, and quantum theory, respectively. Feynman is the best at giving understandable explanations of physical principles. Highly recommended.

Fowles, Grant R. *Analytical Mechanics*. New York: Holt, Rinehart & Winston, 1962, 1977. Gives a good intuitive feel for mechanics. Chapters cover fundamental concepts and vectors; Newtonian mechanics and rectilinear motion of a particle; general motion of a particle in three dimensions; noninertial reference systems; central forces and celestial mechanics; dynamics of systems of many particles; mechanics of rigid bodies and planar motion; motion of rigid bodies in three dimensions; Lagrangian mechanics; dynamics of oscillating systems. Appendices include short summaries of complex numbers, series expansions, special functions, curvilinear coordinates, and matrices. Excellent intermediate-level mechanics text. Essential bedside reference.

Goldstein, Herbert. *Classical Mechanics*. Reading, MA: Addison-Wesley, 1950, 1980. The classic work in the field of classical mechanics. Survey of elementary principles; variational principles, LaGrange's equations; two-body central force problem (Kepler's laws), Laplace-Runge-Lenz vectors; kinematics of rigid body motion, Euler angles, Cayley-Klein parameters, quaternions; rigid body equations of motion, tensors, precession of the equinoxes; small oscillations; special relativity; Hamilton's equations of motion; canonical transformations; Hamilton-Jacobi theory; canonical perturbation theory; introduction to Lagrangian and Hamiltonian formulations for continuous systems and fields. Five appendices, including Euler angles in alternate conventions.

Green, Robin M. *Spherical Astronomy*. Cambridge: Cambridge University Press, 1985. An all-new relativistic version of Smart's classic work. Chapters cover basic formulae; celestial sphere; reference frame; geocentric coordinates; direct measurements of right ascension and declination; two-body orbital motion; planetary and satellite orbits; heliocentric and barycentric coordinates; precession and nutation; time; proper motion and radial velocity; mean and apparent coordinates; astrographic plate measurements; stellar distances and movements; elements of radio astronomy; radio astrometry; planetary phenomena and surface coordinates; eclipses and occultations; binary stars; tensor methods; astronomical constants. An essential bedside reference.

Harwitt, Martin. *Astrophysical Concepts*. New York: John Wiley, 1973. Astrophysics, random processes, relativitistic, and quantum effects. Contains an interesting treatment of tachyons, or faster-than-light particles.

Kane, Thomas R., Peter W. Likins, David A. Levinson. *Spacecraft Dynamics*. New York: McGraw-Hill, 1983. Kinematics, direction cosines, Euler parameters, Rodrigues parameters, rotations, angular velocities; gravitational forces, two particles, body and particle, two bodies, centrobaric and proximate bodies, force functions; simple spacecraft, rotational motion; complex spacecraft, potential and kinetic energy, dynamical equations, lumped mass models, finite-element methods. Two appendices.

Misner, Charles W., Kip S. Thorne, John Archibald Wheeler. *Gravitation*. San Francisco: Freeman, 1970, 1973. The classic work in the field of general relativity. Spacetime physics, geometrodynamics; special relativity, electromagnetic field, electromagnetism and differential forms, stress-energy tensor and conservation laws; curved spacetime, differential geometry, differential topology, affine geometry, geodesic deviation and spacetime curvature, Newtonian gravity, Riemannian geometry, Bianchi identities; Einstein's geometric theory of gravity, equivalence principle, variational principle; relativistic stars; the universe and cosmology; gravitational collapse, black holes, Schwarzschild geometry; gravitational waves; experimental tests of general relativity; Spinors, Regge calculus, superspace, beyond the end of time.

Royal Observatory. *The Explanatory Supplement to the Nautical Almanac and Astronomical Ephemeris*. London: Her Majesty's Stationary Office, 1973. The classic work in the field of navigation. Astronomy, navigation, timekeeping, derivation of almanacs explained. Many formulas and tables. A hard-to-find but essential reference.

Smart, W. M. *Textbook on Spherical Astronomy*. Cambridge: Cambridge University Press, 1931, 1980. The classic work in the field of spherical astronomy. Spherical trig, planetary motions, time, determination of position at sea.

Taff, Laurence G. *Celestial Mechanics*. New York: John Wiley & Sons, 1985. Newtonian gravitation explained. Topics include continuous distributions of matter, the two and three body problems, coordinate and time systems, corrections to coordinates, general precession, proper motion, orbit transfers, oblate spheroids, Laplacian-type initial orbit determination, Gaussian-type initial orbit determination, perturbation theory, differential corrections, stellar dynamics including kinetic theory, Monte Carlo calculations, hydrodynamics and thermodynamics, and binary stars.

Taylor, Edwin F., John Archibald Wheeler. *Spacetime Physics*. San Francisco: Freeman, 1963, 1966. An excellent treatise on special relativity. Chapters cover the geometry of spacetime, momentum and energy, the physics of curved spacetime.

Wertz, James R. *Spacecraft Attitude Determination and Control*. Dordrecht, Germany: D. Reidel, 1978. Attitude geometry; elementary spherical geometry; Keplerian orbits; planetary and lunar orbits; modeling the earth; attitude dynamics; equations of motion. Uses quaternions for equations of motion (p. 511). Appendices on matrix and vector algebra; quaternions; coordinate transformations; Laplace transformations; time measurement systems; metric conversion factors; solar system constants; fundamental physical constants.

Software Engineering

Brooks, Frederick P., Jr. *The Mythical Man-Month*. Reading, MA: Addison-Wesley, 1975, 1982. Software engineering and testing the IBM 360. Essential reading for anyone creating software.

Date, C. J. *A Guide to the SQL Standard*. Reading, MA: Addison-Wesley, 1987. Describes the relational database language SQL. Data definition and manipulation; embedded SQL; language constructs; extensions. Describes the ANSI standard and includes a critique of the standard. An appendix has a SQL grammar in BNF form.

Date, C. J. *An Introduction to Database Systems*. 2 volumes. Reading, MA: Addison-Wesley, 1986. Describes database architectures, particularly relational databases, including data definition, data manipulation, views, and embedded SQL. Overviews of DB2 and INGRES. Relational data structures, integrity rules. The relational algebra and calculus are developed. Inverted list, hierarchic, and network systems are reviewed.

Johnson, Clarence L. "Kelly," Maggie Smith. *Kelly—More Than My Share of It All*. Washington, DC: Smithsonian Institution Press, 1985. Autobiography of the designer of the Lockheed Blackbirds (SR-71, YF-12, A-12), the U-2, F-104 StarFighter, F-80 Shooting Star, P-38 Lightning, and the Constellation. Why is this included here? Kelly Johnson developed his amazing projects at the Skunk Works with very few people. This book details his 14 rules of operation for creating state-of-the-art aircraft with minimal resources in record time. I think these rules apply to software projects as well.

Kelly-Bootle, Stan. *The Devil's DP Dictionary*. New York: McGraw-Hill, 1981. An interesting and fun dictionary of witticisms relating to computers and data processing.

Lotus. *Lotus File Formats for 1–2–3, Symphony, and Jazz*. Reading, MA: Addison-Wesley, 1986. 1–2–3 and Symphony file formats. Summary of record types, ordered by opcode, alphabetically, and by product. Cell format codes, floating-point format, worksheet column designators. Useful for writing software that can read and write the 1–2–3 file format.

Viescas, John. *Quick Reference Guide to SQL*. Redmond, WA: Microsoft Press, 1989. Covers the ANSI standard SQL language in a dictionary format. A handy reference.

Software Tools

Aho, Alfred V., Brian W. Kernighan, Peter J. Weinberger. *The AWK Programming Language*. Reading, MA: Addison-Wesley, 1988. The AWK language: patterns, actions, user-defined functions, input/output; data processing; reports and databases; processing words, random text generation, text processing, word counts, cross-references, KWIC indexing; little languages, including an assembler, interpreter, graph drawing, sorting, RPN calculator, infix calculator, recursive-descent parsing; topological sorting. The book illustrates the great flexibility of AWK and is enjoyable reading.

American Telephone & Telegraph. *Unix Programmer's Manual*. New York: Holt, Rinehart & Winston, 1986. Volume 1: Commands and utilities; Volume 2: System calls and library routines; Volume 3: System administration facilities; Volume 4: Document preparation; Volume 5: Languages and support tools. Includes the full text of the on-line manual pages. Detailed information on sed, nroff, troff, mm, the C language, lint, sdb, Fortran 77, Ratfor, EFL, make, SCCS, M4, awk, ld, bc, dc, lex, yacc, uucp. The COFF object file format is detailed.

Anderson, Gail, Paul Anderson. *The Unix C Shell Field Guide*. Englewood Cliffs, NJ: Prentice-Hall, 1986. Basic command forms; command shortcuts; job control; history and alias mechanisms; C Shell programming; advanced programming techniques; customizing the C Shell; inside the C Shell; example C Shell scripts. Five appendices.

Bell Labs. *The Bell System Technical Journal, July/August 1978*. Short Hills, NJ: AT&T, 1978. UNIX time-sharing system, the C programming language, statistical text processing.

Bentley, Jon. *More Programming Pearls: Confessions of a Coder*. Reading, MA: Addison-Wesley, 1988. Interesting chapters on profilers, associative arrays in AWK, binary search, self-describing data; little languages, document design, and an algorithm for selection. Enjoyable and interesting reading.

Bentley, Jon. *Programming Pearls*. Reading, MA: Addison-Wesley, 1986. Interesting chapters on writing correct programs, back-of-the-envelope calculations, tool-using, performance monitoring, and other topics from software engineering. Algorithms for insertion sort, Quicksort, searching, heaps, and a spelling checker. Highly recommended.

Bourne, Stephen R. *The Unix System V Environment*. Reading, MA: Addison-Wesley, 1987. History and background of UNIX. Using UNIX; the ed and vi editors; the Bourne Shell; the C programming language; UNIX system programming; document preparation with nroff, troff, col, equ, ptx, spell, style, and tbl; data manipulation tools including awk, cmp, comm, diff, grep, join, sed, sort, tail, tr, uniq, field, lex, and yacc. Appendices describe commands, system calls, C subroutines, adb requests, ed requests, sh requests, troff requests, vi requests, a macro library, and the ASCII character set. A good introduction to the use and programming of UNIX.

Kernighan, Brian W., P. J. Plauger. *Software Tools*. Reading, MA: Addison-Wesley, 1976. Filters, files, sorting, text patterns, editing, formatting, macro processing, and a Ratfor-Fortran translator. The source code to many tools is given in Ratfor (Rational Fortran), a language not unlike C. A good resource about program development and refinement. Highly recommended reading.

Kernighan, Brian W., P. J. Plauger. *Software Tools in Pascal*. Reading, MA: Addison-Wesley, 1981. Filters, files, sorting, text patterns, editing, formatting, and macro processing. The source code to many tools is given in Pascal. A good resource about program development and refinement. Highly recommended reading. An essential bedside reference.

Kernighan, Brian W., Rob Pike. *The UNIX Programming Environment*. Englewood Cliffs, NJ: Prentice Hall, 1984. An excellent introduction for technical people to the UNIX programming facilities. Includes many examples of using pipes, filters, and the many standard UNIX tools. Includes material on yacc, lex, awk, nroff/troff. Highly recommended.

Symbolic Algebra

Buchberger, B., G. E. Collins, R. Loos. *Computer Algebra: Symbolic & Algebraic Computation*. Berlin: Springer Verlag, 1982, 1983. Discusses the basic algorithms of symbolic math, including algebraic simplification, factorization, and zeros of polynomials.

Davenport, J. H., Y. Siret, E. Tourneir. *Computer Algebra—Systems and algorithms for algebraic computation*. London: Academic Press, 1988. How to use a computer algebra system; the problem of data representations (integers, fractions, polynomials, rational functions, algebraic functions, transcendentals, matrices, series); polynomial simplification; advanced algorithms, modular methods, p-adic methods; formal integrations and differential equations. Appendices provide an algebraic background and a case study of Reduce.

Lipson, John D. *Elements of Algebra and Algebraic Computing*. Menlo Park, CA: Benjamin/Cummings, 1981. This work on applied algebra begins with the mathematical foundations of sets, relations, functions, and integers. Algebraic systems are then discussed: semigroups, monoids, groups, rings, integral domains, fields, quotient algebras, and elements of field theory. Algebraic computing is then presented, with arithmetic in Euclidean domains, polynomial arithmetic, computation of GCD, computation by homomorphic images, and the Fast Fourier Transform (FFT).

Wolfram, Stephen. *Mathematica*. Reading, MA: Addison-Wesley, 1988. The definitive reference book for the symbolic math package of the same name. Chapters include a practical introduction, the structure of

Mathematica, advanced mathematics, and Mathematica as a computer language. Appendices include more examples and a reference guide to the language.

Symbolic Manipulation and Artificial Intelligence

Allen, James. *Natural Language Understanding*. Menlo Park, CA: Benjamin/ Cummings, 1987. This artificial intelligence reference work covers the processing of natural languages. Part 1 covers syntactic processing, giving an outline of English and covering basic parsing techniques, features and augmented grammars, and deterministic parsing. Part 2 covers semantic interpretation and semantic networks, and part 3 discusses context and world knowledge, including knowledge representation, discourse structure, and belief models. Part 4 deals with response generation, question-answering systems, and natural language generation. Two appendices cover logical rules of inference and symbolic computation using LISP or Prolog.

Bratko, Ivan. *Prolog Programming for Artificial Intelligence*. Wokingham, England: Addison-Wesley, 1986. This volume of the International Computer Science Series covers the Prolog language; lists, operators, arithmetic; controlled backtracking; operations on data structures; advanced tree representations; problem-solving strategies; heuristic searching; AND/OR graphs; expert systems; game playing; pattern-directed programming; a simple theorem prover.

Clocksin, W. F., C. S. Mellish. *Programming in Prolog*. Berlin: Springer Verlag, 1981, 1984. Logic and functional programming. Algebraic and symbolic manipulation. Predicate calculus. Prolog language report.

Feigenbaum, Edward A. *The Handbook of Artificial Intelligence*. Los Altos, CA: Kaufmann, 1981. 3 volumes. LISP, natural language, MACSYMA, automatic deduction and inference.

Kluzniak, Feliks, Stanislaw Szpakowicz. *Prolog for Programmers*. Orlando, FL: Academic Press, 1985. Logic, metamorphosis grammars, Prolog syntax; implementation notes, tail recursion optimization. Includes Pascal source for Toy-Prolog.

Nilsson, Nils. *Principles of Artificial Intelligence*. Palo Alto, CA: Tioga, 1980. Production systems, predicate calculus, resolution refutation systems, rule-based deduction systems.

Sterling, Leon, Ehud Shaprio. *The Art of Prolog*. Cambridge, MA: MIT Press, 1986. Logic programs (facts, queries, rules); database and recursive programming; unification; the Prolog language; arithmetic; structure inspection; meta-logical predicates; cuts and negation; extra-logical predicates; pragmatics; nondeterministic programming; search techniques; parsing with definite clause grammars; game-playing programs; credit evaluation expert system; equation solver; a compiler.

Winston, Patrick Henry, Berthold Klaus, Paul Horn. *LISP*. Reading, MA: Addison-Wesley, 1981, 1984. Understanding symbol manipulation; basic LISP primitives; definitions, predicates, conditionals, and binding; recursion and iteration; association lists, properties, and data abstraction; definition using lambda; printing and reading; optional parameters, macros, and backquote; list storage, surgery, and reclamation; examples involving arrays and binary images; examples involving search; examples from mathematics; the blocks world; rules for good programming and tools for debugging; answering questions about goals; object-centered programming, message passing, and flavors; symbolic pattern matching, expert problem-solving using rules and streams; interpreting and compiling augmented transition trees; procedure writing programs and English interfaces; implementing frames; LISP in LISP; using Common LISP; LISP primitives.

INDEX